Changing Subjects

Over the last thirty years, feminist literary criticism has changed the study of literature. These twenty autobiographical essays by eminent feminist literary critics explore the process by which women scholars became feminist scholars, articulating the connections between the personal and political in their lives and work. They describe the experiences that radicalized women within academia and without, as students, professors, scholars, political activists, women. From these diverse histories a collective history emerges of the development of feminism as an intellectual and social movement, as a heuristic tool, as the redefinition of knowledge and power.

Co-edited by Gayle Greene and Coppélia Kahn, editors of *Making a Difference: Feminist Literary Criticism*, this book presents a history of the field through the eyes of those who have created it. Offering a spectrum of experiences and critical positions that engage with current debates in feminism, it will be valuable to teachers and students of feminist theory, women's studies, and the history of the women's movement. It will interest feminist writers and scholars in all disciplines and anyone who cares about feminism and its future.

The editors: Gayle Greene is Professor of English at Scripps College; **Coppélia Kahn** is Professor of English at Brown University.

Changing Subjects

The Making of Feminist Literary Criticism

Edited by
Gayle Greene and Coppélia Kahn

London and New York

First published 1993
by Routledge
11 New Fetter Lane, London EC4P 4EE

Simultaneously published in the USA and Canada
by Routledge
29 West 35th Street, New York, NY 10001

Typeset in 10/12pt Garamond by Datakey, Cornwall, England
Printed in: Great Britain by Clays Ltd., St. Ives plc.

British Library Cataloguing in Publication Data:

A catalogue record for this book is available
from the British Library

Library of Congress Cataloging in Publication Data:

A catalogue record for this book is available
from the Library of Congress

ISBN 041508685X

0415086868 (pbk)

Contents

Notes on contributors

Barbara Christian is Professor of African-American Studies at the University of California at Berkeley. Her essays on black women writers have appeared in many literary and academic journals. She has done extensive curriculum development in African-American Studies and Women's Studies for high schools and has taught writing for many years. She is the author of *Black Women Novelists, the Development of a Tradition, 1892-1976* (1980) and *Black Feminist Criticism, Perspectives on Black Women Writers* (1985).

Rachel Blau DuPlessis' recent publications include *The Pink Guitar: Writing as Feminist Practice* (1990), *Tabula Rosa* and *Drafts 3–14* (1987 and 1991). She edited *The Selected Letters of George Oppen* (1990) and, with Susan Friedman, co-edited *Signets: Reading H. D.* (1990). She is the author of *Writing Beyond the Ending: Narrative Strategies of Twentieth-Century Women Writers* (1985) and *H.D.: The Career of that Struggle* (1986).

Elizabeth Deeds Ermarth is Presidential Research Professor and Professor of English at the University of Maryland at Baltimore. During the academic year of 1992–3 she will be Overseas Fellow at Churchill College, Cambridge. Her publications include *Realism and Consensus in the English Novel* (1983), *George Eliot* (1985), and *Sequel to History: Postmodernism and the Crisis of Representational Time* (1992).

Jerry Aline Flieger teaches French literature, contemporary theory, and women's studies at Rutgers University. She has written extensively on psycho-analysis and feminist theory. Her publications include *The Purloined Punchline: Freud's Comic Theory and the Postmodern Text* (1991) and *Colette and the Fantom Subject of Autobiography* (1992).

Judith Kegan Gardiner is Professor of English and Women's Studies at the University of Illinois at Chicago and an editor of *Feminist Studies*. Among her publications are *Rhys, Stead, Lessing and the Politics of Empathy* (1989) and essays about English Renaissance literature, modern women writers, and feminist and psychoanalytic theory.

Gayle Greene is Professor of English and Women's Studies at Scripps College, Claremont, California. She has published on Shakespeare, women writers, and feminist literary theory. Her most recent publication is *Changing the Story: Feminist Fiction and the Tradition* (1991) and she co-edited *The Woman's Part: Feminist Criticism of Shakespeare* (1980) and *Making a Difference: Feminist Literary Criticism* (1985).

Carolyn Heilbrun, author of *Writing a Woman's Life* (1988) and *Hamlet's Mother and Other Women* (1990), has retired from her position as Avalon Foundation Professor in the Humanities at Columbia University. She is writing a biography of Gloria Steinem.

Margo Hendricks is Assistant Professor at the University of California, Santa Cruz. She is co-editing *Women, Race, Writing in the Early Modern Period* with Pat Parker (forthcoming from Routledge).

Molly Hite is Associate Professor of English at Cornell University. She is the author of *Ideas of Order in the Novels of Thomas Pynchon* (1983), *The Other Side of the Story: Structures and Strategies of Contemporary Feminist Narrative* (1989) and the novels *Class Porn* (1987) and *Breach of Immunity* (1992).

Gloria T. Hull is currently Professor of Women's Studies and Literature at the University of California, Santa Cruz and an established Black feminist scholar, teacher and poet. Her most recent books are *Color, Sex, and Poetry: Three Women Writers of the Harlem Renaissance* (1987) and *Healing Heart: Poems 1973–1988* (1989).

Ann Rosalind Jones directs the Comparative Literature Program at Smith College. She is the author of *The Currency of Eros: Women's Love Lyric in Europe 1540–1620* (1990).

Coppélia Kahn is Professor of English at Brown University. Her publications include *Man's Estate: Masculine Identity in Shakespeare* (1981) and articles on Shakespeare, feminist theory, and Renaissance drama. She has co-edited three anthologies, most recently *Making a Difference: Feminist Literary Criticism* (1985), with Gayle Greene.

Linda S. Kauffman is Professor of English at the University of Maryland, College Park. She is the author of *Discourses of Desire: Gender, Genre, and Epistolary Fictions* (1986), and *Special Delivery: Epistolary Modes in Modern Fiction* (1992).

Shirley Geok-lin Lim is currently Professor of Asian American Studies at the University of California, Santa Barbara. She received the 1980 Commonwealth Poetry Prize for *Crossing the Peninsula* and has published another three collections of short stories and poetry. She is co-editor of *The Forbidden Stitch: An Asian American Women's Anthology* (1990).

Nancy K. Miller is Distinguished Professor of English at Lehman College and the Graduate Center, CUNY. Her most recent book is *Getting Personal: Feminist Occasions and other Autobiographical Acts* (1991).

Carol Thomas Neely is Professor of English and Women's Studies at the University of Illinois. She is the author of *Broken Nuptials in Shakespeare's Plays* (1985) and co-editor with Gayle Greene and Carolyn R. S. Lenz of *The Woman's Part: Feminist Criticism of Shakespeare* (1980).

Carolyn Porter, formerly Director of the Women's Studies Program and the Beatrice M. Bain Center for Research on Women and Gender, is Professor of English at the University of California, Berkeley. She is the author of *Seeing and Being: The Plight of the Participant Observer in Emerson, Adams, James, and Faulkner* (1981) and of numerous articles on American literature.

Leslie W. Rabine teaches French literature and women's studies at the University of California, Irvine. She is the author of *Reading the Romantic Heroine: Text, History, Ideology* (1985).

Madelon Sprengnether is Professor of English at the University of Minnesota where she teaches both critical and creative writing. She is co-editor of *The M(o)ther Tongue: Essays in Feminist Psychoanalytic Interpretation* (1985) and author of *The Spectral Mother: Freud, Feminism, and Psychoanalysis* (1990).

Bonnie Zimmerman is Professor of Women's Studies at San Diego State University. Her publications include articles on George Eliot and on lesbian literature and theory, and a book, *The Safe Sea of Women: Lesbian Fiction 1969–1989* (1990).

Acknowledgements

We wish to thank Avi Wortis, who suggested that we do this book; Tania Modleski, for her sensitive, helpful reading of the manuscript; and Janice Price, for her continuing support and encouragement. This project couldn't have been accomplished without the help of feminist friends and scholars across the country, many of whom are represented in these pages. We offer special thanks to our contributors for patiently taking their essays through repeated revisions and also to those whose interest and friendship has sustained us: Elizabeth Abel, Janet Adelman, Christina Crosby, Rena Fraden, Elizabeth Minnich, Vicki Ratner, Elizabeth Weed. Finally, we express our appreciation to those who, for one reason or another aren't represented here, but whose work has made a difference to our thinking about feminism: Myra Jehlen, Carey Kaplan, Annette Kolodny, Jane Marcus, Wendy Martin, Lillian Robinson, Ellen Cronan Rose, Roberta Rubenstein, and Jean Wyatt. We are grateful to Scripps College and Brown University for sabbatical and research support.

August 1992

Berkeley, California
Providence, Rhode Island

Introduction

This anthology is an effort of remembering and historicizing, a collection of individual stories that, taken together, comprise a collective story – histories that make a history. It is a way of saying "I" that is also a way of saying "we." Over the past twenty years, a generation of feminist scholars has come of age. Feminism as an intellectual and social movement, as a heuristic tool, as the redefinition of knowledge and power, has shifted the grounds of literary study and altered the profession itself. We are now in a position to assess this movement and to see ourselves as part of a historical process.

The impetus for this book came from conversations we had with Carol Neely and Madelon Sprengnether in the spring of 1988 at the annual meeting of the Shakespeare Association of America. We agreed that feminism had transformed our lives and our scholarship. We saw it as a growing point that enabled us to connect our deepest passions and energies with our work, to think more deeply and originally – and we wanted to understand how this had happened for others in the generation that had come of age with us. We wanted to articulate the vital connection feminism makes between lived experience and theory.

At that moment, a general impulse of retrospection was stirring. Several histories of feminist criticism and of the women's movement were being published; MLA Special Sessions and conferences were beginning to focus on historical assessments of feminist criticism; and more was to come. Yet feminism inside and outside academia was – and still is – enduring a backlash: the feminization of poverty, the anti-choice movement spearheaded by Operation Rescue, the "glass ceiling" of opportunity for women in every field, the shoring up of the traditional family and its roles for women by the Reagan and Bush administrations – all threatened to undo the gains women had made. Our lives may have been transformed by feminism, but other women's lives hadn't, and the women's movement itself seemed imperilled, faltering, self-divided.

So we sent out a call for papers. We asked women to examine the processes that made them feminists and transformed their scholarship to feminist scholarship; to articulate the radicalizing experiences that enabled them to connect the personal and the political. We asked them what difference feminism had made to their writing and teaching, to their relations with colleagues, students, the profession, and the world outside academia. We asked how questions of race, ethnicity and gender interacted with feminism, and what differentiated the first generation of feminist scholars from the younger generation. Finally, we asked our contributors to discuss the challenges that face feminism, and to speculate about its future. We sought personal, anecdotal stories, but we asked contributors to *theorize* them so as to bring out their historical and political dimensions.

These essays tell the story of second-wave feminism, a story you can read in history books, but narrated here in the first person. It begins in the civil rights and anti-war movements, in resistance to the chauvinism of male activists; it gains strength from the formation of consciousness-raising groups where women learned to speak, to realize we were not alone; it culminates in the building of an intellectual and social movement. The story continues in accounts of the isolation, anguish and confusion that the women's movement named and clarified; the sexism, casual and blatant, that women in academia have commonly experienced; the lawsuits and tenure battles.

Though these essays tell similar stories, they also tell many different ones, and make it clear that feminism was never the simple, monolithic entity it is sometimes seen to be. Women from a variety of backgrounds, with diverse interests, talents, and passions, identified themselves with the women's movement. For some, the route was political activism; for others, teaching, motherhood, consciousness-raising or feminist reading groups. Certain key texts are mentioned frequently: Simone de Beauvoir's *The Second Sex,* Doris Lessing's *The Golden Notebook,* Kate Millett's *Sexual Politics,* Betty Friedan's *The Feminine Mystique.* Several women recount how they abandoned dissertations on male authors as their interests shifted to women writers who were then less known, less respected; others tell how they moved toward feminist analysis of the male canon. Several discuss the difficulties of constructing or of even conceiving a career in the male-dominated professoriate. Many are self-conscious about the autobiographical mode, and careful to distinguish components of identity – class, race, politics, family, religion – rather than assuming that identity is simple or unified. All, we venture, would agree with Elizabeth Ermarth's statement, "To say 'I' is to say something profoundly social, as distinct from merely 'individual.' "

While we asked contributors to articulate connections, in fact many of them ponder disconnections – a useful reminder that divisions were inherent in feminism from the start. They seem to come with the territory, because being a woman in our culture means being divided. Defined as objects, we aspire to be subjects; negotiating "ambiguously hegemonic and ambiguously nonhegemonic" positions (as DuPlessis puts it), we are simultaneously the inheritors and the critics of culture (as Woolf puts it). In the fifties, the decade in which most of us came of age, the decade that produced us and produced feminism, conflicts and contradictions were exacerbated as the post-war economic expansion that pushed women into the workplace collided with the ideology of domesticity that insisted they stay home – the ideology Friedan called "the feminine mystique."

Some of these divisions are healthy and productive. They're what we've grown on; they've taught us what we know. Negotiating such minefields (as Annette Kolodny long ago characterized the feminist project) keeps us versatile, agile. Analyzing and interpreting their feminisms, the writers in these pages participate in the debates that have structured feminist scholarship: the Franco–American divide between Lacanian/Derridean theories of the split subject and an American confidence in history, authenticity of voice, and empathetic reading; the question of essentialism; the encounter between white middle-class feminists and feminists who are of women of color; the uses and misuses of "theory." And rather than disappearing with age (most things don't), dividedness takes new, unforeseen forms as feminists move into positions of seniority. Bonnie Zimmerman describes "a shift between viewing from the center and viewing from the margins" and Leslie Rabine speaks of contradictions between the "disrespect, rebellion, and irreverence" we feel as feminists and the "institutional politics" we're forced to practice as tenured academics.

We cast as wide a net as we knew how to, inviting nearly twice as many essays as we finally received. The shape of this volume is partly determined by who was available, who had the time, interest, and inclination required for such a project. Some wanted to join us but were prevented by prior commitments – indicating both the success of feminist criticism and the exhausting professional responsibilities that have come with it. This is but one history of the making of feminist literary criticism; there are and will be others. Our goal was to get on record the two decades in which feminist literary criticism arose and burgeoned, by calling on what we think is its distinctive power – the power of a theory to change lives.

Gayle Greene
Coppélia Kahn
February 1992

Chapter 1

Looking at history

Gayle Greene

LEAVING SHAKESPEARE

It's by no means clear how a girl like me, coming of age in the California suburbs in the 1950s, got hooked up with Shakespeare in the first place. When I think about high school – the homecoming games and proms, the local drag strip we cruised searching for action, the Mel's Drive-In where we hung out, boy-crazy, clothes-crazy, decked out in crinoline petticoats, charm bracelets, bobby sox, pony tails – it seems a bizarre and eccentric attraction. It was an affair of the heart, I know that: for me, anything interesting or worth doing, anything that makes me do real work – is about love. Not all my loves have been happy or productive, though – far from it: in fact some of the strongest have been tormented and destructive. This thing with Shakespeare – what was it?

I'd been intrigued by *Hamlet* in high school, but it wasn't until my freshman year at college that I was really bowled over by a Shakespeare play – *Richard II*. I was barely 17, at the University of Chicago, homesick and lost, and I read *Richard II* in a humanities course. Though this course had little to do with Shakespeare, or with much of anything else as far as one could tell, when I heard the language, really heard it, it was like a spell. I was hooked, caught, cathected, transfixed by that spectacle of ruined royalty, entranced by that sweet sound. I suppose there was something in Richard's adolescent self-pity that validated my own: I too was ready to sit upon the ground and tell sad stories of the death of kings, sure as I was that all was vanity, and certain, also, that I'd been deprived of a birthright. What else could explain my unsatisfactory existence? I was not as critical of Richard as I'd later be, though I was not completely uncritical of him either. I sensed even then affinities between his problems and my own. I had read other plays, but it was Richard, Richard, that ravished me, that struck a chord so deep that it drew me back again and again.

When I think about what else drew me to Shakespeare in those early years, I recall Lawrence Olivier, stunningly blond and anguished in black tights, James Mason, looking distant and Roman in a toga: all that tortured nobility, so tragic, so eloquent – so *male*. I thrilled to Mark Antony's pronouncement over the body of Brutus, "this was a man," and to Hamlet's words to Horatio, "give me that man / That is not passion's slave, and I will wear him / In my heart's core, ay, in my heart of heart, / As I do thee." It didn't occur to me that all this homosocial intensity was obliterating me: the men were grooving on the men and so was I, and it took me years to notice my own absence – such was my alienation from my experience. It was years before I thought about the women in the plays, riveted as I was on those dazzling men, and then it was only working on *The Woman's Part* that succeeded in focusing my attention on them. I suppose falling in love with those heroes was a version of falling in love with movie stars, which I did plenty of in those days – except that it was a more respectable passion, one that I sensed might get me further than a crush on Jimmy Dean. Doubtless that attraction to anguished and inaccessible masculinity was about my father, always a powerful and disturbing presence, or absence, in our so-called family, someone I hadn't a clue how to think about.

Our family went through what a lot of families in the suburbs in the 1950s were going through – that suburban loneliness you could die of, that sense of not being connected anywhere, to anything. But our loneliness was exacerbated by my parents' unconventional arrangements and their politics. We were not a happy family; my parents were always in the process of separating, and, when I was ten, they finally did, leaving my mother that most miserable of anomalies, a woman alone in the suburbs in the fifties, in her forties. My father was mainly away, even when he was around, and he was a womanizer, a philanderer, who was nevertheless oddly devoted to his children and in other ways a nice guy (it took some talent not to get rich as a doctor in those California boom years, but he was an old-style GP who didn't insist on collecting payment when his patients were poor, as they often were). He was Jewish, my mother was not, and when the marriage finally came apart and she changed our name, I was completely confused – I became aware of being Jewish at precisely the time it was denied that I was Jewish, whatever "Jewish" meant. Moreover, at the height of McCarthyism, my parents were lefties, the few friends they had living under shadows, some blacklisted; yet my parents didn't identify wholeheartedly with politics either, so we were lefties and not lefties. We were quite simply without the consolations of any kind of group identity, even oppositional. In those years when everyone was conforming and when, as an adolescent, I wanted nothing more than to belong, conforming was never an option, since I'd been taught so thoroughly that everything out there – the ideology of happy families, of a greater America – was fucked. We were rootless, headless, godless, adrift, and there seemed no way of conceiving of alternatives, no way to imagine any other way of being or living.[1]

I turned, for a sense of other possibilities, to reading. But what I found there was not very helpful: the "tiresome, hysterical pretentious Jewess" of Durrell's *Justine,* Caddie of Faulkner's *The Sound and the Fury,* "doomed and knew it," Hedda Gabler, fatally fixated on the pistols of her father the general, doomed Brett, doomed Gudrun – all male-authored except for Scarlet O'Hara, whose spunkiness I found irresistible, but who also turned out to be doomed. I found myself, disastrously, in Madame Bovary and Anna Karenina. God knows why they were a comfort, these intense, fragile creatures living at the edge of experience – I suppose it was all that exquisitely expressed anguish: they did their despair so beautifully. I was also drawn to the women of Austen and Eliot, who had more interiority and were occasionally even allowed to survive, but I found their happy endings unlikely. I didn't mind the idea of marriage to Mr Knightley, but it seemed implausible. By now we know about those death and marriage plots, where they get us, but at the time, in my teens and twenties, this was all there was.[2] The books I needed – the feminist fiction and theory that would help me make the connections between the confusions I was living through and something out there – were only then being written, and it was decades before I would find them (*Martha Quest* was published in 1952, *The Golden Notebook* in 1962, *The Second Sex* was translated into English in 1953: I did not read these until the late sixties).

There was never any doubt that I would study literature: it was the only thing I'd ever really – wholeheartedly, unequivocally – loved. I muddled through two undergraduate majors, in English and Comparative Literature, fulfilling requirements that didn't make much sense (it never occurred to me that they should), living in terror that the computer would spew me out at the last minute and keep me from graduating. (I had transferred to Berkeley my sophomore year, on account of a boyfriend; by October we'd broken up; this ought to have taught me more than it did.) I never got to know a professor, I never had a woman professor in the five years it took to the MA, and "woman writer" wasn't a category in the curriculum. But in spite of the Berkeley English Department I continued to love reading, and in spite of two dreadful Shakespeare lecture courses I elected to take a senior seminar in Shakespeare, where, turned loose on a play of my choice, I turned to Richard, Richard again, and sunk once more into that sweet despair.

To this day, I don't know whether the decision to go with Shakespeare rather than the novels I lived on was a bad or a good choice – whether it was a choice that reflected (as many of my choices did) alienation from my deepest needs, or whether it actually expressed those needs. It must have expressed something deep – Shakespeare seemed to be something I very badly needed to do, since, when I found myself at Columbia a few years later (a move which, I'm happy to say, was not precipitated by a man), where I was surrounded by exciting activity in the nineteenth century and a vacuum in the Renaissance, it would have made more sense to work on the novel than to persist in a Shakespeare dissertation, a project that turned out to be self-directed. (No one wanted to touch it. The resident Shakespearean said it was "too modern and psychological" and that I "couldn't possibly master all the scholarship" and the resident Miltonist was afraid of offending the resident Shakespearean – though he eventually did read and rubber-stamp it and set up a defense committee and smuggle me out the back door.) It now strikes me as stubborn and perverse to have persisted in doing Shakespeare with everyone advising against it. Perhaps it had to do with Steven Marcus scaring me off George Eliot by naming every German philosopher she'd ever read and assuring me that I'd have to master all of them to write on her. Mastering the

Shakespeare scholarship seemed like a piece of cake by comparison (and from what they all said, the dissertation was about "mastery"). Or perhaps there was a lurking fear that working on a woman writer would make me second-rate. Or perhaps it was a deeper fear of those doomed, desperate women that drove me away from those novels I none the less devoured.

I now think that my determination to work on Shakespeare had to do with power. Not in any simple or obvious way – not in the way E. M. Forster's Leonard Bast, or Rita in the film *Educating Rita*, latch on to culture as upward mobility; more in the sense of identifying with the male, wanting to be my father. The thing is, our family was so marginal, and I was on the losing side even of it. I knew I didn't want to be my mother, an abandoned wife and mother, without resources, dependent on a man. Although she had stayed with us children, and although she was the more attractive of my parents, I felt complimented when people said I looked like my father: he was the doctor, he had the Yale degree, he had position, power, women – freedom; she had us. So it was inevitable that I identify with him, and perhaps also inevitable that I work on Shakespeare. Mind you, my father was never even remotely impressed by my doing graduate study in literature – "In all that time you could have been a real doctor" was his comment when I finally got my Ph.D. – so working on Shakespeare wasn't in any obvious way about pleasing him. It was just that I felt that doing Shakespeare would in some way validate me, would prove I was an intelligent person, and I had a fierce need to prove myself an intelligent person. One of the sad ironies of my life is that I expend enormous energies trying to get the attention of people who turn out not to have been looking, over what turns out not to have been the point.

But there was power of another sort that Shakespeare seemed to offer: it had to do with order, with the edifices built by his language, structures I found shelter in – his works seemed a tower of male strength, what Mrs Ramsay calls the "admirable fabric of the masculine intelligence" (Woolf 1955: 159). I suppose it was understandable, given the shifting sands of my childhood, that I'd flee anything resembling postmodern uncertainties and seek a solid place. Oh, it was always already crumbling, this place, I knew that – that was part of its fascination: but it still seemed to represent something more certain, more clarifying, than anything around me, than the prospects of growing up female in the fifties, than the misery of my mother as she whittled herself down to the confines of her life. I've sometimes wondered how much my attraction to Shakespeare had to do with those wasteful, tormented affairs that consumed large parts of my twenties, thirties, and yes, even forties, where I sought validation in brilliant, articulate, narcissistic men who turned out to be using *me* to validate *them*, for whom I functioned mainly as an admiring audience. Still, painful as much of that was, I did not make the usual mistakes: some sort of conditioning that was marching my friends – compulsively and often disastrously – through the steps of marriage, motherhood, divorce, seemed to have been left out of me. Though I thought I wanted to marry (someday, someone, never now), conventional domestic arrangements held a kind of horror for me – houses, entrapment, babies. I did feel an occasional twinge of envy for the matching dish sets and stem-ware of my married friends (you could tell those of us who "lived together" from those who were married, in the middle classes in the sixties – by our mismatched dishware), but they didn't seem worth the price, those dishes.

One thing I knew, nothing was as it was claimed to be – and for this, I found corroboration in Shakespeare; for always in his plays, though I was drawn to the grandeur, the splendor, I was driven to ferret out the soft spots, to find the rifts and cracks in the structures. What fascinated me about Richard and Brutus and Othello was the way the fine language masked insecurity, the way those dazzling talkers used words to cheer themselves up, to shore up their realities, while in fact their self-delusions left them wide open to self-deceptions and the lies of others. The thing is, I always knew that people lied: the happy fifties masked insanity, a suicidal military stockpiling. The war in Viet Nam came as no surprise, though what did surprise me was that people imagined their protests might halt it (this early cynicism combined with shyness to cut me off from sixties activism in a way I now regret). I always knew that my father lied, but, more importantly, I knew that my mother lied – in pretending to be all right when she was really coming apart, in telling us to love our father when she hated his guts, in trying to inculcate virtues of love and loyalty in us from a situation that travestied them. So I went for and found in Shakespeare's plays confirmation of my deepest sense of reality – that words were unreliable, that people could build facades and get trapped by them, could get confused and ensnared by their own stories. On this, in *Richard II*, in *Julius Caesar*, in *Othello*, in *Troilus and Cressida*, I wrote obsessively. I was struck by the pairings of worders against worders – Richard and Bolingbroke, Brutus and Antony, Othello and Iago – winners and losers differentiated by their ability to wield words. I eventually wrote my (self-directed) dissertation on *Julius Caesar* and discovered that Shakespeare had honed in on something very big, as he so often does, and was intuiting a cultural moment – no less than the revolution in attitudes toward language that was occurring from the medieval to the modern world, the transition from sixteenth-century belief in language and rhetoric to seventeenth-century scepticism, nominalism, and the plain style.

I guess, in an odd way, "mastering" the master was a way of incorporating his power, harnessing (if not exactly understanding) some of the forces that were driving me, demystifying some of that male mystique. I think what I really needed was time and a safe place from which I could take stock – of myself and possibilities – before I could see what I needed to do next. Shakespeare gave me this. I got tenure from him, developed skills of writing and editing, used him to explore certain questions. I learned from him the way language functions in constructing identity and how this process has social (if not political) implications; I learned about systems (value systems, social systems, philosophical, epistemological, and aesthetic systems) and how at times of stress these are prone to come apart; and I learned a lot about power from him – and long before new historicists or poststructuralists or deconstructionists were naming these issues. His plays corroborated my sense, gleaned from a life on the margins, of the contingency of systems and the arbitrariness of convention, of language as a code to be broken: all of which turned out to be fundamental to feminism. I learned what I needed for my next move, to feminist theory and fiction, and when I learned this I left him.[3]

I now work on Doris Lessing, Margaret Drabble, Margaret Laurence, Margaret Atwood, Toni Morrison, Alice Walker, Paule Marshall – contemporary writers whose novels include me and speak to me as no other literary works do, and whose protagonists survive, often alone, to tell their tales. The route I've taken, from a canonized male writer to women writers, has been travelled by other feminist scholars – in fact it describes the trajectory of feminist scholarship, which began with the study of the canon and shifted to the study of women writers. I think for me it was related to recognizing the influence and importance of my mother, accepting my mother in me, realizing that it was okay to be her. It took me years to figure out that though my mother never finished a degree, she was really the smart one, the strong one, in ways that counted. It took me years to understand that I could never be my father, and more, that I didn't want to. I think this was necessary before I could turn to women writers with a sense that I wasn't doing something second-rate – could approach them with the love and intensity that I'd first brought to Shakespeare.

But in a way, my relationship with Shakespeare has been the most lasting and stable one I've ever had with a man. It was a connection, a kind of wonder, a sort of faith – and faith was something sorely lacking in my life. Probably it was faith in some things I'd have been better off not believing in, but I wouldn't have traded it for a wilderness of critical theory: I wouldn't have wanted my Shakespeare parcelled out in little "isms" – poststructuralism, new historicism, cultural materialism, Marxism, no, not even feminism. It seemed to offer something beyond what was available to me as an adolescent going through a confused coming of age in a low, dishonest decade, and though I probably stayed with him too long, as I tend to do in relationships, it made certain things possible.

It may also, of course, have made other things impossible. Perhaps it did keep my lid on when it should have been blowing off – as the study of literature tended to (was intended to) produce political zombies in those days; perhaps if I'd written that George Eliot dissertation I'd have found a faster route to feminism. I know that it took Simone de Beauvoir, Doris Lessing, Sheila Rowbotham, Juliet Mitchell, Kate Millett, Shulamith Firestone, and Adrienne Rich to show me the connections between the roles my mother and father had played out and the social and political structures out there in the world; it took feminist theory and fiction to make me understand the sexual politics of my interactions with lovers, professors, advisors (yes, even with Shakespeare) – to make me see that the political was personal and was what hurt.

My mainstay writer now is Doris Lessing, and I know exactly why. What draws me to Lessing is her articulation of the problems of women and men in our time and her illumination of connections between those problems and the times; her ability to pierce the veil of hypocrisy, the veneer of official versions, and to deconstruct systems (colonialism, capitalism) and to demonstrate (my old theme) that "listening to the words people use is the longest way around to an understanding of what is going on" (1966: 7). Here were women – Martha Quest, Anna Wulf – who were not only facing the sorts of problems I was facing, struggling with their sense of themselves, with commitments to work and to men, but who corroborated my deepest sense of reality: that the most important conversation going on is not usually the one that is being verbalized, that the "small ironical grimace" is what signifies – "you have to deduce a person's real feelings about a thing by a smile she does not know is on her face, by the way bitterness tightens muscles at a mouth's corner" (1974: 62). Here was confirmation that if I was inhabiting "another room" (in Lessing's term), so too were others.

*

The above was written for a seminar on "Gender and Cultural Difference," chaired by Madelon Sprengnether at the International Shakespeare Conference in Tokyo, August 1991. I'd had no intention of publishing it here: it seemed to be more about my relation to Shakespeare than to feminism, and I had something else I wanted to say about feminism – I wanted to write as "we" rather than "I." Urged by Madelon (and others – Carol Neely, Tania Modleski, Roberta Johnson, Janet Adelman, Shirley Garner) that the essay really did belong in this anthology, I've come to see that the "I" of this reminiscence and the "we" I want to talk about may have more to do with each other than I'd realized, that by connecting them I might be making the kind of connection that we were asking our contributors to make – connections that are by no means easy.[4]

The Tokyo paper ended with a tribute to Shakespeare, as I supposed it had to, given the occasion. But this is the way I really want it to end – though it's less an end than a transition:

Here was confirmation of my sense that if I was inhabiting another room, hearing another conversation, so too were others. It was, of course, the women's room, where the women were – at least the women I knew, who had always been having another conversation, inhabiting another culture, and whose relation to the dominant culture was just then being articulated by feminist theory. I still turn to books for validation – I think most people who study literature do – but it is validation of another sort, that has less to do with the "male approval desire filter"[5] and more to do with – what? Something closer to, something more like, what I can only call a center. Something less mediated by the law of the father.

What I love about contemporary women's fiction is the way it can empower women, the way it empowered me. I came to feminism through reading and teaching feminist fiction and theory; it was this that showed me connections between my life and the world, connections that were a lifeline because they made me less isolated and meant that change was possible: my confusions weren't a personal affliction, a private calamity, but were "shared, unnecessary, and political" (in Adrienne Rich's term, "Translations"). It is connections like these that I try to teach my students. It is connections like these that we sought in this collection of essays.

LOOKING AT HISTORY

Feminism happened when women learned to say "I" – when we learned what Adrienne Rich called the courage to say "I" (1979b: 45). This required that we unlearn much of what we had been taught, that we de-condition ourselves as women socialized to subservience – being dutiful daughters, dancing attendance on men, putting the needs of husbands, lovers, children first. It necessitated personal and professional risks, often costing marriages, relationships, jobs, promotions – as the essays in this volume testify. Once we got our Ph.D.s – which was for some of us no mean feat, since writing flew in the face of our own and others' expectations – then, becoming feminist scholars meant retooling and not only learning a new theoretical vocabulary but in many cases *inventing* that vocabulary. And – pardon my nostalgia, I'll keep it to a minimum – it was terrific. It is difficult to overstate that heady sense of possibilities as we set about re-creating our lives, as we felt ourselves becoming authors and directors of our stories (see Miller, chapter 2, pp. 37–8). We imagined that our writing was part of an on-going collective effort, that it might make a difference. We imagined, naïvely, that our "I" was "we"; "we thought all women were us, and we were all women" (DuPlessis, chapter 6, p.101).

Since then we've realized the limits of that "I" and "we"; contemporary theory has rendered suspect the view of personal experience as a site of authoritative discourse and exposed the essentialist, appropriative implications of saying "we." In some sense the questions Coppélia and I asked our contributors – What experiences made you a feminist scholar and how did your feminism affect the way you teach and write about literature? – flew in the face of current theoretical positions, in assuming that writing grows out of experience and expresses a self, since both "self" and "experience" are discredited categories. "Yet it remains true," as DuPlessis says, "that feminist criticism exists, that it came from the women's movement, ... that some of the 'we' in or around these pages did some of this: invented and sustained a major intellectual renaissance – possibly even a 'paradigm shift' – in the past twenty-odd years" (chapter 6, p.97). It also remains true (though narrative itself has been called into question) that stories, stories about the self, stories by women and about women's selves, had enormous power and continue to have power in the creation of feminist consciousness.[6]

At a time when feminism has lost much of its political edge and is undergoing assaults from all sides, it is important that we learn to say "I" and "we" again, though "I" and "we" are not so simple.[7] In the years since Coppélia and I began this anthology, feminism has come to seem even more endangered, more cut off from a popular and a political base, more threatened by conservative tendencies from without and by divisions from within. "Better get it on record before it disappears," as Ann Jones quipped when I told her that we were working on this collection, a remark which has haunted me. As Annette Kolodny urges, we need "to take responsibility for recovering our history," lest others write it for us (1988: 464).[8] Rich's injunction in 1979 – that we "come together telling our stories" – has a new urgency (1979a: 13).

Feminism has already disappeared once in this century, and we are now living through the second backlash that's occurred within fifty years. The similarities between the first reaction, immediately after women won the vote, and what's going on today are chilling. In fact the word "postfeminist" – which sprang to the pages of the *New York Times* in the notorious 1982 article (Bolotin) that described young women as disaffected with feminism, as seeing feminists as man-hating, masculine, lesbian, militant, and hairy-legged – was actually first used in 1919, when (as Nancy Cott tells us) "a group of female literary radicals in Greenwich Village" founded a new journal declaring an interest "in people ... not in men and women"; they called their stance "postfeminist."[9] Assuming that women's rights are all won, women forget; and worse than forgetting, they make "feminism" a dirty word, a "term of opprobrium," as Dorothy Dunbar Bromley said in 1927.[10] By the 1950s there were fewer women in higher education – fewer Ph.D.s, fewer women on faculties – than there had been in any decade since 1900.[11]

"Postfeminism" today is not just a media hype, though the media have gleefully pushed it: backlash is evident in the attitudes of the young, in the erosion of civil rights and gains made by women and minorities, in the virulent reactions against change both within the academy and without.[12] It is further evident in tendencies to blame feminism for everything from the breakdown of the family to the increase in violence against women – in the "prevailing wisdom" that "it must be all that equality that's causing all that pain" (Faludi 1991: x).[13] What equality? one might well ask, when old inequities continue and new ones exist for which new terms – "the feminization of poverty," "the glass ceiling" – have been invented. "We've managed to enter a postfeminist world," as Wendy Kaminer says, "without ever knowing a feminist one" (1990: 1).

In 1985, Betty Friedan described "the new generation" of women as "each thinking she is alone with her personal guilt and pressures, trying to 'have it all,' " women "almost as isolated, and as powerless in their isolation, as those suburban housewives afflicted by 'the problem that had no name' whom I interviewed for *The Feminine Mystique* over twenty years ago" (1985: 89). Anita Shreve's interviews with women in consciousness-raising groups, fifteen years later, demonstrate how women who have struggled to "have it all" find themselves burned out and alone, and how even those whose lives were transformed by the women's movement now dissociate themselves from feminism (1989: *passim*). Ruth Sidel's *On Her Own: Growing up in the Shadow of the American Dream* analyzes the discrepancy between what young women expect of their futures – their fantasies that they will move into prestigious upper-middle-class jobs like those portrayed in the media – and the low-paying dead-end jobs that are actually awaiting them (1990: *passim*). What such studies show is the dead-end of career feminism, the bankruptcy of a feminism imagined as "having it all," and the increasing isolation and bewilderment of women who seem to lack even the terms to analyze their situations – though "the problem" is no longer without "a name," since feminism has been naming it for twenty years. They also confirm – what one senses working with students – that young people have bought into an ideology of individualism and materialism that incapacitates them from challenging the system or even from realizing that it is in need of change.

These are bad times for women – and for children and minorities and poor people and old people and working people and what's left of the left; and this larger problem, a system losing its grip and thrashing about in search of scapegoats for its failures, is probably not something feminist scholars can single-handedly change. But the difference between the first wave of feminism and this second wave is precisely in the existence of feminist scholarship, of a large and diverse and vital body of work that constitutes a significant oppositional force. It is here that we've presented fundamental challenges to the structures and institutions of society – marriage, the family, gender roles, the academic disciplines – and to the structure of knowledge itself. There was no equivalent to this in the first wave of feminism. In this, critical theory has been an invaluable tool, for it has provided means to dismantle epistemological categories and reveal systems as systems, as conventional rather than "natural." This means that feminist scholarship is extremely important; far from being irrelevant, as academics are too prone to feel, we have a real mission. Our task as teachers and scholars is to develop critical and political consciousness in those who are coming of age in a world dominated by Republicans and reaction and cynicism and fear.

Yet it's discouraging to see how little feminist awareness has filtered out beyond the walls of academia, how badly feminism is misrepresented and misunderstood. Out there in the so-called real world, most women go their ways, working in underpaid dead-end jobs, continuing in exploitative relationships, and generally living as though the women's movement had never happened. Most women – if my students and non-academic friends are any indication – have no understanding of what the women's movement is about. Most have accepted the media smear of feminists as bra-burning, hairy-legged, man-hating fanatics and have no sense that feminism might have anything to do with the problems they face in their lives. I remember when Gilligan's new research on teenage girls, articulating the crisis of confidence that hits girls at age 11 – a crisis from which most never recover – made the *New York Times* (7 January 1990: 23ff.), a very intelligent doctor friend of mine reacted the way we used to with our conversion "clicks"; how she xeroxed the article and took it around to the nurses in her hospital who similarly thought it was big news – these same nurses who would never in a million years identify with feminism. But Gilligan's work has been around for a long time, long enough to have drawn fire from feminists who have been blasting away at it for its essentialism, its class bias, etc. Of course her assertions don't apply equally well to all women (whose do?) but how is it that we haven't realized how useful her differentiation between the way women (some women) and men (some men) approach problems might be to the many women

struggling in the professions, isolated in male-defined hierarchies and environments that convince them, when they approach a decision differently from their
male colleagues, that they are crazy and alone, as women in the 1950s were
convinced they were crazy and alone? Seems like we've failed to communicate.
Or maybe we just haven't cared.

I remember talking to women at the women writers' conferences in Dubrovnik
in 1986, 1988, and 1990. It's becoming more and more the case that what goes
on between the talks is more interesting than what goes on in the talks; usually
what I return with these days is a wry sense of the sociology of a conference.
Anyway, I spent a lot of time during those weeks talking with women from
Yugoslavia, Switzerland, Germany, Hungary, England, Italy – some of them
graduate students, some of them lecturers, most living on shoestring budgets,
developing their feminist scholarship and fledgling women's studies programs at
considerable cost and risk. These women had taken great pains and expense to
get themselves to this "international" (US-dominated) conference, and many of
those I talked with did not feel their efforts were well rewarded. Many were
mystified by papers on the repositioning of female subjectivity, on subtle delin-
eations between Professor X's and Professor Y's ideas of subjectivity, theories
spun off other theories that seemed to touch down nowhere. I heard outrage at
how rarely these papers addressed questions of social significance or social
change. While these women were looking to feminist scholars in the US, where
the women's movement is still stronger than anywhere in the world, we were
purifying our theoretical apparatus, refining our relation to Derrida and Lacan,
fine-tuning our definitions. I'm not saying that such definitions are without point
– only that they are not the whole point. I came away feeling that the sense of
disappointment and betrayal that I heard from European women was justified,
and that it pointed to a major failing of academic feminism in the US.

Marianne Hirsch and Evelyn Fox Keller begin their anthology *Conflicts in
Feminism* with the observation:

> A decade ago, we thought of ourselves as part of – even in the vanguard of –
> a movement that then seemed capable of changing the world. We thought of
> feminist theory as an arm of that movement, as providing a radically new, and
> potentially revolutionary wedge for rethinking, and accordingly, for reshaping
> the social, political and economic world in which we lived.
>
> (1990:1)

They conclude with the admission that "however illuminating the essays here may
be about the nature of the conflicts that currently engage feminists, what remains
unexplained is why feminist theorists find themselves with so little forward
momentum at this particular moment in time" (385). This is a real question: at a
time when it's more urgent than ever that we make ourselves heard, we seem to
have lost our voice. As bell hooks says, the feminist movement has not "had an
ongoing radical focus which addresses many people... it is our task (and here
when I say 'our' I mean any of us who are committed to revolutionary feminist

movement) to work at challenging and changing the focus, the direction of future feminist movement" (1990: 1).[14]

Following hooks' precedent, I use "we" in the following pages to refer to those of us who are committed to change. I'm assuming that despite the prob-lematization of this pronoun, despite the rifts within feminism, there is this much agreement: that we who still call ourselves feminists still agree that we want change, and our notion of change is not fundamentally different from what it was.

CHANGING THE FOCUS

We – feminists in academia – inhabit an environment that is unbelievably hostile to what we do. This has got to be remembered, and it can hardly be overstated. Feminist criticism grew up in and was shaped by institutions dominated by men and dedicated to a tradition that has never served our interests; and in many ways, it shows. What has happened with women in academia is a microcosm of what has happened with women in society – and it is what always happens, historically: a few women are let in so that there are a few women in visible positions who can be pointed to as evidence that women have made it; meanwhile the majority of women are left where they always were. This means that much of what has succeeded in academia has been allowed to succeed because it's the kind of feminism institutions can live with. A theoretical discourse that's preoccupied by increasingly subtle deconstructions of subjectivity and experience is unlikely to be much concerned with changing people or experience; it's no accident that this is the going thing.

Feminist scholarship provokes as much, if not more, rage and hysteria today than it did in the mid-seventies, when Carol Neely and Carolyn Ruth Swift Lenz and I began work on *The Woman's Part*. This is evident in that 1988 *PMLA* attack on feminist criticism of Shakespeare by Richard Levin, enthusiastically supported in letters in subsequent issues,[15] which demonstrated, among other things, that despite the fact that the male power-base of institutions remains substantially unchanged, and despite reactionary forces proliferating against us, the old boys really do believe that we have taken over. And this turned out to be the tip of the iceberg, for attacks on what is now termed "political correctness" have made it clear how much opposition there is to radicalism in the academy, how real and dangerous the backlash is.

Yet it would be simpler if the enemy were always this obvious, the guys who attack us in public forums: what's more insidious is the enemy who has outposts in your head, as Sally Kempton argued in that wonderfully sassy early feminist essay "Cutting Loose." DuPlessis admits to anxieties "to 'prove' something (unknown) to someone (unknown)" (Chapter 6, p. 100); Carolyn Porter struggles with questions of "male identification" (Chapter 12); Betsy Ermarth warns of the power of the patriarchal compliment that takes you aside and seduces with the promise, "you are not like other women" (Chapter 17, p. 233). Jane Tompkins describes her initial embarrassment encountering "women's studies" ("how pathetic, I thought… . And in such bad taste," 1989: 121). Miller describes the loss of status incurred when one turns from "real" scholarship to the study of women writers (Chapter 2, p. 39) – a loss I can vouch for in the change I felt in peoples' attitudes when I left Shakespeare for contemporary women's fiction, although this was the boldest move I'd ever made. "You are too good to need to do that, to jump on that bandwagon," I was warned by an eminent Shakespearean whom I'd long admired. (He was wrong, it wasn't a bandwagon but a backwater, in the sense that it bounced me off the gravy train of grants and goodies that come with a conventional slot; there would have been much more respectability in staying with Shakespeare than moving in with that dubious lot – contemporary writers, *women* writers, what's more.) The signals reach us, directly and indirectly, through cajolery, flattery, warning, implicit and explicit – if we heed them we are rewarded, if we resist, we are dropped; and they are so subtle and persuasive that we may bend to them without noticing, without noticing how they have bent us out of shape.

At a time when traditional gender roles and relations are being energetically reasserted, there are strong incentives for not identifying ourselves as feminists, or even as women. The "feminine" has always been viewed as unprofessional, and now, as women are actually moving into the professions, it is more than ever suspect. At a time when feminism is being declared the root of all evil from the right and being dismissed as passé from the left (what these wildly contradictory positions have in common is the erasure of feminism), at a time when feminism is the new "F-word" both within academia and without, even feminist scholars will find ways of avoiding it in book titles, course titles, program titles. Susan Bordo suggests that the "gender scepticism" implicit in the essentialism debate may be a way of allowing us to eradicate "gender" as an analytical category rather than admit to our own ambivalences (1990: 148); Hester Eisenstein suggests that "having failed to create a feminism that captures the imagination of women, we question whether women exist" (UCLA Conference, 4 May 1991). While it has been important to interrogate the language of identity and be clear about the implications of saying "we," pronouns may not be the most burning issue of the day.[16] Given the virulence of anti-feminist and racist backlash, this is no time to become transfixed by our own ingenuity.[17]

It is strange, as Bordo points out, that white feminism, "now critically scrutinizing (and often utterly discrediting) its conceptions of 'female' reality and morality and its 'gendered' readings of culture *barely more than a decade after they began to be produced*" is being so fiercely attacked as " 'resistant' to recognizing its own fictions of unity" (1990: 141-2). As Bordo suggests, "where once the prime objects of academic feminist critique were the phallocentric narratives of our male-dominated disciplines, now feminist criticism has turned to its own narratives, finding them reductionist, totalizing, inadequately nuanced, valorizing of gender difference, unconsciously racist, and elitist" (135). Being a feminist literary scholar seems more and more to be "a matter of keeping abreast of the current repudiations," as Molly Hite says (Chapter 8, p. 125). But I sense a self-defeating tendency in much of this, a critical implosion that has the sound of a grinding halt. I wonder, also, if turning in on ourselves with this fierce self-scrutiny isn't a form of self-erasure, an analogue to our obsession with thinness, a way of assuring ourselves and others that we'll take up less space – a kind of professional/pedagogical anorexia.

I'm by no means advocating that feminist criticism divorce itself from theory or be "untheoretical," though I do think we need to think about theory more broadly and enlist it more judiciously. Actually, there is no such thing as an untheoretical position, though there are untheorized positions – feminists have long known this – but theory has a more general meaning than we in literary criticism have come to think. It means, or at least it used to mean and still does mean to people outside lit. crit., "a lifting of thought to a more abstract, often more systematic level in an effort to provide a framework or grounding for interpretation and/or explanation" (as Elizabeth Minnich defines it). In fact there are more kinds of theoretical positions than are dreamt of in our current philosophies, as Barbara Christian and bell hooks remind us.[18] The fact that "theory" has come to be so narrowly associated with the ideas of Lacan, Derrida, Barthes, says something about what's happened in literary studies, where (once again) a group of white male-authored canonical texts is at the center.

In 1985, in the Introduction to *Making a Difference,* Coppélia and I urged that feminist scholarship ally itself with poststructuralism. But now I wonder: in this argument for alliances, who's being allied with whom, and for what? I wonder if this wasn't (at least partly) a pitch for intellectual respectability, for legitimization – a pitch which was never even necessary, even within these terms, since American feminism has from the beginning cut its teeth on ideas from France, as the essays in this volume demonstrate. (Ann Jones, Leslie Rabine, Jerry Ann Flieger, Molly Hite, Betsy Ermarth, Carolyn Porter describe how crucial theory was in their development, how it opened up questions and categories and provided tools for reconceptualization: the usual categorization of French feminism as "theoretical" and American feminism as "pragmatic" collapses under such testimonies.) It seems a great waste of time to expend further energies establishing our credentials, demonstrating how feminism fits in with or around Lacan, Derrida, Lyotard, or how we're superior to our benighted compatriots (Showalter and Gilbert and Gubar are the favorite targets).

I'm not the first to worry that theory has become the new standard-setter, the source and center of professional prestige,[19] or to wonder how it happened that "theory" got to be defined as something that takes precedence over feminist theory, when – as Miller asks – "isn't the discovery (Beauvoir's) that femininity is produced by a complex concatenation of discursive and non-discursive events as exciting as the proposition (Foucault's) that sexuality (as it turns out, male) is inseparable from the effects and articulations of power?" (1991: 65). (Why, right here at Scripps, at a women's college dedicated to the education of women, my course in feminist theory was refused credit as "the senior seminar": the senior seminar is in "real" theory and is taught by a white male.) Nor am I the first to wonder how "cultural studies" got defined as something different from "feminist studies": what else has feminist scholarship ever been but the study of culture? I'm troubled that we may be consenting to this hierarchy when we urge alliances, or when we urge feminists to "get theory" (as Tompkins did, 1989: 22). Why do we not insist, rather, that these guys seek alliances with *us,* that they learn our language? Because this is not an option, because we are still second-class citizens; because (as Miller notes) "the perception of authority diminishes in direct proportion to the speaker's proximity to feminist discourse" (1991: 66).

So what it comes down to, again, is power, who's at the center, who's King of the Mountain. The issue is legitimization, validation – personal, intellectual, institutional power – with theory as the means, in a set of moves that reinscribes traditionally gendered relations. Since only those who do theory are invited to speak in prominent places, get offered glitzy jobs, high salaries and other perks, is it any wonder that everybody's doin' it, and that our students are spinning out imitations – often rote, formulaic, and mindless for all their ingenuity – as fast as they can? Who wouldn't want to be a star? The problem is not with "theory" *per se* or with theory at all, but with the enlistment of theory in this scramble for power and position.[20]

At a conference on Feminism and Representation (Providence, 1989), for example, the stars came late, left early, and collected large honoraria, while the rest of us talked for free. The two-tiered structure, with plenary sessions for the stars and lots of little seminars for the peons, was a statement about hierarchy; but what was more troubling was the high positive correlation between stardom and incomprehensibility and that there were so many aspiring starlets in the seminars who were doing such convincing imitations of stellar incomprehensibility. Since most of the stars left right after they had given their papers there was no opportunity for dialogue, though there was much discontented muttering of the sort I'm venting here – and perhaps the fact that such muttering is making its way into print suggests that the tide is turning.[21]

The question is, once we've "got theory, " what do we do with it? What's it for? Who's it for? What Tey Diana Rebolledo says of Chicanos applies as well to feminists: there's a risk that in using theory to legitimize ourselves we may actually be "privileging the theoretical discourse" in a way that "de-privileges ourselves" (1990: 348). Theory serves us well as a tool of radical critique of the systems that subordinate us, but it does not serve us well as a tool for personal power and higher salaries (though what I do mean – "us"?). In the early days of feminism, I remember a lot of talk about the dangers of co-optation; I don't hear a lot of that kind of talk any more, now when the disconnection of theory from the political and its connection to the star system endangers us more than ever. As hooks suggests, "Living as we do in a culture that promotes narcissism, that encourages it because it deflects attention away from our capacity to form political commitments that address issues rather than identity," we often seem "more engaged by who was speaking/writing than by what they were saying"; such "cults of personality" have "severely limited feminist movement" (1989: 164). Stardom is about hierarchy, self, career, commodification; it is not about dialogue or action or collectivity or the political (except in the most strategic, self-serving sense).

I realize it's not always easy to distinguish between those uses of theory that have social and political value and those that do not, when everyone who uses theory claims to be radical ("subversive" and "oppositional" are fashionable words, but increasingly void of political content); and I realize also that this is a judgment that will vary according to where one is. There is always the risk of dismissing something as incomprehensible or inconsequential because you haven't worked it through sufficiently to see its implications – but I think it's important to take that risk, to try to differentiate between criticism that's useful and not useful, to ask (as Modleski says) "what's in these developments *for feminism* and for women?" (1991: 5). As Jouve says, "you are still in the same business as the artists themselves. The business of making sense of life"; "Unless criticism springs out of genuine analysis of the real world, and in its turn affects it … then it inhabits the realm of fantasy" (1991: 9,8).

I am a literary critic who is concerned with social change. The books I've found most valuable in my work on contemporary women's fiction in the past several years – Rachel Blau DuPlessis' *Writing Beyond the Ending*, Molly Hite's *The Other Side*, Rita Felski's *Beyond Feminist Aesthetics* – enlist theory to illuminate the relation of literature to change. DuPlessis demonstrates ways that twentieth-century women writers challenge the gender ideology inscribed in narrative forms; Hite describes ways that these challenges are as radical as those of canonized "postmodern" male writers; and Felski examines the problems of defining a "feminist aesthetic." In *Changing the Story* I analyze feminist metafiction as emerging from a decade of rapid change for women and developing narrative strategies that allow readers to work through processes of change. Such approaches enlist theory, or theories, to interrogate cultural assumptions and categories, to explore interactions of literary conventions with social conventions, with an eye to feminist politics.

I'm urging that feminist scholars write with a clearer sense of responsibility to a social movement, that we try to revitalize some important connections – between ourselves and our audience, our writing and its effects. That we think about reaching people outside academia who might actually read our books if they were more interesting. I'd urge that we ask, of our books, articles, and conference papers: Is this a necessary or useful idea? To whom is it necessary or useful? Am I saying this to clarify some idea or information or to insert myself into a critical discourse whose purpose I have not questioned, perhaps, even, to place myself beyond accountability by being so ingenious that no one can possibly understand me?[22] I'd urge that we stop dancing attendance on those who still have power to confer rewards and benefits (and there are endless versions of this insidious game), that we envision our audience not as that patriarch in our head who may finally confer approval on us, but think of ourselves, rather, as reaching people to whom *we* have a responsibility, whom *we* might empower, whether or not they can do us any good. I'm not saying that everyone needs to leave Shakespeare to work on women writers: it's important that feminists not abandon the canon and the study of pre-modern periods to those who have traditionally held them. But I do think that everyone needs to do some equivalent to "leaving Shakespeare" in terms of thinking through questions of purpose and audience – who are we writing for and why – and that we try to balance career-building with concern for collectivity.

I'd urge that the tyranny of trends, the new for its own sake, be resisted – and I can't help associating this with the planned obsolescence of consumerism, the three-minute attention spans of students educated by television, and the flash and trash of show-biz, which academia seems to resemble more each season.[23] That we exercise some independence of judgment and not let novelty and ingenuity be our standards. Nor do I think that practical criticism ought to be despised just because it isn't spinning out a new theory, a theory that often, as Christian suggests, rides roughshod over the complexities of the literature itself (1987: 53, 59). I'd even argue that it's okay to love literature, to teach that reading can be a pleasure, rather than being hard, closed, and the possession of an elite. I'd go further and say that reading can serve radical ends – and in fact it will do so the more effectively, the more accessible it is.

REINSTATING THE SUBJECT

In the years since Coppélia and I began this project, the autobiographical mode has become more prominent. Miller notes that though "the authority of experience" was basic to feminist inquiry from the start, most academic feminists have used a depersonalized, academic style, in order to pass, but that some also deployed experimental, autobiographical, and personal modes; this created "a contrapuntal effect, breaking into the monolithic and monologizing authorized discourse" (1991: 14–15). Miller cites DuPlessis' "For the Etruscans," Carolyn Heilbrun's *Reinventing Womanhood*, Carolyn Steedman's *Landscape for a Good Woman*, Patricia Williams' "On being the object of property," Ann Snitow's "A gender diary," bell hooks' *Talking Back*, Cherríe Moraga's *This Bridge Called My Back*, and others, as evidence of a "turning point in the history of critical practices" (p. x). She poses important questions (pp. 2-3): Why is this form of writing appearing now? Is this a gendered form? Is it trivial, self-centered? Oppositional or recuperative? Is it "antitheory" or "a new stage of theory"?

Miller speculates that the surfacing of such writing now has to do with "the waning of enthusiasm for a mode of Theory, whose authority … depended finally on the theoretical evacuation of the very social subjects producing it" (p. 20); and everything I've said here indicates my agreement. But I'd emphasize – as she does – that personal criticism, rather than a practice pitted against theory and reinforcing the usual binarisms (personal against public, female against male, concrete against abstract), may be imbricated in theory in a way which broadens the notion of theory; and that, far from turning in on itself in a response which is trivial, self-indulgent, "merely personal," such writing is "engaged" (1991: 24). Saying "I" may provide the condition of a new kind of contract, "the chance for a vividly renegotiated sociality" and "an enlivening cultural criticism" (xix, 25).[24] Personal criticism need not be solipsistic, soloistic, self-indulgent, or naïve, "a search for that lost, pure, true, real, genuine, original, authentic self,"[25] but may demonstrate – as Biddy Martin and Chandra Talpade Mohanty describe the essays in *Yours in Struggle* – how "individual self-reflection and critical practice might translate into the building of political collectivity" (1986: 210).

To say "I," to "get personal," is a way of centering ourselves, grounding ourselves; to articulate the relation of that "I" to the social and political forces that have shaped us is a way of making that "I" more than personal, of re-envisioning the personal as political – it is a way of saying "I" while also saying "we." The essays in this book speculate about the collective implications of saying "I." Zimmerman re-thinks "experience" in a way that differentiates it from individualism: "I am not a separate being with my own private and personal experience; my experience, my selfhood, is constituted by others .... when I think of experience as relational and socially constructed, not as personal and individual, I can still use experience as a meaningful category on which to base my politics" (Chapter 7, p. 118). Ermarth differentiates "the person," which "exists socially and discursively," from "the individual," and suggests that, viewed this way, saying "I" allows individual expression at the same time that it "posits that expression in collective terms"; this is "not a soloist's achievement, but, instead, a power conferred by a constituency" (Chapter 17, pp. 236–7). Her analysis resembles hooks' description of what "southern black folks" know:

> That the self existed in relation, was dependent for its very being on the lives and experiences of everyone, the self not as signifier of one "I" but the coming together of many "I's," the self as embodying collective reality past and present, family and community ... . It is this collective voice we struggle to recover.
>
> (1989: 30–1)

Hite argues – and demonstrates in her essay – that "for a writer aware of the contradictions in her own socially constructed 'self,' the project of 'self-writing' is invariably a self-conscious one," "a canny, duplicitous exercise" (Chapter 8, p. 122).[26]

Reinstating the subject is important for reasons explained by Joan E. Hartman and Ellen Messer-Davidow, in a brilliant new collection of essays, *(En)Gendering Knowledge*, that argues for the necessity of a "feminist social epistemology." The essays in this volume demonstrate why feminist inquiry needs to remain linked to an investigation of the ways reality is constructed – to a sense of "knowers as social agents, knowing as social practice ... knowledge as productive of social consequences" (Hartman and Messer-Davidow, 1991: 2). This entails acknowledging the knower as part of the process by which knowledge is produced, inscribing ourselves into our discourse, "activat[ing] our identities" (Harding, 1991: 103), and presenting our knowledge as "corrected by critical reflection and self-reflection" (Hartman and Messer-Davidow 1991: 22). To own our social locations, to reveal "the differences [our] own race or sexuality, class and gender, have made in the knowledge [we] produce" (ibid.: 2), is to "generate new ways of seeing the world" (Harding:113), whereas to disown ourselves and hide behind a fraudulent objectivity is to perpetuate the paradigms of knowledge we wish to challenge. Yet white feminists have been more willing to scrutinize other groups – working-class women, women of color – than to turn the same lens on ourselves: "Why have 'we,' individually and collectively, been so unwilling or unable to take a good look at ourselves?" (Bammer, 1991: 245). Hartman and Messer-Davidow demonstrate how crucial "looking at ourselves" is to the project of feminism, how important a feminist social epistemology is to restoring agency, to reinvigorating "our capacity as agents to act as well as to know" (p. 6), in order that we may "rejoin what we put asunder in the early days of the Second Women's Movement: our intellectual inquiry and our social activism" (p. 1).

The essays in *Changing Subjects* join self-reflection and critical practice in the rebuilding of connections – between personal and political, between academic and non-academic, between writers and readers, between theory and praxis. It is my hope that they will participate in the broadening and enlivening and politiciz-ing not only of theory, but of feminist scholarship and feminism itself – which is, after all, the point. I hope that this history, this sort of history, may play some small part in the revitalizing of political purpose and collectivity – that by seeing where we come from we may see more clearly where we are going – and that feminism may have the powers of adaptation and resistance that will enable it to continue as a force in history.

NOTES

1 Marge Piercy's "Through the Cracks" captures this "isolation and dead-endedness" of the 1950s: what was "lacking" was "a sense of possibilities": "there was little satisfaction for me in the forms offered, yet there seemed no space but death or madness outside the forms"; "nowhere could I find images of a life I considered good or useful or dignified"; "I could not make connections" (1974: 208, 215, 207).

2 I did not realize it, but I was not alone in seeking in fiction for the meaning and connections missing from my life: Doris Lessing, Margaret Drabble, Gail Godwin, Marge Piercy, Erica Jong write of characters growing up in these years who turned to reading this way.

3 It wasn't this simple, of course. I am omitting a good deal, making it all sound much clearer and cleaner than it was. I am leaving out the pain and confusion and loneliness – what it was like plodding through a Ph.D. program with the certainty that what awaited me when I got out, in the mid-seventies, would be unemployment; what it was like to be buffeted about by those strong sexual attractions against which there seemed no defense, that combined with the coldness of Columbia to leave me feeling unfit for life, let alone able to imagine a future. Perhaps this is what narrative does, looks back from an end and selects the steps leading to that end; or perhaps that pain is the subject of another story. The truth is that both stories are true – that despite the anguish of those years, there was this thinking, writing being struggling to survive and make sense of it. I write therefore I am. Of course there was also a lot of luck (though there was a bit of

bad luck too), and a lot of white middle-class support to fall back on – both financial and emotional – from a family that, despite its fuck-ups, had a way of coming through.

4 bell hooks notes "how deeply connected that split [between public and private] is to ongoing practices of domination... . That's why I think it crucial to think about the points where the public and the private meet, to connect the two. And even folks who talk about ending domination seem afraid to break down the space separating the two" (1989: 2). Jane Tompkins describes personal criticism as a challenge to the dichotomy between public and private which "is a founding condition of female oppression" (1989: 123).

5 Which "instructs by quiet magic women to sing proper pliant tunes for father, lover, piper who says he has the secret." Honore Moore, quoted in Miller (1991: 36).

6 Rita Felski argues that "the autobiographical novel continues to remain a major literary form for oppressed groups, as a medium for confronting problems of self and of cultural identity which fulfills important social needs" (1989: 78,169). In *Changing the Story* (1991), chapter 2, I demonstrate the ways feminist writing, fictional and theoretical, helped shape the women's movement.

7 But as Nicole Ward Jouve suggests, it is precisely "because subjecthood has become so difficult, has been so deconstructed, that there is need to work towards it. This is particularly so for women" (1991: 11). Jouve speaks of "the need to speak as a subject, and as a subject bent on self-knowledge. We have lost ourselves in the endlessly diffracted light of Deconstruction... . For we [especially women] have been asked to go along with Deconstruction whilst we had not even got to the Construction stage. You must have a self before you can afford to deconstruct it" (7). Or, as Miller puts it, "only those who have it can play with not having it" (1982: 52).

8 At the conference "What Ever Happened to Women's Liberation?" (UCLA, 3–4 May 1991), historians expressed this concern. Paula Giddings suggested that we need to write our own history or history will be written for us; Alice Echols described the tendency of histories of the sixties to erase the women's movement; she cited Todd Gitlin, James Miller, Tom Hayden, Stuart Burns as "marginalizing us better than the movements did." Adrienne Rich refers to "the erasure of women's political and historic past" wherein the "history of women's struggle for self-determination has been muffled in silence over and over" (1979a: 9,11).

9 Cott (1987: 282, 365, n.3) cites *Judy* 1, no. 1 (June 1919); *Judy* 2, no. 3 (1919). The Arthur and Elizabeth Schlesinger Library on the History of Women in America, Radcliffe College, Cambridge Mass; Cott, 1987: 365, n. 23.

10 "Feminist – New Style," *Harpers*, 155, October 1927, 152–60; in Chafe, 1972: 92, 278. Lillian Hellman described "the emancipation of women" as "stale stuff" (1969: 35).

11 Cott, 1987: 218. See also Showalter, 1988: 822–41.

12 See Kaminer (1990: chapter 9), Rosenfelt and Stacey (1987: 341–61), and Faludi (1991).

13 Kaminer also discusses tendencies to blame the women's movement for the problems of women (*passim*).

14 Annette Kolodny refers to the erosion of "the originating revolutionary potential of feminism" and the "severing of the link between feminist literary inquiry and feminism as a political agenda" (1988: 457). Cora Kaplan describes feminism as "cut off ... from what women are actually writing and from a political movement" (1989: 19, 21).

15 *PMLA* 103 (1988), 125–38, and 817–19; and 104 (1989), 77–9. The article and the letters, as well as my response to the essay and other responses, along with responses to those responses, are published in *Shakespeare Left and Right* (Kamps 1991). It was an attack that, given its stupidity, generated an inordinate amount of attention.

16 Naomi Scheman suggests that the reason we need to be clear about saying "we" is "not out of a desire for theoretical sophistication but out of the need to overcome the white solipsism that has blocked alliances between white women and women of color. Such

alliances – and theories of gender that facilitate them – needn't be grounded in similarities... . Rather, they can be grounded in our interconnectedness, in how our very different ways of being constructed as women have implicated each other" (1991: 189). I find Scheman's distinction between assuming similarities and assuming interconnections useful in thinking about identity politics.

17 As Deborah McDowell says, "we have become much too comfortable with radical language," which can "sometimes be an act of substitution" for "radical action" (1989: 25). Hooks notes that the subject of race is being mystified by the "buzz words" "difference, the Other, hegemony, ethnography" which have replaced "more commonly known words deemed uncool or too simplistic, words like oppression, exploitation, and domination," and which enable race to be "talked about, as though it were in no way linked to cultural practices" (1990: 51, 54).

18 As hooks suggests, "Increasingly, only one type of theory is seen as valuable, that which is Euro-centric, linguistically convoluted." "Rather than expanding our notions of theory to include types of theory that can be produced in many different writing styles ... the vision of what theory is becomes a narrow, constricting concept" (1989: 36).

19 See Christian (1987: 51–2). Kolodny also describes the shift in prestige to institutes of critical theory and explains it in terms of "high-powered men ... bent on fleeing not only an increasingly feminized professoriat but ... an increasingly persuasive feminist practice ... the male 'muscle' of the profession aimed at theory *in order* to distinguish itself from a feminism that had never been systematically theory-driven." But when feminists came on over to theory, this produced "a new move 'against theory' " (1988: 455–6).

20 Although Paul Lauter notes that "literary theory has proven remarkably easy to assimilate to the structure of American university life; indeed, it has become a strong re-enforcement of existing academic norms. The practice of literary theory in no sense challenges the individualistic, production-oriented forms of the American academy, much less the marketplace ideology and the organizational structures into which the colleges largely guide their students"; "And it helps maintain a hierarchical relationship between the privileged discourse of the academy and practical criticism, mainly carried out in the classroom. In that regard, the obscurity of language that has come to characterize most theoretical writing is no unfortunate accident but rather an essential element" (1991: 141). Scheman suggests that "incomprehensibility serves in fact to protect the structures of privilege we take ourselves to be so brilliantly skewering" (1991: 194).

21 Lauter describes how "at one of the most crowded sessions on criticism at the 1982 [MLA] convention three rather complex, not to say obscure, papers were presented. At the end, with an unusual amount of time left, the chair asked for comments or questions. A heavy silence spread through the room. No one spoke. People shifted disconsolately. The session finally ended." Speaking up, Lauter notes, "presents far too high a risk" (1991: 13). Tey Diana Rebolledo describes "a typical talk" at "a recent Chicano Studies Conference": "the speaker begins, 'This paper will focus on the ideology of cultural practice and its modes of signifying.' S/he then spends twenty minutes discussing how the works of whatever theoretical greats s/he selects will define, inform and privilege the work s/he is doing. Such names as Jameson, Said, Williams, Hall, Burke and other contemporary *meros, meros* (mostly male) will be invoked over and over. The speaker is then sent a note by the chair of the panel that there is no time left. And whatever the Chicano/a writing or phenomenon that was to be discussed is quickly summarized in two minutes. The talk is over" (1990: 347–8). Such virtuoso performances issue into nothing – not even talk.

22 As Angelika Bammer suggests, "we should be particularly conscious of our acts of selection in relation to language": are we using difficult language "because it is appropriate to the complexity of our analysis? Can we make complexity accessible in order to

permit communication?"; for such questions really come down to the question, "when is our language a means of exchange, and when is it a tool of domination?" (1991: 253–4).

23 As Jouve notes, "the cult of the new, in the past twenty years, has been a sign of vitality: it has also done a great deal of harm. The pace of consumption has been too fast, generating panic, the constant need for more, the greed to be stimulated and to absorb and digest and move on" (1991: 8).

24 Elisabeth Young-Bruehl credits feminism with the fact that "I" has "made its way" into academic discourse and suggests that "those scholars, who, writing from multicultural or suppressed cultural perspectives, construct their work around the scrupulous observation of their 'I's' are creating the most compelling texts in academia today" (1991: 15, 18).

25 This is Trinh T. Minh-ha's term, "Not You/Like You: Post-Colonial Women and the Interlocking Questions of Identity and Difference" (in Anzaldúa 1990: 371).

26 I find Hite's defense of narrative more useful than Kauffman's dismissal of it – but of course, as an editor of this collection of essays, I would. I was troubled, among other things, by Kauffman's indiscriminate lumping together of everything one doesn't like – "personal criticism," self-help books, essays solicited for this volume – as representative of "individualism"; and as a literary critic concerned with social change, I'm not sure I'm ready to ditch narrative trajectories that have moral lessons.

REFERENCES

Anzaldúa, Gloria (ed.) (1990) *Making Face, Making Soul: Creative and Critical Perspectives by Women of Color*, San Francisco: An Aunt Lute Foundation Book.

Bammer, Angelika (1991) "Mastery," in Hartman and Messer-Davidow (eds) (1991), 237–58.

Bolotin, Susan (1982) "Voices from the Post-Feminist Generation," *New York Times Magazine*, 17 October, 28ff.

Bordo, Susan (1990) "Feminism, Postmodernism, and Gender-Scepticism," in Linda J. Nicholson (ed.) *Feminism/Postmodernism*, New York: Routledge, 133–56.

Bromley, Dorothy Dunbar (1927) "Feminist – new style," *Harpers*, 155 (October), 152–60.

Chafe, William (1972) *The American Woman: Her Changing Social, Economic, and Political Roles, 1920-1970*, London: Oxford University Press.

Christian, Barbara (1987) "The Race for Theory," *Cultural Critique* (spring), 51–63.

Cott, Nancy (1987) *The Grounding of Modern Feminism*, New Haven: Yale University Press.

de Beauvoir, Simone (1952) *The Second Sex*, New York: Vintage.

DuPlessis, Rachel Blau (1985) *Writing Beyond the Ending: Narrative Strategies of Twentieth-Century Women Writers*, Bloomington: Indiana University Press.

Echols, Alice (1991) "History as Politics," UCLA conference, "What Ever Happened to Women's Liberation?" 3–4 May.

Faludi, Susan (1991) *Backlash: The Undeclared War Against American Women*, New York: Crown.

Felski, Rita (1989) *Beyond Feminist Aesthetics: Feminist Literature and Social Change*, Cambridge, Mass.: Harvard University Press.

Friedan, Betty (1985) "How to Get the Women's Movement Moving Again," *New York Times Magazine* 3 November, 26ff.

Giddings, Paula (1991) "Memory as Resistance," UCLA conference, "What Ever Happened to Women's Liberation?" 3–4 May.

Greene, Gayle (1991) *Changing the Story: Feminist Fiction and the Tradition*, Bloomington: Indiana University Press.

—— and Coppélia Kahn (1985) "Feminist Scholarship and the Social Construction of

Woman," in Greene and Kahn (eds) *Making a Difference: Feminist Literary Criticism*, New York: Methuen, 1–36.

Harding, Sandra (1991) "Who Knows? Identities and Feminist Epistemology," in Hartman and Messer-Davidow (eds) (1991), 100–15.

Hartman, Joan E. and Ellen Messer-Davidow (eds) (1991) *(En)Gendering Knowledge: Feminists in Academe*, Knoxville: University of Tennessee Press.

Hellman, Lillian (1969) *An Unfinished Woman: A Memoir*, Boston: Little, Brown.

Hirsch, Marianne and Evelyn Fox Keller (eds) (1990) *Conflicts in Feminism*, New York: Routledge.

Hite, Molly (1989) *The Other Side of the Story: Structures and Strategies of Contemporary Feminist Narratives*, Ithaca: Cornell University Press.

hooks, bell (1989) *Talking Back: Thinking Feminist, Thinking Black*, Boston: South End Press.

—— (1990) *Yearning: Race, Gender, and Cultural Politics*, Boston: South End Press.

Jouve, Nicole Ward (1991) *White Woman Speaks with Forked Tongue: Criticism as Autobiography*, London: Routledge.

Kaminer, Wendy (1990) *A Fearful Freedom: Women's Flight from Equality*, Reading, Mass.: Addison-Wesley.

Kamps, Ivo (ed.) (1991) *Shakespeare Left and Right*, New York: Routledge.

Kaplan, Cora (1989) "Feminist Criticism Twenty Years On," in Helen Carr (ed.) *My Guy to Sci Fi: Genre and Women's Writing in the Postmodern World*, London: Pandora.

Kolodny, Annette (1988) "Dancing Between Left and Right: Feminism and the Academic Minefield in the 1980s," *Feminist Studies* 14, 3 (fall), 433–66.

Lauter, Paul (1991) "The Two Criticisms – or, Structure, Lingo, and Power in the Discourse of Academic Humanists," in *Canons and Contexts*, New York: Oxford University Press, 133–53.

Lessing, Doris (1962) *The Golden Notebook*, New York: Ballantine.

—— (1964) *Martha Quest*, New York: New American Library.

—— (1966) *Ripple From the Storm*, New York: New American Library.

—— (1974) *The Summer Before the Dark*, New York: Bantam.

Levin, Richard (1988) "Feminist Thematics and Shakespearean Tragedy," *PMLA* 103: 125–38.

McDowell, Deborah (1989) Interview with Susan Fraiman, *Critical Texts: A Review of Theory and Criticism*, 6 (3): 13–29.

Martin, Biddy and Chandra Talpade Mohanty (1986) "Feminist Politics: What's Home Got to Do with It?" in Teresa de Lauretis (ed.) *Feminist Studies/Critical Studies*, Bloomington: Indiana University Press, 191–212.

Miller, Nancy K. (1982) "The Text's Heroine: A Feminist Critic and Her Fictions," *Diacritics* 12 (2) (summer) 48–65.

—— (1991) *Getting Personal: Feminist Occasions and Other Autobiographical Acts*, New York: Routledge.

Minh-ha, Trinh T. (1990) "Not You/Like You: Post-Colonial Women and the Interlocking Questions of Identity and Difference," in Anzaldúa (ed.) (1990), 371–5.

Modleski, Tania (1991) *Feminism Without Women: Culture and Criticism in a "Postfeminist" Age*, New York: Routledge.

Moore, Honore (1991) *Polemic #1*, quoted in Miller (1991).

Piercy, Marge (1974) "Through the Cracks", *Partisan Review*, 41: 202–16.

Prose, Francine (1990) "Carol Gilligan Studies Girls Growing Up: Confident at 11, Confused at 16," *New York Times Magazine* (7 January), 23ff.

Rebolledo, Tey Diana (1990) "The Politics of Poetics: Or, What Am I, A Critic, Doing in This Text Anyhow?" in Anzaldúa (ed.) (1990).

Rich, Adrienne (1979a) "Foreword," *On Lies, Secrets, and Silence: Selected Prose, 1966-1978*, New York: W.W. Norton.

—— (1979b) "When We Dead Awaken: Writing as Re-Vision," in *On Lies, Secrets, and Silence*.

Rosenfelt, Deborah and Judith Stacey (1987) "Second Thoughts on the Second Wave," *Feminist Studies* 13 (2) (summer), 341–61.

Scheman, Naomi (1991) "Who Wants to Know? The Epistemological Value of Values," in Hartman and Messer-Davidow (1991), 179–200.

Showalter, Elaine (1988) "Women Writers Between the Wars," in Emory Elliott (ed.) *Columbia Literary History*, New York: Columbia University Press, 822–41.

Shreve, Anita (1989) *Women Together, Women Alone: The Legacy of The Consciousness-Raising Movement*, New York: Viking.

Sidel, Ruth (1990) *On Her Own: Growing up in the Shadow of the American Dream*, New York: Viking.

Tompkins, Jane (1989) "Me and My Shadow," in Linda Kauffman (ed.) *Gender and Theory: Dialogues on Feminist Criticism*, New York: Basil Blackwell, 121–39.

Woolf, Virginia (1955) *To the Lighthouse*, New York: Harcourt, Brace, & World.

Young-Bruehl, Elisabeth (1991) "Pride and Prejudice: Feminist Scholars Reclaim the First Person," *Lingua Franca* (February) 15ff.

Part I

Decades

Chapter 2

Decades

Nancy K. Miller

The year 1990 was Year Zero of the post-Cold War world.
Richard J. Barnet, *The New Yorker* 1991

I am convinced that the politics of saving the family will be the politics of the 90s.
Gary L. Bauer, The *New York Times* 1991

Meaning is in for the 90s. It's got a beat and you can dance to it.
Bob Holman, The *New York Times* 1990

There's something almost irresistible about decades, about taking them as an index by which to measure social change or to identify the spirit of an age: the culture and values of a generation. The seductiveness of decades is exceptionally powerful at their turn – even more so at the end of a century, not to say a millennium. Of course it's a lot easier to name a decade when it's over, than when it's just begun. In the United States the eighties, everyone seems to agree, were a time of greed – junk bonds, leveraged buy-outs, and S. & L. scandals. If that's what we're coming out of, what, in the aftermath of the Gulf War, not to say the Thomas confirmation hearings, are we heading into?[1] A recent cartoon, which appeared in the *New Yorker* (3 September 1990), underlines the difficulty of finding the right emblem. Two men in hard hats are standing in a lumber yard. One says to the other: "Well, Al, the sixties was *peace*. The seventies was *sex*. The eighties was *money*. Maybe the nineties will be *lumber*." What will the nineties be? If not lumber, what? One's guess depends on one's vantage point: let me begin with my own.

Maybe I'm attracted to decades because I was born with one, or almost. But since decades rarely follow the neatness of chronology, I don't think the difference really counts. In any event, for me, the sixties were my twenties, the seventies my thirties, the eighties my forties. I feel particularly lured into thinking by decades now because we've entered a new one and because I've just turned 50: this is a decade I cannot fail to take seriously, which is also to say personally. In what follows I reread these decades autobiographically, and at the same time through the grid of academic feminism: trying to keep alive the tension between the detail of my experience and the history of feminism in the institution, and ending with a look at the dilemmas confronting us as feminists in the nineties.

This attempt to hold the individual and the institutional together through an autobiographical narrative should be seen both as a continuation of earlier modes of feminist performance – which emerged from the empowering conviction that "the personal is the political" – and as a renewed practice within the current collective academic project to construct feminist *archives*: to produce a retrospective that acknowledges the singularities of its subjects; not merely their positionalities. In other words, the subject of this autobiography is speaking not only as an "as a" – as a white, middle-class, heterosexual, New York, Jewish, *type* – but also as a bundle of idiosyncratic bits that specify as they embody those tropes of identity.

Like most decades, mine coincide imperfectly with units of ten. I date academic feminism conventionally with the first publications that in the United States mark its beginnings – Mary Ellman's *Thinking About Women* (1968) and Kate Millett's *Sexual Politics* (1970) – but for my own part I begin before that beginning, in my unconscious struggles over issues of gender and power (those terms were *not* in my vocabulary at the time) in the early sixties.[2]

BEFORE FEMINISM: 1962–1968

In the 1950s, as Rachel Brownstein remembers it, we dreamed of going to Paris:

> Ideally, one would be Simone de Beauvoir, smoking with Sartre at the Deux Magots, making an eccentric domestic arrangement that was secondary to important things and in their service. One would be poised, brilliant, equipped with a past, above the fray, beyond it, foreign not domestic. (And ideally Sartre would look like Albert Camus.)

> (1982: 18)

It's 1962. I've just turned 21 in Paris. For my birthday, my roommate at the Foyer International des Etudiants has given me a copy of the *Lettres portugaises*, which she has inscribed with a message that invites me to consider how wonderful it is to be like the *religieuse portugaise* – young and passionate – and concludes: "dis 'fuck you' à tous les garçons [she was learning English from the Americans who ate downstairs at the Foyer's student restaurant] et aime-les." This edition of the letters, in which the typeface imitates handwriting, is illustrated by Modigliani drawings of women looking unhappy, or at least withdrawn poignantly into themselves. Modigliani is an artist whose images of elongated women I find entrancing. I am knocked out by these letters. They are written, I think, by a real Portuguese nun, Mariana Alfocarado, seduced and abandoned by a real, if anonymous, Frenchman, and obsessing about it. I identify completely, even though I'm of course not Portuguese (not to mention a nun). I have only begun to meet Frenchmen myself and I can tell already that I'm out of my depth.

I'm also studying for my MA with the Middlebury Program in Paris and taking a year-long seminar on Laclos. Antoine Adam, an authority on the early history of the novel in France, standing in front of the lectern in a huge amphitheater of the Sorbonne, produces a weekly lecture on *Les Liaisons dangereuses*. I'm supposed to write an essay on it; the choice of topic is up to me. The program has assigned me a tutor whose task it is to oversee the writing. I'll call him M. Souilliez. He lives on a dark street in the *cinquième arrondissement*, on a steep incline, somewhere near the Sorbonne, maybe behind the Pantheon. It's April. A first draft of the *mémoire* is long overdue; I haven't begun the outline (the outline, "le plan," is at the heart of the French educational system). I have spent Christmas in Italy with an American boyfriend on a motorcycle; Easter vacation with my roommate at her home in Tunisia where I have discovered, among other things, the art of leg-waxing with lemon and sugar. I don't know how I'm going to write this essay, let alone an outline for it.

In despair I go to see the *répétiteur* one evening in his apartment. We sit in the living room and talk about *Les Liaisons dangereuses*; we talk, that is to say, about sex. I am inwardly panicked because I cannot come up with an essay topic, so I try to appear worldly and unconcerned, and with studied casualness hold forth on sex and love, and men and women. Suddenly, I get an idea: I'll write on the women in the novel, how each of them is betrayed by the images others have of them and that they each have of themselves. I sit at a table opposite M. Souilliez and start to make an outline. I'm inspired, excited. As I write, he gets up and walks around the room. I forget about him – I'm so happy that I at last have an idea! Then as I sit at the table, I feel a hand on my breast. M. Souilliez, standing behind my chair, has reached down and slipped his hand through my blouse around my left breast. I stop writing.

Despite the fact that I realize the moment I feel the hand feeling me that I have been chattering away about precisely these kinds of moves in the novel, it hasn't really occurred to me to make the connection between seduction (not to say sex) and M. Souilliez.[3] I am now nonplussed. I try to imagine that I'm Madame de Merteuil, not Cécile, even though I feel a lot more like a schoolgirl than a libertine (that's Cécile's problem in a nutshell, of course). I don't want to have to go to bed with M. Souilliez (he's "old" and not, I think, my type) but I also don't want a bad grade. The hand is still moving around inside the blouse. I remove the hand and sigh. "Oh monsieur," I say, pausing, and hoping for the world-weary tone of the Marquise in my best American *jeune fille* French, "j'ai déjà tant d'ennuis sans cela."

He goes no further, shrugs (in a Parisian gesture which seems to mean either: it's your loss or you can't blame a guy for trying), and lets me leave. I race down the stairs out into the street and up the Boulevard St-Michel to the Foyer. When I get back to my room, I begin to wonder how much harm I've done myself. I finally write the essay – "La femme et l'amour dans *Les Liaisons dangereuses*: la trahison de l'être par l'image" – and wait for the grade. The comments in the margins alternate between, "b," *bien*, and "md," *mal dit*. In general, I seem to have more insights than argumentative force. I take too long getting to the point: "what you say is true and interesting, but what's happened to your outline?" ("Le Plan.") I expect the quotations to do the work of commentary (they should play only a supporting role). And my favorite: "Never hesitate to be clear." In the light, I suppose, of these weaknesses, and despite a very nice overall comment (he thinks

I'm smart), I get a mediocre grade on the essay (my own fault, I tell myself, for doing it all at the last minute; it really wasn't very good, anyway).

In 1968 when, having returned to New York, I decided to apply to graduate school, I went through my box of "important papers" and discovered the MA essay. I looked at the grade on the title page and it suddenly seemed to me – correctly, as it turned out – that the number grade (French style) was the equivalent not of the "B" on my transcript, but an "A"; the number had been mistranscribed. In 1968, it still didn't dawn on me to be angry about M. Souilliez's hand down my blouse. By then, flirting with a libertine incarnation of my own (I took the sexual revolution seriously), I congratulated myself instead, Merteuil-like, for having played the right card (didn't I get an "A"?). Recently, I ran into an old friend I knew when I was first living in Paris. I asked her if she remembered my scene with the tutor. "Oh yes," she said, "at the time we thought that sort of thing was flattering."

*

I sometimes think that I have missed everything important to my generation: 1968 in Paris, 1968 at Columbia. The sixties really, although I did hear the Beatles sing on (pirate) Radio Caroline, "I Want to Hold Your Hand."

*

DURING FEMINISM: 1969–1977

I'm in graduate school at Columbia and feminism is in the streets ... at least in a mainstream kind of way.

26 August 1970 is the first annual nationwide "Women's Strike for Equality." Friends and I join the march down Fifth Avenue to celebrate the fiftieth anniversary of suffrage. Kate Millett publishes *Sexual Politics* and makes the cover of *Time Magazine*. At Town Hall, it's Germaine Greer and a panel of women critics and writers *et al.* (*The Female Eunuch* came out in the States in 1971) versus Norman Mailer. Mailer can't understand why women would become lesbians. After all, he opines, men can do to women what women do to each other – 90 per cent – and then some. In disgust, Jill Johnston walks off the stage and embraces her lover – to Mailer's despair: "C'mon Jill, be a lady" – in sight of the audience.[4]

There is, in general, lots of writing and talk about female orgasm, how many (multiple, preferably), and what kind.

In January 1971, after reading an article by Vivian Gornick in the *New York Times Magazine* about consciousness-raising groups, some friends and I start our own group.[5] At our first meeting, we are amazed by our commonalities. In particular, we talk about how we don't want to be like our mothers, who, we feel did not know what they wanted. What do we want? The specifics are not clear but the project involves taking charge of one's own life. It is nothing less than a fantasy of total control: not only having what we want, but on our own terms and our timetable. The point of the group as we see it is to help each other bring this about: not to be a victim.

What does this mean for graduate school? In graduate school, where the men are the teachers and the women the students, it's harder to say when things begin (certainly not in courses); it's more about things coming together – personally. One day, the man who was to be the second reader on my dissertation, an eighteenth-century specialist, a man in his sixties, takes me aside to issue a dire warning: "Don't try to be another Kate Millett" – *Sexual Politics* was originally a Columbia English department Ph.D. thesis – "she wasn't first rate to begin with." This man, who had co-edited a popular anthology on the Enlightenment, taught a course on eighteenth-century French literature (from the anthology) in which, to see whether we had done the reading, he would pull questions out of a hat and match them with some hapless student. This had something to do with why I didn't want him as my advisor. But he did tell great stories: in fact, the account he gave of Julie de L'Espinasse's life, the way a real woman (and a great letter writer) "died of love," sealed my fate: of course I was going to "be" in the eighteenth century.

In June 1972, fortified by our ongoing weekly discussions in the group, I take the plunge. I'm going to get serious about my work (no more reading, it's time, I'm 31 years old – old!): write the dissertation.[6] I buy an electric typewriter, second-hand filing cabinets on 23rd Street, and a door that when placed on top of them makes a desk; I also declare my thesis topic (equipment first): "Gender and Genre: An Analysis of Literary Femininity in the French and English Eight-eenth-century Novel." In those days in the Columbia French department this is also called a stylistic structural analysis. I am going to analyze nine novels according to the principles of narratology and rhetoric: Propp and Greimas, Riffaterre and Genette, Barthes and Kristeva. I am going to do this, I say, as a feminist.[7]

I had become a feminist and a structuralist together. That's a little condensed: this happened in a single temporality, but on separate tracks. Feminism, for me, meant the group, *Ms. Magazine*, feminist fiction, and a whole set of what today we might more portentously call cultural practices. It meant a revolution in relation-ships – between women, between women and men – and one's perception of the real, in material and symbolic terms (even if we didn't talk that way). Feminism had to do with our lives. And yet despite pockets of local activity – the annual Barnard "Scholar and Feminist" conference, the occasional undergraduate offer-ing – the academic institution was impervious to the dramatic changes occurring in social relations wrought by 1968 and by feminism. Affirmative action began officially in 1972, but its immediate effects were (and remain) almost invisible (as far as I know the tiny number of tenured women has not changed at Columbia since the early seventies).

In 1972, as I remember things, the phrase "feminist criticism" was not yet an acknowledged working category, at least not on the fifth floor of Philosophy Hall where formalism reigned supreme.[8] There was literary criticism and there was feminism (feminist perspectives, the phrase often went). They could illuminate each other, but they were separate: separate but equal? I liked to think that criticism and feminism worked together. After all, I used to argue, both are modes of critique: the one of the ideology that regulates the relations between men and women in culture and society; the other, of modes of criticism blind to their own ideology about literature and art. It's hard to see now, but in the early seventies structuralism, as it was understood in American universities, seemed to mean a break with a reactionary past: the men's club model of lit. crit., practiced today by people like Denis Donoghue and Helen Vendler. This "science of literature" was exciting, enabling; it provided a new language: a dream of transparency. In the rupture of the continuity binding literature to the world – but whose world? – at last we could see what was going on. I can still remember the moment when in a study group I understood Saussure's model of the sign: never again would I confuse the word and the thing; sign and referent; signified and signifier (little knowing that Lacan had already turned this upside down).[9] This epiphany was on a par only with the thrill of discovering binary oppositions and how they organize cultural universes. Lévi-Strauss delivered the truth of this fact in person in the Barnard College gym in 1972 (this gives an idea of the jet lag that characterizes the intellectual traffic between France and the United States).[10] What I mainly remember from this event was the conviction (his, then rapidly mine) that binary oppositions were embedded functionally in the brain. For me, it all went together perfectly with Beauvoir's magisterial analyses of the polarizing operations that opposed man as Same to woman as Other (Beauvoir herself, of course, relies heavily on Lévi-Strauss's paradigms), and even with the lowly housewife's "click" that Jane O'Reilly dissected famously in *Ms*. In both cases, the principles of analysis rescued you from the murk of ambiguity (not to say personal confusion) and privileged authority (the variously tweeded "I"s and "we's" of a fifties legacy). Between the capacious categories of narratology and the stringent lines of feminist hermeneutics, there was no text we – a new "we" – couldn't crack. It was a heady moment.

Is it true that there was no problem in articulating feminism and structuralism together? Yes and no. It's probably that combination of enthusiasms that British reviewers of the book (about French and English eighteenth-century novels) my thesis finally became – *The Heroine's Text* (1980) – found so deadly: structuralist jargon and feminist ideology. I kept seeing the same story everywhere, they complained. Well, yes, that's the whole point (which American academics – at least the feminist ones – generally got). Those objections to my language and approach (plot summary, as the unkinder put it) bothered me less (even if they were insulting and sort of true) than a certain feminist refusal of the project for "ideological" reasons. There were those who felt (i) that all formalism was male, hence incompatible with feminist analysis, and (ii) that the task of feminism was to respond to the issues of "real" women. In that sense I was indeed guilty as charged. Women were strikingly absent from my dissertation. When I chose the expression "literary femininity" I meant it to mark my distance from anything real and to sound theoretically advanced (to ward off the ambient disdain that "working on women" generated): women in fiction, but with an emphasis on narrative; female destiny, with an emphasis on plot. This was my way of showing my difference both from Kate Millett (the incarnation of "strident" feminism) and from the mode of "images of women" that had already begun to emerge in English studies. Any historical considerations were necessarily foreclosed. On the one hand, the historical seemed like an antiquated belief in the referent; on the other, the invocation of the historical as the truth value of literature, the dominant mode of eighteenth-century studies, was the very thing I wanted most to escape from and oppose.[11]

And of course I was dealing with respected male authors, major figures (with the exception of the bad boys Sade and Cleland, forgiven because of outrageousness and sex), and famous books. It was the canon, although the term wasn't bandied about at that point. And women authors? The entire time I was a graduate student, during lectures, reading for seminars, for the thesis, I never once asked myself the question of female authorship, despite the fact that I must have read some women writers for course work or exams: Marie de France, Louise Labé, Marie-Madeleine de Lafayette, Germaine de Staël (the last two known then of course as Mme de …). Besides, by the time I started writing my dissertation, the Author (male) was Dead, intentions a fallacy, and all I cared about was The Text. I blamed – if I blamed – texts for the representation of women, not authors. And not even texts: texts were prisoners of ideology just as men were prisoners of sex.

After my thesis defense it was reported to me that the sole woman on the jury (one of Columbia's classic tokens) had praised me for "sitting on my feelings." I've never been absolutely sure what that meant: that I was tautologically angry because feminist, but my writing was cool and "scientific"? Or that through the elaborate veils of my narratological tables she could tell I really cared. About what? About the logic of "female plot" that killed off heroines – exquisite cadavers as I called them in my first article – at the story's close?

What I really cared about then, I think, had as much to do with my own plot as with the fictional destiny of women in the eighteenth-century novel. At stake, if buried, in the ponderous prose of my structuralist feminism was the inscription of my plot: my own "coming to writing" – "as a woman" – to invoke the language of a feminist literary criticism that was to flower after the mid-seventies.[12] Despite the hierarchies and abuses of academic conventions, I saw writing a dissertation as something radical, but also literary: as becoming the heroine of my life. Despite the so-called feminization of the profession, my getting a Ph.D. felt like a violation of gender expectations. In 1961, having gathered my ideas about appropriate intellectual and domestic arrangements in the America of the late 1950s, it seemed natural for my college boyfriend to get a doctorate; I was slated to get an MA and teach high school French, unless of course – my mother's fifties fantasy for me – I married very well and got to be a woman of leisure who spoke French only in Europe. When, a decade later, I started writing and saw the pages pile up on my desk – a lot of the time spent at my desk involved admiring the *height* of the chapters – it seemed miraculous: as though someone else were responsible for producing the work. The man I lived with at the time, who had mixed emotions about my passion for the enterprise, did a drawing of me sitting with my hands thrown up in the air, as if in astonishment, watching the pages – produced by my cat pounding away at the typewriter – fly upward with a life of their own. But when my typist met me with the final version of the manuscript, I burst into uncontrollable tears on Broadway at 116th Street: I suppose that's part of what I was "sitting on" during the defense.

Part, but not the whole story. I was not, of course, merely a tearful heroine overcome by the events taking place around her. I was also the author of her destiny. I had a very clear sense of having done the work and wanting to own it. And so, in 1973, inspired by the example of Judy Chicago, I renamed myself. I had been using my ex-husband's name – I married briefly and unhappily in the mid-sixties – and the idea of seeing the signifier of my misery embossed on my diploma seemed suddenly and thoroughly unacceptable. At the same time, the idea of returning to my father's (also my "maiden") name seemed dangerously regressive. Not bold enough to go all the way and call myself Nancy New York, or to pick a name that pleased me out of the phone book, I took my mother's name, Miller. It was not lost on me that this was still to take a man's – my grandfather's – name, nor that I was taking the name of my worthiest adversary, my mother.[13] Despite these contradictions, it seemed an irresistible solution.

I will admit to a certain nostalgia for the gestures of those years in feminism that we have now come to take for granted, like being called Ms. I sometimes long for the conviction we had then that changing the language counted for something.

FEMINIST LITERARY CRITICISM: 1978–1989

> And why don't you write? Write! Writing is for you, you are for you; your body is yours, take it.
>
> Hélène Cixous, "The Laugh of the Medusa"

By the fall of 1978, when after having taught my first course – a graduate seminar – on (French) women authors, I wrote "Emphasis Added" (the second of my essays on women's writing), I had both regressed to and returned from the Portuguese nun. I had fully lived out Simone de Beauvoir's analysis of the *grande amoureuse* – the woman hopelessly and desperately in love – and changed literatures. I wrote this essay, which takes its examples from Lafayette's *La Princesse de Clèves* and Eliot's *The Mill on the Floss*, in total solitude, in the aftermath of a story with a Frenchman that had turned out badly (let's just say that I had renunciation thrust upon me). When I discovered – by teaching the letters in a course on women writers – that the Portuguese nun was really a man (a literary hack) in drag, I was more embarrassed at my ignorance, I think, than disappointed. Besides, I didn't need her any more: I didn't need to be in love to write. That was half of the story; the other half was falling in love with the Princess of Clèves: the heroine and the novel.

When I say that I fell in love I mean both that this book swept me away and that it took me somewhere. Working on "Emphasis Added" six years after starting to write my dissertation was like a second coming to writing. The dissertation was still sitting on my desk waiting to be revised, transformed (one hoped) into the tenure book. It seemed to me that I needed to do another kind of writing in order to talk about women writers; but the old task demanded its due and the two projects were at odds with each other. As it turned out it was writing the new essay that allowed me to finish the old book, to finish off a certain past with the flourish of an epilogue. Those few pages are the only part of that book I can still bear to read.

I wrote the epilogue to *The Heroine's Text* in a single sitting, in rage against an anonymous and extremely hostile (female) reader's report. I wish – or I think I wish – I still had a copy of the report. As I recollect it, the reader complained, among other things, that I didn't seem to realize that the novels I analyzed were written by men. This felt at the time an outrageous objection to make to me, of all people! Still, I had to ponder the remark and it led me to make the point explicitly at the close of the book: that these novels were written by men for men through the double fiction of the female reader and her heroine. It also led me to think about my complete failure to consider what difference women's fictions would have made to my argument about the limited arrangements of closure that I called the heroine's text. That was a point less easily fixed. It seems to me now that a lot of the energy that fueled my writing after the epilogue came from a desire for reparation: how could I not have taken female authorship into account from the beginning?

The move to working on women's writing had a double effect on my career and on my sense of myself as a feminist critic. Once I started working on women writers and on feminist criticism as literary theory, I felt myself to be instantly losing status. Not within the feminist community at large, of course, but within the little world of French departments that I was used to. (I'm still not sure whether this is true, or just what I worried about.) No doubt this anxiety also was bound up with the fact that at the same time (that is, before coming up for tenure) I began to "leave the century" – what would it mean not to "have" a period? But that is the matter of another reflection about the organization of literary studies.[14]

At one point, a feminist critic brought me up against this anxiety of authority as we were returning from a conference in which I had given a paper on women's autobiography: "You've always worked on women, haven't you?" she asked. Panic stricken, I cringed inside myself: she was right. Male authors, but women all the same. I never would be taken seriously. Not for me all the stories of the first, "real" tenure book "for them," and how one then saw the light: and worked on women. This was not, it turned out, what she was getting at, but it fueled my paranoia. If I had always been a feminist in my work on male writers, "working on women" seemed to make me into a different (read "lower") order of feminist: soft instead of hard, marginal instead of central. None the less, that was where I was going; nor was I alone. For me to have resisted the turn to women's writing would perhaps require greater explanation than my seduction by it. Despite, or perhaps because of the excitement, even the scandal, of *Sexual Politics*, and the success of Judith Fetterley's *The Resisting Reader* in 1978, the trend in feminist literary studies in the eighties was moving massively toward the study of women's writing.[15]

Again I am struck with the difficulty and strangeness of evoking a time when just *saying* "women's writing" had a radical edge to it. When I began to "work on women" in the late seventies I had no idea of what that was going to mean for me and more generally for developments in feminist theory. In personal terms it meant a new sense of self-authorization that changed my relation to all of the issues in the profession – especially to "theory" – and changed my identity within it. I think this is because in North American feminist criticism, by an interesting process of slippage, authorial subjectivity (itself implicitly constructed on the model of the heroine) became a homologue for female agency. Through these effects of substitution, it became possible for me, a reader of novels (alternately, a critical heroine), to cast myself (at least in my own eyes) as a feminist theorist. Or so it seemed at the time. By the early eighties, the metaphorization of feminist theory had been accomplished. This process, which can be tracked, if a little too neatly, by two titles that seem to echo each other – *Madwoman in the Attic* (1979) and *Honey-Mad Women* (1988) – was emblematic of the decade's intellectual style.[16] Although differences of position separate these two powerful works, their authors Sandra Gilbert and Susan Gubar, on the one hand, and Patricia Yaeger, on the other, all rely importantly on intertwined metaphors of literary identity and female experience to make their case.

The eighties also saw the widespread formalization of Women's Studies Programs, many of which had come into being in the late seventies throughout the United States. In 1981, when I moved across the street from Columbia to Barnard as the director of their fledgling Women's Studies Program, it seemed to me (and this was part of what allowed me to take an administrative job that I was otherwise unprepared for) that the rise of feminist scholarship as an institutional force derived at least in part from the sense of self -, but finally, collective authorization, that "working on women" provided. From my office with the decorator-purple (we hoped subversive) walls, I wrote a book-length collection of memos, characterized by the rhetorical turns of feminist righteousness, demanding courses and lines in a mode called "bullets" and taught me by a colleague from Political Science; my memo style, she explained, was too narrative.

By 1985, however, that interlocking sense of personal conviction and political solidarity – speaking "as a feminist" *for all women* – had already begun to erode seriously within the feminist community. This was the moment when white mainstream feminists finally began to pay attention to internal divisions that of course had been there from the beginning. The publication, for instance, in 1981 of *This Bridge Called My Back: Writings by Radical Women of Color* clearly marks the terms of dissent from the discourse of unity. By 1985, the date I assign only somewhat arbitrarily to this crisis in representativity, women of color refused a definition of feminism that by the whiteness of its universal subject did not include them, and poststructuralist critics looked suspiciously upon a binary account of gender with referential claims; did we really want to posit a *female* experience as the ground of women's identity?[17] Not to be left out, mainstream academics (male and female), who saw themselves as upholders of literary standards, trounced feminist critics for confusing aesthetics and sociology. Couldn't we tell art from women? This last position, which has continued to thrive in the 1990s, in many ways announces the colors of the 1990s to date: a return to a 1950s Cold War ideology that takes the form on the academic front of an intertwined belief in Art and the Individual.[18]

AFTER FEMINISM? 1990–

Bob Dylan is clearly the first rock-and-roller to reach 50 as a meaningful artist.

Dave Marsh, *New York Times*, 19 May, 1991

I became a feminist critic along with a certain history: as it was being made around me. By this I mean that my decades of intellectual formation coincided with those of another chronology, a chronology of social revolution. I said earlier that I had missed '68. That's true if we think of '68 narrowly as a single apocalyptic event, or even as a network of events with specific locales: the Sorbonne, Berkeley, Columbia. But '68, we know, can also be seen as a trope: the figure of diffuse political movements, including feminism, that came to restructure the social imaginary. In this sense '68 didn't miss me.

Teresa de Lauretis has argued famously that feminism's unique method was what in the United States we referred to as "consciousness raising" and that she prefers to call, through translation back from Italian, the practice of "self-con-sciousness"(1986:8). And certainly it was in the space of this group work that I began for the first time to make sense of my life as a good daughter of the patriarchy. What flowered from those moments and flashes of insight were the elements of an analysis – a reading – that would make a larger kind of sense when articulated collectively. The decades of the seventies and eighties saw the invention of new social subjects,[19] critics and readers who, in the cultural aftermath of '68, created the feminism we now look back on. Whether one calls this the institutionalization, or as I prefer, the textualization of feminism, what matters is the fact of that construction: the library of feminism's literatures.

But, you may say, this sounds so elegiac, as though what matters to you were solely the invention of feminism's noble past, or worse, its future anterior: what feminism will have been. It's true … . At 50, like Lot's wife I seem rigidly turned toward the past. What have I left behind? Despite the fashion look-alikes, it's not the sixties and I don't have to worry about M. Souilliez's hand down my blouse. It's not the seventies and I don't have to hide my rage in writing from my judges. It's not the eighties and I'm not running a Women's Studies Program. Still, you point out, sexual harassment is an ever-present feature of academic life for students, and they, like our younger colleagues, continue to undergo Lucy Snowe's command performances. You're just giving us a personal narrative of escape from certain penalties of youth and more vulnerable professional location. What is it exactly that you miss?

I confess: I look back wishfully to the seventies and the extraordinary conjunction of structuralism and feminism that fed both my writing and my life. But, most of all, I miss the passion of community (what we took for community), and our belief that things would change. In *Conflicts in Feminism*, Evelyn Fox Keller comments on her attachment to this period:

> If I were to name one feature of feminist theorizing in the seventies for which I am openly nostalgic, it is the conviction then widely held that there was important work to be done – work that could be supported in the name of feminism not because all feminists held the same priorities, but because that work had a radical thrust from which, we believed, feminists – and women – would generally gain some benefit.
>
> Hirsch and Keller (1990:384)

The loss to contemporary feminism of the energy which emerged from that conviction cannot be underestimated, even if the reasons for it are important.[20] Keller adds: "We have learned well the lesson that differences can be suppressed; I suggest we need also to learn that commonalities can be as facilely denied as they were once assumed." Perhaps this is what lumber for contemporary feminism will entail: a rebuilding of alliances on new grounds. Reconstruction after our civil wars.

*

Having arrived at this point, I should now adopt a more confident, visionary tone and scan the cultural firmament for signs of things to come: portents for feminism in the nineties. But that would require that I feel either prepared to speak for feminism, or willing, as I have been so often in the past, to predict what its next moves might and should be. I seem instead to be more at ease reviewing (even teaching) the history of a feminist past than imagining its future; waiting, as the decade unfolds, to see what the critical subjects we have created in our students will bring about. The nineties in this sense are theirs and lumber what they make of it.

That would have been a graceful way to end, and because not altogether unpredictable, rhetorically satisfying: a return to the pedagogical relations with which I began, only with me no longer the student: not me as the object of a botched "seduction," or sitting at the master's feet. Me as the teacher. Yes, but a little disingenuous too. As if the matter of generations and the transmission of feminism's body of knowledge were an easy matter; as if I had forgotten the painful ironies of the feminist classroom in which female authority is regularly contested.[21]

The ending I want here will have to deal with what links a singular and a collective destiny, the tangled figures of representativity: what is and isn't unique in the construction of a subjectivity.

I have been personally identified with academic feminism over two decades, emotionally and intellectually attached to the crises of its development. The intensity of that cathexis may explain why I cannot see clearly where "we" are going. To some extent my uncertainty is also an effect of feminism's historicity: its self-critical movement into middle age; the pondered doubt of retrospection; the shattering and dispersal of pronominal empire. But it probably would be more accurate to acknowledge that the failure of vision I experience emerges at least in part from the panic of *my own* aging. The panic, which occasionally assumes the shape of impatience (notably with our official pieties), has something to do with the ways in which feminism over the years has irrevocably shaped the plot of my life – the trajectory and detours of my own story, my personal disappointments; the disappointments of history.[22] It has to do as well with the infrequent stories of women's lives after fifty.[23] Is there life for a female academic after the feminist plot of tenure and promotion?

I can't see from here how that life-writing is going to turn out. For the time being, however, I find myself needing to resist the lure of feminism's self-authorization. This has meant, among other things, the experiment of an explicitly autobiographical criticism: an attempt to free myself from the compulsion to represent feminism (feminism's founding gesture) as though I had no differences from its positions. I'm not saying that "as a feminist" I no longer believe in our interventions; nor have I stopped "working on women" *for women*. Rather that for me this work now requires another language and another set of conventions for performing it.

NOTES

1 I wrote this essay in the fall of 1990 in the shadow of operation "Desert Shield," which then seemed the most powerful historical marker to date of the decade to come. As I revised in January 1991, "Desert Shield" had become "Desert Storm," and then (in anonymous Army lingo) "Desert Calm." Now, one year later, it's just the Gulf War (sometimes Persian) minus the metaphors. I published this essay with "Desert Storm" as the historical marker for the opening of the 1990s in the *South Atlantic Quarterly* (winter 1992), 91:1.

No sooner had I finalized this version of the essay for the current volume than we became the witnesses to the confirmation hearings for the appointment of Clarence Thomas to the Supreme Court. These included the testimony of Anita Hill about her experience of sexual harassment. It seemed both necessary and oddly fitting, given the nature of this piece and its location in an archive of feminist history, to place the hearings as the decade's inaugural domestic event. It will be especially interesting to see what the country's belated "discovery" of sexual harassment will mean for the future of feminist activism, and whether the theatricalization of women's "issues" will lead to a renewal of the women's movement, not to mention a renewed commitment to social change.

The impossibility of "writing to the moment" has never been more poignantly clear.

2 The books that electrified me then were Doris Lessing's *The Golden Notebook* and Simone de Beauvoir's *Mémoires d'une jeune fille rangée* (which I read in Paris in 1964 in a copy lent to me by Hester Eisenstein). They gave me clues to other ways of being a woman but I wasn't ready to *do* anything about it.

3 In a recent book on Simone de Beauvoir that Carolyn Heilbrun gave me for my fiftieth birthday, Judith Okely, a British anthropologist who is exactly my age, describes her encounters with Frenchmen in Paris *circa* 1961, encounters that seemed eerily familiar. I was struck by her account of spending the night – without losing her virginity – with a man who "over breakfast" asked her "to read aloud the seduction scene from Laclos's *Les Liaisons Dangereuses*" (1986:13).

4 *Ms. Magazine* includes this event in its time line for 1971. In its coverage of a debate between Deborah Tannen (*You Just Don't Understand*) and Robert Bly (*Iron John*) the *New York Times* (3 November 1991) looks back to the 1971 event for a point of historical comparison. My memory of the event differs somewhat from the reporter's (Esther B. Fein) account, but our sense of the gulf separating the 1970s from the 1990s is shared.

5 Four of us – Hester Eisenstein, Bethany Ladimer, and Naomi Schor subsequently became feminist scholars; one, Ellen Sweet, an editor at *Ms. Magazine*; another, Elizabeth Silk, a therapist committed to women's issues.

6 Actually, writing the dissertation seemed a solitary undertaking of such enormous moment that I withdrew from the group and indeed from therapy in order to "work." (I returned to both after "finishing.") Holed up in a tiny room in a ground-floor tenement in the Village, I wrote, cut off from the pleasure of the support that had gotten me there in the first place. I guess that was my idea of being a scholar (though I did watch daytime TV for relief).

7 Rereading this after having seen a three-hour profile on Richard M. Nixon on public television, I try to think about what it might mean to have been writing a dissertation during the Vietnam War and Watergate. I learn that on 23 June 1972, as I was, perhaps, drafting an introduction to "Gender and Genre," Richard Nixon was having a conversation with H.R. Haldeman about diverting the FBI. I easily remember spending hours watching the Watergate proceedings on TV in total fascination and indignation, but I can make no connections between the privacy of the desk and the public scenes.

8 My memory here turns out to be slightly at odds with the history of feminist criticism in English studies, where the Chicago MLA of 1970 is the scene of feminist criticism's originary event: a session sponsored by the Commission on the Status of Women in the Profession (formed in 1969) at which Adrienne Rich read "When We Dead Awaken." Fraya Katz-Stoker published "The Other Criticism: Feminism vs. Formalism" in 1972, in Susan Koppleman Cornillon's pioneering anthology, *Images of Women in Fiction: Feminist Perspectives*. Carolyn Heilbrun and Catharine Stimpson's "Theories of Feminist Criticism: A Dialogue" took place in 1973 and was published in 1975 in Josephine Donovan's now classic *Feminist Literary Criticism: Explorations in Theory*. If datably, as we look back, 1972 emerges as the beginning of feminist criticism's published history (this is the date with which Jane Gallop begins her new history of feminist criticism, *Around 1981*), it still remains true, I think, as Elaine Showalter describes that moment in "Women's Time, Women's Space: Writing the History of Feminist Criticism," that in its origins feminist criticism derived more from feminism than from criticism (1987: 37).

9 Not to mention Derrida. We have to keep in mind that there is always a time lag in these things; poststructuralism, with a whole new set of emphases, had already unsettled structuralism in France. Colonials necessarily live according to belated cadences.

10 I was amused to see that Marianna Torgovnick, whom I did not know at the time, also remembers this moment as having the aura of truth (1990: 210–11).

11 A colleague of mine used to do a wonderful imitation of a former teacher who, in teaching Montesquieu's *Persian Letters*, would intone in a singsong (complete with

full-blown American accent): "Dans chaque lettre il y a une idée, et l'idée c'est la liberté."

12 Hélène Cixous's " The Laugh of the Medusa" appeared in an issue of the journal *L'Arc* devoted to Simone de Beauvoir in 1975. An extraordinary manifesto of what was to become known as "French feminism," it was here that Cixous invoked the wonders of "écriture féminine" with all the contradictions and ambiguities we have since pondered. I found its cadences almost mesmerizing at the time. Jane Gallop (1989) has a succinct account of this moment.

13 Not my grandfather's real name either, which may have been Middlarsky, but the Ellis Island rendition of an immigrant's desire to be a "Yankee": from Pinchas to William.
    I kept Kipnis as my legal middle name and made the initial K. part of my new signature. My father, who was a lawyer, took care of the change for me and never said how he felt about it. My thesis advisor, however, who took the conventions of the patriarchy very seriously, was, to my great amusement, shocked. The woman typing the dissertation, a student at General Studies, who was rapidly changing her life, also changed her name (a lot more creatively), and I felt quite pleased to have inspired her to do it.

14 At a departmental party recently I was deep in conversation with a female colleague. We were interrupted by a male colleague, who asked what we were talking about. When we foolishly revealed the truth about the subject of our absorption – our haircuts (we go to the same haircutter) – he was jubilant: "Oh," he said, "I always wondered what women talked about when they were alone." I guess I didn't look at him as witheringly as I hoped since he went on to pursue his interruption. Did I, he wanted to know, have a period? Being what is called "peri-menopausal," I had to work very hard not to answer in terms of my newly haywire cycle. I censored my "sometimes" and said no, since he was merely looking, as it turned out, for someone to serve on an orals committee. But it's true that not having a period can be a problem.

15 The splitting off of work on men's writing from women's has had serious repercussions on the history of feminist criticism and on the feminist critique of canon formation. This has meant, among other things, not noticing a lot of very interesting work, like that of Nancy Vickers on the Renaissance and of Naomi Schor on French nineteenth-century literature, to cite two well-known examples. Elaine Showalter, who played an important role in fostering the distinction, maps the shifting currents of women's writing/men's writing, and the turn to "gender" in the introduction to *Speaking of Gender* (1989).

16 My book *Subject to Change* (1988) clearly belongs to this project (and in this sense already seems dated to me: it bears its date in history). It's my impression that the prestige of feminist literary theory, or at at least the appeal of its metaphors, will continue to wane in the 1990s, to be replaced by feminist theories emerging from philosophy (this is already implicit in some 1980s work, even in Yaeger's), science (Donna Haraway's cyborgs, for instance), and psychoanalysis (here it's more a matter of a shift in emphasis). This change also has to do, on the one hand, with the shift *toward* gender and "gender bending," redefinitions of lesbian configurations, and, on the other, *away from* the attempt to identify female specificities altogether.

17 This view was most famously summarized by Jonathan Culler's conversion of Peggy Kamuf's "writing like a woman" to "reading as a woman" which "deconstructed" the experience model, recasting it as a trope. It is less frequently noticed that Culler at this point (*On Deconstruction* was published in 1982) deals here uniquely with the feminist criticism of men's writing.

18 I'm thinking here of Helen Vendler's attack on feminist critics in "Feminism and Literature" which appeared in the 30 May 1990 issue of the *New York Review of Books*. And the vicious posturing of Camille Paglia, for whom feminism seems to represent a betrayal of the values of the sixties.

19 de Lauretis brilliantly analyzes the implications of this process in " The Technology of Gender" (1987).

20 I recognize that nostalgia itself has been subject to feminist suspicion, especially by a younger generation of feminists. Biddy Martin, for instance, in her critique of Adrienne Rich, writes in "Lesbian Identity and Autobiographical Difference(s)": "The ultimate formulation of a politics of nostalgia, of a return to that state of innocence free of conflict conceived as women's primary emotional bonds with one another, enacts its own violence, as all dreams of perfect union do" (1988:87). I also think that for those of us who lived the seventies in our thirties the nostalgia is a regret for a productive *reality*.

21 I'm thinking here of the questions rehearsed so cogently in the introductory essay of *Gendered Subjects: The Dynamics of Feminist Teaching*, "The Politics of Nurturance" (Culley *et al.* 1985).

Part of the problem has to do as well with the *Bildungsroman* of the feminist critic: can she accede to cultural authority when the role of the female intellectual seems to require disassociation from feminist causes: Susan Sontag, for instance, and, most recently, her grotesque self-appointed rival, the media-created anti-feminist, Madonna wannabe, Camille Paglia?

22 Probably the most important piece of this fallout involves my not having had a child – not, as it turned out, entirely by choice. This had everything to do with feminism in the 1970s. Deborah Rosenfelt and Judith Stacey comment sharply:

> The reaction to the fifties' cloying cult of motherhood freed millions of women like us to consider motherhood a choice rather than an unavoidable obligation, but it may also have encouraged many to deny, or to defer dangerously long, our own desires for domesticity and maternity. One of the ironic effects of this history is the current obsession with maternity and children that seems to pervade aging feminist circles, a romanticization that occasionally rivals that of the fifties.
>
> (1987: 351)

(The key notion here for me personally is "defer dangerously long"; the romanticization they point to applies as well.) But Ann Snitow, speaking as "the child of this moment" in "A Gender Diary," underlines the fundamental contradiction of this conjuncture (the seventies rereading the fifties): "I don't think the feminism of this phase would have spoken so powerfully to so many without this churlish outbreak of indignation" 1990:31). This will have to remain the subject of another essay, and I hope an edited book, on what this double truth of liberation and deferral has meant to women and feminists of my generation: the nineties rereading the seventies.

23 This is a central piece of Carolyn Heilbrun's *Writing a Woman's Life* (1988).

REFERENCES

Brownstein, Rachel M. (1982) *Becoming a Heroine: Reading about Women in Novels*, New York: Viking.

Cixous, Hélène (1975) "Le rire de la Méduse," *L'Arc* 61.

Culler, Jonathan (1982) *On Deconstruction*, Ithaca: Cornell University Press.

Culley, Margo, (ed.) (1985) *Gendered Subjects: The Dynamics of Feminist Teaching*, Boston: Routledge & Kegan Paul.

de Beauvoir, Simone (1962) *Mémoires d'une jeune fille rangé*, Paris: Gallimard.

de Lauretis, Teresa (ed.) (1986) *Feminist Studies/Critical Studies*, Bloomington: Indiana University Press.

—— (1987) *Technologies of Gender*, London and New York: Routledge.

Donovan, Josephine (ed.) (1975) *Feminist Literary Criticism*, Lexington: University of Kentucky Press.

Gallop, Jane (1988) *Thinking Through the Body*, New York: Columbia.

—— (1989) '1975: French Feminism,' in *A New History of French Literature*, Cambridge, Mass.: Harvard University Press.

—— (1992) *Around 1981*, New York and London: Routledge.

Gilbert, Sandra, and Susan Gubar (1979) *Madwoman in the Attic: The Woman Writer and the Nineteenth-Century Literary Imagination*, New Haven: Yale University Press.

Heilbrun, Carolyn (1988) *Writing a Woman's Life*, New York: W. W. Norton.

Hirsch, Marianne, and Evelyn Fox Keller (eds.) (1990) *Conflicts in Feminism*. New York and London: Routledge.

Katz-Stoker, Fraya (1972) "The Other Criticism: Feminism vs. Formalism," in Susan Koppleman Cornillon (ed.) *Images of Women in Fiction: Feminist Perspectives*, Bowling Green: Bowling Green University Press.

Lessing, Doris (1981) *The Golden Notebook*, New York: Bantam.

Martin, Biddy (1988) "Lesbian Identity and Autobiographical Difference(s)," in Bella Brodski and Celeste Schenck (eds.) *Life/Lines: Theorizing Women's Autobiography*, Ithaca: Cornell University Press.

Miller, Nancy K. (1988) *Subject to Change: Reading Feminist Writing*, New York: Columbia University Press.

Moraga, Cherríe, and Gloria Anzaldúa (eds.) (1981) *This Bridge Called My Back: Writings by Radical Women of Color*, New York: Kitchen Table, Women of Color Press.

Okely, Judith (1986) *Simone de Beauvoir*, New York and London: Virago/Pantheon.

Rich, Adrienne (1979) "When We Dead Awaken: Writing as Re-Vision," *On Lies, Secrets, and Silence*, New York: W. W. Norton.

Rosenfelt, Deborah, and Judith Stacey (1987) "Review Essay: Second Thoughts on the Second Wave," *Feminist Studies* 13, 2 (summer).

Showalter, Elaine (1987) "Women's Time, Women's Space: Writing the History of Feminist Criticism," in Shari Benstock (ed.) *Feminist Issues in Literary Scholarship*, Bloomington: Indiana University Press.

—— (ed.) (1989) *Speaking of Gender*, New York and London: Routledge.

Snitow, Ann (1990) "A Gender Diary," in Marianne Hirsch and Evelyn Fox Keller (eds.) *Conflicts in Feminism*, New York and London: Routledge.

Torgovnick, Marianna (1990) *Gone Primitive: Savage Intellects, Modern Lives*, Chicago and London: University of Chicago.

Vendler, Helen (1990) "Feminism and Literature," *New York Review of Books*, 30 May.

Yaeger, Patricia (1988) *Honey-Mad Women: Emancipatory Strategies in Women's Writing*, New York: Columbia University Press.

Chapter 3

History/My history

Gloria T. Hull

For myself and my readers, I need to make very clear at the outset that what I am recounting here is my own personal, unique story. Iterating this seemingly obvious fact frees me up and gives me latitude not to have to be representative, "correct," or anything else externally constructed or imposed. It gives me the space to delve into myself and my history and honestly present what I find. Until recently, I wished that mine was a different narrative, one which more closely adhered to the prevailing meta-stories and added greater glory to these valorized texts.

I have wished to have been more racially active, more sexually courageous, more intrepid politically – in general, grander and more heroic. But desires such as these constitute one way that we have silenced and rejected ourselves and thereby colluded in the process of simplifying our history, reducing what it was to some near-mythical idea of what it should be. I myself needed to become thoroughly comfortable with this realization before I could even begin to write this essay. Making this statement is also a reminder that, if we have learned anything from the hard-won growth of these past ten years of militantly diverse feminisms, it is that no one of us can speak for any all of us.

My roots as a feminist scholar probably go as far back as the lessons I imbibed from my iron-willed, independent mother and my endurance-oriented poor Black southern culture, as well as the strong, resourceful and individualistic qualities I perforce developed as an abuse survivor. For the first part of my life, these essentially interior characteristics were all the radicalness I possessed. I went through the segregated educational system as a model student, producing "A's" and extracurricular achievements and making no waves. However, my personal circumstances predisposed me toward feminist consciousness and I was ready for feminist movement when it came.

A convenient place to begin charting the construction of my present feminist identity and practice is June 1966, when at 21 I graduated from college *and* got married – both in that same florid month. I had received a three-year NDEA fellowship for graduate study in English at the University of Illinois – which I had initially accepted without telling my fiancé, who was expecting me to join him at Purdue University in Indiana. Clearly, I knew enough to know that these two gender-coded paths – marriage and a professional career, especially one requiring marital separation – were at odds with one another and that I was treading on tricky ground. It is interesting to me that I accepted the fellowship in secret, but not at all surprising that I was determined enough to do so – even in that backhanded way. Obviously I feared reprisal, opposition, disapproval for gender overstepping, but not enough to scare me into line.

I went with my new husband to Purdue for the summer (where I worked as a university secretary), and then found an apartment and set up for school in Champaign-Urbana that fall. The plan was for us to live and study separately during the week and to connect on weekends. It didn't work. He wanted a wife – and kept making the considerable drive over to see me during the week, leaving his books and chemistry lab experiments to suffer – thereby graphically impressing upon me the unworkability of my scheme. I gave up after only *one* semester.

Looking back, I see myself searching for the office in which I resigned my fellowship and officially withdrew. I walked into it and conducted my business *alone*. The handling was strictly routine, matter-of-fact. There was no one to ask, "How come? Why are you doing this?" Nothing. At this point, I was the only Black woman I knew at the university. Had I had some kind of support, any kind of model, a good friend even, I might have persevered. My mother and everyone else only saw rightness, naturalness in my personally coerced and socially constructed move ("Of course, *he* wants *his* wife to be with *him*"). I suppressed my own feelings of anger, outrage, injustice. I felt that what was happening was wrong, but could not articulate a totally coherent, persuasive analysis – even to myself.

In January 1967 (the following semester), I began a teaching assistantship at Purdue, and some months later made a foggy decision to have a baby. The decision was foggy, but the baby was very solid – as was the love I felt for him when he arrived. I carry images of us getting up on cold Indiana mornings, packing our new son and all his diapers and milk bottles in a portable crib, leaving him with the babysitter. I knew I was not being the white American ideal of the perfect mother and I felt guilt, which I shut off. But, as always, there was the part of me which realized that enough was wrong with "the way things were" and how the standards were constructed to keep me keeping on.

My husband began a post-partum affair – which I followed sometime later with one of my own. This response proved my ability to say (if only to myself), "Just because you're a man, you don't have the right to do this and make me take it." In the sphere of sexual politics, this is the language and consciousness of the black blueswomen who viewed sexuality as personal power, to be exercised as one ("damn well") pleased. As they saw it, though the "equipment" differed, this is one definite area where men and women were created equal. Resisting from this consciousness constitutes an analysis of gender roles and sexual conventions, with or without an elaborating critique.

*

Sometime around 1969 to early 1970, I decided to write my Ph.D. dissertation on women in Byron's poetry – Byron the flamboyant, younger-generation Romantic poet. Why Byron? Why women? Ultimately, I have to regard this as one of those nascent feminist moves, arrived at in ways which are impossible to fully explain. I am sure that I was trying to make something relevant out of an essentially *ir*relevant and alienated/ing process, a motivation which lay at the heart of Black/Ethnic Studies and Women's Studies, neither of which I had had any contact with at this time (which was very early for me *and* the two movements). Byron was aristocratic and canonized – but he was also a social, political and sexual rebel. And women figured prominently enough in his life and work to render that an acceptable topic, luckily for me as I groped for toeholds of meaningful connection.

Writing this essay, I pulled out my copy of the dissertation, looking to get some sense of what it was I did or thought that I was doing. One of the first things I noticed is that I was boldly hedging my bets. From the Abstract:

> By utilizing a biographical-critical approach and *by assuming a feminine viewpoint which is somewhat different from the traditionally masculine view*, this study traces Byron's development as a man and artist as it is seen through his handling of women in his poetry.
>
> (my current italics)

And in the Introduction, I write:

> [This thesis] is also intended as a step in the direction of providing a body of criticism about women in society and literature; and it takes a view of them which is different, *in certain respects,* from the traditionally masculine view which has been almost the exclusive perspective.
>
> (again, my current italics)

From somewhere, in 1970–1, I had gotten the idea to provide "a body of criticism about women" (recognizing their absence) and was positing a "femin*ine*" – if not femin*ist* – critical perspective. I was able to foreground women, to see Byron through them, and to make a few original observations about how female characters function in his poems. My committee was all white-male and traditional New Critical. As was true throughout my early career, these men really helped me by not too actively standing in my way.

*

Thus far, all the characters in this narrative – other than the main ones – have been white. The setting was white, almost all the people were white, white everything and everywhere – except when we were visiting back home in Louisiana or selectively watching television, where the Civil Rights/Black Power Movement was now being relayed. Isolated though I was, its impact was psychically revolutionary. One Sunday morning in 1969, I washed my hair as usual and then "impulsively" decided to go natural with it. Actually, the scene was quite funny (if one overlooks the sad irony). There I was in front of my bathroom mirror with this weird bleached, leftover straightened hair standing out over my head and me without a clue as to what to do with it. I got help from the one natural, militant sister I knew, summoning her via the telephone even though we were only slightly acquainted.

This decision to wear my hair in an Afro was, of course, a rejection of one definition of gender/woman/the feminine in favor of another, a rejection of white for black. More suggestively, it could almost (though not quite) be read as a rejection of gender *for* race; and this indicates the crying need African American women have always had to think and feel both race and gender into one body/for-mulation/framework.

Of further relevance here is the fact that my favorite pop song this year (still 1969) was a recording entitled "Black Pearl" by Sonny Charles and the Check-mates. It begins:

> Black pearl, precious little girl
> Let me put you up where you belong
>   ('Cause I love you)
> Black pearl, pretty little girl
> You've been in the background much too long
>
> You've been working so hard your whole life through
> Tending other people's houses, raising up their children too
> Hey, how 'bout something – for me and you
> Here in my arms you're gonna reign supreme
> No more serving, baby, they're gonna serve my queen
> It's our turn for happiness and our day has come
> Living for each other and answering to no one.

The refrain is repeated, and then comes another verse whose lyrics are stereotypic-ally romantic without the overt racial and political references of the first stanza. However, it ends with

> You'll never win a beauty show, no, they won't pick you
> But you're my Miss America, I love you.

I was crazy about this song – in a kind of sentimental way – and anyone not familiar with it would really need to *hear* it to get the full flavor of those smooth, black male voices, urgent, mellow, soulful. Here was a construction of African American womanhood. I certainly knew that analyzing gender for Black women necessitated a racial framework; hence my positive response, especially to the historically allusive lines about work, *et cetera*. However, I cannot remember to what, if any, extent I balked at the romantic diminution of "little girl" or the female pedestalization. If I did, these negative reactions were effectively outweighed – at least on the emotional level – by the revisionary racial message and the call for loving and valuing Black women (however it was couched).

*

We left Purdue in March, 1970 when my spouse completed his doctorate and accepted a position in Delaware. I was ABD, writing my dissertation, doing housework and needlework – busy, but in a way bored and isolated. I did not like being the dependent wife even though my husband did not require me to play the corporate spouse role. As Blacks, as historically working-poor individuals, we both brought oppositional consciousness and our feelings of being different to this situation. It was during this period of gender-role dissatisfaction that I read for the first time Betty Friedan's *The Feminine Mystique*. I cannot recall how I found my way to this book (which was published in 1963). I know that I was clandestinely combing the library card catalog for "lesbian" and "homosexuality" in 1971–2, but do not remember doing the same for "feminism" and "women" in 1969–70.

Even with my current knowledge of all that is lacking in Friedan's analysis, I have to admit that her work deeply affected me (as it did other Black and Chicano women my age and slightly older). Looking at it now, I am still struck by its clear passion and radical persuasion:

> The real joke that history played on American women is not the one that makes people snigger, with cheap Freudian sophistication, at the dead feminists. It is the joke that Freudian thought played on living women, twisting the memory of the feminists into the man-eating phantom of the feminine mystique, shriveling the very wish to be more than just a wife and mother. Encouraged by the mystique to evade their identity crisis, permitted to escape identity altogether in the name of sexual fulfillment, women once again are living with their feet bound in the old image of glorified femininity. And it is the same old image, despite its shiny new clothes, that trapped women for centuries and made the feminists rebel.
>
> (Friedan 1963: 102)

It goes without saying that, because of my education, feminist tendencies, social positioning, and personal circumstances, I could identify with what Friedan was saying. Furthermore, she gave me data and tools to supplement what I was already grappling with.

In my memories of 1970, I couple *The Feminine Mystique* with another telling book, *Don't Cry, Scream*. It is an early (1969) volume of poetry by Black Arts writer Don L. Lee (later Haki Madhubuti), which a vendor brother from Indianapolis sold to me shortly before I left Purdue. *Don't Cry, Scream* is a classic of late 1960s to early 1970s Black, radical poetry, full of contempt for "whi-te" and whitewashed Negroes and of praise for the new "Blackman" and his Black woman. It is also blatantly sexist and homophobic, which I must have seen – and yet it represents the site of Black cultural nationalism from which I was also working as I moved further into Black consciousness and into the study and teaching of Afro-American literature.

Also, during this 1970–1 time, I finally admitted to myself (and to my husband) that I was seriously missing and yearning for women, who had been my best friends and lovers ever since third grade. I did not realize how important this contact with women was until it was no longer there – as it had so effortlessly been in undergraduate school. There, I had a girlfriend (more or less secret) and a boyfriend (very public), sorority sisters, and post-curfew dormitory parties with my suitemates where we drank Bacardi rum and did Mae West imitations and pseudo-striptease dances in our babydoll pajamas. Neither at this point nor in college was I theorizing female sexual expression through categories of straight, bisexual or lesbian. What I now sensed was that the richness I wanted was no longer there, and I felt secure enough in the "allrightness" (if not rightness) of my desire to acknowledge and (at first furtively) seek it. This represents one more of those areas where I knew deep within myself that what the world said about this matter was not the final word.

Against this troubled backdrop and after beginning my first academic appointment in the fall of 1971, I left my marriage and almost-four-year-old son in 1972. Three years ago, I wrote a poem about this leavetaking, in which I experienced the pain which I could not then allow myself to feel. Entitled "Counting Cost," it reads in part:

Walk out the door

Too much pain
too much limitation –
Leave that woman-thing
        that mother-bind
behind

. . .

Walk out the door –

Away from meals
of fried pork chops and frozen string beans,
of the feminine mystique turned black – and blue
Needing a larger self
a whole, new way of being
in that tragic drama
where all the characters
play the parts of ghosts
and end up dying
as the world turns,
as the curtains fall

Cry all the unshed tears many long years later
Look the damned and bloody monsters
        in their midnight face
Count the cost
Feel the pain

. . .

(Hull 1989: 116, 118)

I think it is very important for us to remember that – however instinctive, coherent, examined or unexamined – many of us were making difficult and painful choices in our feminist evolutions. As we remember and reconstruct these histories, it is crucial that we not forget this aspect and fall into making up neat, intellectual stories which leave out the messiness and the blood. With my son – who eventually came to live full-time with me – a beautiful young man now in graduate school, I can look back upon the anguish and forward with joy, feeling a great deal of thankfulness that everything worked out as well as it has.

*

From this point, I am tempted to analyze my development as an expansion from private to public, taking what I had learned on the private–personal level and applying/manifesting it in a public mode. Perhaps, though, the most pivotal realization may have been that it was possible to do academic work which was meaningfully connected to myself and the "real world" realities which concerned me. Another way to say this is to posit that we had to chant "Black is beautiful" and "Sisterhood is powerful" before we could declare that they were also legitimate scholarly subjects. Gestures of self-esteem seem to be fundamental prerequisites to any kind of revolutionary change. Thus, as I began to focus on African American literature, I possessed a basic understanding of gender which informed my reading and which I could use to critique the male bias of the literature and criticism. The more deeply I delved into the field, the more radical I became.

My first article – written c. 1973–4 and published in 1975 – was an examination of "Black Women Poets – From [Phillis] Wheatley to [Margaret] Walker." Vexed with the condescending lip service paid to Wheatley, the silence about Frances Harper's feminist poems, the blatant worshipping of only three or four Harlem Renaissance male poets, and the general lack of perceptive attention to Black women writers, I essayed a nascent intervention into what I read as a sorry state of affairs. It was quoted from and reprinted, apparently filling a gap as one of the few materials available with a gendered, female-valorizing perspective on Black American women. In 1974, I also began contributing one lecture night on Black Women's Literature to our newly establishing Women's Studies program at the University of Delaware. This activity represents my first formal feminist work. It is important to note that my knowledge of feminism, as is true for most others of my generation, was not *learned* in any classroom, but forged by us from within and without the academy. It was literally impossible to have taken the courses which I now delight in teaching and sitting in on occasionally – "Feminist Theory," "Methodological Perspectives on the Study of Women," "Black Women Writers and Literary Criticism/Theory," and so on down a gratifyingly long list.

In an individual way, I was getting in closer touch with the predominantly white women's movement – but only through reading. With both fear and boldness, I used this reading to make connections. For (a brief, comic) example: Sometime in the first half of the 1970s, I read a poem by one Rita Mae Brown in the magazine *Women: A Journal of Liberation*. Called "Dancing the Shout, or the Song Movement

Sisters Don't Want Me to Sing," it was about her love for women. Thinking she was Black, I wrote her a cryptic note saying something to the effect that her song sure sounded good to me. She answered with an extremely nice letter (which I still have in a box someplace) telling me she was not a Black woman and communicating quite a bit of who she was. I remember this episode with amusement and always think fondly of Rita Mae, whom I later met and whose novel, *Rubyfruit Jungle,* I loved.

My emotional and psychic identity-consciousness as a bisexual woman who often lives a functionally female-centered/lesbian life (but has married a second husband and nearly a third), has certainly fueled my predisposition toward and continuing commitment to feminism and feminist scholarship. There was something inside myself that the lesbian/feminist materials I began to read could hook. From my own experience, I knew the facts and felt the urgency of the stories and analyses. Understandably, at the onset of my overt radicalization, I stressed the lesbian side of my sexual continuum, "passing," as it were, in this uni-dimensional way. However, now that I have begun to complicate my sexual identity by acknowledging its full and ever-present range, the "bi-ness" has begun to assume more radical implications and overtones.

In the past three years, I have been out in my classes as a bisexual woman professor, but cannot yet definitively say with what impact. For me personally, it has been good. It has cleared the air of speculation and misconceptions, and kept me from being put in one box or the other. I suspect that it probably has not given students on either side of the aisle as much as they might have wanted or could have used – except perhaps for the bisexual ones for whom it is a rare and happy affinity. In my research and teaching, I treat sexuality, analyzing it as a factor in the life and productions of the writers I study and making sure that figures other than simply heterosexual ones are included. The current, laudable efforts to define bisexual identity will further give all of us much-needed information with which to work.

*

What there was to read in the early 1970s still astounds me with its beauty and abundance. To remind myself of this writing, which almost singlehandedly formed my feminist awareness, I went to my shelves and casually pulled down books. Mostly, they were thin volumes with dates and "acquired in New York City" inscriptions (Delaware did not have them). There were writers who became famous and others who did not, but whom I bought, read, and profited from indiscriminately before any market-place hierarchizing could have occurred. I waxed affectionate and nostalgic with the feel of these books as I randomly skimmed them, noting the scraps of yellow paper which marked poems and passages that personally moved me or that I had used in my very early lectures when this was the only material available (before wider publication, mainstream texts, and convenient anthologies). A few of them were unevenly mimeographed productions with unnumbered pages. Many featured frank photographs of the authors and their children, friends and lovers. I found line-sketches and artwork of women nudes, a few misspelled words and grammatical slips, female-suggestive erotic covers, beautiful raw creativity, anti-capitalistic copyright pages, words of hope and fire – all for mostly $1–1.50.

Among a surprisingly slim stack of seventeen titles, there were three from the Oakland, California Women's Press Collective – Pat Parker's (peace and rest to her soul) *Child of Myself* (1972), Judy Grahn's *Edward the Dyke and Other Poems* (1971), and *Eating Artichokes* by Willyce Kim (1972), this latter sporting a picture of a young, very thin Grahn in pencil-striped shirt and pants. In *Edward the Dyke,* I reacquainted myself with Helen, Ella, Nadine, Carol, Annie, Margaret and Vera of the powerful "Common Woman" sequence as well as with the other polemical, love and lyrical pieces in a wide variety of forms. In *Child of Myself,* there were poems with check marks by their titles or first lines, indications that I had read them to classes and (predominantly heterosexual) community audiences when I needed some incisive humor wonderfully encoded in African-American voice. One of the most used:

You can't be sure of anything these days.

> you meet a really far out man –
> tells you,
> he's been on his own for years
>> opens car doors for you
>> carries packages for you
>> protects you from evil doers
> Says he wants an intelligent, creative
>> woman to be his *partner* in life.
>>> you marry and find

> the dude is
>> too weak to pick up a dish
>> too dumb to turn on a burner
>> too afraid to do laundry
>> too tense to iron a shirt
> & to top the whole thing off –
> he tries to cover his incompetence,
> by telling YOU –
>> it's women's work.

You can't be sure of anything these days.

(Parker 1972: [7])

This poetry was direct, hard-hitting, aural/oral, meant for communal consumption, calculated to effect personal and social transformation – just as was the work of the Black Arts movement. In poets such as Parker and Audre Lorde, the revolutionary racial and feminist currents converged.

Yellow slips and inked annotations in volume 2, number 1 (1974) of *Woman Becoming* (Pittsburgh, Pennsylvania) likewise remind me that I used the last two lines of Karen Marsden's poem, "plastic wrinkle war," to preface (or conclude) a rap about ageism and commodity standards of female beauty. There is a chapbook by alta, whose work is characterized by outraged and outrageous honesty. I own her *Burn This and Memorize Yourself: Poems for Women*, with its double-imaged, mirror photograph of her on the cover. However, what I pulled from the shelf was her *Letters to Women*, Shameless Hussy Press, Berkeley, California – no date and a credits page which includes this directive: "for underground reproduction without profit, there is no copyright. For moneymakers, this is copyright, and you gotta pay." I especially liked the second stanza of her "letter to lyn" for its searingly graphic imagery and vocative claiming of self:

I see soul pain eyes
hidden in blue shadow
fur lashes deny the real
hair/ acceptable above the brow
not below the knee
        i see your eyes, sister
        i see your soul
you call your breasts wrinkled lemons,
hide them under ½ inch foam, learn
to like your thighs only to hear
you have ugly feet.
how long will we listen to men
who tell us they love us?
who call us frigid or maniac & turn away?
how long will we stand as dolls on a shelf
      buy me   buy me
      one house & i'm yours.

           i'm *mine*, sister.
           how about you?

                                 (alta)

And there is one of those quiet lesbian poems – beginning "full your breasts down on me/ full in my fingers" – whose concrete simplicity touched me.

From Times Change Press comes a publication by Barbara O'Mary, *This Woman: Poetry of Love and Change* (1973). Its back cover blurb communicates not only its content, but also its aesthetics, feminist assumptions, and the understood audience:

This book is a journal. It tells of a year of intense change – involving Barbara's lovers male and female, her daughters, her job, her politics, her fears, her visions. Barbara's poetry is simple, intimate and honest. We identify with it immediately, as it clarifies our own experience; we take it personally.

Among this early formative reading, the most precious of all for me was *The Black Woman: An Anthology*, edited by Toni Cade (Bambara), which I acquired in October 1970, the year it was published. This book was the closest cognate I had to a course on Black American feminism. It gave me theory, analyses of current issues and cultural works, poetry and fiction, by writers such as Nikki Giovanni, Kay Lindsey, Audre Lorde, Paule Marshall, Alice Walker, Sherley Williams, Joanne Grant, Abbey Lincoln, Frances Beale, Toni Cade herself, Verta Mae Smart-Grosvenor and Pat Robinson.

In its uncompromisingly radical female and racial perspectives, *The Black Woman* taught me how our position could be both thoroughly feminist and for-real Black, and the new thing that emerged when the two were conceptualized together. For instance, in one of her essays, Bambara, through her always inimitable style, takes the contested issue of gender roles and breaks it down Black:

> Keep the big guns on the real enemy. Men have got to develop some heart and some sound analysis to realize that when sisters get passionate about themselves and their direction, it does not mean they're readying up to kick men's ass. They're readying up for honesty. And women have got to develop some heart and some sound analysis so they can resist the temptation of buying peace with their man with self-sacrifice and posturing. The job then regarding "roles" is to submerge all breezy definitions of manhood/womanhood (or reject them out of hand if you're not squeamish about being called "neuter") until realistic definitions emerge through a commitment to Blackhood.
>
> (Bambara 1970: 109)

Marshall's "Reena" is massively marked up with three colors of ink – red, black and blue – jogging me to recall that this brilliant and provocative story was the subject of the first professional paper I ever presented (to the College Language Association Convention, New Orleans, Louisiana, 1973). I think I called it "Afro-Caribbean Perspectives ..." to fit the convention theme, but am sure that, whatever else I did, I focused heavily on its examination of "what it has meant, what it means, to be a Black woman in America."

In addition to the scattered pile of books in front of me, I know I read others I cannot now recall: like Shulamith Firestone's *The Dialectic of Sex* or Del Martin's and Phyllis Lyon's *Lesbian/Woman* or fiction by Ann Allen Shockley or more popular (aboveground and underground) women's or Black texts which were current at the time. I can see how deeply influenced and permanently marked I was by the kind of reading which I have briefly discussed here, particularly by its passion and poetry. To it, I can trace the beginnings of my insistence upon clarity, concreteness, foregrounded experience, visible political commitment, emotion and expressive beauty (qualities which usually characterize African-American women's literature). No matter what I read – poetry, fiction, literary criticism, cultural criticism, theory – I want these attributes, and when they are not present, I acutely feel the lack of their grace and power. I understand my impatience with too much intellectual abstraction, my chariness about the (to me, irresponsible and even dangerous) way that some people "play" with disembodied ideas.

*

Connecting with Barbara Smith in December 1974 proved to be a significant event for me with positive, long-term consequences. We were both wandering around the Modern Language Association annual convention in New York City wondering why in the world we were wasting our time being there. Having begun our work on Black American women writers, we were vainly searching for relevant sessions and making frustrated, irreverent jokes about the usual "old boy" fare from which we had to choose. We ended up hanging out in our rooms and in offbeat restaurants, talking with what Zora Neale Hurston called "hungry eagerness" about our writers and Black feminist literary criticism. The very next year, I joined her as the second Black woman on the MLA's Commission on the Status of Women in the Profession. Membership on the Commission connected us to areas and possibilities of the profession and helped to provide resources to launch projects and form scholarly community. The 1975 convention in San Francisco was a different story. There were relevant sessions and other Black feminist scholars with whom to talk.

The work of recovery and valorization had soundly begun, fueled by the inception of the first courses on Black women writers (for example, Alice Walker's at Wellesley College), by the early harbingers of the contemporary United States' Black women's literary renaissance (for example, Toni Morrison's *The Bluest Eye* and *Sula*), and by the scholarship beginning in other fields (for example, Angela Davis's "Reflections on the Black Woman's Role in the Community of Slaves," *The Black Scholar,* 1971). Mary Helen Washington's *Black-Eyed Susans: Classic Stories by and about Black Women* was published by Doubleday in 1975. Critics such as Washington and Deborah McDowell continue to be commentators whom we can admire and learn from. In this first collection, Washington debunked stereotypes about Black women which, she said in her Introduction, "abound like weeds in this society," made a case for viewing the Black woman "from the special angle of the black woman writer," provided a thematic framework for studying the literature, and advanced her own perceptive bits of interpretation (pointing out, for instance, that Sula and Pauline Breedlove could well be read as "hidden artists"). Barbara Christian's important *Black Women Novelists: The Development of a Tradition, 1892–1976* appeared in 1980. As I sit here reconstructing this history from the unsystematic upsurges of my memory, I realize that sweeping revisionary trends are being localized in certain individuals and events and that what occurred in my world is only one small piece of a large and complex story. I certainly wish to acknowledge that many people in many places galvanized these currents.

Associations with Florence Howe, the Reprints Advisory Committee of the Feminist Press, revolutionary colleagues, and so on all fed my feminist knowledge and literary politics. More specifically, I became professionally radicalized about the condition of "minorities and women" in the academy. When I was hired for my first job at the University of Delaware in 1971, I was even "greener" than grass. Operating in isolation and totally without mentoring, I included my employment as church pianist and university secretary on my curriculum vitae and did not even know that salary negotiation was possible, let alone that my rarity as a commodity might be worth something. My good fortune was to have been allowed to pursue the path of my development. It was not until I came up for promotion and tenure in 1976 that I saw myself being undermined in ways so commonplace that they are nasty clichés – ways which included questioning the worth of my scholarship because it focused on Black women and Afro-American literature and appeared in non-"recognized" journals. Being able to analyze what was personally happening to me as a widespread professional problem was immensely helpful, and it left me with a useful edge of "outsider" awareness.

By the early 1980s, I had defined the Black feminist critical approach I used to the point of being able to state it (though with some postmodern hesitation about fixity and absolutes) as a set of "fundamental tenets." These were that (i) everything about the subject is important for a total understanding and analysis of her life and work; (ii) the proper scholarly stance is engaged rather than "objective"; (iii) the personal (both the subject's and the critic's) is political; (iv) description must be accompanied by analysis; (v) consciously maintaining at all times the angle of vision of a person who is both Black and female is imperative, as is the necessity for a class-conscious, anti-capitalist perspective; (vi) being principled requires rigorous truthfulness and "telling it all"; (vii) research/criticism is not an academic/intellectual game, but a pursuit with social meanings rooted in the "real world"; (viii) good criticism can be "life-saving" for the Black women who produce and read it; (ix) the writing does not need to be rigidly traditional in style, but can be creative and poetic; and (x) a holistic envisioning of a broad audience can often be more exacting, useful and liberating than more schizophrenic conceptualizations (Hull 1982: 193–4).

During the 1980s, most of us engaged in Black feminist literary criticism learned to use some version(s) of this methodology well. (Here I have given my own formulation, but I believe that the basic ideas were generally widespread.) Our development has moved in the direction of increasing refinement, sophistication and problematizing, both to foster our own growth and continued excitement about our work and to maintain the place of this work within the academy.

The other significant result of my meeting with Barbara Smith was, through her, becoming associated with the Combahee River Collective/Black Feminist Retreat group. Earlier I had joined the newly formed National Black Feminist Organization and attended one conference, but had not enjoyed any sustained/sustaining contact with other Black feminists. Affiliation with this group provided satisfying interaction with other Black feminists in communal and activist ways which included the academic–intellectual but encompassed much more. Once or twice yearly between 1977 and 1980, fifteen to twenty of us met in cities along the north-east corridor from Boston to Washington, DC. Other participants included Lorraine Bethel, Cheryl Clarke, Demita Frazier, Ellie Johnson, Yvonne Flowers, Phyllis Bethel, Sharon Page-Ritchie, Gwen Braxton, Linda Powell, Beverly Smith, Carroll Oliver, Audre Lorde and Julie Blackwoman.

At the retreats we tried out our creative and critical work on each other; shared our latest reading; discussed books, music, and films; planned (and sometimes executed) ways to spread Black feminism among Black women; formed nucleus groups for politically and culturally active projects; talked about ourselves and our lives; and engaged in stringent social critique and analysis. I probably do not need to say that we also drummed, danced, loved, laughed a lot, did rituals and made gorgeous meals.

Shortly after the onset of my participation with this group, I began to associate with another circle of exciting women – including Alexis DeVeaux (poet and writer), Konda Mason (then manager of Sweet Honey in the Rock) and Michelle Parkerson (filmmaker and writer) – who operated in the arenas of art, theater, and music. These women, too, helped me to create a brand of cultural nationalist black lesbian/feminism by keeping the lesbian/feminism tied to race and culture and to beautiful Black women. Compared with white "dyke wimmin's" culture, our dress, behaviour, activities, music, habits and habitats were quite different. We grew dreadlocks, multiply pierced our ears, wore dark lipstick and African garb, lived vegetarian, visited the Caribbean every chance we got, and so on.

Overall, the grounding I received from these "lifestyle" dimensions of my feminism was every bit as crucial for forging my identity and praxis as a black feminist literary critic as were the seemingly more direct and overtly intellectual sources. In many instances, the two came together. We carried with us – and sometimes talked about – power, particularly personal power as concept, being, and practice. It went with a confident valuing of self and belief in our ability to cause effects in the world. Related to it was the equally large notion of spirituality. Loosely defined, it nevertheless gave embodiment and therefore accessibility to an important area, provided a name and legitimization to a part of us which existed and could then be consciously used and developed.

Spirituality is still a keystone of my feminist endeavors. I discussed it, for example, in my work on Alice Dunbar-Nelson and Georgia Douglas Johnson, and it is my major current interest. It is also something I am increasingly learning to use in my teaching – as subject matter and as one dimension of a feminist pedagogy. This latter has to do with what my colleague Bettina Aptheker calls creating a favorable learning environment by opening hearts, unblocking energies, and freely exchanging them.

*

Presently, in 1991, I am pointedly seeking ways to keep my whole life, including my work as an African-American feminist professor and literary critic, personally fulfilling and socially useful. At midlife, the old motivations (parental praise, superiors' approval, tenure, raises, etc.) do not carry the same force. Consequently, I find that I am oftener being self-reflective and also thinking/feeling more deeply about the people and circumstances with which I interact as I go about my business.

I am concerned about the current crop of graduate students, whose slow and fearful progress, calculated choices, capitulative attitudes, and ultra-careful behavior baffle and even distress me. They are in certain ways sharper and brighter than I think I was or can recall most of my cohorts as being, but some quality of daring and enthusiasm seems to be absent. I can remember being scared but not timid, reticent but not inhibited, cautious but still confident. I ask myself: has the terrain changed so much? Are we in some sense more forbidding than our old professors? Is this a problem which I help to create? I remind myself that the 1990s are not the 1970s. Women's Studies – though still vulnerable – and feminist scholarship have been institutionally recognized. There is now a generation for whom feminism is largely an intellectual pursuit. There is no longer the same precise need for the consciousness we carried of being infiltrators and subversives, even though the appalling developments around "political correctness" should remind us radicals and progressives of certain realities which it is better never to forget.

I watch with interest the dynamics of race and scholarship concerned with it. One particular focus is how women of color will deal with the sobering difficulties of conducting work about each other. I encounter women of color of one race who decide to study a writer or writers from a different race – only to falter in impatience and frustration when they textually and emotionally encounter their previously unknown blind spots. I have also found myself being increasingly observant of those white women scholars of roughly my generation who made their reputations on, in most instances, good work about Black or Third World women. They have, of course, earned the authority of their positions, but I wonder about the "closedness" (sometimes bordering on arrogance) which accompanies it in some of them – how that attitude came to be and what it might indicate, not only about the white women themselves, but about all of our relationships with each other as academic feminists.

As I write this set of current concerns, I hope that I do not sound smug, self-righteous, or mean-tempered. What I really feel is troubled and thoughtful – in something of the same way I ponder whether we are, in the final analysis, truly justified in saying that our teaching and writing – as we generally do them now – constitute "political work." I had a greater sense that this was so when there was a more activist edge and more extensive contact between those of us who were academicians and those of us who walked other ways in life. Maybe we cannot do everything (and I myself see personally how hard it is to simply keep the head above water). However, I believe that just yearning to impact beyond the academy probably adds something fine to what we do. When I think about my own wishes, I know that I am seeking appropriate new ways to connect with receptive audiences and affirm the Black feminist values important to me and the literature which embodies them. I hold on to this one certainty and see where it takes me.

REFERENCES

alta (n.d.)*Letters to Women*, Berkeley, CA: Shameless Hussy Press.

Cade (Bambara), T.(1970) *The Black Woman: An Anthology*, New York: New American Library.

Friedan, B.(1963) *The Feminine Mystique*, New York: W. W. Norton.

Hull, G. T. (1982) "Researching Alice Dunbar-Nelson: A Personal and Literary Perspective," in G.T. Hull, Scott and Smith (eds) *All the Women Are White, All the Blacks Are Men, But Some of Us Are Brave: Black Women's Studies*, Old Westbury, N. Y.: The Feminist Press.

——(1989) *Healing Heart: Poems 1973–1988*, Latham, N. Y.: Kitchen Table: Women of Color Press.

Parker, P. (1972) *Child of Myself*, Oakland, CA: Women's Press Collective.

Chapter 4

Imaginary gardens with real frogs in them
Feminist euphoria and the Franco-American divide, 1976–88

Ann Rosalind Jones

When I think about the present state of feminist literary theory at the same time that I think about my history as a feminist, I come up with some bad news – feminist literary studies are in a state of violent division. Then, on reflection, I end with some news that seems better: the stakes – as always – are changing. I've been disturbed by the bitter debate in literary studies between feminists oriented toward theory, especially French theory, and feminist critics reading women writers, past and present, in archeological or celebratory ways. Toril Moi's 1985 book *Sexual/Textual Politics* typified the Anglo-American/French divide that Betsey Draine compared in 1988 to the contest between the two women in the judgment of Solomon, fighting over who was entitled to claim the baby in the king's custody. Draine admits that her analogy is an uncomfortable one: why should an Old Testament monarch be figured as the judge over who has priority in feminist theory and criticism? But she is right to say that the debate has taken on the quality of ancient myth, with each side exaggerating the shortcomings and flattening out the intricacies of its opponent.

None the less, there is a real debate. American feminists have worked in an empirical, activist mode that privileges practical politics, historical context and empathetic reading. Most of them began with direct political experience, in consciousness-raising groups and on-the-street activism. As critics, they began by analyzing sexist ideology in male writers' representation of women, they celebrated the work of new feminist novelists and poets, they excavated lost women writers; *then* they turned to reflections on what they had been doing and why. Differently, the women theorists whose work has most often been imported from France rejected activist feminist politics during the 1970s; they refused to be labeled as feminists because the term sounded too much like any other liberal political affiliation. Their work began in interdisciplinary critical theory, framed in elite academic settings. One of their first points of reference was Derrida's critique of philosophy, his argument that the assertions of metaphysics, from ancient Greece to contemporary speech-act theory, are couched in vocabularies which, like all language, are labile, interplays of terms that depend on each other rather than any link to external reality to produce meaning. The Derridean axiom most directly useful to French feminists was that claims to truth in western thought are built upon hierarchies of value through which one term is shored up by a negative opposite that it can neither acknowledge nor do without. For a thinker such as Hélène Cixous, this view of thought in language offered an entering wedge into the sexual politics of culture. The logic through which man defines himself as woman's superior can be exposed, reversed and displaced; and rigid gender binaries themselves can be transcended (1975a, 1975b).

Psychoanalysis was also appropriated by Frenchwomen for a particular argument, its focus on language as a system of constraints rather than a medium of power for female speakers and writers. Freud argued that the price we pay for our entry into culture, an entry that disrupts the natural mother–infant bond, is the internalization of patriarchal conscience in the Oedipal process, a process redefined by Lacan to stress culture as the Law of the Father, through which infantile pre-linguistic fantasies of omnipotence are replaced by a subject position imposed by codified public language. In this linguistic prison-house, no one can speak of the desire for the mother she or he has lost; women become objects of fantasy for men and are themselves marginalized in language because of the privileged status it allows the phallus as symbol of paternal authority. But the unconscious persists; it disrupts the Symbolic order, in the form of symptoms, resistances, derangements of official public discourse. In the work of Julia Kristeva, this disruptive force, the semiotic, belongs to men: it is visible in Bellini's artistic practice (Kristeva 1977) and audible in the modernist linguistic experiments of male writers such as Mallarmé (Kristeva 1974a) and Céline (Kristeva 1980). But Kristeva has shown little interest in women writers or any writer not part of the modernist canon. And when, in the late 1970s, she proposed semiotic resistance as a model for political activity, recommending free-form rejection of the reigning order rather than any pragmatic attempt to seize power and occupy the Symbolic order from within, she left feminists on this side of the ocean wondering whether such a project had any political purchase at all (1974b).

From the French or Francophile theoretical perspective, on the other hand, American feminist criticism is seen as naïvely confident about women's rational self-determination and their power over language. We assume, it is said, that women writers can express their experience in transparent language, that feminist reading can produce solid interpretations of what writers intended to say, and that gender differences are the proper subject of feminist investigation. Franco-feminist theory, in contrast, defines literary texts as sites of unconscious or deliberate resistance to the laws of language, proceeds on the assumption that texts are open to a variety of readerly explorations rather than capable of a final interpretation, and envisions the dissolution of gender oppositions, a mobile polysexuality, as the goal of psychic liberation. Both positions question the humanist framework of earlier literary studies, according to which great books are written by a sovereign subject in full possession of himself – typically a white, ruling-class, heterosexual, male self. But American feminist criticism has wanted to register women's claims, at various historical moments, to some of that sovereign subjectivity, to centralize women as authors rather than to dissolve historically under-acknowledged feminine identities into a mobile continuum of free play in which language and genders oscillate, undisturbed by any imbalance in lived social power.

Betsey Draine rejoiced in 1988 that feminists in the United States were working to meet the French halfway, or more than halfway: that deconstruction was being brought to history, that notions of identity and agency in language were gaining complexity. But I want to resist tossing the American baby out into trans-Atlantic waters. I want to suggest that the history of feminism as a political movement in this country has materially shaped our critical habits, and that this history may now be providing new ways of formulating critical projects in the 1990s. I'm going to try narrating the shifts in American feminist criticism in an autobiographical way – that is, by presenting the history of my own involvement with feminism as a typical case. No absolutely typical feminist literary academic exists. But as I've thought back in an autobiographical/historical way, as the editors of this anthology asked speakers at the March 1990 Scripps conference on feminist scholarship to do, I've come to the conclusion that my particular past is not merely idiosyncratic. It resembles many other academic women's trajectories and, on reflection, it turns out to be coherent and incoherent in ways that surface in many other American feminists' life histories. So – allowing for nostalgia and screen memories both – here's the story of an American feminist politicized in the late 1960s, living a kind of intellectual schizophrenia at graduate school through the 1970s, and teaching in a women's college through the 1980s.

In 1964, when I was an undergraduate studying comparative literature at the University of California at Berkeley, the Free Speech movement began. Students occupied plazas and college buildings to keep the university administration from prohibiting political activity on campus. Four years later, in 1968, I was living in Paris when what the French call "the events of May" occurred: students and factory workers joined in a strike that paralyzed the country and forced new elections. I was radicalized by what seemed possible at both those moments: to block police power by keeping the campus cops from arresting a protester and driving him away, to force a government to liberalize its policies and replace its representatives, and – above all – to act in concert with other people in spontaneous and astonishingly effective ways. We kept the police car from driving away; the general strike paralyzed the country. But I also recall that the spokesmen for the Berkeley students were almost invariably men. Mario Savio was a philosophy student who quoted Aristotle to denounce the university deans; in France, from his various hideouts, Danny Cohn-Bendit talked to newsmen on behalf of the student–worker coalition. In Berkeley we women students listened and cheered; in Paris I helped silkscreen posters to call people to meetings. Men theorized in those movements; women got arrested and roughed up by cops, as men did, but they weren't in charge of strategy or speeches to the press.

That was what was so different about the feminist consciousness-raising groups that began forming in New York in the late 1960s: women did the talking. Following the model of self-criticism practiced in the villages of Mao's China, we met to analyze what we were up against in a world run by men. It's hard to describe my fearful excitement, my sense of sailing over the edge of some unknown abyss, when ten of us met for the first time in an Upper West Side apartment to define what we wanted to do – which was to talk together about what we couldn't talk about elsewhere: our resentment that our time was never our own because we were expected to care for the psyches of all the people in our lives, our fear that we weren't competent to do the kind of academic and professional work our men seemed to be doing more confidently, our unease about concentrating on our own oppression when there were so many other kinds of suffering going on – in the American South, in Viet Nam, in Latin America – as our leftist lovers and husbands were happy to remind us. But we met anyway, every Thursday night for a year. We took turns speaking; we listened; and we interpreted.

Each meeting began with someone raising a problem she'd faced that week, something she thought was related to sexual politics – sexual come-ons from men on the street, being the person to do all the emotional work in a marriage, panicky inability to concentrate at a library. The other nine of us would listen, mention similar events in our own lives, analyze what the commonality we were discovering implied about our conditioning and the division of labor in a sexist society. So there was a move from a single pained story to group comment, and from there to a general conclusion about how we were positioned as women and how we could change that positioning (Shreve 1989).

I want to argue that we were evolving a hermeneutic, that is, a systematic way of interpreting our own statements. But in contrast to deconstruction and psycho-analysis, we were interpreting the discourse of an oppressed group: not the masters of western metaphysics, not the socially privileged, articulate patients of an analyst like Freud. There were no Rousseaus or Doras in the group. But there were gaps and contradictions in what any one of us said; there were hesitations and uncertainties. A typical opening remark was "I don't think this is really important, but … "; another was "I don't know how to say this." As listeners in the group, we felt a responsibility to fill in gaps, to explain contradictions as the result of old conditioning and new desires, to hear uncertainties not as a symptom of the instability of language in general but as a symptom of imposed silence, of the shame that operated in paralyzing ways when a woman tried to articulate her dissatisfaction. We assumed a fixed referent for what any one of us was signifying: a social order that disempowered women. And we were anti-psychoanalysis for concrete reasons. Those of us who were in therapy were encouraged to interpret our unhappiness as a neurotic response to early life in dysfunctional families; no shrink was likely to propose that *most* families in the 1950s and 1960s had been dysfunctional for women, even or especially those they'd been conditioned to construct for themselves – although Betty Friedan had made the point resoundingly in *The Feminine Mystique* in 1963. What we did instead was to listen to each other on the assumption that we were deeply sane, that what we needed was not endopsychic readjustment but changes in the way we were treated and could act in the world.

Listening in consciousness-raising groups was a subtle process, not easy for those of us who were good students (or father-identified daughters of academics, like me) who were always the first to make a comment in class, always fast off the mark in a discussion. I learned to shut up and keep listening, to say, "You haven't used up your twenty minutes, do you want to say more?" or "Wait, give her a chance to finish!" (people said that to me a lot at first) or "You know, this doesn't sound so strange, it sounds like what Sara was saying last week." None of these responses characterizes deconstructive reading or the celebration of the decentered text. Our goal was to define a center we could share, to take conclusions and final sentences as statements of truth rather than artifices of closure, to look for the repeated, typical response rather than the idiosyncratic text in process. Yet we were certainly producing a new text, or, better, since the dynamic was oral, a new signifying process. The point was to turn it into engagement with the recalcitrant world of required femininity, heterosexual relationships, and all those dishes someone had to wash. The conclusions we drew began being taken back home: arguments were heard all up and down Broadway about the power relations encoded into housework, about unequal distribution of psychic work, about the distinction between really listening and waiting for the other person – the woman – to stop talking so that you could make the point you'd intended to make before she started to speak. The group exhilarated me because we were elaborating a new communicative medium, a set of rules for giving a woman the time she needed to make her point and for orchestrating the circle of listeners so that everyone had a chance to respond. That is, we were transforming socialized reticence into group-assisted sense. We were also redefining what a secret was. By breaking down the mystifying division between private life and public discussion, we were rewriting the etiquette about what was speakable and what wasn't.

None the less, there were crucial silences in that group. We were all white, all middle-class, and all (at least at the moment) heterosexual – a homogeneity we were blind to at the time. The assumption that we were all straight extended to our lovers as well; never a word was breathed about bisexuality or lesbianism. No one talked about money or lousy jobs, no one talked about the class and academic privilege some of us had more of than others. We worked on a communal assumption that our meanings, once uttered, were transparent, that our routine at meetings made what we were feeling directly accessible to group understanding. Eventually, though, a theory–practice split complicated the process. Consciousness-raising was intended as a first step, the psychic precondition for political work; but in our group (and many others) feelings stayed the issue. We worried about our failure to take the next step. We kept planning political interventions, but, with the exception of one feeble picket line outside an art film theater, our actions never materialized. Still, we were doing important work: collaborating on the articulation of a felt political knowledge of our being-in-the-world as women. That was the accomplishment of consciousness-raising in the late 1960s.

It seems clear to me now that the first stages of feminist literary work corresponded to this process of empathetic analysis. Early critics read women characters in men's books as we read each other in the consciousness-raising group: as women placed in oppressive circumstances. The method was not to blame Shakespeare's Cressida or Thackeray's Becky Sharpe but to understand, perhaps better than their authors, what they were up against. Even more, we read women writers as if they were ourselves: aware of their situation, angry, lucid. Sometimes, of course, this was true: the Redstockings were publishing brilliant polemical pamphlets, Valerie Solanas came out with her "SCUM Manifesto," academics such as Anne Koedt writing "The Myth of the Vaginal Orgasm" showed what committed feminist research could do. The first collections of poetry from the movement stressed genuineness of voice above all, in titles such as *No More Masks* and *I Hear My Sisters Singing*. A title that didn't exist but could have is *Our Voices, Ourselves*. It's certain that the phonocentric emphasis in American feminist criticism, the celebration of the "real woman's voice," came partly out of the consciousness-raising process: we wanted to speak, we constructed occasions to speak, we heard ourselves quavering out difficult sentences, we waited to hear a supportive response. CR groups were de-repressive, permission-granting structures that opened up a new oral medium.

But they weren't permanent. One way or another, we all moved beyond the group in 1970. That year I found myself in the kind of contradictory work situation that ought to have produced some kind of enlightenment or at least a sense of the ironies of late capitalism. It didn't, though; at the time, my practice was exceeding my theory. In 1969, after a lot of debate and many feminist demonstrations, New York State legalized abortion (the Roe versus Wade decision of the Supreme Court wasn't written until 1971). This meant that abortion clinics could open in New York; and one immediately was opened, by a twenty-five-year-old woman who had studied philosophy in England and met a New Orleans doctor who knew the new aspiration technique. I heard through the feminist grapevine that this clinic needed counsellors, so I showed up for an interview. When I had the interview at the clinic, I said I wanted the job because it seemed like "perfectly unalienated labor" – being paid to do something that I wanted to do in the first place. The clinic was a new physical space where a new social practice was being evolved. Again, women were talking and listening to each other, and although most of the doctors were men, the administration and the counsellors' collective were run by women. We were a motley group, much more so than my CR group had been: black and white, professional nurses and long-skirted counter-cultural types, New Yorkers and mid-Westerners. Our reactions to each eight-hour shift varied widely: some of us quit from burn-out, some had nightmares and wanted to invent mourning rituals, others developed a black-humorous hilarity. But most of us felt triumphant that we were women taking care of women. Kristeva's conviction that any political action, any take-over of worldly power by women, will simply reproduce the mastery structures of the masculine Symbolic was not affirmed by the consistently feminist yet diverse counselling styles at the clinic.

At the same time I was teaching English part-time at Queens College. At Queens, the department was run by men; the secretaries were required to tell young women teachers how to dress ("no trousers unless you wear a jacket that covers your rear end"); and the syllabuses were relentlessly male-authored. I taught novels by men, plays by men, essays by men: Flaubert and Dickens, Shakespeare, Orwell. Unwed mothers appeared fairly often in these texts and invariably met bad ends. But the tragic Gretchen in Goethe's *Faust* and Hardy's Tess of the D'Urbervilles had nothing in common with the women I was seeing at the clinic on weekends, from teenagers to mothers of five who'd flown into Kennedy airport from all over the country. These women were saving themselves from the catastrophe of involuntary maternity that apparently appealed to male writers so much, as one of a heroine's few pathways to tragic stature. Yet I did not imagine changing my book lists. I taught my students how to write coherent paragraphs and read symbolism, not how to focus on heroines or their absence. I do remember asking one sneakily feminist question about the angelic little Biddy in *Great Expectations*. "Why," I said, in my best Socratic manner, "is this character so good?" (meaning she was unbelievable). To which a Queens sophomore, a well brought up Catholic boy, said, "Well, girls just *are* nicer than boys." What happened next I don't recall, but it wasn't the discussion of gender ideology, social conditioning and reader expectations that we should have had. My clinic job was practical feminist politics; the teaching seemed to go on in another realm entirely. At Queens we held moratoriums to talk about Viet Nam, but no one talked about giving a course on women writers.

At this point in feminist criticism, not surprisingly, the "images of women" approach, that is, the analysis of men writers' representations of women, became deeper and sharper. Misogyny was discovered in the masterworks; woman-hating was recognized not as an occasional flicker in this male writer or that but as a substratum of most American and European writing. The book that offered this argument most spectacularly, Kate Millett's *Sexual Politics* (1969), was further exceptional in that it bridged the gap I'm recalling in my own intellectual life: Millett's best-selling attack on Henry Miller and Norman Mailer, the expatriate modernist and the all-American writer, was written as a Ph.D. thesis at Columbia. I, however, had just spent a year there writing an MA thesis on Michael Drayton, a 1590s poet remarkable for sonnets in which he alternately idealizes and attacks a female beloved named "Idea," without ever asking any questions myself about power, fantasy, the writer's control of the woman through language and rhetoric, his articulation of sex as violence through which he declares himself a man. But feminists continued and deepened this kind of work throughout the 1970s: misogyny was read as a deep-set cultural construction, as the bedrock for certain aspects of national identity-formation in the United States, and as a kind of community ritual in European culture. At this point, Claudine Hermann was writing her *Les Voleuses de langue*, which appeared in France in 1976. The Franco–American divide was not yet in evidence in that book, perhaps because Hermann taught in the United States. But her analyses of male writers and official discourses in French were written from a deeply critical perspective that had a good deal in common with American work such as Annette Kolodny's study of US pastoral, *The Lay of the Land*, to name one example.

Where were the women writers? Everywhere, being dug out of the past in reaction against the supremacy of the male-authored canon. Kate Chopin is a good example of the ways in which a writer censored in her own time, and then minimized by critics who labeled her as a regional novelist, became more and more readable for feminists. Women were also beginning to be heard as critics: I think of Fraya Katz-Stoker's attack on formalism in Susan Cornillon's anthology, *Images of Women in Fiction* (1972), of the delighted rediscovery of Woolf's *A Room of One's Own*, and of the careful research through which literary historians such as Ellen Moers and Elaine Showalter exposed the ways that economic necessity forced women to make their way into the networks of nineteenth-century popular publishing, proved how widely read they were at their time, and demonstrated how firmly elitist academic criticism had effaced them from readability. Women were also writing for a popular reading public: Erica Jong, Marge Piercy, Marilyn French, Rita Mae Brown. And modernists such as Jean Rhys and Doris Lessing were being read differently, with an eye to gender politics.

I, however, maintained my academic schizophrenia. When I started my Ph.D. at Cornell, having decided to go on with Renaissance literature, I wrote a massive dissertation on five male love poets without posing a single question about the women they complained of and praised. In fact, the only twentieth-century input I responded to was literary theory, a major issue at Cornell in the 1970s. We read Lévi-Strauss, we read Lacan, we read Roland Barthes and Jacques Derrida. Theory conferences every year imported Marxists such as Jameson, deconstructors such as Paul de Man, Lacanians such as Lacoue-Labarthe; question and answer periods were riveting, shifting from ecstatic appreciation to hostility and incomprehension. But feminism as theory was absent from the Romance language and comparative literature circuit. *Diacritics*, Cornell's theory journal, published an issue on feminism and deconstruction in 1975, but with the exception of Marxist theory (occasionally taught by a comparatist from Guyana via Cambridge, who quit and went home to help run the government in 1976), theory was approached as a philosophical issue rather than as a political project. A good deal remains to be figured out, I think, about the reception of French theory in American departments of language and literature: how it positioned its American readers in gender terms, how young male academics welcomed it as a kind of liberatory terrorism that left their older humanist colleagues (also men) in the dust – without necessarily posing more directly political questions about whose interests on or beyond the campus this new Oedipal warfare and critical dispensation might serve.

Another form of pressure at Cornell came from the writing program, where several poets-in-residence – all men – were making statements that infuriated their women students. One would-be poet was advised, "We're all human; poetry is universal. You're stepping down from that level if you write as a woman." Another student, asking a seminar leader why they read no women poets, was told "I can't teach what I don't read." The name of his course was Great Modern Poets. It was in reaction against such serenely masculinist assumptions, not against the glamour of theory, that a third group, crucially important to me, came into being. Ten women graduate students met in an unofficial seminar on feminist literary criticism throughout the winter and spring of 1976-7. Half were in the poetry-writing program; half were studying theory and criticism. That summer we assembled an account of the group, called "To the Woman Who Reads and Writes" (published in *The Ithaca Women's Anthology* the next year). As I write this, I'm using that piece of collaborative writing to think about what this group worked through.

In some ways we lived out a microhistory of feminist criticism. Beginning with angry rejection of the all-male canon read as universal truth, we came to male-authored criticism with deep suspicion. This suspicion made the deconstruction of critical blindness, such as Shoshanna Felman's analysis of Balzac's male critics, useful to us (1975). So was the debate over whether women's poetry was merely confessional (Sylvia Plath and Anne Sexton were the cases in point), because it prompted us to ask whether the term "confessional" would have such a negative connotation if it were applied to male poets – and why, in fact, it never was. The public/private division was coming under attack again, this time as a literary-genre problem rather than a CR group issue.

We also asked what a feminine style might be. In this, we were responding to feminist inquiry about language in the United States (for example, Adrienne Rich's *Dream of a Common Language*) and in France, although we didn't yet know the manifestos of writers such as Hélène Cixous, Annie Leclerc and Luce Irigaray. But the poets in the group wrote so differently from one another that we never arrived at generalizations about female language. It was a topic for conjecture rather than a uniform practice. Our writers of lyrics took on similar themes: patriarchal culture as obstacle, the unspoken ways in which young women (us) sensed and used their bodies, poetic language as concrete magic. But their particular histories – a Canadian, a midwesterner, a Scotswoman, a Californian, some straight, some lesbian – unfailingly distinguished their treatments of any topic. Heterogeneity was the rule. In fact, sharp disagreements arose about the language in which we would present the collaborative text describing the seminar: was "collective" too political a term, was a line about lesbianism inclusive enough to end on? The question of style arose in another way for the literature students, because we wondered whether, in spite of the sense of discovery and frank speaking in the group, we would have to "write like little men" to succeed in academe.

What we were looking for in our reading, we said, was a new language, by which I think we meant a convincingly elaborated articulation of women's sense of new social and cultural possibilities. We approached texts with a utopian demand – and we were usually disappointed. The satire and melancholy of Margaret Atwood's poems, the wild anguish of the Portuguese text *The Three Marias* (I quote) "left us cold." But another kind of reading began to develop, one more self- and institutionally critical. Some of us disliked the way Ai and alta, for example, used street slang in direct, explicit statements. They seemed too straight from the shoulder. Where was the poem? But we then turned the question back on our own ignorance: could we discover how their circumstances as black poets accounted for their disregard of the rules of nuance and negative capability sacred to the poetic theory of the high academy? How much of that myth had we internalized? The mix of academic and popular feminist publishing in the United States meant that we were confronting texts that challenged the expectations we'd derived from high modernism.

This challenge was important, the result of the publication of women's writing of the moment by seat-of-the-pants local presses as well as by academic and popular companies. Small publishing outfits all over the country, and the sense of editors such as Suzanne Juhasz that we needed to be reading black as well as white women, prevented the kind of monopoly established by elitist presses such as des femmes in Paris. And the critique of masculine power in France focused on the centrality of the phallus in culture and language, not on the predominance of men in the modernist canon. Kristeva read late nineteenth-century male writers such as Mallarmé and Lautréamont as a liberatory avant-garde in *The Revolution of Poetic Language*; Cixous celebrated Lewis Carroll, James Joyce and Jean Genet; writers such as Marguerite Duras, interviewed by Alice Jardine in a recent issue of *Yale French Studies*, were eager to be accepted into the modernist canon promoted by publishing houses such as Minuit and Seuil. In answer to a question by Jardine, Duras responded – more or less – "What's the problem with the canon? I'm in it" (1988). I wonder how critic–theorists such as Cixous and Kristeva would have responded to a French equivalent of the outpouring of texts by the Feminist Press, Naiad, South End Press, Kitchen Table Press, Off Our Backs, and the other alternative presses that came and went through the 1970s in this country.

Eventually, the Cornell group moved toward a reading stance that now seems to me to be the most valuable result of the year's work: the expectation that we were going to be surprised. We were no longer sure of our criteria; we found them insufficient to explain our responses. Again, our practice was outpacing our theory. That productive uncertainty came from reading new work, pre-canonized and pre-judged; the unpredictable variety of new writing by women kept us off balance. Toward the end of the group account, I read,

> we find that our practice (the internal dynamics of our own group) has superseded our theoretical elaboration.... . What we have now to develop is the theory that has been part of our work, the silent workings of intellectual production that we have made manifest, viable and real, not because of, but rather, in spite of our institutional affiliations.

I am not celebrating a golden, pre-theoretical Eden here. I am remarking, though, that at the moment that this group began to sense the need to formulate a basis for its methods, we defined the audience for that definition as ourselves – not as male colleagues or academic media curious about our undertaking. One of the tensions in the critical debate that has preoccupied us for the past five years is certainly a desire to explain ourselves to the institution – that is, to male colleagues who have put themselves in the center again by asking us to account for ourselves (or offering to do it for us). Separatism may have been a problematic dimension of early feminist work, but it had its uses. The Cornell "ovular," as we called it, knew who its audience and political constituency were: other women in the academy and, we hoped, some outside it.

Theorizing has hardly been lacking throughout the decade since that piece was published. But institutional affiliations have a very different meaning now. I want to give you the history of one more group, in order to make some final suggestions about the success of academic feminism – about the fact that the academy now tolerates, even welcomes, certain forms of feminism rather than looming up as the monolith that provokes it. In 1977 I took a job at Smith College. Two other women who were just beginning jobs in the same area suggested setting up a feminist reading group, and I leaped at the chance. This group typified a new stage of feminist work for me: it was interdisciplinary. We included four literary critics, two sociologists, two graduate students in education, a psychologist and a linguist. We read a lot of different material, although not novels – they were too long, no one had time for them. Instead, we discussed articles on object-relations theory, on socio-linguistics, on women's moral judgments and their supposed fear of success. As part of a network of feminist scholars throughout the Pioneer Valley, a hotbed of women's studies and political activism in the 1970s, one of our first moves was to infiltrate a conference of Catholics promoting disarmament and attacking abortion; another was to cheer for a local women's slow-ball team, the Hot Flashes.

But the warmth and light began to dim over the issue of critical theory. Our linguist, one night in the winter of 1978, suddenly turned on us literary types. "You talk about language all the time," she said, "but I don't understand anything you're saying. What are your premises? What is the phallus? Why don't you ever ask *me* about women and language?" She was angry, and she was in tears. The group drifted apart, even after – or perhaps because – we literary theorists presented a session on Lacan and the French femininity-theorists. One woman who'd left to become a faculty wife at Notre Dame (she'd finished a Ph.D. in education, but the big first academic recession was beginning) came back for a visit and shook her head at us in wonder, saying "You all talk in paragraphs. My women friends in the Midwest can hardly get out a sentence." What was happening, I think, was that French-oriented critical theory was becoming a master discourse, an intricate vocabulary that laid claim to total pan-disciplinary understanding. Some of us had become unable to imagine any other way of talking; and we were driving people away.

Another incident, in 1986, brought the conflict to a head for me. Several organizers of the Five College seminar on women in the Third World decided to begin by reading Gayatri Spivak's dense commentary on the short story "Draupadi," by a Bengali writer, Mahasetva Devi; at the last minute, we threw in an article by Mark Cousins purporting to explain deconstruction. The meeting was a catastrophe. Women from various fields, some of them activists in their fifties, others new arrivals in the area, objected violently to the opacity of all three texts. I found some of their objections convincing. One woman, an African-American literary critic, said, "I don't mind difficult reading, but isn't this approach finally just a way of focusing on the oppressor all over again?" Others asked, less temperately, how any of this theory was relevant to clitoridectomy in Ethiopia or the blindness of women working on assembly lines in "free" trade zones in the Philippines. Finally a woman who'd been a member of the previous study group stood up, declared, "Deconstruction is an empty yuppie theory; we need to read Fanon, not Derrida," and left the room. It wasn't easy to think through what had happened, but we couldn't simply accuse our critics of anti-intellectualism. I think we were being brought right up against the non-fit between deconstruction as a critique of the language of philosophy and the feminist ethic of knowing the other woman in a politically productive way.

That fiasco made me nervous about what I was doing. So did my teaching, though in a much more positive way. The first year I was at Smith, a colleague in French proposed that we team-teach a course in twentieth-century women writers. I was delighted; we put together a bilingual course which we taught to sixty students whose enthusiasm was dizzying. Marilyn knew Colette and Monique Wittig, as well as Christiane Rochefort, a popular feminist writer whose comic satires and utopian fictions deserve to be better known in the US; I taught Woolf, Atwood and Toni Morrison as critical experimenters with language. The next year we sometimes switched around; Marilyn taught the Anglo-Americans, I taught the French. Many academic women protest at the strains of working at elite graduate institutions, especially of being the only over-worked feminist in a field. I was luckier; I have to say how much pleasure and intellectual give-and-take these undergraduate courses gave me, especially at a college where a lot of other feminists were teaching similarly. These courses for sophomores had nothing to do with my Renaissance research, but teaching in that politicized undergraduate context finally made me start thinking about women writers of the Renaissance. Perhaps I also had an expiatory motive: after all those years of reading sixteenth-century men on women, I felt it was time to look at the women poets who'd been writing in response to them.

So Comp Lit 222, Twentieth-Century Women Writing, was the stimulus that eventually brought my book *The Currency of Eros* into being – although teaching three courses a term and advising totally engaging honors students made the project look as though it was going to illustrate Derrida's concept of infinite deferral forever! None the less, it was teaching, in a climate of feminist excitement, that finally directed my research toward women writers. So did the work of social historians and cultural critics such as Mary Poovey and, later, Nancy Armstrong, who used Foucault to read conduct books for women as discourses of power that simultaneously defined proper behavior for women and provoked resistance to social prescriptions. But the more Renaissance writing by women I read, the less sense it made. That is, it became a more and more uneasy bedfellow to my theoretical assumptions. Lacanian theory posited women's marginality to language; deconstruction posited their oppression in the violent hierarchies that shore up masculine identity; social history suggested that they were increasingly disempowered and silenced in early modern Europe. Yet I was finding extraordinarily interesting poets, women unpublished since the 1580s (but known to 1980s feminists, who were unfailingly generous with titles and advice about how to lay hands on a fragile pamphlet or a rare edition). By the time I had to write an introduction for the book, the contradiction between oppressor theory and the non-victim status of eight of a possible dozen poets was driving me to despair.

In fact, it drove me to feminist film theory, which was itself revising the strictures of semiotic analysis based on Lacanian premises. In 1987 a British Marxist-feminist, Christine Gledhill, wrote a wonderful article, "Pleasurable Negotiations," appropriating for feminism the concept of negotiation elaborated by Stuart Hall and other analysts of popular culture at the Birmingham Centre for Contemporary Cultural Studies. Negotiation as a description of active, critical response to cultural systems such as television and film gave me a way out of the theoretical impasse to which my reading of sixteenth-century women had led me, a strategy for moving beyond the oppressor/victim opposition Regina Marant-Sanchez mentioned at the Scripps Conference. For the Birmingham Marxists, following Gramsci but concentrating on viewer responses, negotiation means a two-way street, the process through which readers respond in partial, self-interested ways to the ideologies encoded into cultural forms. Hall defines three negotiating positions: one that accepts dominant ideology, one that redirects it to serve the interests of a subordinate group, one that contests reigning assumptions by re-articulating them in an alternative framework – as, for example (this from Gledhill), a woman's reading of a cinematic heroine as a model of active sexuality rather than the preconstructed object of the male gaze. As I present this solution, I may seem to be pulling a red rabbit out of a hat. But since the 1970s, British and American materialist feminists had been providing historically specific, nuanced accounts of cultural forms (the detective novel, the Romantic lyric, Victorian feminist tracts, the domestic novel). I'm thinking of the work of Kate Belsey, Cora Kaplan, Judy Walkowitz, Judy Newton, all of whom combine deconstructive and psychoanalytic insights with a focus on social pressures as limit and as challenge to women reading and writing. Gledhill does the same thing in her theoretical synthesis, and I think her revision of semiotic theory is typical of a new tendency in some recent American feminist criticism. So I'm going to end with three mini book reviews – and then, for fun, with three poems from the Cornell ovular.

In these three recent books, I see a new emphasis: on the liberatory maneuvers women have evolved to remain intelligible within cultural codes, their strategies of compromising with but also exposing and opposing the Symbolic order. The new books and the 1977 poems work out similar negotiations, I think. First, there's Patricia Yaeger's *Honey-Mad Women*, subtitled *Emancipatory Strategies in Women's Writing*. She does not reject contemporary French theory but she proposes a project that goes beyond it:

I want to begin to define a countertradition within women's writing, a tradition that involves the reinvention and reclamation of a body of speech women have found exclusive and alienating. The goal of this study is not to dispute that language is dangerous for women, but to ask whether we can identify contexts in which women find language empowering, in which women speak of their pleasure and find pleasure in speech.

(1988: 2–3)

She goes on to suggest a variety of joyful verbal processes and thematic clusters in a variety of prose and poetic texts by women, including Charlotte Brontë, Eudora Welty, and the contemporary (and, importantly, pre-canonized) American poet Mary Oliver. Without underplaying the coercive pressures of male-derived genres, Yaeger builds on critics as diverse as Mikhail Bakhtin, the theorist of popular festivity, and Hannah Arendt to argue that feminist readers must "make room" for new and utopian uses of language by women, for, as she puts it, "the positive ideology" of content and "the intersubjective dimension of collective dreams."

Another recent book formulates one "collective dream" as the feminist goal of understanding mother–daughter relationships. Marianne Hirsch's *The Mother–Daughter Plot* combines sympathetic analysis of women's texts with psychoanalytic insights, particularly from object-relations theory, into contradictions and gaps in such texts, especially the feminist daughters' tendency to speak about mothers and for them, rather than attending to maternal articulations of the relationship. Hirsch reads three time periods symptomatically, identifying disidentification with mothers as well as fantasies of pre-verbal fusion with them in a range of texts from the 1860s to the 1970s. Her readings are deconstructive yet sympathetic. Like Yaeger, she uses French theory but criticizes its limits; and she ends with a celebration of Toni Morrison's *Beloved* as an innovatory maternal text. Hirsch defines her own position historically, narrating her engagements as daughter and mother, as a participant in consciousness-raising groups, and as a member of academic seminars in which feminine filiation was a troubled issue (1989: 25–6). That is, the critic acknowledges her political and intellectual past and her familial roles as sources of her theory. This exploration of a social identity formed through feminist contacts is very different from the suspicious procedures of deconstruction, with its ironic awareness of its own implication in the oppositions it analyzes. Hirsch, rather, offers her own history as the basis for her readings, refusing neutral mastery and simple empathetic responses alike.

Finally, Elaine Showalter points toward a new inclusiveness in feminist readings, that is, the scrutiny of masculinity as well as femininity as a social construction. In *Speaking of Gender*, she collects essays on men and on women, on the interaction of sexual typing and gender transgression in drama, fiction, poetry and criticism itself. What men writing in this collection do is not easy for academic critics of their sex. I suspect that an untenured man analyzing machismo or homosexuality in canonized texts by men risks as much as a feminist working on little-known women writers, perhaps more; he's rocking a very big boat. Showalter acknowledges that drawing men into the terrain of feminist criticism entails risks of other kinds, too: that they will take over, that women as readers and writers will be marginalized yet again. But her move beyond disciplinary and gender separatism is an interesting one, a strategy for infiltrating textual studies of all kinds. If femininity and masculinity are mutually defining terms, the power dynamics between them need to be approached from both sides, by critics of all sexes. Her conclusion emphasizes the political dimension of this third direction for literary and cultural criticism:

> Like other aspects of literary analysis, talking about gender without a commitment to dismantling sexism, racism and homophobia can degenerate into nothing more than a talk show.... But ... the genuine addition of gender as a central problem in every text read and thought, whatever the era and whoever the author, could also move us a step further toward post-patriarchy. That's a step worth trying to take together.

(1989)

I like the tentativeness of that ending, and its insistence on collaborative effort. Those are two threads that have held my history as a feminist critic together. And to end the story happily, I'll reproduce three of the poems from the *Ithaca Women's Anthology* – not as models for what feminine writing was or should be, but as early versions of the departures I've recorded here. These are confident poems, dancing in language, aware of its limits but optimistic about its potential. The first explains certain men to certain women; other things happen in the next two. All three texts, I think, mobilize the political critique, the linguistic adventurousness, and the joyful utopianism I've encountered at ongoing moments of feminist criticism in the United States. From 1977, in memoriam – but may nobody from that ovular rest too much in peace:

"Primer for a Woman about to Enter the Academy for the Study of Poetry"

Susan Carlisle

Beware of beard
that seems solid black
trimmed by a lexicon
or any other
invaluable tool.

Beware of the grey beard
wearing grey trousers
who mumbles in middle
english, quotes harold
bloom at breakfast.

Be wary of fragrant
briefcases that drift
slightly open,
bulging as if with
wrenches but starved
for fresh paper.

Watch too for attaché
cases with violent
latches that always
thrash open
when you are about to read
a poem.

Beware of ivy
that whispers its name.

Be prepared
for perpetual pipes,
exotic syntax, tweed
that will twist down
the long oak table
like a lecture, endless,
like crabgrass

Don't look for lesbians
in the O.E.D.
You'll find only sapphists
unnaturally engaging
like Sappho
in "vice."

If you search for sapphists
in the library
you'll find lesbians
and Sappho smiling
from her glistening beach
beckoning from her thin
wedge of air
on the shelf.

If you see too many
cylinders, penises, knives
in a poem it's not
your imagination.

"Bed"

Kate Kazin

I want you my pearl
but I am your oyster:
a wet find,
a sweet urchin;
four sponges
and two brimming shells:
two sets of waves, love's ocean talk
and always
an extra arm.

"Notes for Another Coven"

Jenny Aberdeen

A spell is news:
what needs to be said
again, to change things,
magic language,
seeming to preach
like the old one

but being fire
out of flesh once
burned
stoned
drowned
or silenced somehow
of other women.

We gather again
in this room
witches, women who know
to cackle in argument and mirth,
who know
that to call the devil
by his true name
is to watch him
melt, muttering
to a dwarf-
professor.

Black tatters of our academic gowns
still cling to our shoulders; we hold

the housewife's brookstick: we'll
be whole! we cry. We'll be at home
in the mind.

Gather, witches, women who know
we will burn now
only with our own flame
sparking from one to another.
We will not be silent.
We will float now, we will fly

wearing the tall black hats
of our welsh great-grandmothers
the magic broomsticks between our thighs,
the rent gown billowing behind us

speak now
    what needs to be said
speak now
    what needs to be said
in your mouth a new word waits
in your mouth a new word waits
for you to find it.

REFERENCES

Cixous, Hélène (1975a) "Sorties," in *La Jeune née* (with Catherine Clément), Paris: Union Générale d'Editions, 10/18. Translated as *The Newly Born Woman* by Betsy Wing, Minneapolis: University of Minnesota Press, 1986.

—— (1975b) "Le Rire de la Méduse," *L'Arc* 61: 39–54. Translated as "The Laugh of the Medusa" by Keith Cohen and Paula Cohen, *Signs* 1 (summer), 875–99.

Draine, Betsey (1988) "Refusing the Wisdom of Solomon: Some Recent Feminist Literary Theory," *Signs* 15 (1) (autumn), 144–170.

Duras, Marguerite (1988) Interview with Alice Jardine and Anne Menke. In "Exploding the Issue: 'French' 'Women' 'Writers' and the 'Canon'?" *Yale French Studies*, no. 75, *The Politics of Tradition: Placing Women in French Literature*, 239–40.

Felman, Shoshanna (1975) "Women and Madness: The Critical Phallacy," *Diacritics* 5 (4): 2–10.

Gledhill, Christine (1988) "Pleasurable Negotiations," in E. Deidre Pribram (ed.) *Female Spectators: Looking at Film and Television*, London: Verso (Questions for Feminism), 64–89.

Hermann, Claudine (1976) *Les Voleuses de langue*. Paris, des femmes, translated by Nancy Kline as *The Tongue Snatchers*, Lincoln: University of Nebraska Press, 1989.

Hirsch, Marianne (1989) *The Mother–Daughter Plot: Narrative, Psychoanalysis, Feminism*, Bloomington: Indiana University Press.

Kristeva, Julia (1974a) *La Révolution du langage poétique*, Paris: Seuil. Translated by Margaret Waller as *Revolution in Poetic Language*, New York: Columbia University Press, 1984.

—— (1974b) "Oscillation du 'pouvoir' au 'refus'," interview with Xavière Gauthier, *Tel Quel* 58 (automne), 98–102. Excerpted in Elaine Marks and Isabelle de Courtivron (eds) *New French Feminisms*, Amherst: University of Massachusetts Press, 1980, 165–7.

—— (1977) "La Maternité selon Giovanni Bellini," in *Polylogue*, Paris: Seuil. Translated as "Motherhood according to Giovanni Bellini" by Thomas Gora and Alice Jardine in *Desire in Language: A Semiotic Approach to Literature and Art*, New York: Columbia University Press, 1980.

—— (1980) *Les Pouvoirs de l'horreur: essai sur l'abjection*, Paris: Seuil. Translated by Leon Roudiez as *Powers of Horror: An Essay on Abjection*, New York: Columbia University Press, 1982.

Moi, Toril (1985) *Sexual/Textual Politics: Feminist Literary Theory*, London: Methuen.

Showalter, Elaine (ed.) (1989) *Speaking of Gender*, New York and London: Routledge.

Shreve, Anita (1989) *Women Together, Women Alone: The Legacy of the Consciousness-Raising Movement*, New York: Viking.

"To the Woman Who Reads and Writes," group essay (1978) *Ithaca Women's Anthology*.

Yaeger, Patricia (1988) *Honey-Mad Women: Emancipatory Strategies in Women's Writing*, New York: Columbia University Press.

Chapter 5

Radical optimism, maternal materialism and teaching literature

Judith Kegan Gardiner

My mother, a paient attorney, knows bright babies when she sees them, which, fortunately, is one hundred per cent of the time. Mothers who claim that their infants recognize them are often wrong, say psychologists, but their children develop faster and more happily because of these positive expectations. Such recognitions, which begin as fictions and become facts through our actions and relationships, provide a model for some of the ways I think about feminist teaching and scholarship. In this model, one benefits from advancing others with whom one identifies; it is possible to feel optimistic because one is an agent of social change and possible to continue acting because one feels optimistic about the potential social results.

My mother and father were partners in their own law firm. As I grew up in the 1950s, I read in a corner and never learned proper girlstuff like how to use make-up or pin pincurls. I did learn typing and shorthand so that I could always get a job. None the less, I knew that men and women could sometimes work together in gratifyingly intellectual ways and on reasonably equal terms. "That's no family. That's a debating society," one teenage friend said, both admiringly and critically, after dinner at my house.

By the late 1960s, I was a graduate student with a baby daughter, living in Nashville, Tennessee, and finishing by mail a dissertation for Columbia University about Ben Jonson's poetry. In that manageably mid-sized, border southern town I joined a group of activists and discovered racism and sexism and US imperialism. These white and black activists believed in standing up and being counted – as frequently as possible; I helped form the Nashville Committee for Decent Housing, Nashville Women for Peace and Social Justice, and the Nashville Committee to End the War in Viet Nam, groups with overlapping memberships. I also supported the local Students for a Democratic Society and the Southern Student Organizing Committee. The people with whom I demonstrated also picnicked together and enjoyed the foreign film society and chamber music concerts. Besides students and teachers, they included hippie candlemakers, conservationists, Unitarians, and a small, dedicated band of Quakers. For a year I taught English and world literature at Fisk University, a distinguished, predominantly black institution. The civil rights movement was winding down, the anti-war movement was winding up, and the women's movement had yet to appear. My first feminist "click" of recognition came at a Vanderbilt faculty party at which the men spoke about literature only to one another, ignoring anything said by me or the other women. Still, it was easy and pleasant to feel part of a progressive community there. We met, marched, and picketed, wrote leaflets and spoke on radio talk shows, and all this symbolic activity felt effective. We were not simply joining pre-existing discourses but changing the terms of public discussion and so ending a war, modifying local housing policies for the poor, and limiting overt racial discrimination. At the same time, some of us were beginning to think of ourselves as women with things in common.

With a completed Ph.D. and another daughter, I applied for academic jobs. The head of one English department at a prestigious private university bluntly told me that he would not even look at my job application or letters of recommendation because he did not wish to hire women. At another fine university, the chairman of the English department phrased his rejection more diplomatically, though insider friends told me he meant the same thing. I therefore felt lucky to land an assistant professorship of English in 1969 at the University of Illinois at Chicago, a big public university where I still teach, in a department with many female colleagues. I promptly joined New University Conference, the somewhat tamer faculty auxiliary of Students for a Democratic Society. When the men in this Marxist group began complaining that the independent women's movement was bourgeois and divisive, I and the other women in our chapter defended the women's movement, even though we didn't know much about it, and became what we defended. We split off, recruited students, and joined the Chicago Women's Liberation Union, an umbrella organization for workgroups of socialist feminist activists. When the United States bombed Cambodia in 1970, students organized "liberation schools," and our university's women's union held a Susan B. Anthony Women's Liberation Teach-In where we formulated a program of "demands" around which we've organized for the last twenty years, winning most of them in scaled-down forms. We wanted a Women's Studies Program and founded one, teaching on overload for years before we received institutional funding. We wanted free full-time childcare on campus for everyone who wanted it; we got a small, Piagetian, sliding-fee childcare center. We wanted a Women's Research Center and a Student Women's Center and only now are about to see these goals realized.

To prepare for all this, we began meeting weekly to study women's movement literature. We were too busy and activist-oriented to think of this as a consciousness-raising group, but we did support one another and change the ways we thought about being women. I was teaching full-time and still doing all of the cooking and most of the laundry, shopping, cleaning, and evening and weekend childcare in my household. I taught literature, mostly basic undergraduate courses, and tried to move classroom chairs into circles over the objections of the janitorial staff. I didn't publish for a long time, a luxury today's beginning academics don't have, but I did go to a lot of meetings of both women's and mixed political groups. The campus group involved in collectively teaching our introductory Women's Studies courses often discussed racism and tried to recruit women of color, with sporadic success. A woman in the first group was named George, had short hair, lived with a female friend, and found much of our conversation irrelevant. Years later I realized she was probably a lesbian, a kind of person I didn't know how to see until some outspoken lesbian students joined the teaching collective. Such teaching collectives included faculty, students, staff, and sometimes community women, and they were dedicated to being non-hierarchical, non-competitive, and mutually empowering.

At first, as we eagerly read the new feminist scholarship and rediscovered authors such as Virginia Woolf, Simone de Beauvoir and Tillie Olsen, we were indeed equal in the knowledge necessary to teach about women in society, history and literature. We divided all tasks and responsibilities among ourselves and made decisions, slowly and sometimes painfully, by consensus. Each session of the teaching collective, the women's union, and other groups that I attended ended with "criticism/self-criticism," which we thought we were learning from the Chinese and their exemplary democratic revolution. (I went to China for a few weeks in 1976 and was much impressed with what appeared to be young people's revolutionary zeal.) Despite occasional grandstanding and mutual minor intimidations, we were self-conscious about process and eager to do right. We were committed to democratic and egalitarian procedures, and we agreed that empowering as well as informing our students and ourselves was rightly a goal of our teaching. We agreed, too, that we needed to overcome our own and our society's sexism, racism, classism, imperialism, homophobia and other barriers to the decent life and satisfying community we could sometimes imagine. I'm still a democratic socialist, a materialist feminist, and a progressive eco-feminist, and I still sometimes stand on streetcorners holding signs, these days mostly defending abortion clinics and protesting American military adventures in other countries.

Meanwhile, I had to start publishing to win tenure and so keep my academic position, which I enjoyed and which was clearly preferable to the secretarial jobs I'd held before and during graduate school. Reading for interdisciplinary Women's Studies courses drew me to psychology and psychoanalytic theory, as did watching my daughters grow. I joined a seminar of analysts and literary theorists who discussed literature from a psychoanalytic perspective. After reading those first important early 1970s anthologies such as *Sisterhood is Powerful* and *Woman in Sexist Society*, I also began reading feminist theory and then feminist literary theory. In 1976 I helped found the Newberry Library Feminist Literary Criticism Group, a city-wide study group that still meets. I also belong to an English department faculty group that discusses ideas that have become fashionable since I was in graduate school, ideas such as semiotics, deconstruction and Lacanian psychoanalysis. Thus, as I shifted from being a "new critic" who explicated Renaissance English literature by men to a feminist critic interested in modern writing by women, my journey was not a solitary one. Now I go back and forth between centuries, writing on topics that range from self psychology, to television's versions of intimacy, to women writers from Aphra Behn to Doris Lessing.

But if my various study groups challenged me to confront new literary, psychoanalytic and feminist theories, it was the classroom that tested their usefulness. Students at the University of Illinois at Chicago are mostly from working-class and lower-middle-class families. They average thirty hours a week of paid work while carrying full course loads. They are ethnically and racially diverse, often politically conservative, yet frequently sceptical about authority, including the authority of their teachers. I like my students; I like teaching them; and, in so far as I want to change the world, teaching and writing, although neither the most direct forms of political action nor the only ones I engage in, have certain advantages. Analyzing verbal structures is what I am trained to do, and power in this society has a great deal to do with who says what to whom, and how. The university English classroom allows me and my students to discuss not only literary styles and genres but also the way the world works and how some people write and feel about their situations now, and how others did in the past. Literary texts cannot escape being exemplary, representative and representational. That is, they present specific characters and events in ways that imply they stand for more general matters. If as a feminist I believe that the personal is also political, then teaching literature means teaching the personal, individual instance in relation to public discursive power and judging individual texts in terms of esthetic values that only make sense in specific social contexts. That means, for example, considering Janie's poetic powers in *Their Eyes Were Watching God* in terms of the story-telling traditions represented in the novel. It also means talking about Shakespeare's conflicts about sexuality in the sonnets in terms of his and other Renaissance attitudes and customs rather than simply explicating his metaphors.

I taught some warm, wonderful "Women and Literature" classes for which only women signed up. I also volunteered for English Department survey courses and Honors College seminars that enrolled men and women who would not otherwise have taken courses with a feminist orientation. These students spoke freely in class, and some said, for example, that Jews control the world's money supply and that AIDS is God's punishment for homosexuality. While respecting the students and their rights to their opinions, I wanted them to see for themselves why such views are erroneous and dangerous to them as well as to the groups they malign.

Such conflicts about values both inform and trouble my teaching and scholarship. I had learned from Quakers and Communists. The New Left politics that formed my ideas were idealistic and moralistic. They encouraged me to regard certain things as unjust, such as bombing people in other nations because our government did not like their government, and to protest these actions not because I was a victim but because, as a citizen, I was responsible for them. The women's movement, however, was based primarily on identification politics, on women saying that we ourselves are oppressed and are going to do something about it – change minds, laws, ourselves, you, the schools and other institutions.

In my literary criticism, too, I was thinking about feminist values in terms of larger ideological structures. In an essay on "Gender, Values, and Doris Lessing's Cats," I argued that the good, the true and the beautiful, love, freedom and justice all traditionally mean different things for men and for women in part because they are embedded in larger ideological systems – such as Christianity, liberalism, and Marxism – that are all sexist, but in differing ways. Since for esthetics there are no agreed-upon values that determine what is great literature, traditionalists rely on a self-reinforcing canon of masterpieces that show what other great works should be like. These traditionalists fear feminist challenges to such a canon and charge that we feminist critics are "swept up in ideological approval of third-rate work." They assume that they know, and we don't, what is first and what is third rate, and that such ratings make sense; they also condemn feminist literature classrooms like mine for their allegedly "univocal moral rhetoric of liberation," when in fact we struggle in class to present multiple viewpoints that are explicit about the connections they make between aesthetic categories and their moral and political implications (Vendler 1990: 20, 23).

Like my teaching, my scholarship also oscillated between the male-dominant tradition of canonical English literature and new feminist approaches. Moreover, because I was raising daughters, analogies among teaching, reading, writing and mothering seemed attractive to me, as did theories like Nancy Chodorow's that placed a special value on the mother–daughter bond and that explained differences between contemporary American men and women with reference to the institution of female mothering. Although I was not at first much older than my students, in the heady days of early feminism many young women expected special maternal nurturance from their Women's Studies teachers and were as angry as teenage daughters when they felt that we let them down. In an essay "On Female Identity and Writing by Women," I used such familial analogies to connect the psychologies women in our culture often form with the kinds of writing they produce. I thought that twentieth-century English and American women writers might treat a woman character as though she were a daughter, thus involving the author in a process of self-definition and empathic identification at the same time that she shaped the character artistically. Such metaphors can be limiting; at the time they seemed illuminating, connecting what I felt about my own roles as teacher, daughter and mother with my understanding of other women's creative processes. I wanted to understand what, if anything, was distinctive about contemporary English and American writing by women. I also wanted to understand the relationships among readers, writers, texts and characters, and to figure out what gender had to do with them.

I saw the concept of empathy as central to understanding such relationships because it is the mental process through which we can understand – and begin to care about – the thoughts and feelings of other people. And although women in our culture are expected to be more empathic than men, the concept is not limited by gender. A "politics of empathy," I claimed in my book *Rhys, Stead, Lessing and the Politics of Empathy*, 1989, might help us bridge some of the gaps between reading and writing, teaching and criticism, and representation and action. I suggested that especially for some twentieth-century women writers, an autobiographical sense of outrage at the oppression of women, the poor and the colonized grew into empathy. This empathy with the situation of other oppressed people then fostered the desire to change unjust social conditions – in part by writing about them and so putting readers through the same empathic process. Such empathy therefore seemed to me a necessary precondition for efforts to alter history for the benefit of women and other oppressed people.

Views like mine have recently come under attack as "essentialist," which means their critics think such views imply that all women have some things in common simply by being biological females. They think that feminists like me who describe patterns common to some women and their literary works are covertly prescribing that all women must fit such patterns. For example, bell hooks warns against the "impulse towards unity and empathy that informed the notion of [women's] common oppression" and so "provided the excuse many privileged [white, middle-class] women needed to ignore the differences between their social status and the status of masses" of working-class women and women of color (1984:6). My students are not very privileged, but many of them, whatever their own class, race and ethnic background, are eager to see themselves as different from the world's "masses." They do not invariably assume that poor or foreign or ethnically distinct women are like themselves, but they do not see such differences as valuable or legitimate either. It is because of such attitudes that fostering empathy seems to me potentially progressive rather than imperialistic. Thus, like many other Women's Studies and literature teachers, I try to help students see some commonalities in women's situations in contemporary culture, like our vulnerability to widespread violence and sexual objectification, and I also try to make such analyses nuanced and specific, repeatedly asking students: what does this mean, what does this matter, and who benefits from this being the way things are thought and said and done?

In my view, empathy should allow one to understand the constraints endured by other women, not to assimilate their experiences to one's own. Only by trying to understand other people, I think, will one work for social change rather than solely for individual advancement; only by working with other women for goals meaningful to each particular group will new female identities be formed that are local, powerful and capable of correcting their own exclusionary practices.

Literary identifications provide one model for expanding upon identification politics and encouraging the internalizing of standards whereby an individual's sense of identity depends on feelings of integrity, of doing right or good. But if identification politics make the most sense for a group, like women, with some oppressions in common, what can and should structure our actions and identifications when we ourselves are the oppressors rather than the oppressed, when we ourselves are unjust? What – besides being overpowered – will get a privileged group to change? People rarely like losing their advantages, and people who feel that they are losing power often behave badly. All Americans these days may feel we are losing economic and political power, but perhaps the overlapping categories of men, white people, adults and the economically secure feel it most acutely. One reason that the old have fared relatively better than other poor people is that the young believe they'll be there one day. Men do not think they will ever be women or whites, blacks, but literature may help people empathize across such lines, may help us imagine what it would be like to be in the other person's position. To be politically effective, I think, we need an empathic feminist perspective that defines our self-interests so that they include the other's and include doing right by the other (and vice versa).

The Reagan–Bush–Thatcher decade of the 1980s polarized literary as well as political discourse in English. Conservatives attacked feminist and liberal humanist ideas as disruptive of permanent truths that they thought upheld their values. I began to teach postmodernist feminist theories that also attacked liberal and humanist ideas, including 1970s-bred American feminisms like mine (see Nicholson 1990; Weed 1989; Moi 1985). For example, Denise Riley deconstructs the category of "women" for falsely implying that all women have common interests, and Judith Butler warns against "feminist theory" taking "the category of women to be foundational to any further political claims without realizing that the category effects a political closure on the kinds of experiences articulable" (Butler 1990b: 325; see also Butler 1990a). Many of my students furiously rejected such texts, in part because they felt excluded by the difficult language and in part because they had often just come to see themselves as feminists and hence found the category of women an important organizing principle in their lives. For them, issues about what is "essential" and what is "human" are crucial in ways that the theories did not always address clearly: what obligations are entailed in thinking of themselves as women, as Americans, as people, and so on? In order to clarify these theories for my students, I found myself justifying their strategies and so once again became, at least in part, what I defended. Now I try to develop practices for teaching literature and feminist theory that foster empathy as a useful though partial means toward moving myself, my students and our discourses beyond both identity politics and purely oppositional postmodernism. I think of such practices, metaphorically and self-warningly, as both maternal and materialist, and of the beliefs that uphold them as still, if wryly, radically optimistic.

Yet I realize that my views, along with similar American feminisms, may still be dismissed as "essentialist," and I want to explore some reasons why the term "essentialism" has now begun to function the way "communist" once did to disqualify whatever is so labeled from serious consideration. Of course one might justly worry about theories that insist women must by nature be full-time child-rearers, but such conservative notions are not the feminist views that the anti-essentialist theorists attack. I speculate that the current popularity of anti-essentialism points to deep fears in our intellectual engagement with contemporary culture (also see Bordo 1990; de Lauretis 1989; Fuss 1989). Anti-essential-ism, as I see it, over and above its creditable uses to denaturalize sexual roles, is a form of anti-materialism. Some people argue so fiercely against biologism that they apparently desire to avoid biology altogether. But to be any kind of materi-alist feminist, as I am, requires some acknowledgement of at least two biological facts, not dependent on sexual difference, which are, I would claim, literally essential: first, humans are embodied; second, humans are mortal. In contrast, anti-humanist anti-essentialism appears as a form of idealism shaped by a fear of individual mortality.

Human mortality is a biological fact. Fear of mortality, however, is a social fact. All people die; not all people are afraid of dying. I speculate that the contemporary fear of dying is related to several things. One is an attenuated sense of personal, embodied agency caused by the defeats of the left in the last decade and more generally by the nature of postmodern capitalism which stresses information as more important than production. If we think of ourselves as information circuits or as computers, then it is painful to realize that we are dependent on our fallible mortal "hardware" for consciousness and existence. And if we compare ourselves as thinking machines to computers, we acknowledge how speedily our generations are outmoded, how deficient are our memories, how difficult we are to upgrade.

Anti-essentialism covers over a fear of mortality, but I surmise that this fear springs less from the stable facts of human embodiment than from a current crisis precipitated by the fear of meaninglessness, which is related for the left, even more than for the right, to a crisis of values. Presumably dying is not so terrifying to those who feel they have accomplished something good and been able to pass it along to future generations. Postmodernist anti-humanism makes such opti-mism seem naïve and misguided. If we don't believe in progress, we may suspect we will give less to our children and students than we received from our parents and teachers. This fear of the future as a fear of mortality is related to a nonbiological mortality, the dying of United States capitalism as the dominant international force and therefore also the waning of our national identity. Ameri-cans joke anxiously about the vigorous "young" Japanese and Korean capitalist economies and fear advanced technology's revenge against our own society in the form of environmental pollution. I think the left may now be more afflicted by the sense of being citizens of a dying world order than is the right. We leftists always knew capitalism was doomed – and rejoiced that it would be replaced by a more humane and just system called socialism. The collapse of Stalinism heartens the right who believe that if Russians and Nicaraguans say they want it, capitalism must be in the ascendancy, must, in fact, be the final and perfect world order that will end the fluctuations of history. We on the feminist left scorn such ethnocentric vanity but are more doubtful now than we used to be about how truly democratic socialism might work. We reject the right's identification with a macho, triumphant and fictionalized Western Way of Life, but we may find our own progressive thinking imaginatively stunted and less convincing than before, especially if our utopian longings continue to picture a peaceful, classless, gender-balanced "four-gated city" like those in Doris Lessing's or Ursula LeGuin's fantasy fictions. I think such a suspicion of humanist equality, a suspicion that fuels "anti-essentialism," impedes feminist utopian longings. My students were appalled when I suggested they envision a future society made up of equally-affluent, androgynous tan bisexuals speaking Esperanto, but they were also confused about which differences among people would and should remain in non-oppressive societies – races, religions, languages? Even in today's society, would they be progressive defenders of "difference" if they wore lavender T-shirts while listening to rap music and eating tacos – or do such symbolic gestures succumb to shopping mall liberalism, where "differences" between people are accepted so long as they are solely consumer choices?

Because it is so hard to picture a positive future for ourselves and our society, the anti-essentialist anti-materialist fears aging as well as death, and instead opts for endless fluidity and process. Many of today's postmodernist faculty as well as students are in fact younger than we first-generation, second-wave feminists. To us they may seem caught in a Peter Pan syndrome of the young who fear growing old. One can only keep all options open by not testing some of them. Only through such a youthful stance of generalized opposition can one valorize "subversion" or "opposition" without clearly defining what the alternatives are to the present, what of present arrangements might be desirable to maintain, and what of the infinite alternatives to present arrangements seem now to us the most desirable – and for whom.

The old left could use anger against oppression as well as moral sympathy to galvanize action. Confronting scarce resources, leftists knew that the enemies of most people were the few who expropriated their resources, including the oppressed's bodies and labor power, for their own advantage. Such knowledge, joined to what seemed relevant action, mobilized group solidarity and even joy. Those of us who think we helped end the American war in Viet Nam, legalize abortion, and so on, are more likely to believe in social action and the efficacy of symbolic protest than those people with progressive values who have come to maturity always losing, being outvoted by right-wing politics and made to feel silly, ineffective and unrepresented by the media. Without the cohesions of group success, the not-old, not-new, but what's-left-of-the-left left seems to have fear as its only successfully mobilizing emotion. Thus the most effective progressive groups of the recent American past have been anti-nuclear and pro-environmental, all claiming the extinction of humanity or the death of the planet as the evils against which it is still possible to enlist group action. Thus another consequence of the anti-essentialist fear of mortality is a coalescence around survivalism as the only value that everyone can agree on. I do not want to demean a lively and hopeful ecological politics, but merely to point out that one of its attractions is that pro-environmentalism has an easily comprehensible and nostalgic referent in unspoiled, non-human "Nature" – the nature of the prettiest calendars and posters – and hence that this social movement has not found it necessary to articulate alternative power relations to those currently in existence in order to garner popular support.

The appeal to survival can be made more vaguely, too, as the non-negotiable, covertly humanist appeal of even the most sophisticated postmodernist. For example, Donna Haraway playfully and ironically delineates the "informatics of domination" under which we live (1990:203). When she wishes to appeal for action, however, she assumes that we agree with an unquestioned and untheorized set of values. The "dominations of race, gender, sexuality, and class" (199) are self-evidently bad, whereas "liberation" is obviously good (191). Most frequently the value she appeals to, without elaboration, is "survival": for example, "the task is to survive" (212) and "survival is the stakes" (219). These impassioned comments tend to clinch arguments and to seem self-evident. But they are not self-evident at all. Is it the physical planet we are worried about saving? The universe has many planets left. Is it humanity, so destructive to our own and other species? And if so, how justify this claim without the most literal humanism. Is it women, or people of color, or the laboring classes who are threatened with genocide? What system of domination could survive without the productive and reproductive work of those it dominates? Is it the nation or the religious group? And should all such entities survive, even those that oppress others and their own members? And if, as I suspect, "survival" in appeals like Haraway's means the continuance of all the speaker finds good and rewarding about human social existence, then the issue is not simply "survival" at all but rather the more complicated problem of defining values and political practices that can allow all people to live in conditions that fulfill such values. Thus I find a hidden humanism in postmodernist antihumanist critiques, a hidden humanism that would be more useful to feminists if were openly acknowledged and discussed.

Currently I see postmodernism as where we live; its theories define our problems, but it cannot define our goals or solve these problems. Postmodern theory is valuable in persuading us that representation is important to those who would alter life under capitalist patriarchy. Representing foetuses as cell masses or as murdered babies may profoundly influence women's legal options. Postmodernists are sometimes accused of thinking that discourse is everything. However, we might instead agree that language is more important now than it used to be and that it more fully sustains power in global capitalism than in earlier economies. This development may be bad for us as citizens or workers, but it is good for English, the imperial language of advertising, rock music, Hollywood, and air controllers – and for us as American teachers of literature. Language is always important, but differently in different contexts. For eastern Europeans freed from overtly repressive regimes, the idea of getting to the truth and correcting official lies may have a profound liberatory potential unavailable to us Americans for whom the endless simulations of commercial infotainment dissolve the possibilities of truth. In this situation, the American feminist teacher of literature can strive for communicative engagement with students without assuming that her values will be, or always should be, theirs.

In other words, I've suggested that postmodernist vagueness about values comes from a theoretical anxiety about liberal, humanistic and Marxist values that is unwarranted and limiting. If humanism can be racist, imperialist and oppressive in assuming that diverse people should be like the dominant classes, anti-humanism can also be racist, imperialist and oppressive in attending chiefly to elite language practices in elite books and journals and in dissolving all group identities that could serve to mobilize progressive action: it is our specific values and practices in specific instances that should be the test of such things, not polarizing categorical statements. All relations of power cannot be abolished in society and probably should not be. All "oppositional strategies" are not equally progressive. We need to define who can justly exercise what kinds of power and when. "Liberation" is not an unequivocal goal either but depends on defining who should be freed from what and with what possible consequences for others: the growing number of nationalistic discourses should make us pause over definitions of "freedom." Only through democratic processes can such issues be resolved, but even such a statement necessarily depends on prior assumptions about human rights, including minority rights. Feminist democratic practices will require mechanisms for contending about groups and boundaries, for deciding who can make decisions for whom: the feminist literature classroom, like the interdisciplinary Women's Studies class, can take at least a small part in such discussions, and the particularistic democratic political processes I imagine here have their analogies in the literature class, where we talk about the hypothetical situations of specific, imaginary and hypothetical people who live only in discourse, but in discourses that shape our realities.

Meaning is more important than mortality, and our students' generation must believe in the possibility that they can make meaningful changes in their society and lives, in order for there to be a better world for them – a conclusion I come to not just from observation of world events but specifically from my particular vantage point of mother–daughter engagement. Both my daughters are now young adults. Carita majored in American Studies and English in college and, after courses in Shakespeare, Hemingway and other canonical subjects, wrote a senior thesis about cookbooks; Viveca was a comparative literature major who heard lectures about deconstruction and wrote a thesis about supermarket romances. For both of them, studying literature meant focusing on a broad cultural nexus composed of market factors and economics, representation and fantasy, genre and literary styles, differences among women, and various postmodernist theories. Meanwhile, my mother, still going to work each day as a lawyer, is becoming more forgetful, more someone who needs sometimes to be mothered herself. It is as a sandwich generation person, then, meditating on meaning through the mother–daughter nexus, that I now define the future I see for feminist literary criticism as one engaged in teaching for change.

Although my maternal metaphors for teaching and reading literature are only analogies, they indicate my personal investment in a future that matters, in identification, commitment and a belief in the effectiveness of my believing in the effectiveness of myself and other feminists.

REFERENCES

Bordo, Susan (1990) "Feminism, Postmodernism, and Gender-Scepticism," in Nicholson (ed.) (1990) 133–56.

Butler, Judith (1990a) *Gender Trouble: Feminism and the Subversion of Identity*, New York and London: Routledge.

——(1990b) "Gender Trouble: Feminist Theory, and Psychoanalytic Discourse," in Nicholson (ed.) (1990), 324–40.

Chodorow, Nancy (1978) *The Reproduction of Mothering: Psychoanalysis and the Sociology of Gender*, Berkeley: University of California Press.

de Lauretis, Teresa (1989) " The Essence of the Triangle or, Taking the Risk of Essentialism Seriously: Feminist Theory in Italy, the U.S., and Britain," *differences* 1.2 (summer), 3–27.

Fuss, Diana (1989) *Essentially Speaking: Feminism, Nature & Difference*, New York and London: Routledge.

Gardiner, Judith Kegan (1982) "On Female Identity and Writing by Women," in Elizabeth Abel (ed.) *Writing and Sexual Difference,* Chicago: University of Chicago Press, 177–92.

——(1987) "Gender, Values, and Doris Lessing's Cats," in Shari Benstock (ed.) *Current Issues in Feminist Scholarship*, Bloomington and Indianapolis: Indiana University Press, 110–23.

——(1989) *Rhys, Stead, Lessing, and the Politics of Empathy*, Bloomington and Indianapolis: Indiana University Press.

Haraway, Donna (1990) "A Manifesto for Cyborgs: Science, Technology, and Socialist Feminism in the 1980s" in Nicholson (ed.) (1990), 190–233.

hooks, bell (1984) *Feminist Theory from Margin to Center*, Boston: South End Press.

Moi, Toril (1985) *Sexual/Textual Politics: Feminist Literary Theory*, London and New York: Methuen.

Nicholson, Linda (ed.) (1990) *Feminism/Postmodernism*, New York and London: Routledge.

Riley, Denise (1988) *"Am I That Name?" Feminism and the Category of "Women" in History*, Minneapolis: University of Minnepolis Press.

Vendler, Helen (1990) "Feminism and Literature," in *New York Review of Books* 37.9: 31 May 19–25.

Weed, Elizabeth (ed.) (1989) *Coming to Terms: Feminism, Theory, Politics*, New York and London: Routledge.

Part II

Reading/writing against the grain

Chapter 6

Reader, I married me
A polygynous memoir

Rachel Blau DuPlessis

Doing this in the first place. No innocence in the autobiographical. What with its questions of saying "I" and the issue "what I" and how that "I" negotiates with various "selfs"; and the question how much (a lot) is unsaid or repressed. With resistance to the cheerful myths of disclosure; with suspicion of narrative in the first place, and no self-justifying memories to legitimate "me" rather than anyone else. If I cull my journals from the eager, pressured past, that self with its "experiences" is postulated as the authentic one, and this one as the processor of that truth. Finally, don't much like to take some, or any, "me" as exemplary, which is, after all, one of the casts of an autobiographical essay.

Yet it remains true that feminist criticism exists. That it came from the women's movement and is in a continual constructive dialogue with both that movement and others for social justice. That academic fields involving the study of literature were thereby overturned, remade (though not, of course, exclusively by feminism); that a maenadic pleasure sometimes accompanied; that professional careers were on the line; and that some of the "we" in or around these pages did some of this: invented and sustained a major intellectual renaissance – possibly even a "paradigm shift" – in the past twenty-odd years.[1] It would be irresponsible never to speak about it. Indeed, I hope many more people do, including those not, as it happens, published here. This is an historical exercise, not a confessional one.

The "I" implicated here is very precise, yet more than half unspeakable. Its descriptors are not mere political trading chips. They are vectors, interlocked with energy, joy, imbalance, determination, depression – themselves not free-floating emotions, but situated and socially formed. "I" can be said to be an off-white feminist, resisting even "enlightenment" Judaism, a radical but middle-class US inhabitant in a professional job category. A person mainly gendered female, who maintains an imaginary bisexuality, and a polygynous curiosity about the feminisms I and others have traversed. Who benefits from many world-economic interests which I abhor. I am a non-biological real mother. Am a heterosexual married property owner. Poet, critic and essayist. My writing space is saffron orange with a light blue ceiling. I use a Mac Plus. If I had not become a feminist, I would not have been able to write much or to think anything especially interesting in any original way. I would not have been able to create the works that came through me and go under my name.

Chronology is time depicted as traveling (more or less) in a (more or less) forward direction. Yet one can hardly write a single sentence straight; it all rebounds. Even its most innocent first words -- A, The, I, She, It – teem with heteroglossias. And, remember: there is always more to remember. If you choose to believe that this is memory; it is also fabrication once it is words. Some files are too far back in closets. Some things, some names are lost. Narration becomes judgment: it's hard to resist this. To put things in an order is to lose some connections, gain others. To "develop" (express, expound) is to distort, says I, at my most anti-expository, but what of minimalist aphorisms of obliqueness which others tax as unreadable? The texture of everything is reduced to nothing by the erosion of time, then boldfaced, barefaced, is recreated. Sentences structure. Cause mainly precedes effect, but effect effectuates selections of cause. Cause and effect affect. Can be affectation, a knowingness. My tone is turning arch. Also compressed. I am already leaving things out. Memoir is already seduction, not the least is self-seduction. I am both pleased and uncomfortable to be telling you all this.

Way before, or, up to 1967: inscribed female (as well as other things). "Gee – I am living in a patriarchal family!" True. Favored daughter therein. But no dialectics, no dialogue, no interchange. Just a narrowly defined set of achievements: reading and writing: a little person of the book. It was the 1950s, and certain things seared me, although my parents were a middle kind of liberal (justice for some vague all) with a fervor around secular humanism (struggling against prayer in the schools, of which there was an inordinate amount, aware of First Amendment issues, giving much to the Ethical-Humanist movement). Terrifying to me were the Rosenberg trial and executions. The McCarthy assault on civil liberties. And the silent seepage of the knowledge of the Holocaust. What is the pattern there? The knowledge of the potential criminality of state power. Confirmed during the Civil Rights, Viet Nam War and Watergate eras.

College, Barnard, luckily had an ideological commitment to neutralize (if not undermine) feminine conditioning: "You can have it all, girls! have a career, have a family!" Bless our robust cheerleader, President Millicent Carey McIntosh, with her link to the feminism of Bryn Mawr in the early twentieth century. If we laughed then, we were hardly to laugh last. A major contradiction lay between the culture's incessant (and our internalized) demand for instantly ratifying engagement and marriage, and any sense of independence, self-definition, autonomy, social commitment. Our rebellions could only be enacted in often damaging affiliations with various "scenes": Beatnik/bohemian. Theatrical male homosexual (as a female hanger-on; lesbianism was a bogey woman my friends and I scared each other with).[2] Poetry: as a muse-figure "trying" to write. (In fact, I later learned you don't "try" to write; you write.) And doing sex – this decision for autonomy, independence and pleasure still hooked us into simulacra of the marital loop. In those days (pre-pill), no one got legal birth control without being married.

As always the contradictions between what we wanted and felt we had an inchoate, ill-defined "right" to (sexual choices), but couldn't get and were prevented from having, began a process of political arousal.

A minor contradiction for me lay between my being poetically awakened by the Donald Allen (ed.) *New American Poetry* (with Allen Ginsberg, Robert Duncan, Robert Creeley) versus the Georgian poetic craft that passed for the only contemporary in the academy. My "creative writing" class was accurately speared by classmate Erica Jong in one of her books for its staging of narcissistic hypocrisy in which two men, a guest and the teacher, insisted that "women can't (really) write." No blood and guts (a miraculous amnesia about menstruation, abortion, childbirth), no drunken bouts at 3 a.m., no – in short – male freedom. For at least two of the women students so jeopardized, such preening assurance seems to have thickened their resistance, increased the soupy ferment contributing to early feminism.

The Golden Notebook, and *A Room of One's Own*, books read in 1964 when I was roiling around as a out-of-water female fish in early graduate school (so too *The Feminine Mystique*) named something extremely precise and acted like diagnosticians honing in on some disease one hardly knew one had, so self-denying were the symptoms/sufferings.[3] It is clear that my narration right here and now of this "before" has placed a premium on a kind of parzivalian innocence; I am implying that I wandered, with a baffled charm, into many structured ritual sites, but unerringly neglected to ask any questions. But this is not true. All the time I was asking inchoate and depressed questions of the gender and sexual systems, something like the educative "What's going on here?" without always noting the wounded (but powerful) King at the center. For I was deeply discontented with the feminine, with most females, with womanhood, with women's roles, with my gender-future (however tidy and rosy and controlled I had once tried to make it), and this discontent had something to do with sex – by which we meant sexuality and gender all mushed together. In fact, in our sexual acting-out we were probably uttering the "word" gender before we knew it. It was pre-feminist somaticizing.

I also kept on asking which was I, the woman or the artist, with a relentless and lacerating binarism. It was the greatest pain and grief in my life, the sense that I had to choose, that one precluded the other, and that I was a bad woman for wanting an artistic career, a bad artist because I was a woman and couldn't work out the terms of any art. It was as if I were still placed in a *Bildung* vs. romance nineteenth-century novel: by my contemporaries, my men and boys, my mentors, such as they were, and my colleagues. And by me. Self-repression and cultural censorship of females were in interlock. My resistance came destructively, in not writing, in long silences around writing, in baffled and punishing blockage. This went on for years. I even said (I was proud to articulate this then, but it was, in fact, a nadir) that "I did not want to have my psyche female." I learned gradually, including in dream and in vision, that my muse was indeed (a) woman. An actual figure appeared – silent, smiling.

True to Essentials Documentary of a Real Dialogue. Place: Columbia University, Butler Library, card catalog room. Date: 1964 or 1965. Characters: prissy little good girl RB, and ET, Professor of English, female, scholar of the old school.

ET: How are you doing in graduate school?

RB: I love it, it's wonderful.

ET: You know, sometimes women don't have an easy time of it as professionals, getting a Ph.D. is hard, things happen, there is prejudice, I wonder if you have run into any of that.

RB: I don't know what you are talking about.

In 1966-7 after taking my (Ph.D.) "orals" and thereupon having a breakdown characterized by a tidal wave of insomnia and a thick lump in my throat "imaginarily" impeding my speech and breath, I was appointed as a Preceptor in the Columbia College English Department. Apparently the decision to appoint women was one highly contested and debated, very rancorous. Although, or because I was one of the first three women ever to be so honored, my suspicion cut deep. Happily, I did not believe for even one second that we were the first or only three women Ph.D. candidates with the requisite credentials, that no other females before us could have been called to serve in That Department of That College.[4] My suspicion of the gesture was deeply radicalizing, beyond tokenism. But being there, on the job, contributed to a token mentality, bemused, anxious at the pressure to "prove" something (unknown) to someone (unknown). We were taken with that astonishing jocular mix of "seriously" and "not seriously" which was so destabilizing. For "them," I was perhaps some odd pawn; for me, I was the whole chess set, though still lying around in a box.

The radical movements were in increasing ferment, and I identified deeply with Civil Rights and with anti-war activism. The Columbia University campus was a most vigorously fermented site, with the issues of the increasing complicity of the universities in the military-industrial complex, issues of class and race and privilege, questions of the (mis)use of state power, the legitimating and sorting functions of education, especially given the Viet Nam War. We constantly exploded level upon level of liberal contradictions. And during the Columbia Strike (spring 1968), I was, true to my liminal form, not inside the buildings with the strikers, but just outside, attending the watchdog "Ad Hoc Faculty Group," which held an open forum throughout, a committee of the whole, which, if self-important, still provided more political education than I had ever had. And just outside, on the night of the police bust (a punitive police riot, in fact), I was, for one terrifying moment, encircled by mounted policemen on rearing horses.

First feminism, 1968–73: consciousness-raising and the personal/professional project. What then happened – what was the time frame in that spring that seemed to go on forever and mean everything? At one point (I think – in semester terms – fall 1968, but possibly spring 1969), feminism simply came to campus – Kate Millett (a Ph.D. candidate and NOW activist writing her thesis –

Sexual Politics) and Harriet Zellner (an economics student) brought it to Columbia from a mysterious "downtown." I thought, in a jealous fascinated tone of which it is impossible to give the palimpsests and nuances – "O the Blacks have organized, now it's the women. The *women* are going to organize?!" but I recognized even in the first dubious, snide and suspicious glance that politics had, finally, come to where I was, to my contradictions. And woman/women was what, or where, I was.

I still do not understand, given my overt slapdash rejection, how in the world I ever got to that first meeting.[5] But once I was there, it was the Great Awakening (Showalter 1987: 35).[6] A giant room filled to the brim with women – many of whom were prepared to testify: brilliant, angry, articulate witnesses to overt prejudice, sexist remarks, invidious discouragement, hostile intellectual atmosphere, sexual suggestiveness, instructions: "go home to your children," charges of "lacking seriousness," prejudice in the award of financial aid or TAs – the whole gamut of sexual and gender discrimination and second-class citizenship "despite" shining Alma Mater's light. It was a conversion experience; the scales fell from my eyes, my glance fell upon things and saw them new. The experience was powerful, energizing, defining, the birth of commitment and conviction. I became a feminist.[7]

And became one of the activists in Columbia Women's Liberation. The every detail of which was a passionate engagement to justice and equality for women, and the re-defining ourselves as productive, not sidelined or blocked by gender. "Woman" was a political, an economic category. With Ann Sutherland Harris, I counted up and sorted the percentages of female faculty at Columbia, adducing reasons and prejudices. We were one of the first such reports in the country, and our dismal statistics became news in *The New York Times*.[8] We seemed to be making a mixture of radical and liberal feminism: equality of access was a primary and stated goal – getting "in" – to our profession of choice, to the rewards as structured. But in the same breath, that "in" was called into question. We were newly in love with women, with ourselves, with each other, with our possibility for changing everything: marriage, beauty, writing, media, law, opportunity, education, stereotypes, art, history, childcare, sex, divisions of labor. We thought all women were us, and we were all women. Of course we knew better even then, but wanted, I think, to share with all women the power of our effervescent politicization. I remember pro-choice marches; Lucinda Cisler's bibliography about women that revealed there was "a" field there; the odd sit-in (March 1970) at the *Ladies Home Journal*; Congress to Unite Women (May 1970) and the "issue" of lesbianism; a sign, "remember our brothers at Kent State" when women too had been killed there (Echols 1989: 195-7).[9]

So the ferment of the 1960s exploding in spring 1968 and beyond was a combustible politicization which made me both "68er" and feminist.[10] It also confronted me with two ideas, each to have great impact on my intellectual work. First, the idea that culture itself was a political instrument, that not only subject matter, but also structural and formal choices were part of ideology; that language, hegemony, discourse, form, canon, rightness and wrongness, allowable and not allowable were historical, relativized and interested concepts.[11]

The second idea was directly indebted to my reading of *Sexual Politics*; by this time (1970) I had my doctorate, and had gone off for two (isolating) years to Lille, France (Université de Lille III, where my colleagues told me that they had already had feminism in France a long time ago, and didn't need any, merci). I began tracking Millett's reading and branching out – beginning with the Brontës, Elizabeth Gaskell, George Eliot, Woolf's *A Room of One's Own* (again and with marxistante eyes; impossible to read it too often), Stowe's *Uncle Tom's Cabin*, Lessing's *Four-Gated City*. In a kind of electric intellectual shock, I began to see the feminist cultural project. No more and no less than the re-seeing of every text, every author (male and female), every canonical work, every thing written, every world view, every discourse, every image, every structure, from a gender perspective.[12]

In 1972–3, I was teaching, in a nagging career discomfort, four courses per semester at Trenton State College.[13] Towards the end of the year, I was told I would not be reappointed "Because you are a woman, and we do not know what your husband will be doing next year." Despite my letter of appointment reading otherwise, I had been moved to a one-year terminal contract. All so kind, and meant kindly, the evocation of husband and all, and, of course, actionable. The denial of my right even to "compete on an equal basis." Their denial compounded mine. After mulling over how much he, the Chairman, didn't mean it, and how dumb it was of him to say that, and how nice he really was, how bad I'd make him feel, how much I didn't want to be there, and how uncomfortable I was with all of this, I brought a sex discrimination suit before the New Jersey State Commission on Civil Rights. When they took the case, their findings revealed that I was being paid a couple of thousand dollars less per year than my exact contemporaries, two young men, on paper precisely comparable to me. This difference was a small fortune in 1973. I won the case, the difference in pay, and an injunction against the college directing non-discrimination.

Second feminism, 1973–9: the cultural project. Reading women writers; writing out of/into women. Suddenly, the feminist critical project extended to my creative work. Suddenly, on 2 January 1973, I awoke to my own poetry: "Idea: to retell myths involving women as radical reinterpretations of them." I began with Orpheus and Eurydice – he the figure of the poet, she, a dead nothing. Where had that come from? Where, indeed. Experiences of anger. The sense of being culturally marginal. Entombed. At a career dead end. Couldn't write, no success with poetry, none with critical book, none with jobs. A couple of miscarriages already under my belt; there would be eight. The dream life of the cave. My poem says it is not Orpheus who turns back to Eurydice, but rather she who turns away from him, because she wants to go deeper into the living cave.

It was my Douglass College student Valerie Napawanetz who, after reading the poem, gave me a gift from the mythology course she was taking.[14] It was a copy of H. D.'s "Eurydice," a poem I had not known, although I was in an intertextual relation with it. And the facts of this encounter are astonishing. Since my own poem (altering and tampering with the hegemonic myth) had changed what what was culturally legible to me, I could read and identify H. D.'s project. Working on my own poem, I gained intellectual tread, formulated the thesis of the revisionary relationship to hegemonic culture that fueled some of my critical work. Writing a (feminist) poem allowed me to write (feminist) criticism; "Eurydice" led to *Writing Beyond the Ending*.[15]

I had been trying to write about Pound and Williams, to "rewrite" my dissertation: a dead task. Dead and commanding. Dead and authoritative. Dead and obligatory. Having read Robert Duncan's illuminating essays on H. D. contextualized in a feminized and heterodox modernism (published in *Caterpillar* in 1967–8), I had never accepted the mandated ignorance of H. D.'s work, but did not bother to examine her power, for I had internalized the priorities and hierarchies of study and excellence: *Cantos*, worthy; *Helen in Egypt*, unread. But in 1975, after reading Susan Stanford Friedman's "H. D.: Who Was She?" in the context of my developing work on women poets, I was finally propelled to begin serious study of H. D.[16] I needed a woman, a poet, and a modernist, and I needed her badly. Despite the fact that one of "my" first ideas of feminist criticism was the re-reading of every cultural artifact (and, indeed, I have had real feminist fascination with Humanities courses), I tilted (with my whole generation) toward the startling discoveries of women writers, female "voices," precisely because they had been culturally buried. This project was revendicatory: we were recovering something, we were claiming it. This began as "equal rights" criticism – women writers could be shown to "compete on an equal basis"; yet "women" were not made equal, and the position quickly modulated into the discovery of particularities in women's writing precisely based on various readings of female social and psychological specificities and differences (from males). Of course there was an investment in unifying or totalizing the idea of "woman." As a real intellectual and cultural idea, it had just been won from a morass of prejudice, contempt and misogyny, and needed self-solidarity, which slid (often too easily) into the notion of affirmation and unity.

What else did early feminist criticism of women writers feel like? If we found textual marks of wholeness, it was because we sought personal and social wholeness (in a spiritual sense, yes, but also as legal redress – to be made whole). If we sought heroes both in the women writers and in their personae and characters, it was because we had few. This first hermeneutic circle was driven by deep necessity; one must now read it contextually, with empathetic understanding. However, I always distrusted victim-to-apotheosis narratives in early feminist criticism. Writing itself was a complex claim to agency, and reflecting upon the transformative energies of women writers, I called their processes of biographical and literary selection and transposition "the career of that struggle." As a writer I yearned for, yet as a critic I suspected the notion of authenticity; finding "the" woman's voice, as if it had – or could have been – preserved in atlantal perfection through the ages. This yearning for originary or organic moments of wholeness could be an enabling myth towards writing, but it was not useful for the critical analysis of writing. So I was constantly skirting what has been called "cultural feminism." For me the significant moments of feminist criticism were psycho-social analyses of literary production; "gynocriticism" was always a subset of that approach, in my view. Writing was a complex species of ideological negotiation, processing, transposition of cultural materials in a social matrix: that idea persists in all my critical work.

I got my first "real" job (at Temple University in 1975), taught undergraduate "Women in Literature" and composition endlessly, and had begun (1974) writing about Rich, Rukeyser and Levertov, an article scrutinized by Ann Calderwood's demanding editorial eye for *Feminist Studies*. When Ann no longer wanted to edit the journal she had begun, I and Judy Walkowitz, a historian – convinced that *Feminist Studies* was a feminist institution – helped initiate a major transition (meetings upon meetings) to a collaborative and collective board, with Claire Moses as Managing Editor, the journal housed at the University of Maryland, College Park. I was an active member of the central Editorial Board for about fourteen years, from 1974 to 1987.[17] With someone – was it Judith Stacey, was it Rayna Rapp? – I wrote the statement of purpose with its echo of Marx's "Theses on Feuerbach":

> The feminist movement has demonstrated that the study of women is more than a compensatory project. Instead, feminism has the potential fundamentally to reshape the way we view the world. We wish not just to interpret women's experiences but to change women's condition. For us, feminist thought represents a transformation of consciousness, social forms, and modes of action.

Modulations of second feminism, 1979–84; essays and trials; getting some work done. In 1976–7, pursued by some happy daemons of voice, pressure, intensity, anger and desire, I put aside everything I should have been doing, and everything I knew about the academic reward system, and wrote my first essay, "Psyche, or Wholeness," a response to Erich Neumann's *Amor and Psyche* (DuPlessis 1979).[18] Thereafter, having given a seminar on the vexed question of a female aesthetic at the 1979 Barnard Scholar and Feminist Conference, I wrote two other curious works, more and more committed to their disclosures, pace, discursive variety and praxis of bricolage. "For the Etruscans" was followed by a double homage to Duncan and H. D. – "an essay on H. D. and the muse of the woman writer" (DuPlessis 1990b). The essay form permitted me to say what I wanted, and how, to link and to leap. Reader, I married me.

"Etruscans" has had a career of its own. It has been taken as an example of "the" female aesthetic. However, what it says is that women, like other members of "(ambiguously) non-hegemonic" groups, are driven to use structural, rhetorical and epistemological tactics that run counter to normative ones. In it, a particular female person makes analysis, has dreams, outcries, offers doubled-voiced montages, mats of citation, longing, grief, and curiosity in/out of the situation of acute feminist attention. Its (apparent) inclusiveness and its fragmentation, its heteroglossic glissades are consciously oppositional and critical. The essay makes no special claim for *a* or *the* female aesthetic (or even *female* aesthetic), but its rhetoric can arouse to hope for change of consciousness and ideology, can move the reader (at least temporarily) into a utopian space. Doing that kind of work offered an artistic extasis that also proposed some serious principles about the polyvocal, the multi-generic, the interested, the non-objective.

It seemed that one needed, as a feminist, to invent an endless number of forms, structures and linguistic ruptures that would cut way beyond language-business-as-usual and narrative-business-as-usual, which always seemed to end up with "the same" kind of binary, "patriarchal" normalcy. Experimental writing of all sorts had always been crucial to the feminist project of cultural change: of revolution, not revision. It seems to me that feminism (with other socially based cultural movements) is the necessary completion of modernism. (Of modernisms, both "high" and "post- .") Writing cannot make these changes alone; but writing exerts a continuous destabilizing pressure, and, in both analytic and formal ways, creates an arousal of desire for difference, for hope. If consciousness must change, if social forms must be re-imagined, then language and textual structures must help cause and support, propel and discover these changes.

When I first began to justify my essays, I called the mode "free-fall open prose writing which has speculative, critical, autobiographical material all together."[19] The word "free-fall" is a datum of early naming; risk, pleasure, and dreams of flying intermingled in the first feel of doing this work. But from the very beginning, I knew I was making principles of art integrate with principles of analysis in ways that aroused readers to feeling, understanding and response. By shifting among stances and genres (from the citation of interrupting shouts to the telling of dreams to speculations about texts), there is a play among the subjectivities contained in my "I." The genres, with their own histories, tones, codes, social meanings, subjects of study, create the plurality of "I," dissolve "I" back into them. This is much more than the matter of "assuming a personal voice" (that is, in the essays), which is not ever what I have said I was doing.[20] I backed into an understanding of some of the "theory" behind this practice: poststructuralist multiple subjectivities; interrogations of the One, the Center, the Same; issues about the dialectics between semiotic and symbolic (postulated) arenas of language use; social dialects and genres in relation. For me, the texts began as gestures of emancipation and interrogation; they were not contained or incited by theoretical postulates.[21]

The same astonishing work sheets from the summer of 1979 that produced "Etruscans" also produced the thesis, the set of working terms, and chapter sites for *Writing Beyond the Ending*, a book on which I had already been engaged (DuPlessis, 1985). The study defines one major project of twentieth-century women writers: the critique of the (heterosexual) romance plot and of the classic relation of romance and quest, by the invention of narrative strategies that erode and replace the heterosexual couple as adequate fictional ending.[22] This book was written from a fecund cross between feminist humanism and the neo-Marxist analysis of Raymond Williams and – a special debt – Virginia Woolf. Some of its hidden aims for myself were to create rich mixes and readings of writers (Dorothy Richardson! Olive Schreiner! Zora Neale Hurston!) that were precise, synthetic, and illuminating, and to create succinct exemplary notions of strategies beyond the conventional ending. I worked by specific studies of women authors, "female traditions," the identification of special relations of women to dominant traditions, the discovery of new legibility of "lost" works; the identification of concerns, allusions, cultural and linguistic stances read via gender. But I worried about the totalizing of the thesis – the argument that black and white, lesbian and heterosexual, British, North American and Canadian authors all saw the necessity of this critique of narrative – yet the use of a plurality of examples from different groups was a principle of the book for me. There was an unspoken tension in my thinking about these manifestations of sameness in different groups, yet this thesis and argument seem at the same time to be one of the achievements of the book.[23]

The curious thing – I am almost embarrassed to say this – is that I was simultaneously writing a scholarly and critical book on one kind of modernism (indebted to realist and humanist conventions) while I was inventing another use of another modernism, in post-realist and post-modernist essays, published throughout this period. This doubleness of motifs has so far run through this memoir: being a radical and liberal feminist simultaneously; being simultaneously a token woman which led to compliance, and a resistant one, which led to critique. And now simultaneously assuming humanist and postmodernist generic and analytic modes. Not to speak of being a critic and being a poet. But in praxis, these are not frozen binaries. I'd call them working contradictions.

Indeed, there has been a crucial interactive pattern to the production of my feminist work. My poetry propelled my criticism, criticism propelled poetry, and essays were originally born in a growth spurt between them. Essays then further incited my main critical book, and even my next one, on H. D. The three genres I use offer (at least) three different and related subject positions, answerable to different social expectations and writing forums. But they were not separate tracks. Discoveries made in one mode led the way to work in another. I cannot say it strongly enough: writing long poems ("Eurydice" and "Medusa") opened my career as a critic, opened it intellectually, for the ideas in *Writing Beyond the Ending* on kinds of mythopoetic practices – ideas of "breaking the sentence and breaking the sequence," displacement and delegitimation – were underwritten and enabled by my poetic practice. My turn to the essay form, an eccentric detour and divagation if ever there was one, allowed me to find a thesis for my first critical book. The point is – poetry is intellectual work, criticism is poetic work, and if these do not come as a necessity – a personal and cultural necessity – what good are they? My poetry (a somewhat hidden thing, a somewhat unrewarded thing, a slowly written thing), my essays (a dangerous, satisfying, sometimes misinterpreted thing) made me a feminist critic. Were part of my feminist criticism.

In 1980, I went through that peculiar hazing process of feminist members of my generation: I was denied tenure at Temple University, and, while the signals were mixed, one of the then powerful voices ran an exasperating condemnation of all feminist work in which my "appropriation of H. D." and the fact of my essays loomed large. Of course, it is true that the essays were intemperate and maenadic work, though not that they were poorish art or unanalytic intellectual documents. This tenure battle was, of course, no joke. I worked with intransigence to reverse the decision, and gained yet a little more political education. My "risks" were patent: I produced both creative and critical writing in a new field; I worked with other women to build a new feminist journal; the field was "political" – that whole story. But the cultural necessity of feminist work gave me the drive and the justification. It was just me; this is what I was doing. So there we were.

1984 to now; polyvocal poems and the pluralist feminism-plus of cultural studies. My poetry does not resemble hegemonic feminist or women's poetry or mainstream poetries in its form or its poetics. I draw on avant-garde traditions in written and visual texts, always working with metonymic exposition and the possibilities of collage. Virtually unpublished throughout the 1970s, I said "I was too feminist for the objectivists, and too objectivist for the feminists." Not until 1977, in the little magazine *Montemora*, did my work in poetry begin to find any audience. *Wells* was published in 1980 (by Eliot Weinberger), a very pure, heavily revised book. It was unreviewed and went through no normal path of critical acceptance. However, people taught and wrote about certain poems, particularly the "myth poems." I think it's the Xerox machine that did it.

For some of the poetics and some of the intransigence, I was indebted to the work of the "Objectivist" poet George Oppen, many of whose writings in poetics occurred in his self-chosen form: personal letters. With a perspective on archival work about unduly marginal figures which I developed from work on H. D., I engaged from 1980 to 1990 on a large-scale editorial and textual project: *The Selected Letters of George Oppen* (Duke University Press, 1990), which presents materials important (in my view) to contemporary poetry and poetics. My interest in the critique and dissolution of the canon (note the working contradiction) is not focused only on women writers.

In *Wells*, I wrote the lyric: in notions of the pure hit of the singular, singing voice that we think of as its characteristic. Yet I was also suspicious of those seductions, especially the ideology of beauty-in-poetry, which seemed bound up with rigid positioning of female figures, and therefore a peculiarly negative matter for a female writer. Consequently, I began making two other kinds of works in poetry. The first was a critical or analytic lyric (that is, "Crowbar," not trobar) under the rubric of *The "History of Poetry"*: rewriting stances central to the positioning of women in the anthologized history of poetry as we know it. The second kind of poem (begun in 1984), on the analogy of the term "working papers," could be called "working poems"; I call them *Drafts* (DuPlessis 1987 and 1991). My current poetry continues this post-lyric, creolized writing: epiphanic moments are flattened and undercut; narratives are multiple and dissolved; heteroglossia is maximized; the symphonic space is the site of anarchic, wayward collages of language and investigations of textual markers. I became a "mail-order" contributor to the *HOW(ever)* group in San Francisco (far from my home); Kathleen Fraser, Frances Jaffer, and Beverly Dahlen created a newsletter-format magazine which linked modernist experiment by women with innovative writing by contemporary women. To see, at least, where I'd been, as my feminist humanism and my feminist postmodernism debated modernist experiment, I collected ten years of my essays (mainly published by small press journals) in *The Pink Guitar* (DuPlessis 1990b). Since a number of the essays concerned Pound, Williams and Eliot, as well as Duchamp, at least I have finally *really* "rewritten" my dissertation.

Now we are up to the present, and my tone will probably, therefore, change, if it hasn't already. It is clear that reading gender needs to be further elaborated by analytic interplays among studies of race, class, sexualities, religious culture and other psycho-social forces and determinants, and by studies of the manifestations of these markers in culture and text. Feminist cultural studies, feminism(s)-plus (for this is the direction) is based on establishing a plural relationship among the marked categories; this is the polygyny I now try to embrace. None of these markers is static and already understood, but each is created in political, cultural, social and historical interactions whose activities, contradictions and textual manifestations need critical scrutiny. Thus, I feel situated in what Susan Stanford Friedman has recently termed Post/post-structuralist feminist criticism, a criticism that (like Nancy Miller's) does not scant intention, agency, thematics and the impact of material conditions, while it makes nuanced readings of language and linguistic play, the partial and interested claims of any reality, and the careers of master narratives (Friedman 1991: 465–90). This is what it now means to me to be a "feminist reader." Working in this matrix, I need now to write a critical book about modern poetry, its cultural narratives and social debates. Perhaps I will. Luckily here, as in my other work, I won't be alone.

NOTES

1 The concept comes from Thomas Kuhn (1962); it has been applied to feminism by Catharine Stimpson and others. His model of growing contradictions and discontinuities in the way one's knowledge holds together, issuing in major intellectual discomforts, provoking a sudden conversion experience which changes the shape of knowledge, and which then gets institutionalized, is echoed in my experience and my narrative.

2 I am not proud of this; I record it as a datum of the time. A feisty, energetic woman with trouble entering the heterosexual marital economy "feared" she was a lesbian. Homophobia and sexism rampant on a field of green. I hung a copy of Pontormo's "Three Graces" on my wall; these were young men duplicitously drawn as women, breasts stuck on male bodies: this was one vow of androgyny – not to be consumed in emotional ground wars, not to be colonized by men.

3 From the first, the Lessing intrigued me formally; the notebooks separate and fused were

like a structural coup expressing my sense of the multiple dimensions of being situated as a woman politically, sexually, artistically, relationally.

4 Except – when I look at the profile of the three and with all due respect to us, I see we were all – please forgive me – daddy's girls, and possibly had certain elements of psychic safety and reassurance to the appointers, aside from whatever credentials. Luckily, I was in France that first year, and my replacement was Lillian Robinson, not one, I believe, to have fallen, then or at any time, under the "paternal" rubric.

5 Robert DuPlessis recently reminded me that he had encouraged me to attend. It is impossible to put this datum in without setting up the oddest reverberations of all sorts ("She's saying her *hus*band ... WHAT?"); therefore, of course, I am putting just this detail in.

6 In the interests of the sociology of knowledge, it is also worth listing the number of feminist critics who emerged from that Columbia matrix – I don't mean Columbia Women's Liberation, but the English and French Departments: my unsystematic count reveals in English Nina Auerbach, Louise Bernikow, Carolyn Burke, Barbara Christian, myself, Kate Ellis, Judith Kegan Gardiner, Sandra Gilbert, Myra Jehlen (as junior faculty), Nancy Milford, Kate Millett, Lillian Robinson, Catharine Stimpson, Louise Yelin. And Alice Jardine, Nancy Miller, and Naomi Schor were in the same academic generation in the French Department. Carolyn Heilbrun, on the faculty during this ferment, was herself becoming a notable and influential feminist critic. Forgive me if my list is incomplete.

7 I could have written "I was born again, a feminist." Although I am more than somewhat uncomfortable, and even campy, in invoking this New Testament structure of feeling. There was, for instance, no messiah. Luckily. Also "born-again" implies a first baptism prior to the renewal; but for a long time we thought we were engaged in the invention of feminism. Later, more slowly, we understood the degree to which many feminisms had already occurred. And had to a large degree been erased or distorted. Even now, we are learning how our feminism must be "feminism(s)" – see Elizabeth Meese (1990).

8 Ann was proudly sent off by Columbia Women's Liberation in spring 1970 to provide testimony before the House Special Subcommittee on Education for hearings on Section 805 of H.R. 16098 to prohibit discrimination against women in federally assisted programs and in employment in education. With Linda Nochlin, she curated an important – a staggering – exhibition, Women Artists 1550–1950.

9 I am insisting, here, on the integration of political and social arousals into the cultural work of feminist literary criticism.

10 "68er" is Meredith Tax's phrase, in an article in *In These Times*.

11 Therefore I responded strongly to the Marxist work of Fredric Jameson and Raymond Williams, the latter a real influence on *Writing Beyond the Ending*.

12 I was in France, not at the MLA in 1971, and did not hear first-hand either Adrienne Rich's or Tillie Olsen's essays. They none the less became central, definitional statements when I read them in *College English* (1972), contributing much to my formulation of feminist cultural projects. The subtle layers of personal and political thinking characteristic of the work of both writers has been exemplary to me.

13 Another instructor, Paulette Williams, stayed one semester. We had lunch. She said "I dream of a work, a work of many women speaking a kind of poetry, with many colors, like a rainbow, and dancing and singing ..." I said, "O it sounds wonderful – you should do it." She went off to San Francisco, and as Ntozake Shange, did it. Indeed she did.

14 The professor of the course was feminist classicist Froma Zeitlin. I was on another one-year terminal contract (1973–4) at Douglass College replacing Elaine Showalter, whose women writers course was already on the books. Teaching my version of a "Women in Literature" course further spurred my desire to write about women's writing.

110 Rachel Blau DuPlessis

15 My other "myth" poem, "Medusa," written 1974–8, was another complicated undertaking. Because it was about rape, but not only sexual rape but also the rape of vision by patriarchal ideology, it failed numerous times, fell into tendentiousness, and resisted becoming art. My stubbornness in negotiating the completion of this poem over the four years it was in question taught me a great deal about being an artist.

16 I had the pleasure of working in H. D.'s manuscripts and archives, always, I would argue, a vital move for an enriched understanding of figures whom one is trying to recontextualize and put on the critical agenda. My work on H. D. issued in a book, *H. D.: The Career of that Struggle*, an anthology, *Signets: Reading H. D.*, with my friend and colleague Susan Stanford Friedman, and several essays in *The Pink Guitar*.

17 A member of the central Editorial Collective until 1982, the Associate Editor for Creative Work from 1982–7. I am still affiliated with the journal as a Consultant/Reader. I was convinced that feminist artistic, creative, and visual work was a central component of our intellectual revolution. So I was the artistic member of the board, with an eye for covers, who fought for a more open, "voicy," essay style as part of the canon of acceptable work, who insisted that poems and fiction be represented.

18 One might say it is the answer to that other me who did not want to have her psyche female.

19 In a letter of 4 January 1978 to Tillie Olsen.

20 Indeed this writing, right here, differs; it is a memoir.

21 I was not directly influenced by Cixous' "Laugh of the Medusa" but there is no doubt that this is the great manifesto of maenadic writing.

22 In many ways, *Writing Beyond the Ending* began with the example of Showalter's *A Literature of Their Own*; I was quite put out by the readings given of Woolf and Richardson, but intrigued by the question of how to define what women writers had in common, and committed to the cultural studies that have always been the distinguishing marks of Showalter's criticism. As well, my central finding of a critique of heterosexuality would not have been possible without lesbian–feminist criticism, which I knew in part through such little magazines as *Amazon Quarterly*.

23 As anyone knows who has written a book, one of the unspoken difficulties is keeping one's intellectual growth self-consistent, and consistent with the announced thesis, once this is settled. It might be interesting to try to do this otherwise. As is also obvious, I chose to write this book in standard tones and modes of argument; it would have been professionally unstrategic (to say the least) to make another kind of work.

REFERENCES

Allen, D. M. (ed.) (1960) *The New American Poetry*, New York: Grove Press.
Cixous, H. (1976) "The Laugh of the Medusa," *Signs* 1: 4 (summer), 875–93.
Duncan, R. (1967) "Rites of Participation, II," *Caterpillar* 1 (October), 6–34.
DuPlessis, R. B. (1979) "Psyche, or Wholeness," *The Massachusetts Review* XX (spring), 77–96.
——(1980) *Wells*, New York: Montemora Foundation.
——(1985) *Writing Beyond the Ending: Narrative Strategies of Twentieth-Century Women Writers*, Bloomington: Indiana University Press.
——(1986) *H. D.: The Career of that Struggle*, Bloomington: Indiana University Press.
——(1987) *Tabula Rosa*, Elmwood, Ct: Potes & Poets Press.
——(ed.) (1990a) *The Selected Letters of George Oppen*, Durham: Duke University Press.
——(1990b) *The Pink Guitar: Writing as Feminist Practice*, New York: Routledge.
——(1991) *Drafts (3–14)*, Elmwood, Ct.: Potes & Poets Press.
Echols, A. (1989) *Daring to be Bad: Radical Feminism in America, 1967–1975*, Minneapolis: University of Minnesota Press.
Friedan, B. (1963) *The Feminine Mystique*, New York: W. W. Norton & Co.

Friedman, S. S. (1991) "Post/Post-Structuralist Feminist Criticism: The Politics of Recuperation and Negotiation," *New Literary History* 22 (2): 465–90.

——and R. B. DuPlessis (1990) *Signets: Reading H. D.*, Madison: University of Wisconsin Press.

Kuhn, T. S. (1962) *The Structure of Scientific Revolutions*, Chicago: University of Chicago Press.

Lessing, D. (1962) *The Golden Notebook*, New York: Simon & Schuster.

Meese, E. (1990) *(Ex)tensions: Re-figuring Feminist Criticism*, Urbana: University of Illinois Press.

Miller, N. (1988) *Subject to Change: Reading Feminist Writing*, New York: Columbia University Press.

Millett, K. (1971) *Sexual Politics*, London: Rupert Hart-Davis (first published 1969).

Olsen, T. (1971) "One Out of Twelve: Writers Who Are Women in Our Century," *Silences*, New York: Delta.

Rich, A. (1971) "When We Dead Awaken: Writing as Revision," *On Lies, Secrets, and Silence: Selected Prose 1966–78*, New York: W. W. Norton.

Showalter, E. (1977) *A Literature of Their Own: British Women Novelists from Brontë to Lessing*, Princeton: Princeton University Press.

——(1987) "Women's Time, Women's Space: Writing the History of Feminist Criticism," in Shari Benstock (ed.) *Feminist Issues in Literary Scholarship*, Bloomington: Indiana University Press.

Woolf, V. (1929) *A Room of One's Own*, New York, Harcourt Brace Jovanovich.

Chapter 7

In academia, and out
The experience of a lesbian feminist literary critic

Bonnie Zimmerman

I have never written a professional essay in which I reflect directly upon my own life, although most of my scholarly writing flows more or less directly from my personal values and experiences. So this essay has proven to be the most difficult writing assignment of my career. What are the ideas, events and experiences that made me a feminist critic – or, more specifically, a lesbian feminist critic? More important, what are the meanings I have placed upon these experiences?

Experience has become a suspect concept in feminist theory. Claims to "the authority of experience" no longer carry the weight they once did. Experience itself, we are told, only derives meaning when we reflect upon it, which means it is heavily mediated by ideology, language or discourse. There is no pure experience in which to ground our ideas, no perfect authority with which to justify our politics. Connected to this questioning of experience is our questioning of the category "woman." If there is no essential, monolithic, uniform woman, then there can be no such thing as "woman's experience." Merely changing the singular to plural – from "woman's" to "women's" experience – does not help, since we still assume a unifying "womanness" from which to generalize about diverse women. What is that womanness, that unifying experience or set of experiences, that makes it possible for us to draw a feminist theory out of our lives?

Such thinking has had dramatic effects on contemporary feminist thought. On the positive side, it has made us far more aware of how one group of women has generalized from its experience to that of all women, resulting in the erasure or distortion of the experiences and perspectives of all other groups. It has made us wary of duplicating patriarchal thought about an "essential" female nature. It has deepened our initial understanding of the pervasive influence of language and ideology on consciousness and behavior.

But the undermining, or deconstructing, of experience has its troublesome side as well. If we cannot speak from our experiences as women, from what or where can we speak? If there is no category "woman," how can there be feminism or women's liberation? What do we make of the strong, unshakable feeling most of us continue to have that we do experience the world as women? Experience seems to resist our every attempt to dethrone it.

For lesbians, these contradictions (if indeed they are such) are particularly compelling. Throughout the twentieth century, lesbians have been excluded from the category "woman." Lesbians have been marked by the signs of masculine gender, and defined as unsexed women, trans-sexuals, men's souls trapped in women's bodies, bulldykes and butches. Even lesbians who conformed to the outward trappings of conventional femininity might be scrutinized for flaws – perhaps too ambitious or career-oriented, not sufficiently subservient or attentive to men, or prematurely feminist. In the early years of the women's liberation movement, lesbians were purged from some feminist organizations, and lesbian issues continue to be derided as a "lavender herring" – a deviation from the true path of feminism. So lesbians know well how arbitrary and partial is the category woman. Consequently, Monique Wittig, perhaps the most radical of lesbian theorists, claims that lesbians are not women (Wittig 1981: 47–54). Lesbians deconstruct that essentialist category. Many other contemporary lesbians, particularly separatists, reject the very word as unredeemably patriarchal, opting instead for such variant spellings as "womon" or "wimmin."

But if lesbians cannot or choose not to belong to the category woman, can we claim "lesbian" as a more meaningful category or identity? How can we develop a politics and theory that draws upon lesbian experience, or lesbian existence? What makes such concepts any more meaningful than that of women's experience? Are we not vulnerable to the same charges of false universalizing or essentialism? On the other hand, without some kind of general acceptance of lesbian as a category, there can be no lesbian identity, lesbian community, lesbian culture, lesbian literature, lesbian theory or lesbian criticism. And yet, I feel sure that all these do exist.

My own history convinces me that "experience" is still a useful concept, and necessary to any understanding of the development of feminist theory and literary criticism. Similarly, our belief in the centrality (if not authority) of experience has been crucial to the development of lesbian feminism, as it has to the feminisms of women of color. It is still experience, not language or discourse, to which we appeal when testing the hypotheses posed by any feminist theory. Accordingly, I must pay due attention to the experiences that turned me into a lesbian feminist literary scholar.

Mine is one of those embarrassingly stereotypical radicalizations of the late 1960s. I could be one of the secondary characters in any novel by Marge Piercy, Marilyn French or Alix Shulman: the woman in the consciousness-raising group who doesn't have an individual personality or voice, and who comes out about two-thirds of the way through the plot.

I became a feminist (although I didn't use that word for many years) because of the gap between my expectations of who I could be as a bright, college-educated, middle-class Jewish woman, and my experiences of discrimination and deeply internalized self-doubt. In 1968, when I first heard of "women's lib," I was 21 years old. I had just graduated *summa cum laude* with a degree in philosophy (which I deliberately selected because it was not a "women's subject"). I had managed to become one of the boys intellectually, but, much to my surprise, my emotions, my subjective self, were a textbook model of traditional female social-ization. I was young, and I wanted desperately to be saved from an undefined future. Fortunately (from a vantage point two decades later) no Prince Charming was around to heed my call. I would have to save myself.

This gap between my intellectual authority and my emotional vulnerability was the space in which my feminism flourished. Because I had always respected ideas – because I still believe that if a theory makes sense, one should seriously consider living by it – once introduced to the basic concepts of the second wave of feminism, I had no choice but to rethink and redirect my life. Every feminist text I read made sense; every feminist idea resonated to my own experiences.

Because of the time at which I encountered the women's movement – 1969–70 – there were no courses or teachers to fuel my feminism. I entered graduate school and joined a consciousness-raising group in the same month. We graduate students (and a very few courageous, mostly untenured, faculty) were our own teachers; we designed the first Women's Studies courses. The sources of our feminist thinking necessarily were our own lives and the texts we were both rediscovering and creating. But because we were all graduate students, all white, and, at that moment, all heterosexual (a situation that would very quickly and dramatically change), the feminism and Women's Studies we created was so partial and limited that it has required continual redefinition during the twenty years since. We did our best based upon our experiences, but our best and our experiences were inadequate to the task.

The early women's movement, we might remember, quickly polarized into socialist or Marxist tendencies, and radical tendencies. At that point in history, we were desperately trying to determine "the primary contradiction": was class the source of all exploitation, as Marx claimed, or was sex a deeper and more primary oppression? I now recognize this form of thinking as yet another manifestation of western dualism and absolutism, another attempt to demand intellectual allegiance to one totalizing theoretical position. But twenty years ago, the quest for the primary contradiction seemed all-important to my generation of feminists. As socialist feminists we read Bebel, Engels, Juliet Mitchell. As radical feminists we read Roxanne Dunbar and *No More Fun and Games*, Shulamith Firestone, and "The Fourth World Manifesto." We all read Simone de Beauvoir and Doris Lessing. Although the women who belonged to my "we" were almost all white, we originally had been radicalized by the civil rights movement and the Black Panthers, and so we also read Malcolm X, Eldridge Cleaver, Assata Shakur, and later Angela Davis.

But around 1971, the earth quaked beneath my feet once again. Impelled by both feelings and ideas – my growing passion for women and my acceptance of a radical critique of heterosexuality – I "came out" as a lesbian, and my life changed even more profoundly. Within a year, my ideas had moved conceptually 180 degrees, from Marxist feminism to radical feminism to lesbian separatism. I don't know to what extent I freely chose to become a lesbian and to what extent the women's movement simply allowed me to claim an identity already "planted" in my soul: I suppose for me the process involved both inclination and opportunity. But the result (for me and many other new lesbians) was a profound sense of exclusion from virtually every institution in US society: family, education, workplace, even the women's movement and feminist criticism. Looking back, I suspect some of that marginalization was self-imposed, resulting in part from the romantic sixties' myth of the outlaw and in part from my own internalized homophobia. I expected to be rejected and misunderstood, and I found that I liked the role of the outsider. Although that phase of my development didn't last long, it had a permanent influence on my work as a critic. It committed me to addressing uncomfortable issues of heterosexism and homophobia within feminism and Women's Studies, and to developing lesbian scholarship – by and for lesbians – as fully as I could.

For this purpose I found sustenance in new texts: in particular, "The Woman-Identified Woman" manifesto, and the many lesbian newspapers and journals that began to appear. Most important among these was *The Furies*, produced by a Washington DC-based lesbian separatist collective that was to have an unparalleled influence on the emerging lesbian feminist movement. Of further significance to me as a literary scholar were Jeannette Foster's *Sex-Variant Women in Literature* and Barbara Grier's *The Lesbian in Literature* bibliography, two reference works that opened up a rich field that I have mined for the past two decades.

No body of literature will ever have as strong an impact on my ideas as that produced in the first few years (roughly 1968 through 1972) of the women's liberation movement. Everything we have written since has been a refinement, development, refutation or reconfiguration of the concepts developed in that pioneering literature. Even the important work on difference that characterizes the feminist theory of the 1980s is not totally new, for the early women's liberation movement had a substantial sensitivity toward class and race oppression that seems to have been muted by later theoretical emphases on "women's nature" and "women's culture."

The generation of feminists that produced these texts – "my" generation – were pioneers. Although isolated individuals preceded us, the wave of political and intellectual activism that began in the late 1960s was one of the great movements of the century. We broke new ground in virtually every area of society. We took risks and created dazzlingly new ideas and interpretations. Because we were pioneers – because we fervently believed (rightly or wrongly) that we had been born anew – we were also ideologues and fanatics, passionate about our new religion. We believed that we were stripping away the lies and myths of the past to reveal the "real truth" about women and lesbians. We were sweeping the house clean. It was that commitment to truth-telling that made us so intense, and so dogmatic at times.

Accordingly, we made a lot of mistakes and did a lot of damage. One of my least favorite memories is of a conference paper in which I severely criticized a popular anthology for failing to include lesbian material. Afterwards, the editor confronted me in tears. Although I felt uncomfortable, I also shielded myself in righteousness. But the incident stayed with me until, very recently, I met her again by chance and apologized for what I perceived as my "bad behavior." To my surprise, she, in retrospect, had come to accept my criticism as something that needed to be said. None the less, I now see that a very fine line exists between raising necessary and constructive criticism, and cleansing one's soul in the blood of the goddess. Hence, I am relieved that the belief in absolute truth, in the authority of experience, has been qualified by new critical theories.

The more recent generations of feminists cannot have this edenic (and apocalyptic) consciousness. What my generation learned through consciousness-raising, they can learn in the classroom. When I began my dissertation in 1972, there were very few formal examples of feminist literary criticism. I used *The Second Sex* and *Sexual Politics* to ground my analysis in theory. Today a graduate student could write an entire dissertation on any number of discrete issues within feminist critical theory. This generation is necessarily better educated, more sophisticated and polished, probably more at home in academia. I suspect it is also less passionate and political than mine, although I now hesitate to judge another person's political commitment.

What light does this recitation of one individual history shed upon the current debate over experience? The Random House College Dictionary defines experience as "a particular instance of personally encountering or undergoing something." Several additional definitions follow, all of which emphasize *personal* process. No wonder a movement that proclaimed "the personal is political" would lay claim to "the authority of experience." What is missing from the dictionary definition, and from some experientially based formulations of feminist thinking, however, is the recognition that a personal encounter, or experience, is never an isolated or solipsistic event. Experience, in "liberal humanist" thought, is perceived as being personal and individual, something that "belongs" to me. My experience – and thus my consciousness, which is also perceived to be internal and self-contained – is a central point to which all other experiences and consciousness address themselves.

Given this conceptualization, it is no wonder that white women would posit white female experience as the personal reference point from which to derive feminist politics and theory. Or that heterosexual female experience should be held up as the norm, with lesbian experience a deviation or variant. If we claim that the personal is political, then the fact that white women in a racist society are likely to be personally racist, and heterosexual women personally homophobic, means that our politics and our theories will be racist and homophobic as well. (I do not mean to ignore the differences of class, age, religion or physical ability. But I do not want every sentence to read like a list of oppressions. Similar points obviously can be made about every category of difference, although each particular difference has its own dynamic, subjectivity, history and politics.)

This balancing act – to speak from the place of personal experience and to scrutinize the assumptions of the universality of that experience – has produced a particularly persistent tension within the feminism of the past two decades. It also has been a persistent tension within my own understanding of my self, my politics and my work as a feminist literary critic. I have defined myself progressively as a woman, as a white middle-class woman, as a lesbian, as a white middle-class lesbian, as a white middle-class lesbian who is also a Jew, and so on. At each moment of redefinition, I have felt torn between difference and sameness, between particularity and generality, between the experience of self and the experiences of others.

It is not surprising that these questions and conflicts should be at the heart of feminist theory, and that literary theorists should be so central to the debates. One of the traditional tasks or virtues of literature has been to mediate between self and other. The text itself is a means of communication between writer and reader; one does not exist without the other. It is, perhaps, rather old-fashioned to claim that this mediation or communication produces empathy, the experiencing of another's being as if it were one's own. Empathy is yet another suspect concept, since, unexamined, empathy results simply in the colonization of the other. If I empathize only with experiences that resemble my own and thus validate my pre-existing assumptions, I merely turn the other into a mirror image of myself. I have appropriated her experiences; she still exists only in relation to myself.

But, in many ways, I am an old-fashioned girl. I still consider empathy a virtue to be claimed for literature. I think it possible that the act of reading can displace or de-center the self, and imaginatively allow the other to take its place. Reading (an act of imaginative displacement) can allow us to be, to use Maria Lugones' felicitous phrase, "world-travellers" – or word-travellers (Lugones 1990: 390).[1] That travel may take place between worlds within the self itself, or between worlds that the self inhabits and those it does not.

I find this concept appealing because I inhabit many worlds myself, some at the center of this society and some at its margins. For many years, as I said, I perceived myself as profoundly marginalized: as a Jew in a Christian world, as an underemployed Ph.D. during the 1970s, as Women's Studies faculty at the MLA, as a lesbian everywhere. Marginalization, at least in radical circles, can be very comforting. It can let you think you're off the hook. As a Jew and a lesbian, I didn't have to take responsibility for other oppressions. As a part-timer or a Women's Studies person, I could scoff at professionalism and academese. But, of course, that is merely sticking my head in the sand. I may be marginal in relation to certain dominant groups in our society, but I exist right at the center of others. Most obviously, I am white and middle-class. And now, amazingly, I am a tenured full professor who chairs a department and has served on a plethora of powerful university committees. Every day of my life I experience a shift between viewing from the center and viewing from the margins, between seeing myself as subject and being seen as object, between defining myself as Self and being defined as Other. Such shifts in perspective can result in psychic headaches. But it also can allow the "world-travelling" that Lugones offers as a way out of solipsistic and arrogant thinking.

One further influence has helped me make some sense of the relationship between self and other, and the continuing usefulness of experience. As I have written, I was an undergraduate philosophy major and, although most of what I studied is irretrievably lost to me, a few vague ideas have remained embedded in my memory. I was particularly fascinated by such topics as the phenomenology of experience, the nature of consciousness, and the relation of the self to the not-self, the other. How can the self ever really know the world, or another self? How can we ever be sure that the not-self isn't just a projection of our own consciousness? As a 19-or 20-year-old undergraduate, I approached this question from a romantic, Bishop Berkeley perspective; I was intrigued by the idea that, as in a novel or film, I might wake up one day and discover that everything I had experienced was a mere dream, or perhaps that I was only a character in someone else's dream. But now I approach the question in a different fashion. If I start from my own consciousness, my own experience – and indeed from where else can I start? – then I run the risk of creating the other, the world, in my own image, as a projection of my consciousness, my experience, my needs, my fears, my prejudices. And if I am teaching students and writing criticism – in short, helping to define a field of study – then I have a great deal of power to perpetuate my own partial and solipsistic view of things.

One idea that has helped me out of this dilemma is that of intentionality: the idea that consciousness is never simple and self-contained, it is always conscious-ness *of* something or someone. Similarly, experience is never private and internal, it is always experience of something or in relation to someone. I am not a separate being with my own private and personal experience; my experience, my selfhood, is constituted by others. If I an not open to others, I am not my self. I have no experiences that are not shaped by the very complex world in which I live. It seems to me that when I think of experience as relational and socially constructed, not as personal and individual, I can still use experience as a meaningful category on which to base my politics. This, after all, is what we meant twenty years ago when we said "the personal is political."

Let me further pursue this line of thinking by looking at the most characteristic lesbian narrative form, the coming-out story. In the late 1970s, several collections of lesbian personal narratives appeared, and since that time some have been reissued and new ones collected. The coming-out story is a classic lesbian literary form. It inscribes the intensely personal story of coming to know one's self as a lesbian, resulting from a lifelong consciousness of difference, a political choice, or simply a *coup de foudre*. Some people complain – and their complaint has some justice to it – that coming-out stories all sound alike, that it becomes boring after a while to read large numbers of them. But that, of course, is the point. Coming-out stories do have certain similarities, because lesbians share certain experiences in any particular society. Of course, once the coming-out story is established as a literary form, we may as likely shape our experience (actually our memory of our experience) to the story as the story to the experience. But there is a core – an event or emotion – that seems constant among great numbers of coming-out stories, whether written, or part of the lesbian oral tradition.[2]

So there seems to be a common "lesbian experience" that contributes to the formation of a "lesbian identity" and in turn, to lesbian culture, community, literature and criticism. Yet to stop there would be to succumb to the tyranny of sameness and fall victim to the universalizing that results from an unexamined exaltation of experience. The self has not yet encountered the other. Sameness has not made room for difference. It is very tempting to think that one's (my) own coming-out story is the only possible version of the story. But I have had to learn to be aware of the nuances that demonstrate how different it is to come out at age 14 with no knowledge of a feminist or gay movement, than (as I did) at age 24 with half one's consciousness-raising group. Or how different it is to come out when one is an African-American or Latina community activist, than an Anglo Women's Studies major. There will be similarities among all these experiences, but the differences will be equally profound. We have no choice but to create a lesbian feminist theory (and literary criticism) that makes room for both the sameness and the difference – based upon multitudes of experiences living as lesbians in this particular society.

To conclude, how would I summarize the connection between lived experience and theory, between my life and my work?

Necessary. Inevitable. Frustrating. Conflicted.

No matter how persuasive the poststructuralist critique of "the authority of experience" – of experience as another discourse – as a feminist and a lesbian I can never discount the influence of lived experience on my work. I can no longer take it for granted; that is, I understand that we must scrutinize "experience" for its ideological underpinnings. Nevertheless, I would not be a feminist critic, a lesbian critic, were it not for the particular shape my experiences have taken in the second half of the twentieth century. I was a women's liberationist and a graduate student, so I became a women's studies scholar. I am a lesbian and an academic, so I write lesbian criticism and theory.

I wrote my dissertation on George Eliot because I cried at the end of *The Mill on the Floss*. I could believe in Maggie Tulliver because I myself had been misunderstood and rejected. Because I could believe in Maggie, I could care about George Eliot enough to live with her words for years to come. At the beginning of my career, my work and my life were intimately and unproblematically connected.

But as my lesbianism became essential to my identity and world view, I could no longer care enough about George Eliot to put her at the center of my life; thus, I never wrote the book I had always expected I would, although my dissertation provided material for a few competent and rather conventional articles that helped me get employment and tenure. Eventually I wrote two essays applying lesbian–feminist ideas to Eliot, but this material would not get published for nearly ten years (Zimmerman 1990a: 126–44).

Instead, I felt compelled to move in another direction. Why? Because I cannot write unless I feel strongly about a subject, and for many years lesbian literature and theory has been all that I have felt passionately about. I cannot write about something that does not move me; I cannot do literary criticism as an academic exercise. I want my ideas to be of use. This means that questions of voice, accessibility, and community of readers are crucial to me. When I began writing my study of lesbian fiction, *The Safe Sea of Women*, I was determined to use the full depth of feminist theory and critical practice, but also to express those ideas in the language of the common reader. To some extent, I believe my chosen voice has prevented some academic readers from taking the book seriously as a theoretical text. Like many others, I have grown skeptical of the imploding of feminist theory, of our new predilection for exclusive languages and hermetic ideas. With the dethroning of experience, feminist criticism, formerly politically motivated, has become much more elitist and professional, as well as more various and complex. I have heard it said that theory cannot be expressed in ordinary language, but I do not believe this to be true. Garbled theory may not be expressible in ordinary language, but clear theory surely can be. And if our ideas are important and valuable, they deserve to be understood.

As for myself, my strength as a scholar is as a synthesizer, organizer and publicizer. And that is a very valuable role to play. My academic writing has always been and will always be politically motivated: I want to advance lesbian consciousness and visibility wherever I am placed, and where I am placed right now is in the academy. That is why I write, and why I write lesbian criticism.

NOTES

1   Lugones offers her concept of world-travelling specifically to women of color, who must traverse the different worlds to which they belong. I acknowledge my presumption in taking the phrase out of her context.
2   I have discussed the coming-out motif in lesbian novels in *The Safe Sea of Women: Lesbian Fiction 1969–1989*. The book references a number of other sources on the coming-out story.

REFERENCES

Lugones, M. (1990) "Playfulness, 'World'-Travelling, and Loving Perception," in G. Anzaldúa, *Making Face, Making Soul: Creative and Critical Perspectives by Women of Color*, San Francisco: Aunt Lute Foundation, 309–402.
Wittig, M. (1981) "One is Not Born a Woman," in *Feminist Issues*, 1 (2) 47–54.
Zimmerman, B. (1990a) " 'The Dark Eye Beaming': Female Friendship in George Eliot's Fictions," in K. Jay and J. Glasgow (eds), *Lesbian Texts and Contexts: Radical Revisions*, New York: New York University Press, 126–44.
——(1990b) *The Safe Sea of Women: Lesbian Fiction 1969–1989*, Boston: Beacon.

Chapter 8

"Except thou ravish mee"
Penetrations into the life of the (feminine) mind

Molly Hite

SOME OPENING PARAGRAPHS

Like the ways to God, the ways to becoming a feminist literary scholar can involve affirmation or negation. I suppose the way of affirmation involves community, even sisterhood (I am thinking back to the days when sisterhood was possible, if not powerful), mentoring, women closing their office doors and going back to their desks and saying "Look—" very firmly, and then it came out, what you always knew or what you needed to know. The problem was that when I went back to college I flung myself into the bosom of the most established patriarchy I had heard of, and although there were women in some of those offices they were basically telling me how to survive that patriarchy, never mind thinking differently. A number of these women were named Sister, by the way, and they weren't powerful. The men were all named Father. My way was the way of negation, and I mean by that to suggest St John of the Cross and not St Theresa, who was a flake according to those suave and soutaned Jesuits with whom I fell in, late, an outsider, alternately oppositional and collusive. I learned feminist scholarship by learning masculinist scholarship.

*

Of all the genres of prose narrative, autobiography is arguably the most debased from the standpoint of literary theory, inasmuch as it appears to presume the primordial integrity of the recorded and recording "self," the linear progress of a coherent and developing "life," and the sunny transparency of a "language" uniquely fitted to the task of enabling reading subjects to observe writing subjects. Traditionally, women's writing has been especially vulnerable to the charge of being merely autobiographical – "merely" in the sense of "uncreatively" or even "unintelligently," as if in the case of the female subject, world became word by a clerical act of transcription or as if the writer embodied herself in language by rolling inkily across her page. Yet recent theories of autobiography have complicated the whole issue of whether there can be anything "mere" about autobiographical discourse by insisting on a gap between the experiencing, writing subject and the object of that experience, that writing. The "I" of autobiography is inevitably a constructed subjectivity, constructed not only by the immediate culture and society at a given historical moment, but also by the writing "I," who is working with a socio-culturally limited menu of narrative conventions, theoretical positions, and ideological implications. When such theories of autobiography are applied to women's self-writing, they often reveal in that self-writing an acute awareness of precisely this subject–object split. For even bourgeois white women in late twentieth-century western societies, the available roles are so constricting that it is difficult to experience them as natural, and for a writer aware of the contradictions in her own socially constructed "self," the project of "self-writing" is invariably a self-conscious one. Women's autobiography is thus – at least potentially – a canny, duplicitous exercise, less an act of unveiling than the calculated assumption of a costume.

*

The first problem is taking yourself too seriously. Write about yourself but not, you know, "your." "Self." Too emphatic. Second person might help. I am not I. I am, on the contrary, you. In a non-universalizing, non-essentializing sense, of course, it ought to go without saying: "you." Life within quotation marks. A familiar, crouching position. In high school you learned not to put that "I" out there where somebody could slice at it, not to stick out: hard if you were close to six feet tall. "You" were. Call me Mary Seton or Mary Beaton or Mary Carmichael. On second thought, don't. Everybody called me Mary until I left Pullman, Washington at the age of 17 and went to New York to become, literarily, Molly. This is too emphatic. This ought to be within quotation marks. Or brackets, or italics, or maybe footnote-sized print. All of this ought to be in footnote-sized print down at the bottom of the page. *This is not a bourgeois white western feminist narrative of personal progress.* Maybe that part should go at the top, like a Surgeon-General's warning.

*

This essay will consider the making of a feminist literary critic. And possibly her unmaking: if you read Dinesh D'Souza (a former Reagan aide who has matching cover polemics on the subject of Illiberal Education in *The Atlantic* and *The New Republic* at the moment of this writing) or the last MLA Job List you'll have gathered we're a dying breed. Dying, even dead, but still wraithily hanging around because the university offers entrenchment to the fashionable, disregarding the fact that they invariably become unfashionable, pouf dresses with tenure among all those resurgent natural shoulders and cultural literacist old school ties. So there's been a certain damping down lately, a certain wilting of the pouf, and this swamp atmosphere conditions any attempt to write anything like a narrative, not to mention a linear narrative, still less a teleological narrative. So where does that leave us?

*

Chloe liked Olivia. They shared an office. Out of this you're going to make a revolution?

DEVELOPMENT

I took philosophy, the Queen of the Sciences. Gender markers to the contrary (the limp-wristed King of the Sciences was Theology), I went for the power, the secret horde, the scholastic Rhinegold those Jesuits had up there under their cassocks. (To be a Jesuit you have to do a graduate degree in philosophy, even if you're specializing in something else. And you have to be a man, of course. Of course of course.) I was the only woman majoring in philosophy during my first two years there. Long seminar table, shiny-jowled priest, sometimes as many as twenty-five surly young men, me. I was there to get a penis of my own, of course. Of course of course. Not always a priest; sometimes it was what they called lay faculty, usually a robust man in coat and tie bouncing with theoretical vigor, theorizing sexuality, the Church as the life (he was a deacon) of the carnal, the teachings of Thomas (Aquinas: we were all on first-name terms) as affirmation of life (he had children), bouncing with jolly repression (young women sought his advice about their boyfriends). There were two older women named Sister, one of whom I took to myself as a sort of outsider's interceding Virgin. Both were stunningly intelligent, self-effacing, despised. There was a third Sister who left the order, insisted on publishing, was purged, became my lifelong friend. And there was another woman, lay faculty, in the outlying department of English (shiny-jowled second-rate Jesuits, dusty men in jackets and ties, women: a woman's field, after all) who was more stunningly intelligent than the Sisters even, who had charisma enough for the entire university, who played Miss Jean Brodie to the girls who feared Hell in their own ravening vaginas, and who was my most important mentor. I lied about not having female mentors; I had a lot of them, still do. Or not lied, repressed; or not repressed, couldn't get that part into the story of my linear, teleological dart under the outspread, brooding, bright, Miltonic wings of that patriarchy.

I think during this part of my education I was insane. I'm not sure when to date the beginning of the insanity. I had left home at the age of 17 to join VISTA, Volunteers in Service to America, the domestic and commensurately messier Peace Corps, part of the War on Poverty that now looks like a period of fuddled benignity in the vigorous middle age of our self-promoting entrepreneurial massacring nation, a prematurely senile lapse into limited but well-intentioned philanthropy. I attribute the good intentions in retrospect. At the time, I saw nothing but hypocrisy. I accordingly became, as we put it then, radicalized, smoking pot in small rooms with draft-evading young men, singing doleful and (we thought) ironic folk songs about our situation, and finally getting bounced for the purest of reasons, demonstrating against the war (Viet Nam). After that there was New York, a great deal of left activity and discussion (a graduate student told me a while ago that the new left failed for lack of adequate attention to theory:

to each her own revisionist history), several years with the listener-sponsored radio station WBAI, a marriage (I tend to leave that out), then the Great Conversion of 1969, *annus mirabilis* of the Second Wave of twentieth-century feminism. Demonstrations, consciousness-raising, some radio programs, the decline of the left and the heady efflorescence of Women's Liberation as the new left, the true left, then meeting women who were redoing history, redoing literature, redoing thinking. At which point I hopped coasts and apprenticed myself to the guys in cassocks.

All of whom knew I was going to Hell, by the way. I wasn't even Catholic. Had never been, no lapses, nothing. I said the Lord's Prayer (oh yes, I said it, we often prayed to that large Jesuit before a seminar) with a silent coda that Catholics in their austere originality have no use for, the part about the kingdom and the power and the glory. That withheld, inwardly muttered sentence became the dimension of my rebellion. It was a momentous falling-off. I think I had a certain amount of clarity, going in, about being there to get a penis for myself. Whatever their fustiness, their outdated ecstasies, their private miseries (and they all had them and exposed them to us like withered dangling stigmata in painful ignorance of what they were doing, being too rarefied to truck with the unconscious or the high modernist iconographies of male hysteria), these men were authentic repositories of the thing itself, Western Culture. And its weapon, Logic. For this I abandoned a great deal, notably my mind: the most exalted and mother-obsessed of the Fathers assured me that he prized my feminine intellect, a welcome addition seeing as the masculine mind by itself is a lonely and weary and celibate tool. From another Jesuit, this one in the English department (I took English classes as holidays stuck judiciously among the philosophy seminars, an interpretation of literature sanctioned by both my philosophy and my English professors), I learned that the Anglican John Donne had at least got right the proper spread-eagled stance toward the deity. God as exemplary rapist, I learned, is a constant in all Western Cultures. My great female mentor hissed under her breath about the Great Mother but we all knew who had the power. All of us may have been insane; I think all of us who were female were at least a little off. We met in offices behind closed doors to whisper our denunciations. We bonded as an impotent oppressed class. I think about all this sometimes. Sometimes I go for months without thinking about it at all. I still haven't decided if anything about it was good for us. For me.

You go to the priesthood to get the tools, and of course you come away with all the ends the tools are designed to reach. I should have known this, being older, being left, being (I thought) feminist, but I wasn't prepared for this terrific longing to be accepted by the Great Father. I ended up graduating from a college where most of my sources of wisdom were confident that I was going to Hell despite the relative probity of my feminine mind. I recrossed the country with my toddler son (where do I account for him?) and my fresh new divorce (ditto) to apprentice myself to more Jesuits at Fordham University. I didn't change my thinking there; I just acknowledged that it had all become unworkable, too much private life in the way of life of the mind. In the way of this disquisition, too. Where does the rest of it go? Where do I put the entropic rundown of that marriage, the nights waitressing in a little red ruffled wet-dream outfit, the baby born on a student loan? Feminism was supposed to be about getting all those things into one sentence.

DIGRESSION

Here is where we make that noise about breaking the sentence and breaking the sequence. I can attach a bibliography if you want. Here is where we claim the obligatory feminization of the écriture, embrace syntactic disruption as the outward and visible sign of phallogocentric collapse. Or is that what we're repudiating now? I lose track.

Being a feminist literary scholar is in many respects a matter of keeping abreast of the current repudiations. We're always killing off the Mother and riding sternly into the future on our newly phallicized hobbyhorses, call it modernity. We're always being reclaimed by that bright brooding masculine dove, and denouncing the bearers of the bad news to the effect that we're doing it *again*. What do you mean, again? To each her own revisionist history.

Alan Bloom, Dinesh D'Souza, the *New York Times Magazine*, if by any perverse chance you've got hold of this, it's as bad as you feared, or hoped. We tenured radicals are pitifully vulnerable. We go in for things like self-criticism. We think conventional linguistic structures are fraught with oppressive ideology, so we write phrases that look hilarious inside other people's quotation marks. We bite our own tails a lot. Too often, we bite them off.

Last I checked in on the repudiation industry we were fighting about Essentialism. Because I am still a product of those seminars, still the student who sold her heritage for a mess of Logic, I watch the fray and murmur: nothing will survive if you use the term that broadly, that's not what an essence is, can't you see you have to make distinctions, use more care and attention, mean what you say, otherwise it's all preening and strutting and flaunting your very long tail?

This is true and I mean it. I care horribly about the way the shaky edifice of feminist scholarship is falling down, again. But my words come from the same universe as the preening and strutting and flaunting. Like these new combatants, this year's, this decade's, I wish to exorcise the soft, the flaccid, the viscous, the sloppy, from feminist discourse. I yearn for tumescent rigor. For this reason I do not believe we have constructed more than temporary alternatives. This year's. This decade's. The edifice comes down very easily, and once again we find we have no home and no safety.

DEVELOPMENT, CONT.

The business of narrative is to get from point A to point B. This is why we talk about linearity. In so far as point B is construed to be Up, we can also talk about teleology. Progress! Growth! Point A is called Then, point B is called Now.

Or, linearly, Here, as in How I Got Here. This part takes us sprinting through graduate school at the University of Washington, where I scuttled along in terror of the known feminists and found myself writing a novel about academic life as pornography in order to go on writing a dissertation for a committee composed of three men. There is another marriage here, and later another baby. This is all you'll hear about them. With a final burst of speed we can return the repressed to my old Jesuit haunts for a year of groveling as junior faculty, then shoot me across the country again to a ten-year span we'll compress into the moment of Now and Here. They asked if I would mind teaching a course on Twentieth-Century Women Novelists. The rest isn't history but anticlimax.

Inevitably this kind of narrative fixates on the individual and ignores the collective. And I did elect to make the obsessive focus of this account my long apprenticeship in phallogocentrism. Me and the boys. It was the wrong focus; it distorts; it throws everything off. I always had lines strung to far-flung and geographically arbitrary locations where other feminists lurked. These lines weren't organized and high-tech enough to warrant being called a network. They were more like the string between tin cans in a child's walkie-talkie. Feminism for me has always been a jerry-rigged apparatus.

It turns out that I have to redirect your attention after the fact. The narrative isn't the important part. It was the wrong narrative. I did not have the correct emphasis, as the projectionist in the Golden notebook (within *The Golden Notebook*) puts it. There is no correct emphasis. There is no real story. You lay out your tracks and shoot along from Then to Now, from There to Here. You miss most of the countryside.

None of this comes as a surprise.

HOW TO CONCLUDE

People in the literary professions believe that stories have some sort of transcendent importance. This is another aspect of our daily life that prompts hilarity and dread in readers of mass-circulation, ostensibly highbrow periodicals. What about Life? they chorus. This next decade is going to be about Life if cultural literacists have anything to say about it. We're going to have to buckle down to the business of living and stop having our savants do it for us. Enough self-reflexiveness. Enough race-class-and-gender. Enough frills: back to the standard model, no pigmentation, no vagina. Back to the real world with its master-narratives of legitimation. Enough stories.

My partner (white, male), who teaches history – the kind with events, not the kind with titles – keeps looking up from a stack of freshman blue books to report on the state of the nation. Think of these reports as regular intrusions into all of the above. I didn't write them as regular intrusions into all of the above because they illustrate poignantly how dangerous it is to venture into postmodernist disruptions – how even linear narratives get derailed with depressing predictability. They illustrate how the story to which readers respond is too often the story they wanted to hear.

"They don't distinguish between a demonstration and a riot," he says. Picture me writing, longhand, about theories of autobiography.

"When they see a sentence about violence done to union members, they always read it as a sentence about unions getting violent," he says. I am deep into my ruminations about penises, men in skirts, and the Western Cultural Tradition.

"They all identify Eleanor Roosevelt as the wife of FDR," he says. "Every one of them. They say he got polio so she had to get involved in politics. Why else would she get involved in politics?"

I put down my pen. "She was considered homely," I volunteer.

He nods. "They all say that, too," he says. "Except they leave out 'considered.'"

"Why else would she get involved in politics?" I say. The news is that it's happening again. To each her or his revisionist history.

I put in that patch of dialogue not only to insist with pained eagerness that other people think stories are important too, but also to show how the meanings we think we've committed to paper aren't the meanings other people read. Although if I had really made that point you couldn't possibly understand it inasmuch as the meanings we think we've committed to paper aren't the meanings other people read. In our discipline (discipline?) we have slogans that make that point. *There are no texts, there are only readings. Authorial intention is unknowable and irrelevant in any case. Slippage is inherent in language; the ideal of perfect communication is a hangover from the Enlightenment.* Perfect communication? Any communication. You are reading this, but you're not reading what I think I've written. I'm not reading what you think you've written. We're each of us alone here within our quotation marks, fetal crouch in the linguistic bomb shelter, post–Enlightenment monads.

Except that monads are a peculiarly Enlightenment invention, born of rationalism and self-reflexivity and a notion of certainty so grandiose and rigid that it makes knowledge the prerogative of the Great Father and his transcendental signifier in the sky. I wouldn't be writing this if I thought you couldn't understand it. I wouldn't. You understand?

Nor do I think this volume is premised on a commitment to the bourgeois narrative of individual progress. To reduce narrative to one form and one function is to fall into one of those odd ahistoricist traps we are supposed to be on the lookout for as feminists. By this token, it seems part of the same old story, that bad news *again*, to assume there is by definition something wrong with feminist narrative. There is by definition something wrong with narrative, which incarnates one story by suppressing numerous others, but that's just narrative and we can live with it, inefficient though it is, on one hand as a purveyor of the truth, on the other hand as an instrument for winning hearts and minds.

As for the correct emphasis, I think we should try very hard not to use that seductive rigidity to shut ourselves up again. "Shut up" being here the modality of silence as well as incarceration. "Ourselves" being here a bland usurpation of that totality "women," as if there were women, as if there were differences and *also* women, as if to generalize were not necessarily to be an Essence. There are lean times ahead.

*

I never got here, as in How I Got Here. Or, not here with the requisite specificity: feminism, literariness, scholarship. There is little in my narrative to suggest a course set for here, now, this persona. The eerie thing about writing autobiography (as opposed, perhaps, to reading it – or as opposed to writing fiction) is that it seems so contingent, as if each step were not a progressive unfolding of the design but only a cautious shifting of weight onto the next patch of tussocky high ground, with sucking mud all around. It's a swamp, this business of living, and it doesn't help all that much to plot routes across it because as far as I can see it doesn't stop being swamp, you don't arrive at a culminating region of sure footing. On the contrary: eventually it pulls you in. I don't know if I speak for anyone else in this generation of feminist scholars *in medias res*, but that's as close as I get to a theory of progress.

Chapter 9

The long goodbye
Against personal testimony or, an infant grifter grows up

Linda S. Kauffman

We lived as usual. Everyone does, most of the time. Whatever is going on is as usual. Even this is as usual, now. We lived, as usual, by ignoring. Ignoring isn't the same as ignorance, you have to work at it. Nothing changes instantaneously: in a gradually heating bathtub you'd be boiled to death before you knew it.

Margaret Atwood, The Handmaid's Tale

I feel like a lot of people have kind of napped through the Reagan years, politically. You know how you feel when you wake up from a nap, sort of real disoriented and cranky and stuff? That's how this time is striking me.... As I looked around I saw things weren't the way they were being described at all. You remember that old 'safety net' thing they used to talk about? You don't hear about that any more. People fell right through.

Laurie Anderson, 16 March 1990

Since this essay is written against the grain of individualism, novelistic discourse[1] and personal testimony, let's dispense with the personal immediately: for 400 years every male Kauffman was a Protestant minister and missionary. Racking his brain to invent the occupation that would be most rebellious and least remunerative, my father became a Bible salesman. I was his side-kick: together we sold Bibles and religious paraphernalia to servicemen in bus stations up and down the Southern California coast, pitching piety and scoring sales, though privately we scorned the suckers. My job: to "look innocent." I was 5. (One item I remember vividly: a trippy 3-D color picture of Jesus that lit up when you plugged it in; to my infant eyes, Jesus looked like a psychedelic cartoon, "turned on" in both senses of the word.) Since he had the I.Q. of a genius, my father disdained bosses and nine to five routines: instead, he worked successively in various kinds of sales, and, as our fortunes declined, as a milkman, cab driver and grifter. My most vivid childhood memories: the glittering marquees on the strip in Vegas, especially the huge cowboy tipping his hat at the Golden Nugget, who reminded me of Howdy Doody, and the Silver Slipper, which reminded me of Cinderella. Another sublime memory is the Long Beach Pike, a pretty seedy scene in those days; my antics amused the carneys while Dad conned the sailors, all of us grifting according to our gifts. From the age of 11, I worked nights in his janitor business, cleaning banks, offices, and the model homes spreading over Orange County, California, in the 1960s like mould on cheese. Although legitimate, this job was the most humiliating: how dare the morons traipsing through these houses look at *me* with pity, while I cleaned around them? While polishing the tellers' windows in banks, I cultivated murderous fantasies, malevolently sizing up the huge fortress-like safes and thinking, "*Let's blow this sucker up, Dad*!" Once he began to drink and gamble in earnest, we successively lost the furniture, the car, finally the only house we'd ever own. My mother and I waitressed for $1.25 per hour each, and ate at the restaurant, since the only staple in steady supply at home was vodka. Once the newspapers and telephone were cut off, we lived in virtual seclusion. Long before Reagan invented the rhetoric of a "safety net" for the "truly needy," we had fallen right through.

Depending on my mood, my past strikes me as having all the makings of an Arthur Miller tragedy or Beckettian comedy. I developed a chameleon-like ability to move up and down the socio-economic ladder, for I was raised to imitate the gentility of my reverend ancestors, despite our chronic lack of cash. In the 1950s, I remember literally being homeless (I was so young, I thought we were "camping"); but eventually we managed to "pass" in the middle class, living largely on credit. No wonder my doctoral dissertation was on Dickens and Faulkner: my family alternately resembled the Micawbers and the Pockets, the Compsons and the Snopeses.

As the last sentence indicates, I clearly believe that our intellectual work as feminists is directly related to our personal histories; that our subjective experiences influence our politics, that our psychic traumas affect our teaching and writing.

So what's my beef?

First, I dislike the "our" in the previous paragraph: among many other assumptions it takes for granted, the one that is probably most accurate is therefore most troubling: "we" all do the same kind of labor, that is, feminist work in higher education in America. Are "we" feminist scholars solipsistically talking only to ourselves?

Second, it's too easy to validate my credentials. My checkered past is too easy to transform into a Nixonian Checkers speech of bathos. By insisting on the authority of my personal experience, I effectively muzzle dissent and muffle your investigation into my motives. "I've suffered more than you" is a false (albeit fashionable) piety, as if we needed to (or could) distance ourselves from bourgeois banalities. It elicits a phony competition to prove that "I was poorer than you." (My mother used to joke, "I was so poor, I didn't have a mother.")

Third: the facts of my life and hard times rearrange themselves generically into one of several novelistic lines, including, but not limited to, the following:

• The nobility of suffering.

That's the first lie: suffering never ennobles, it only humiliates, and – if you're lucky – enrages.

• Ms Horatio Alger: anybody in America can rise to the top with hard work, and fulfill the American dream.

That lie disguises the randomness of existence: it is only by chance that I am not a welfare mother, a stripper, or a waitress. In this light, the fact that I am white and was at least able to forage in the middle class considerably outweighs the fact that I am female. The lie's corollary: I raised myself by my bootstraps; so better had you – what we might currently call the Clarence Thomas syndrome.

- Revolutionary impulses led me to the university.

In fact, I sought the university precisely because I saw it as a haven from the chaos and craziness of "real life"; far from scorning "the ivory tower," I was, I smugly thought, fleeing into one. Unfortunately, carrying on the Kauffman trait of exquisite bad timing, shortly after I arrived at the University of California, Santa Barbara in 1967, police and National Guard patrols put the university under siege: classes were suspended, curfews imposed, students were beaten and arrested. As the Bank of America burned down, the National Guard murdered a student who was trying to *protect* the bank's precious property. Kevin Moran perished, but the bank rose from the ashes with a new fortress-like design within weeks.

- The anti-war movement radicalized me.

I have no nostalgia for those years (1967-71). They were as close as I ever want to come to total chaos: one couldn't depend either upon the students, the police or the National Guard for rationality, much less protection. Incredibly, scarcely twenty years ago some Americans found it normal to be murdering students on campuses, from Kent State to Jackson State, from Augusta to Santa Barbara. Not only did I learn how quickly a police state can become the norm, but I discovered how many Americans would avidly support one.

- Out of the impassioned radical evolved an impassioned feminist.

I owe to my mother whatever semblance of normality my childhood had; I owe my feminism to her fierce insistence that I escape the traps that thwarted her, and to the model my older sister provided of an escape route: studying English literature.

At the time, that solution did not seem nearly so quixotic as it seems in retrospect: in 1972 we naïvely believed that the university was the most egalitarian of institutions, the one most receptive to social change and justice. Instead, it turned out to be among the most reactionary and entrenched. In contrast to law school and medical school, which at least rely on quantitative measurements in evaluation, English departments in those days relied on vaguely F.R. Leavisite criteria involving qualitative response to "felt life." Leavisite standards still dominated English departments in the 1960s and 1970s, and – make no mistake – they still dominate in the evaluations of many full professors to this day.

My sister, Kay Austen, is now an ex-English professor. While tenured at the University of Hawaii, she fell ill. The University seized the opportunity and terminated her in retaliation for her affirmative action work. For the past ten years she has battled paralyzing illness while waging a sex discrimination case of *Bleak House* proportions against the University. Court testimony revealed that the University conspired to deny her health care when her condition was "gravely life-endangering." Testimony also revealed that they considered putting her under surveillance when she was living 6,000 miles away. Whether she ever finally "wins" this case or not, the University remains the victor – precisely by forcing each individual victim of discrimination to go through the long, arduous process over and over again.[2] I want feminist scholarship to reach an audience that transcends the academy, but that doesn't prevent me from mourning the decimation (I use that word literally) of a generation of feminist scholars who have been exiled from academic life by sexual harassment, retaliation and discrimination in the past twenty-five years.

Is it even possible to write against the grain of individualism? When you read my opening gambit, didn't it make you (whether you know me personally or not) want to know more? That is precisely my point: there is something fatally alluring about personal testimony. Even theoretical texts can be co-opted by critics who insist on interpreting in the same old way. It happens to feminists, materialists, poststructuralists alike. One reason I devoted the past decade to writing about love and epistolary fiction was to see whether it was possible to wrest signification away from representation by demonstrating that even love – the emotion that's supposed to be the most private, the most authentic, the most inviolate – is artifice, a construct. The French have known this for a long time: "Some people would never have been in love, had they never heard love talked about," said La Rochefoucauld. Consider Roland Barthes' *Fragments d'un discours amoureux*: Barthes' aim was to emphasize the fragmentary and discursive aspects of the text, rather than to create the lover-as-hero, because:

> If you put the lover in a love story, you reconcile him with society because telling stories is a coded activity. Society tames the lover through the love story. I took Draconian measures so the book would not be a love story, so the lover would be left in his nakedness, a being inaccessible to the usual forms of social recuperation, the novel in particular.
>
> (Barthes 1985: 302–3)

But (here's the grifter's voice again): Americans are hooked on authenticity and sincerity. Ironically, in the English translation, Barthes' "Draconian measures" are co-opted from the title forward: *A Lover's Discourse: Fragments* makes the lover, not discourse, primary; it reduces his analysis to psychology, when his aims were figural and structural. It suggests that we are reading the real sentiments of a lover named Roland Barthes, as if he were merely a love-lorn columnist, some French version of Ann Landers or Dr Ruth Westheimer.

Imagine substituting the word "feminist" for "lover" in the passage above: you reconcile the feminist to society because telling stories is a coded activity, as I tried to demonstrate by highlighting the implied narrative lines in my own history. Society tames the feminist through the story in particular, the allure of personal testimony in general. Are feminists succeeding in finding ways to make their work inaccessible to the usual forms of social "recuperation" – a word that in French simultaneously connotes co-option? Lest you accuse me of setting up a minor strain in feminist criticism as a "straw woman," I am arguing that such recuperation infects not just feminist criticism, but reader-response criticism, psychoana-lytic criticism, materialist criticism, *and even poststructuralism*. Let me take another improbable example: At a conference, Jacques Derrida hears the rumor that he is in analysis; he asks,

> Who am I and what have I done so that this might be the truth of their desire? … This must signify something not negligible in the air of their times and the state of their relation to what they read, write, do, say, live, etc.

> (Derrida 1980: 203)

I have purposely seized upon Barthes and Derrida because poststructuralist strategies are supposed to *preclude* the kinds of responses I am describing. Even if "we" (and here my presumption is glaring) are poststructuralist, postmodernist, anti-humanist feminists, "we" are avid consumers of true confessions, suckers for sentimentality. (As you'll see below, I am not in the least exempt from these lapses myself.) How can I as a feminist describe and account for "the air of [our] times and the state of [our] relation to what we read, write, do, say, live, etc." more precisely? A few symptomatic reflections follow.

One can obviously use the personal voice without forgetting history, society, politics. More difficult to resist is the temptation to view the personal as inherently paradigmatic, the individual life story as coherent, unified, morally inspiring. It makes us see similarity where in fact there are only differences – irresolvable, irreconcilable differences at that. Invocations to personal experience are appeal-ing because they imply that one can surmount injustice and triumph over adver-sity. In fact, most disappointments last a lifetime, and many injuries are irremediable. The older I get, the less I'm able to construct a moral even to my own story that doesn't lie with every word. As Laurie Anderson says about New Yorkers, "There are ten million stories in New York City, and no one knows which is theirs." The air of our times and the state of our relation to what we read, write, do, say, live, involve our saturation in images and in the cult of personality. Protests, movements, ideas are reduced to "Entertainment Tonight" sound-bites; one's image is tagged, marketed, commodified. (*Look what happened to Jesus!*) In the eighteenth century the quintessential medium was the essay; today it is the celebrity interview. We live in a society that no longer nourishes itself with beliefs but with images; the image always has the last word (Debord 1967; Barthes 1985). Have feminists defused the power of the image? Hardly. Can they do so? Probably not. But many have been engaged for the past decade in deconstructing the images in advertising, cinema, literature and popular culture through which femininity is constructed. Other feminists, however, reduce "Theory" to a passing fad, philos-ophy to a season's fashion.

Right now, I'm haunted by one particularly audacious image, publicizing a new magazine called *Allure*. It features a Chinese woman in Maoist dress in a grainy black and white photograph. One spot of vivid color relieves her (primitive, totalitarian) drabness: her lips are a vivid red. The copy reads:

Why 6,000,000 women who used to carry a little red book now carry a little red lipstick. Beauty makes a statement. And when nail polish becomes political, and fashion becomes philosophy, Allure magazine will be there. With reporting about fragrance and fitness, cosmetics and culture, travel and trends. Allure: the revolutionary beauty.

How are we going to confront the fact that feminism has become another product, and that we are implicated in its commodification? That's one thing I hoped *Feminism and Institutions* would do: front the facts of complicity with social institutions, examine the complexities of shifting allegiances and conflicting commitments by engaging men and women in dialogue (Kauffman 1989b). Complicity is not a pleasant topic. One of the sobering discoveries I've made as a feminist is that institutions shape us more than we shape them. No one in 1972 could have predicted that feminism would make such remarkable inroads in our educational, legal, civil institutions. Nor did anyone dream that the Equal Rights Amendment would fail, that the nation would so passionately embrace neo-conservatism, that the world would be gripped again by the fervor of fundamentalism. Despite our desire to believe in the myth of (Enlightenment) progress, such are the facts. One of the profound paradoxes confronting feminists in the 1990s is that despite the massive transformations feminism has wrought, we are facing increasingly intransigent conservative powers that will remain in force far into the next century. (If he lasts as long as Thurgood Marshall, Clarence Thomas will be on the bench until 2031.) I wanted to see if it was possible to protest against feminism's commodification *and* to attack the premises of bourgeois individualism – the cornerstone supporting the American mythology of the individual as a unique, coherent, unified self.

One of the ways that feminism obviously co-operates in promoting that ideology is through literature. The case of Doris Lessing's *The Golden Notebook* is illustrative. The novel, published in 1962, is usually heralded as one of the first manifestos of the modern women's liberation movement. Anna Wulf is represented as suffering a schizophrenic "breakdown" at the hands of sexist society; since her "illness" results in a paralysis of the will and a writing block, evidence of her "cure" is that the novel commences with her novella "Free Women." Fiction is thus reduced to a tragic representation of life; "life" is reduced to a tale of individual malaise. The implicit message is that you cannot change society, only yourself. Such interpretations perpetuate narcissism and personal passivity instead of inspiring political action and social change (Ohmann 1983; Newton and Rosenfelt 1985). In fact, the novel is a sustained critique of subjectivity and of the individual's obsession with the personal. Ella (one of Anna Wulf's multiple "selves") reflects, "How boring these emotions are that we're caught in and can't get free of, no matter how much we want to" (Lessing 1962: 318).[3] Far from focusing on the individual, the novel disassembles the history of the twentieth century, ranging from Stalinist Russia to Algeria, Korea, China, Africa, America and Indochina. Lessing insists that what we call the psyche is influenced as much by social, political and economic traumas as by the personal. Here's an antidote to individualism from Lessing herself:

> When *The Golden Notebook* came out, I was astonished that people got so emotional about that book, one way or another. They didn't bother to see, even to look at, how it was shaped... .What I'm trying to say is that it was a detached book. It was a failure, of course, for if it had been a success, then people wouldn't get so damned emotional when I didn't want them to be.
>
> (Howe 1967: 311–13)

Lessing's only failure, in my view, was to underestimate readers' and reviewers' capacity to fold all attempts to go beyond what is now known as "the representational fallacy" back into the criteria of bourgeois realism – the view of literature as a reflection of individual experience. Elaine Showalter, for example, insists that Lessing "will have to face the limits of her own fiction very soon if civilization survives... .Either she will have to revise her apocalyptical prophecies (like other millenarians), or confront, once again, the struggling individual" (Showalter 1976: 313). But in Lessing's view, it is precisely the ideology Showalter endorses which may lead to apocalypse, for the individual cannot be confronted in isolation, separated from a complex matrix of international politics, environmental issues, multinational economics and global military conflict. Margaret Atwood chillingly depicts the consequences of that ideology in *The Handmaid's Tale*: apocalypse is inevitable if we continue to be sunk in subjectivity. Atwood almost seems to take Showalter's ideas to their absurd but logical conclusion; the novel is a sustained parody of the theory of gynocriticism: "You wanted a women's culture. Well, now there is one. It isn't what you meant" (Atwood 1986:127). In many ways, the same prophecies Lessing made in 1962 are reaccentuated and defamiliarized by Atwood twenty-four years later: organizing military coups, destabilizing governments, resettling "undesirables" and repressing civil liberties have all come to seem "normal." When *The Handmaid's Tale* appeared in 1986, few of us were aware of the extent to which her dystopia was already a reality in some parts of the world: Nicolae Ceausescu forced women to bear up to five children to increase the nation's power, and women were subjected to forced gynecological examinations every three months to make sure they hadn't had abortions. The enormity of these crimes has only come to the world's attention since the Rumanian Revolution in 1989, although Atwood explicitly describes these horrors in the novel's historical note:

> Rumania ... had anticipated Gilead in the eighties by banning all forms of birth control, imposing compulsory pregnancy tests on the female population, and linking promotion and wage increases to fertility.
>
> (Atwood 1986: 305)

Lessing and Atwood wonder what drives people collectively to embrace their own repression. What vicissitudes of psychic life account for the appeal of fascism? Experimental novelists have been trying to lead us away from the ideology of individualism and towards avant-garde conceptualizations for the past seventy-five years, but academic critics have frequently recuperated and reprocessed them like American cheese – bland, but familiar. As a feminist literary critic I want texts to challenge the boundaries of realism, of genre, of narrative, not to subordinate the (anti-representational, anti-bourgeois, anti-narrative) other into the same – the same old story.

In the past decade, many feminists have either challenged or surmounted the dichotomy between Anglo-American New Criticism and French poststructuralism. Many more (myself included) have practically re-tooled in order to incorporate materialist analyses. Didn't we say goodbye to personal testimony, with its valorization of the power and autonomy of the individual psyche, a long time ago? As Teresa de Lauretis observed in 1984:

> What we call "Experience" should instead be defined as a process shaped coequally by the relation of the inside and the outside: Experience has a mobile relation to the reality it encounters, the subjectivity it assumes, and the discursive practices within which it unfolds. Subjectivity is constructed from experience, but what one comprehends as subjective are in fact material, economic, and interpersonal social and historical relations.
>
> (de Lauretis 1984: ix)

In fact, however, the appeal to the personal and the concomitant repudiation of "theory" seems to be making a pretty snappy comeback, presaged in 1983 by Elaine Showalter's "Critical Cross-Dressing: Male Feminists and the Woman of the Year," which warns feminists of the "seductions" of "male Theory" in general and poststructuralism in particular (Showalter 1983). The notion that feminists are being "seduced" by so-called "male Theory" has persisted throughout the decade. Barbara Christian reinforces Showalter's view that "Theory" is a passing fashion when she argues that literature has been taken over by western philosophers who are intimidating people of color, feminists, radical critics, and creative writers with a language "which mystifies rather than clarifies our condition, making it possible for a few people who know that particular language to control the critical scene" (Christian 1989: 229).[4]

In my view, the languages of critical theory are difficult because of their foundations in disciplines which were long isolated from literary studies. That the New Critics actively sought such isolation for ideological purposes has been well documented.[5] But the sentiment is none the less representative of a current *strain* (in both senses of the word) in feminism. Seduced by "male Theory," we have lost touch, so the argument goes, with the revolutionary fervor of the first wave of feminism, and only by once again focusing on our own consciousness, can we recapture the spirit of an earlier age.

But isn't it at least possible that rather than blaming ("male") Theory, we must confront a totally transformed economic and historical moment? The only sure thing about all idyllic epochs, as Raymond Williams once observed, is that they are always gone. Let's face it: that's true of feminist idylls too. Perhaps we should recall some of our mistakes in the idyllic old days, like Patricia Spacks' disclaimer that she did not discuss the work of black women in *The Female Imagination* because she was "reluctant and unable to construct theories about experiences [she hasn't] had" (Spacks 1975: 5). Remember the searing question Alice Walker asked? "Spacks never lived in 19th century Yorkshire, so why theorize about the Brontës?" (Walker 1983: 372). Walker attacked the theoretical weakness and unexamined assumptions of bourgeois individualism in (white) feminist literary criticism. (Below, I discuss some mistakes in my own earlier scholarship.)

In "Me and My Shadow," Jane Tompkins similarly warns that theory is "one of the patriarchal gestures women and men ought to avoid." She argues that "the female subject par excellence, which is her self and her experiences, has once more been elided by literary criticism" (Tompkins 1989: 122).[6] To Tompkins, feminism's function is to facilitate self-discovery about one's victimization at the hands of patriarchy, to idealize woman's superior moral sense, her "Sentimental Power" (Tompkins, 1985).[7]

The cumulative effect of this approach is to discourage investigation of any complicating factors that may weaken the stance of victimization or moral superiority. It avoids the complicated question of collusion and complicity either in one's own oppression, or with institutions. The underlying premise is that writing reflects a world already bathed in the emotional light that the solitary woman projects. This strain of feminism thus resurrects the mirror and the lamp of Romanticism, the movement most closely aligned with the expressive theory of art. The criteria of value are sincerity and authenticity, which inevitably lock us back into the very dichotomies (male intellect versus female intuition; head versus body, etc.) that so many other feminists have spent so much time trying to dismantle. Ironically, the argument that women can only write about themselves has been the cornerstone of *sexist* criticism of women writers since Sappho (Kauffman 1986). This hyperbolically sexualized rhetoric none the less persists, refiguring the feminist as Clarissa, virtuous victim who must vigilantly ward off the masculine seductions of loveless, disembodied "Theory." Nancy Miller confesses, "Barthes has seduced me"; she also refers to "the appeal of a headier (sexier ...) destabilization from deconstructive, psychoanalytic, and neo-Marxist perspectives... .The chapters of this book all testify to my awareness of their seductions" (Miller 1988: 3, 17).[8] If we keep perpetuating this tired rhetoric, feminist criticism *will* – like Clarissa – end up starving itself to death.

What "male Theory" is hurting most, such critics agree, is women's *feelings*. Says Tompkins: "I'm tired of the conventions that keep discussions of epistemology ... segregated from meditations on what is happening ... inside my heart ... I have to deal with the trashing of emotion, and with my anger against it" (Tompkins 1989: 122–3, 138). Christian's words are almost identical: she yearns for the integration "between feeling/knowledge, rather than the split between the abstract and the emotional" (Christian 1989: 229). This integration, she argues, would allow the black woman to "pursue herself as subject" (ibid: 235). Such protests belie a nostalgia for a clear, transparent language that never did exist. Self-division does not result from some plot by theorists to persecute writers.

Instead, the vicissitudes of psychic life are far more complex, as is language's mastery over us, with all its internal tensions and contradictions. The yearnings for integration and unity fly in the face of the discoveries in linguistics, psycho-analysis and poststructuralism about the construction of the subject – namely that we are always *beside ourselves* in multiple senses. Striving for integration through self-expression can only be viewed as a quixotic enterprise when one considers the structure of the unconscious. The political efficacy of such self-regard (in both senses of the word) is also questionable. Moreover, what is happening "inside our hearts" is as much subject to convention as are discussions of epistemology, as my discussion of love made clear earlier. The ideology informing such yearnings for integration is seldom made explicit, nor is it clear how such integration could advance the collective cause of social justice for women, African-Americans, or African-American women.

To return to my discomfort with the use of the collective "we": how can "we" overcome the tendency to be hermetically sealed, like Clarissa in her coffin, in academic obsessions? The last thing I want is for feminism to embalm itself by becoming the new orthodoxy. On the one hand, we maintain that the university is a microcosm of society; that the work we do in academia is political work. I think that is true. Nevertheless, social injustice and racial inequality cannot be conflated with a contest of faculties – a distinction Tompkins, Christian and Miller all blithely ignore. Tompkins confesses that she once told a panel at the Modern Language Association Convention to " 'get theory' because I thought that doing theory would admit us to the big leagues" (Tompkins 1989: 122). Nancy Miller's concept of politics is bounded in a nutshell: the seminar table and fellowship panel: she broods over "problems between 'us' and 'them' [which] loomed large in institutional terms – tenure, promotions, journals, fellowships, etc." We can't do political work within the university unless we constantly remind ourselves that it is a sphere of relative privilege and entitlement – a reminder which makes it difficult to sympathize with Miller's unabashed confession that "To the extent that I was vividly untenured, I of course worried at all times about everyone" (Miller 1988: 13). Beyond the politics of the profession – ranging from Christian's indictment of those whom she perceives as controlling the "critical scene" to MLA panels and academic "big leagues" – lies a vaster political arena and a harsher national mood. The allure of personal testimony makes it easy to conflate the *feminist* with the *academic* perspective. Like looking through the wrong end of a telescope, all one sees is in miniature.

Radical work goes on in universities, but only if one turns the telescope around. One of the advantages of the theoretical project of dismantling traditional disciplines and of undoing the traditional divisions – the *disciplining* of academics – is that the interrelations between culture and society, power and ideology can no longer masquerade as innocent or invisible. Whereas Christian protests that "there has been a takeover in the literary world of Western philosophers from the old literary elite, the neutral humanists" (1989: 225), she does not seem aware that "neutral humanists" is a *non sequitur*, if not an oxymoron. Christian is dedicated to offering new readings to promote a black female literary tradition, but new readings alone will not ensure the preservation of that tradition. Ironically, Marxists, feminist theorists, African-Americanists, and students of popular culture have all contributed to exposing what is at stake in the production of literary texts and movements. One of the most exhilarating facets of reconceptualizing academic study today is the opportunity to help students comprehend this process and to demystify its operation. Continually exposing and undermining the construction of knowledge is vital to every project of redefining feminism. That project is perpetual – and perpetually threatened by co-option and commodification.

One strain of feminism that has been commodified most successfully is the therapeutic model. Tompkins chides those who see pop psychologists such as M. Scott Peck and Leo Busgalia as "mushy" and "sentimental" (Tompkins 1989: 138), but she fails to see how by endorsing them she uncritically perpetuates individualism. What cannot be ignored is how such books promote that ideology: the individual – removed from history, economics, *and even from the unconscious* – is depicted as someone who always has choices, and whose choices are always "free." Adversity is merely the product of a "bad attitude, negative thinking, or low self-esteem." To be a subject (to recognize oneself as a free and unique being) is itself an effect of subjection to ideology. In this light, it is clearly a delusion that by throwing off the straitjacket of formal expository prose, anyone will be revealing her "true," unique self. Writing about yourself does not liberate you, it just shows how ingrained the ideology of freedom through self-expression is in our thinking.

It's worth mentioning the other bestsellers which have proliferated recently, disseminating similar messages: *Men who hate Women and Women who Love them; The Dance-Away Lover; The Peter Pan Principle; Smart Women, Foolish Choices; Men Who Can't Love;* and *Women who Love too Much.* One cannot ignore the ways in which these books exploit feminism as a commodity, complete with sophisticated and expensive marketing research campaigns to target consumers. Indeed, the audience for such books seems to be insatiable. Not only are these books targeted for an exclusively female audience, but they are relentless in their insistence on "normality" – not to mention heterosexuality. In the guise of teaching women how to deal with their feelings, these books feed on the media hype about the so-called "man-shortage." They assiduously avoid analysis of historical and socio-economic factors, reproducing instead the tired stereotypes of Woman as Victim, as masochist, as "Love Junkie" who needs to be "cured" of her "addiction" to love through a strict regimen of group therapy and confession. Femininity as disease: where have we heard that before? These are the books that are seriously engaged in reproducing femininity for mass-market consumption.

What is not negligible in "the air of our times and the state of our relation to what we read, write, do, say, live, etc." is how resilient individualism is, and how relentlessly it co-opts feminism. While we are being exhorted to focus on our feelings, a lot of people are falling through the cracks in our society. It is no accident that the hysterical hyperbole about "family values" reached its apex just as the actual kinship system began to recede (Mitchell 1975:227–31). The same anomaly applies to individualism: the hyperbole about the individual masks an alarming erosion of civil liberties in the United States. The bathtub has been gradually heating for some time now.

• September 1989: the US Court of Appeals overturns a lower court order to shut down the "high security unit" (HSU) at the Federal Correctional Institution in Lexington, Kentucky. Designed specifically to control women convicted of politically motivated crimes, the HSU has been denounced by the American Civil Liberties Union as a "living tomb"; by Amnesty International as "deliberately and gratuitously oppressive"; and by the Soviet Union as a US human rights violation. Gilda Zwerman's extensive research on women in American prisons reveals that this High Security Unit

> utilizes and manipulates the "terrorist" label in order to justify the "special" treatment of political prisoners [and represents] an expansion in the use of incapacitation, surveillance, and deterrence as mechanisms for social control and repression to a degree heretofore unprecedented in the U.S. correctional system.[9]

Along with Alejandrina Torres, a Puerto Rican nationalist, Susan Rosenberg was HSU's first inmate, and remained there for nearly two years. Convicted of carrying weapons and explosives for a radical group, Rosenberg is serving fifty-eight years for a crime that – had she "merely" been a terrorist at an abortion clinic – would have garnered her a suspended sentence.

• 7 October 1989: The Senate passes a House-approved amendment, sponsored by Senator Jesse Helms, preventing federal funding of "obscene" art, and requiring all recipients of National Endowment for the Arts and National Endowment for the Humanities grants to sign an affidavit certifying that the monies will not be used to produce works that contain "depictions of sadomasochism, homoeroticism, the sexual exploitation of children or individuals engaged in sex acts and which, when taken as a whole, do not have serious literary, artistic, political or scientific merit." Reminiscent of the loyalty oaths of the 1950s, the three categories are presented as if they were synonymous "perversions"; who will define "serious merit" remains unspecified. The cumulative effect is to force artists to steer clear of what they think the public might find indecent, which is a far broader category than obscenity.[10] Playwright Arthur Miller observes that self-censorship is already so widespread that it has allowed freedom to be "killed without a trace."[11]

• 6 February 1990: A bill introduced in the Washington state legislature, sponsored by Republican Jim West, would make it a crime for people under the age of 18 to engage in sex, including "heavy petting." The fine: 90 days in jail and $5000, unless they decide to marry.

• 21 April 1990: The Rev. Donald Wildmon and the American Family Association target photographer David Wojnarowicz's work by taking two homosexual images out of context from a larger collage and mass-mailing the enlarged images to every member of Congress, as well as to 178,000 pastors on the American Family Association's mailing list. Wojnarowicz, now dead from AIDS, filed suit and won a Pyrrhic legal victory: Wildmon was asked to send a "corrective letter" to his subscribers and Wojnarowicz was awarded one dollar.

• September 1990 to January 1991: eleven out of fifteen fundraising letters from three leading Religious Right groups targeted homosexuality as the most dangerous menace within America today.[12]

I am not implying that these incidents are unproblematic. They are not equivalent to one another. They may not even be among the worst examples of the current state of affairs. I've purposely included injustices that might not normally be regarded as specifically *feminist* concerns, because it is precisely the interconnection of feminist issues with other injustices that urgently needs our attention in the 1990s. My examples are symptoms of other dilemmas facing the nation: how far are we willing to go in suspending the Constitution to combat drug trafficking, pornography, public health, crime? Wherever we turn, the most vulnerable institutions and individuals are under attack: not just the arts and humanities, but women, children, immigrants, the aged, the poor, the infirm. The aim is to widen the net of surveillance, to create language and action that transforms police campaigns into a " 'war on   ' " (fill in the blank). We no longer question either the desirability or the necessity of surveillance and punishment. What does it say about our society that we can only conceive of social problems and solutions in terms of crime and disease? When the infrastructure of our cities is collapsing, when millions are hungry and homeless, when our financial institutions are imploding, how do we still find the means to siphon off enormous resources to fund preposterous pornography commissions, to put rap singers on trial, to demand urine samples from employees, to persecute those with AIDS? The right has replaced the specter of communism with enemies from within – within the body politic and within the body: leftists and feminists within the university, micrological bogeys, viruses in the immune system, in computers, in the womb (Haraway 1989; Petchesky 1987; Treichler 1988). Under the banner of "normative health," repression is proliferating at a prodigious pace.

I'm conscious of the paradox involved in engaging in a critique of individualism on the one hand, and arguing for the preservation of civil rights on the other. The mythology of individual freedom and choice is inflated in direct proportion to the erosion of civil liberties, which are undergoing the most massive assault since the McCarthy era. That assault is intricately interwoven with an assault on the poor, the disenfranchised, the intellectually, politically and sexually suspect. The right has turned the rhetoric of equality against its citizens: "equal rights for unborn women" and "crime victims' rights," like the "Pro-Life" anti-abortion campaign, cunningly disguise the repression which is actually being promoted. To offer one more example: the Senate Judiciary Committee, whose wisdom and good judgment is so fresh in our minds since the Clarence Thomas–Anita Hill travesty, will soon vote on a "pornography victims' compensation act," which would allow the so-called "victims" of pornography to sue producers and distributors of films, books, etc. "The Accused" is one type of film that could be removed from shelves, since it depicts a gang-rape.[13] For the first time in history, the logic of civil rights is turned *away* from its traditional support of expression: censorship would mean a *furthering* of civil rights (Downs 1989: 60). Feminists can protest against these repressions without necessarily endorsing the ideology of individualism. We can agree that the individual is the product of power, and still recognize that, today in America, that power is becoming increasingly concentrated among fundamentalists and conservatives, whether one turns to education, politics, religion, media, advertising, economics or the law.

What can I as a feminist literary critic do? I can address the misapprehensions of representation: What has led us to view symbols and representations as dangerous menaces, the dissemination of which must be controlled? I can use my own personal history in a critique of the underlying assumptions about person and story, as I have tried to do here. Moreover, I'm the perfect candidate to consider critically "women's ways of knowing" and "sentimental power" because my first book, *Discourses of Desire*, was at some points an implicit endorsement. In one passage, I remark:

> I have tried to expose the devaluation of the sentimental as another form of repression, with ramifications as serious at the end of the twentieth century as sexual repression was at the end of the nineteenth.
>
> (Kauffman 1986: 316)

I now see that such an approach to sentimentality has led in directions I couldn't have predicted – although I now think I should have been able to predict them. Feminism's greatest strength has always been its capacity for self-critique, and it would be a great pity to see that capacity muted by the insistence on consensus. Feminist criticism has confronted numerous dilemmas in the past decade: how to engage in poststructuralist theory without losing sight of the material body? What does it mean to be constituted as a subject in and of language? Which texts (and which ideologies) survive and why? I think we still have the most to learn from the ruptures, limitations, and contradictions in our thinking. In *Special Delivery*, I propose and enact a conscious strategy of what I call "infidelity": one can show how one's own arguments may subsequently become inadequate; one can even confess how one's desires may be in conflict with the theoretical stances one endorses. One can highlight rather than blithely eliding the paradoxes that are irreconcilable, the consequences that are irremediable. As *Special Delivery* went to press, I discovered a similar argument in Sandra Harding's *Whose Science? Whose Knowledge?* In a chapter entitled "Reinventing Ourselves as Other," she exhorts us to provide "traitorous" identities and social locations, and to engage in traitorous readings of the assumptions we make in and about texts (Harding 1991: 288–95). Such assumptions include racist, regional, heterosexist and sexist assumptions. I would add that sexism infects both genders; as a discursive construct, can't we finally put to rest that *bête noire,* "the white male"?

As a feminist, I have not everything to do, but something. Even while endorsing poststructuralist strategies, I cannot wait for the revolution that has no model, to come before I act. (But I *can* continue to deconstruct the terms in which the arguments are framed, and the assumed ideology underlying them.) Rather than contributing to the successful working of the machinery of society, I want my work to be a counterfriction to the machine. Despite the fact that my family were the black sheep of generations of Protestants, I wholeheartedly endorse the word's etymology in *protest.*

We are living in a politically exhausted culture, and still responding to it with exhausted genres. Personal testimony can sometimes be eloquent, but it is not an infinitely inexhaustible genre. Too often it reinforces the blind belief that we are all intrinsically interesting, unique, that we deserve to be happy. My happiness, frankly, is not very important in the grand scheme of things. I never thought feminism was about happiness. I thought it was about justice. The times demand a frontal attack on the complex political alliances – civil, legal, economic, educational, religious – that are acting in conspiracy, explicitly and implicitly, to boil us alive. Atwood is right: it takes effort to ignore, and a united front ill serves feminism at this particular historical moment. While some warn against betraying "mothers," or trashing the "sisterhood," this merely reveals the relentless rhetoric of familialism (another staple of bourgeois ideology) in yet another guise. Meanwhile, far more serious betrayals are unfolding before our eyes. When I began this essay, the Helms debate was just heating up; it already seems long ago and far away. In fact, as you read them, didn't the dates I mentioned seem antiquated? Have they already ceased to alarm us? Now, in September 1991, it is abundantly apparent just how cheap and easy personal testimony is: Clarence Thomas is relying on the same maudlin strategy to silence dissent at the confirmation hearings for his appointment to the Supreme Court. Deflecting every political challenge, every question of intentionality, and every issue of constitutional interpretation, he invokes the supreme authority of personal experience: nobody knows the troubles he's seen because he's from Pinpoint, Georgia, son of a sharecropper. His invocation to personal authority disguises his opportunism, his indebtedness to the civil rights movement he now repudiates, his cynicism. Today's grifters aren't in Vegas; they're testifying in a circus-like atmosphere[14] on Capitol Hill.

Feminism is far more than the effort to "express" "women's personal experience," and its "territory" extends far beyond the bonds of family, beyond the lecture hall, beyond academia. Growing up among grifters, I learned early how illusions are fabricated, how false piety smells. That doesn't mean I have no illusions, no hopes, dreams, etc. It does mean that I want continually to cast doubt on the status of knowledge – *even as we are in the process of constructing it* – a perpetual project. By resisting the flattering temptation to talk solely to and about ourselves, we can concentrate on defying repressions that have already come to seem "normal." The pace of contemporary events is like a speeding convertible; we can ill afford to be enchanted by the rear-view mirror. Rather than mythologizing ourselves or the past, can't we total those disabled vehicles and – at long last – wave goodbye to all that?

NOTES

1 The connections between the ideology of bourgeois individualism and the novel as a genre have been made by Nancy Armstrong, *Desire and Domestic Fiction: A Political History of the Novel*, Oxford: Oxford University Press, 1987; Lennard J. Davis, *Resisting Novels: Ideology and Fiction*, New York: Methuen, 1987; and Linda S. Kauffman (1992), among many other recent studies.

2 In March 1991, Kay Austen won ten years' back pay, ten years' future pay, and extensive damages in the first court ruling to find the University liable for sexual discrimination. Federal Judge Samuel P. King ruled that Austen was subjected to "harassment, retaliation and discrimination" by her department chair, and the judge went on to castigate the entire university: "the record is clear that the University of Hawaii administration closed ranks to support him against her."

3 My views of *The Golden Notebook* and *The Handmaid's Tale* are developed in greater depth in Kauffman (1992).

4 *Gender and Theory* is structured dialogically so that each essay is followed by a critique: see Michael Awkward's "Appropriative Gestures: Theory and Afro-American Literary Criticism," in response to Christian, and Gerald M. MacLean's "Citing the Subject," in response to Tompkins.

5 See Terry Eagleton, *Literary Theory: An Introduction*, Minneapolis: University of Minnesota Press, 1983; Frank Lentricchia, *Criticism and Social Change*, Chicago: University of Chicago Press, 1983; and Janet Batsleer, Tony Davies, Rebecca O'Rourke and Chris Weedon, *Rewriting English: Cultural Politics of Gender and Class*, London: Methuen, 1985.

6 I suspect (and sincerely hope) that I am the "unfriendly reader" to whom Tompkins refers in her essay, because critique is an invaluable aspect of engagement between women who are friends as well as feminists; conversely, by generously playing a role the of "unfriendly reader" of *Special Delivery*, Jane immeasurably improved my book.

7 See also Mary Field Belencky, Blythe McVicker Clinchy, Nancy Rule Goldberger, Jill Mattuck Tarule, *Women's Ways of Knowing: The Development of Self, Voice, and Mind*, New York: Basic Books, 1986. Carol Gilligan's work has also been instrumental in promoting this view; in addition to *In A Different Voice* (Cambridge, MA.: Harvard University Press, 1982), see "Joining the Resistance: Psychology, Politics, Girls and Women," *Michigan Quarterly Review* 29: 4 (fall 1990): 501–36.

8 In *Getting Personal*, Miller recycles the same rhetoric to defend Tompkins and attack Gerald MacLean in their exchange in *Gender and Theory*. For an alternative interpretation, see Mary Poovey's review article in *Modern Philology* (May 1991): 415–20.

9 Cited by Patricia Golan, "American's Most Dangerous Woman?" *On the Issues* 13 (1989): 15–21.

10 *The New York Times*, 10 November 1990.

11 *The Washington Post*, 13 November 1990. The *New York Times* reported on 18 September 1991, that government documents were released which show that the National Endowment for the Arts bowed to political pressure in rescinding the grants it had initially recommended for Karen Finley, John Fleck, Holly Hughes and Tim Miller (*New York Times*, p. Bl, 3). The next day, the Senate voted 68 to 28 to prohibit the NEA from awarding grants that would promote materials that depict "sexual or excretory activities or organs" in an "offensive way". (*New York Times*, 20 September 1991, p. B2).

12 *Right-Wing Watch* 1:4 (February 1991): 2.

13 *The New York Times*, 7 November 1991.
14 Or should I say *peep*-show atmosphere? After this essay went to press, the Senate Judiciary Committee was forced to postpone the Senate vote in order to give the appearance of taking sexual harassment seriously: law professor Anita Hill testified that Thomas sexually harassed her when she worked for him in the Department of Education and the Equal Employment Opportunity Commission – the very agency which is supposed to investigate such abuses. On 15 October, 1991, the Senate confirmed Clarence Thomas's nomination by a vote of 52–48. The same senators who glossed over Thomas's credibility when he insisted that he never discussed Roe v. Wade felt no compunction about trying to destroy the credibility of Professor Hill, labelling her a "perjurer," a "fantasist," and alluding repeatedly to her "proclivities." Ironically, in the kangaroo court of the media, Clarence Thomas "won" because his testimony was passionate and personal: as if suddenly remembering that he was black, he compared the Senate hearings to a "high tech lynching." Anita Hill was deemed too cool, dispassionate, impersonal. Few spectacles so vividly demonstrate the abuses of personal testimony; with this one, I rest my case.

REFERENCES

Atwood, Margaret (1986) *The Handmaid's Tale*, Boston: Houghton Mifflin.

Barthes, Roland (1985) *The Grain of the Voice: Interviews, 1962-1980*, trans. Linda Coverdale, New York: Hill & Wang.

Christian, Barbara (1989) "The Race for Theory," in Linda Kauffmann (ed.) *Gender and Theory: Dialogues on Feminist Criticism*, Oxford: Basil Blackwell, 225-37.

de Lauretis, Teresa (1984) *Alice Doesn't: Feminism, Semiotics, Cinema*, Bloomington: Indiana University Press.

Debord, Guy (1967) *La société du spectacle*, Editions Buchet-Chastel.

Derrida, Jacques (1980) *The Post Card: From Socrates to Freud and Beyond*, trans. Alan Bass, Chicago: University of Chicago Press.

Downs, Donald Alexander (1989) *The New Politics of Pornography*, Chicago: University of Chicago Press.

Haraway, Donna (1989) "The Biopolitics of Postmodern Bodies: Determinations of Self in Immune System Discourse," *Differences* 1(1): 3-43.

Harding, Sandra (1991) *Whose Science? Whose Knowledge?* Ithaca: Cornell University Press.

Howe, Florence (1967) "A Talk with Doris Lessing," *Nation* (6 March), 311-13.

Kauffman Linda S. (1986) *Discourses of Desire: Gender, Genre, and Epistolary Fictions*, Ithaca: Cornell University Press.

——(ed.) (1989a) *Gender and Theory: Dialogues on Feminist Criticism*, Oxford and New York: Basil Blackwell.

——(ed.) (1989b) *Feminism and Institutions: Dialogues on Feminist Theory*, Oxford and New York: Basil Blackwell.

——(1992) *Special Delivery: Epistolary Modes in Modern Fiction*, Chicago: University of Chicago Press.

Lessing, Doris (1962) *The Golden Notebook*, New York: Simon & Schuster, reprinted Bantam Books, 1981.

Miller, Nancy K. (1988) *Subject to Change: Reading Feminist Writing*, New York: Columbia University Press.

——(1991) *Getting Personal: Feminist Occasions and other Autobiographical Acts*, New York: Routledge.

Mitchell, Juliet (1975) *Psychoanalysis and Feminism: Freud, Reich, Laing and Women*, New York: Vintage.

Newton, Judith and Deborah Rosenfelt (eds) (1985) *Feminist Criticism and Social Change: Sex, Class and Race in Literature and Culture*, New York: Methuen.

Ohmann, Richard (1983) "The Shaping of the Canon of U.S. Fiction, 1960–75," *Critical Inquiry* 10: 199–223.

Petchesky, Rosalind (1987) "Fetal Images: The Power of Visual Culture in the Politics of Reproduction," *Feminist Studies* 13(2): 263–92.

Showalter, Elaine (1977) *A Literature of Their Own: British Women Novelists from Brontë to Lessing*, Princeton: Princeton University Press.

——(1983) "Critical Cross-Dressing: Male Feminists and the Woman of the Year," *Raritan Review*, 3: 130–49.

Spacks, Patricia Meyer (1975) *The Female Imagination*, New York: Knopf.

Tompkins, Jane (1985) *Sensational Designs: The Cultural Work of American Fiction 1790–1860*, Oxford: Oxford University Press.

——(1989). "Me and My Shadow," in Linda Kauffman (ed.) *Gender and Theory*, Oxford and New York: Blackwell.

Treichler, Paula (1988) "AIDS, Homophobia, and Biomedical Discourse: An Epidemic of Signification," in Douglas Crimp (ed.) *AIDS: Cultural Analysis, Cultural Activism*, Cambridge, MA: MIT Press.

Walker, Alice (1983) *In Search of Our Mothers' Gardens*, San Diego: Harcourt Brace Jovanovich.

Chapter 10

Feminism, the roaring girls and me

Margo Hendricks

BEGINNINGS

Since 1983, my intellectual work has been intricately connected with notions of "speaking," of making heard women's voices which have been silenced. The women I have centered my research upon I affectionately refer to as the "Roaring Girls": playwrights and dramatic characters who render problematic historical conceptualizations of gender, race, sexuality and class. The original "roaring girl," Moll Cutpurse (Mary Frith), was a seventeenth-century woman who transgressed both social and literary norms. Moll wore a man's jerkin and a woman's skirt, her manner was definitely non-feminine, and yet she never allowed anyone to ignore the fact that she was a woman. In many ways, women playwrights have been forced to follow a similar path in order to achieve some measure of success in the theatre. These women have "mastered" the narrative discourse of two communities; and, like Moll, they too have come to know the paradox of identity.

To some degree, my relationship with academia mirrors this situation. Yet, upon reflection, I am not surprised at what I find myself doing as a career, though laboring in academia was not my original intention when I applied to college. At 28 I entered a state university with aspirations to be a history major and corporate lawyer. A confident first-year student, I enrolled in an upper division Renaissance English literature course. My first examination received a marginal grade, and the professor had the dubious distinction of being the first individual to give me a "C" on a literature assignment. Despite sound advice to drop the course and retake it once I had met the prerequisite, I insisted on completing the class. The outcome of my obstinacy was a fascination with early modern history and culture, and the acquisition of a mentor.

Dr Catharine Gannon was the first academic to provoke me to reflect on the absence of faculty of color in the English department. On her advice I entered the graduate program in English at the University of California, Riverside. One of three students of color (all African-Americans, two nearing the completion of their studies), I pursued my doctorate in Renaissance English literature in an environment made somewhat less problematic by an ethnically and sexually diverse community of graduate students. In addition, I had the support of three individuals who, like Dr Gannon, "saw nothing wrong with a black woman studying Middleton, Marlowe, Shakespeare and others." None the less, despite this enabling environment, I quickly became aware of my "status" as a rarity – a "minority" doctoral student and, more importantly, one who specialized in something other than "ethnic" literature.

For people ideologically identified as "minorities" this academic positionality is a familiar one. One grows accustomed to being invited to speak on minority issues, giving the necessary slant on race and ethnicity. My situation proved to be troubling for those individuals whose own assumptions about the authenticity of experience required, if not a white male, at least a white female. Though on the surface I represented the order of things, with my choice of literary study I had disrupted the validity of cultural identity. Instead of being invited to speak directly to issues of validated ethnic or racial differences, I was continually being asked, "How did you end up in Renaissance literary studies?"

FEMINISM, 1979

My engagement with feminist scholarship, ironically, was instigated not by questions related to racial or class analyses but by an essay on Shakespeare written by Gayle Greene. I was concerned with the growing elitism of feminist theory, the unexamined acceptance of the idea of "naturally based" binary oppositions in critical discourse, and the general absence of attention to historical agency. With the same obstinacy that characterized my refusal to drop the Renaissance literature course, I embarked on a "politically correct" feminist reading of early modern dramatic literature and what might appropriately be conceptualized as "feminist drama." My expectation was that my dissertation would resolve once and for all the tension between Marxist theory and feminism. So I began a study of gender relations in early modern English city comedy.

By the time I completed my dissertation, I had begun to experience a sense of critical disjunction: I was both a feminist and an historian but generally not at the same moment nor with the same degree of clarity. My dilemma arose not only from a perception that historical agency increasingly was being elided in much of feminist theory, but also from the sense that much of this discourse seemed to perpetuate a monocentric definition of history and gender. In other words, as a scholar of early modern English literature and a woman of African ancestry, more often than not I was faced with the erasure, elision, assimilation or obliteration of cultural histories with which I identified. What was even more profoundly disturbing was the sense of feminist inattentiveness to the racialized politics of early modern English colonialism and its long-term effect on the women of Africa, Asia and the Americas.

Principally, and perhaps naïvely, I expected feminist scholarship to incorporate Jean E. Howard's observation that the concern of any type of historical criticism is the "practical business of reading [a] text and the critical business of explaining the terms of that reading" (Howard 1986: 30). As a result of this expectation my own attempt to problematize English city comedy evolved in ways parallel yet often contradictory to most strands of American feminist criticism. The voices of Howard, Lynda Boose, Joan Kelly and Michèle Barrett, however, emerged as a real presence in my writing as I grappled with the metaphors of gender and class. Yet it was when I sought to theorize cultural identity that other, equally powerful voices surfaced: Valerie Smith, Gloria Hull, Cherríe Moraga, Barbara Smith, bell hooks and Angela Davis – all women of color, all willing to challenge a monolithic notion of Woman. In the end, the dissertation reflected not the thematic closure I had sought but an awareness that I had merely scratched the surface of the complexities of social identity.

FEMINISM, 1990

My professional career has come at a time of transition in the academy. Feminist politics has made it much easier to discover, create and strengthen feminist intellectual networks. Yet assumptions about what constitutes intellectual legitimacy continue to reflect traditional gender, race and class ideologies. While a growing number of my peers within early modern literary studies share the views of those who encouraged me to pursue Renaissance Studies, I find that I am still expected to justify my decision. It is not unusual for me to be interrogated, as a white student once did, as to why I did not specialize in African-American literature. Nor is it uncommon for an academic to approach me and begin a conversation about a favorite black woman writer. Most encounters, however, are like the one I experienced at a recent conference where a scholar of Renaissance literature introduced himself during lunch and, after a brief pause, asked my opinion of Henry Gates and his work on the trope "signifying monkey." Within a matter of seconds, I must admit, all of my great-grandmother's instructions about deference to age and wisdom evaporated, and the wall between decorum and irreverence collapsed beneath the weight of my sense of humor. I replied that I was unfamiliar with Gates' work since speaking monkeys did not loom large in the *Faerie Queene* or the *Laws of Ecclesiastical Polity*. Nonplussed, the astute scholar then commented on the problem of race in *Othello*. Amused, I explained that my dissertation examined the relationship between gender and city comedy. His discomfort clearly visible, the scholar muttered a few words in response before making his escape.

These moments are striking examples of the way in which ethnicity and gender automatically signal an intellectual identity. For individuals like the student and the scholar, my intellectual status is determined by the color of my skin, the notation on a birth certificate designating me "female," my sexual orientation, and presumptions about class. The "naturalness" of these categorical constructions not only hold legal and political legitimacy but historical validity as well for the scholar and student. And, as I have come to realize, these essentializing notions are not automatically checked at the gate when people enter colleges and universities.

My intrusion into Renaissance literary studies seriously contradicted preconceptions about appropriate lines of demarcation in university teaching. Additionally, my color and gender seemed to make questionable any possible insight I might have to offer about Shakespeare's or Milton's literary and cultural significance. What I understood and what the student and the scholar did not was the undeniable fact that Shakespeare's and Milton's culture is my own. My education (from kindergarten through doctorate) had been defined by the vision of early modern European humanists. Like the white student and the scholar, my intellect had been "cultivated" by a decidedly eurocentric and patriarchal educational system, even if my sense of myself had its origins in a predominantly black community.

What I also realized, of course, was the complicated intellectual position such politics often produced. And this awareness has become a form of empowerment, permitting me to survive cultural practices informed by racialized and sexualized conceptions of identity (Rothenberg 1990). I use the word "survive" not to indicate a feeling of victimization or marginalization but to suggest the uneasy truce which has developed between myself and academia. Such a truce can, at best, be only a deferral or a disruption in the politics of social identity.

Upon reflection, I now recognize that Moll Cutpurse's fluency in the discourses of two disparate communities was similarly a strategy of survival: her speech was "the dialogue of power and resistance, of refusal and recognition" (Hall 1990: 223). The question which her representation poses for my own theorizing, and for feminism in general, is "How can we stage this dialogue so that, finally, we can place it, without terror or violence, rather than being forever placed by it" (ibid.: 233)? Like Moll, I am fully conscious of the historical limitations imposed on my ability to alter perceptions that make of my sex and color a particular sign. Yet I am equally conscious of the danger of undervaluing the role of historical agency in the production of cultural identities.

Conceptualizations of gender, as well as of race or class or sexuality, have been based on a logic of essentialism. The way we think of ourselves, speak of ourselves, represent ourselves is constituted by our ability to claim a specific biologically based, cultural identity (Hall 1990: 233). I was not born black, nor female nor respectably middle class – these words were spoken at the moment of my birth to distinguish me from someone who is typecast as white, male and working class. From that moment, these labels became descriptive of an historical past and constitutive of an historical present. As points of reference, black, female and middle class have allowed me to produce and reproduce my identity even as they produce and reproduce an ambivalence similar to that of Moll Cutpurse. Even now, when I speak of a women's community or the African-American community I am aware of invoking a specific and exclusive commonality while also paradoxically refracting other aspects of my cultural identity (for example, geographical region, class, professional status and age).

Cornel West suggests that the "new cultural politics of difference" has emerged in response to "the precise circumstances of our present moment" in human social history (West 1990: 19). However, it seems that such politics may come to reify institutionalized definitions of personal identity. To be a "black woman" or a "woman of color" is not just a matter of recognizing differences. On the contrary, it is also, in many ways, a validation of the social processes which gave political and historical currency to the words. For the receiver of these utterances, any interaction between us will bear with it beliefs and assumptions about gender, about African-Americans, about slavery, about racial relations in the United States, about the economic conditions facing people of color, about black women's sexuality and so on.

While cultural politics may be on the ascendancy in academia, in the practical politics of the academy, what hasn't become fashionable is the increased presence of the historical subjects of this discourse. In 1989 23,172 doctorates were awarded to US citizens (of a total 34,319); nearly 8,400 of these doctorates were awarded to women and 2,097 to people of color. These demographics are somewhat deceptive since there is no gender breakdown within the ethnic groups and no indication whether women of color are counted twice. What is also interesting about these statistics is that the majority of doctorates awarded to these candidates occur in three disciplines: education, sociology and psychology. For women, on the other hand, literary studies remain the first choice in doctoral studies. Finally, the number of doctorates awarded to people of color has not kept pace with the number of bachelor's degrees awarded.

Despite the transformative effect cultural politics may have on social and literary theories, the employment status of women and people of color in academia has not reached a level where we might say true progress has been made. Sexism, racism, homophobia and classism will not disappear simply because cultural politics becomes a trope for our books, articles, and MLA special sessions. Nor will the declaration by colleges and universities that they are "committed to diversity" necessarily disengage the hierarchical political economy upon which ideologies of gender, race and class have been and continue to be based. On the contrary, the politics of difference stand dangerously close to reifying an historical marginality for women, people of color, lesbians and gays. Rather than being contingent or disrupted, the meanings of race, gender, sexuality and class as linguistic categories seem to be further stabilized as rhetorical badges of social identities. In the end, feminism and other political criticisms should be concerned about sustaining ideologies which may serve as effective tools for intellectual "crisis management" (Spivak 1990: 97).

FEMINISM, 2000

Since the seventeenth century the capitalist mode of production has generated, defined, circumscribed and recast the political choices available to women. But in their resistance and rebellions, women have acquired an awareness that identity is not just a question of who you are; from a political point of view, the more important query is who ultimately defines that identity. For Moll Cutpurse, who recognized that though her choice was limiting it was also politically extenuating, identity was not something to be imposed upon her by another. Four centuries later, feminist scholarship continues to challenge patriarchal definitions of identity by making "explicit [that] its moral and political aim" is to destabilize the gender hierarchies which Moll sought to resist. In doing so, feminism has greatly transformed the practice of writing social and intellectual history (West 1990: 31). Yet this may not be enough.

Having achieved a measure of academic legitimacy, perhaps it is time, as Barbara Christian suggests, for feminist scholars to "confront the positives and negatives of what it means to become institutionalized in universities" (Christian 1989: 73). Do we risk being implicated in fostering a complacency about difference, about identity, about our relationship to academia? Are we in danger of becoming polarized by the specificity of the "new [academic] politics of cultural identity"? Will institutional legitimacy enhance or undermine the oppositional politics of feminism as it becomes an established discipline within the academy? My questions suggest that, as feminism increases its participation in academic and theoretical debates, it must also evaluate the cost of that participation.

Feminism (and feminist scholarship), therefore, is at an intellectual and political crossroads *vis-à-vis* academia. The continued struggle for social change seems to require a different feminism: one critically engaged with current theoretical discussions, yet resistant to a type of political accommodation or stasis that institutionalization often engenders. Feminist scholars such as Meaghan Morris rightfully argue that, "since feminism has acted as one of the enabling conditions of discourse about postmodernism [and identity politics], it is therefore appropriate to use feminist work to frame these [theoretical] discussions, and not the other way around" (Morris 1990: 16). And, in the past few years, feminist scholarship has achieved a strong presence in literary studies. Yet that presence, increasingly, is more often perceived as part of the trilogy *gender, race and class* and not, it seems to me, as the theoretical "frame" Morris perhaps had in mind.

The future of feminist scholarship, as I view it, will involve developing political and theoretical strategies which will militate against this tendency without undervaluing the interconnectedness of gender, race, class, sexual orientation, age and other social categories which constitute cultural identity. Whether one is a black feminist, latina feminist, Asian feminist or white feminist, in the end the goal of political and intellectual activity is a shared commitment to transforming the lives of women and men. This is the history and practice of feminism.

REFERENCES

Thank you: Jeffry Fawcett, Jyotsna Singh, Don E. Wayne, Patricia Parker, Randy Nakayama, Lynda Boose, Thandeka, Libby Wood, Stephen Orgel, the PAPC Women's Caucus, The Stanford Humanities Center, and the students of my " Literary Patronage and Seventeenth-century Women Playwrights" course – who patiently listened. I would also like to express my gratitude to Gayle Greene and Coppélia Kahn for requesting the essay. Once again, Gayle has provoked me to reflect on my feminism.

Christian, B. (1989) "But What Do We Think We're Doing Anyway: The State of Black Feminist Criticism(s) or My Version of a Little Bit of History," in Cheryl A. Wall (ed.) *Changing Our Own Words: Essays on Criticism, Theory, and Writing by Black Women*, New Brunswick: Rutgers University Press, 58–74.

The Chronicle of Higher Education (25 April 1990), 1.

Hall, S. (1990) "Cultural Identity and Diaspora" in Jonathan Rutherford (ed.) *Identity: Community, Cultural, Difference*, London: Lawrence & Wishart.

hooks, b. (1990) *Yearning: Race, Gender, and Cultural Politics*, Boston: South End Press.

Howard, J. E. (1986) "The New Historicism in Renaissance Studies," *English Literary Renaissance* 16 (1): 13–31.

Morris, M. (1990) *The Pirate's Fiancée: Feminism, Reading, Postmodernism*, London: Verso.

Rothenberg, P. (1990) "The Construction, Deconstruction, and Reconstruction of Difference," *Hypatia* 5 (1): 42–57.

Spivak, G. C. (1990) "Gayatri Spivak on the Politics of the Subaltern," interview by Howard Winant, *Socialist Review* 90 (3): 81–97.

Wallace, M. (1990) *Invisibility Blues: From Pop to Theory*, London: Verso.

West C. (1990) "The New Cultural Politics of Difference," in Russell Ferguson, Martha Gever, Trinh T. Minh-ha and Cornel West (eds), *Out There: Marginalization and Contemporary Cultures*, New York: The New Museum of Contemporary Art, 19–38.

Part III

Legacies

Chapter 11

Mother

Coppélia Kahn

She died on Shakespeare's birthday in 1982, aged either 83 or 85. I'm not sure which, because she concealed her age from me and everyone else, especially her second husband, who was ten years her junior and my father. "Don't pin a number on yourself," she would say to her husband-hunting friends in those long gossipy conversations about bargains and fashions that I overheard while connecting the dots or pretending to read *Mary Poppins*. I never called her mom or mommy, always mother, the more formal term, to keep her at bay linguistically when I hadn't a chance of keeping her out of my room, my bureau drawers, my wastebasket and least of all my mind, which she still inhabits.

This essay is about how my mother shaped me, and without ever knowing it, my feminism. It's an attempt to take personally Virginia Woolf's advice that women think back through their mothers – and given that I spent about forty years consciously organizing my personality so as not to resemble my mother, and trying to escape the relentless battering of her narcissistic ego, it's hard. It even feels dangerous, as though I'm approaching a plague-ridden city from which I had fled, and risk catching the dread disease again. Were it not for editing this book and being inspired by the other essays here, I'd never attempt it. While I lived under her thumb, in terror of her rages, and desperately trying to fulfill her expectations while deviously flexing my own will, I shrank from trying to understand her. It might have brought me closer to her, and the last thing I sought was the sympathy that understanding might bring. I sought, instead, opposition; resistance unto death. She was enemy and oppressor; I her victim. Now that I am 52, a veteran of eight years of therapy and two of psychoanalysis, happy in my second marriage, proud of my grown-up son and absorbed in my vocation as teacher, feminist critic and Shakespeare scholar, I can risk the contagion. For now I can acknowledge how even my strategies of resistance and escape were drawn from her passions and interests. Much of what she loved I love too. She was an anglophile to the core, and it can be no accident that my scholarship focuses on Shakespeare, hallmark of Anglo high culture.

But more importantly, I can interpret my work – on Shakespeare as the poet of *male* experience – through the feminist theory that informs it and see it as a palimpsest for the mother–daughter relationship that I struggled so fiercely, clumsily and painfully to break out of. My work is the site of that struggle. Feminist theories of female personality development – those put forth by Chodorow, Kristeva, Irigaray and others – have excavated that Minoan region of mother–daughter relations, "so grey with age and shadowy," that baffled Freud. Their focus on it has been empowering for many feminists, myself included. The uses and the limitations of this relationship as the basis for a theory of how women are made, not born, are still being tested. Sometimes, the fluid ego boundaries and relational logic attributed to the mother–daughter dyad have been both essentialized and sentimentalized; when historicized, the dyad has also been enlisted to condemn the old cultural habit of blaming the mother. In revisiting this most important relationship of my life through the lenses of the psychoanalytic feminist theory that has helped me break free of it, I cannot hope to avoid blaming my mother; she hurt me too much. (In the ensuing narrative, my father's role is shadowy, ill-defined – as it was in my growing up.) But perhaps with some historical perspective I can understand what made her so possessive of me and so angry at her husband, or how what I thought of as her essential nature was shaped by her experience as a woman and by her profoundly bourgeois aspirations.

*

My mother only twitched the veil hiding her past to afford selective glimpses of it, so what I know is patchy. Born into a genteel, affluent family in British Columbia, she had begun college there, as I now reckon it, during the First World War. In her first year, she met an older man who evidently swept her off her feet. She married him, went to live with him "in the interior" where his work was, in the logging camps, and quickly had two children. Terrible disappointment followed; he didn't provide, he lied, and one day she came home to find the fine furniture she had brought with her being carried out to pay his debts. They separated, and divided the children between them; she took her daughter with her to Oakland, California where her stepfather and mother had moved, to begin a new life. She learned office skills, moved to Seattle, and became what we call a single parent during the Depression, eventually putting my half-sister through nursing school on what she earned as a secretary.

I think she never got over the shock of becoming déclassé and socially marginalized as a single woman with a child, plummeted into the working class when she must have had every expectation of security, leisure and respectability as a bourgeois wife. Her experience during the Depression formed her politics as a staunch liberal Democrat yet also confirmed her bourgeois identity as a woman – and the slippage between the two positions always irritated me. On the one hand, she felt that government owed everyone a fair shake, applauded Roosevelt (whom she worshipped) for the New Deal, and passionately defended "Negroes" and the poor. On the other hand, she held to a grammar of class markers as rigid and antiquated as *Burke's Peerage* and devoted most of her time to finagling, scrounging, and faking the appurtenances of gentility she couldn't live without.

Pink satin drapes in the living room , a Persian lamb coat, subscription tickets to the Seattle Symphony: she got them on sale or second hand, or made them herself, or scrimped on what others would consider necessities in order to have them.

When, near the end of the 1930s, she married my father, it must have seemed to her that the scrimping could end. He was barely 30, college-educated, a working journalist with good prospects. I was born, they bought a house, and within two years the Second World War arrived. Because the marriage was already strained, my father told me decades later, he enlisted in the Merchant Marines; he was too old to be drafted. He hoped that time apart might somehow smooth things out. For my mother had begun to reveal the hot temper, the intolerance for any view different from hers, the implacable willfulness, and the relentless criticism of my father that characterized her as long as I knew her. When he came back, things weren't easy financially, their relations deteriorated further, and though there were some good times, her flashpoint got shorter and shorter, and he seemed paralyzed by it.

Looking back, it seems to me that so much of her anger came from the frustration of her class-bound expectations of what marriage would give her. "A man ought to protect a woman;" "I do things no woman should have to do;" "a woman shouldn't have to work" – these phrases hang in my memory. In the post-war era, of course, women who had pitched into the war effort by taking men's jobs were – not always willingly – retreating into domesticity, settling into the "feminine mystique" of the fifties. The strongest social signals told women to concentrate on child rearing, home decorating and fashion trends. Though my mother (to her credit) detested mere housekeeping and pursued cultural and political interests, for her they were the centerpiece of home, and home was her domain. But my father's income, as the fifties advanced, was increasingly precarious and couldn't easily pay for the mortgage, my music lessons, the car. The scrimping was more necessary than ever. When my mother took a part-time job as "market researcher," calling on people in their homes to survey their consumer preferences, she saw it not as an opportunity to equalize her family role with my father's or to gain experience fitting her for a better job, but as an indignity, a shocking retrenchment, a breach of faith. Hence she clung the more insistently to the class markers: driving a truck, especially if you parked it outside your house, put you beyond the pale, as did bad grammar or unfamiliarity with this season's symphony program.

My mother was smart, attractive, skilled, abundantly energetic: she always looked at least ten years younger than she really was. Even in the fifties, despite the national swing toward home and family, many women worked, and with her clerical skills she could have gotten an office job. But for her, a job like that must have meant returning to the earlier trauma of losing her class status and with it a large measure of her identity as a woman, her claim on respectability made tenuous without a breadwinning man to back it up. So instead she heaped criticism on my father for his unfortunate career moves, and attention on me as I began to turn out well. According to my half-sister (who had grown up and left home before I was born), I was "the smart one" she had failed to be: a straight-A student and precocious reader, I played the piano and got my picture in the paper for honors and awards.

Since the world of work offered my mother no avenue of fulfillment, let alone financial relief, she channelled – drove is a better word – her energies into high culture and raising me. They amounted to the same thing, since I soaked up art museums, chamber music concerts, and the Theatre Guild like a sponge. As her marriage degenerated further, I became the sounding-board for her raging discontent with my father. A teenager trying to be my own person, I felt suffocated by her supervision of me – an only child, a girl – and frightened by the long, bitter, screaming quarrels she instigated. Inevitably, I suppose, we came a cropper on sex.

What must have been her own deeply Victorian upbringing stuck with her, and I imbibed it – as well as the ideas about sex floating around in middle America of the fifties. She never said a thing about menstruation, and, when it came, merely showed me how to use Kotex – but told her friends who, to my puzzlement, congratulated me. I and my girl friends learned the facts of life piecemeal, covertly, sharing whatever printed matter we could get our hands on and trying, with partial success, to figure it out. The only thing my mother ever told me about sex was that if a man tried to kiss me, I should hit him.

So it was no wonder that my normal teenage curiosity, fused with a greater than normal urge to get away from mother, made sex seem the defining experience that would mark my difference from her – my escape and my precious, private triumph. Despite remaining on the outer fringes of high school social life, in a mild sort of way I managed to experiment sexually without her finding out – until without any thought of provocation, I walked up our street with a boyfriend, our arms around each other's waists. Wrath descended: I had disgraced my parents, I had shamed myself. A good girl in all other respects, in this one I was bad. My mother's fury wounded and disabled me, I think, because I was in fact so bound up with her; I was the confidante of her disappointment with my father, her daily companion, for my father worked long hours, and – this I repressed totally – dependent on her for my self-esteem. Sex became a minefield between us. I wanted to win someone's love and love him as my mother hadn't been able to, but I couldn't attack her antiquated *mores* or defend my desires when, especially in this era, I too was so ignorant and guilty about seeking love and pleasure. She, having loved unwisely and having lost so much because of it, thought of sex as a bogey, a deadly trap for a woman. Too inhibited to talk even about kissing, let alone intercourse and pregnancy, what she really feared in that pre-pill era, I think, was that I would become pregnant – the ultimate, unthinkable disgrace for a nice girl, and the ruin of all her hopes for me.

With a mighty leap, I skirted the minefield, or so I thought, by winning a full scholarship to Barnard College and putting the width of a continent between us. She approved and assisted, though she was actually cutting the ground out from under her feet by letting me go "so far away." Why did she let me go? She loved me and wanted the best for me, but again I suspect that her ambitions for me were also shaped by her class-bound conception of what "woman" meant. Her idea of the content of my education was foggy, and she never encouraged me to think specifically of even the usual career tracks for girls – teaching, social work. What I went to college *for* was left unspoken, or unthought; what mattered was that it was a good college and would put me on speaking terms with the better sort of people.

And so I went off to college with a trunk full of homemade clothes (the wrong kind, though) and the expectation of putting behind me the shames, confusions and struggles of home. Whatever Barnard did for me, however, it couldn't keep my mother away even though she could never afford to visit me there. In fact, my growing familiarity with a social scene she couldn't imagine and (despite my attempts to hide it) with sex, impelled her to attempt a long-distance method of control, through letters. At least one per week, sometimes five or six, several or many erratically typewritten pages long, repetitive, incoherent, abusive and ever more critical of me, those letters in effect kept me guilt-ridden, self-doubting, and under her thumb despite the rich culture of New York I revelled in and the intellectual world opening up to me. The letters couldn't have affected me so deeply (I wept, I burned with anger and shame, I went to bed and tried to sleep them away) had I not identified with her, been psychically fused with her at an unconscious level. No matter how bizarre her demands on me, in some sense I tried to meet them, tried to be a good girl. I see now that she had painted herself into a corner: in holding out for the middle-class ease she never attained, she had deprived herself of outlets for her talents and energy, except for her daughter, whom she had unwisely allowed to elude her total control.

Though Barnard was self-consciously and proudly a woman's college, with distinguished tenured women on its faculty, in this period (I graduated in 1961) no college curriculum reflected any concern with gender difference, with women's history or cultural productions. And its ethos was stalwartly gender-blind: Barnard girls were expected to enter the professions and, at the same time, marry professional men, raise families, and be active in community work – as though all those pursuits were just the same for them as for their husbands. Like most colleges then, it acted *in loco parentis* especially with regard to sex. This policy had the unintended effect of turning sex into something both public and seamy. Necking madly in the beau parlors all evening or on the front porch one minute before sign-in time, we were forced to bring desire into the open but look the other way. Once my best friend barely made it to the front door in time and lurched into the elevator, only to realize that her garter belt and nylons were dangling out of her coat pocket.

I can see now that as I proceeded steadily toward graduation, what my mother and I were wrangling over wasn't just sex itself but also what was far more threatening to her: the prospect of someone taking her place as the most import-ant person in my life. (Of course that would be a man; I'm not sure my mother even knew what lesbianism was, and I barely did.) When I announced that I wanted to stay in the East and work after college, my parents proposed, then demanded that I return to Seattle, live with them, and help my father in the educational film business which he conducted out of an office at home. I would be protected from the bogey of sex, my father would get the clerical help he needed, and my mother would regain her household companion. The goal of my education would be to return to the place where I began.

*

When I arrived in Berkeley in the fall of 1962 to begin graduate study in English, I brought with me the award of a teaching assistantship, about $500 in savings, and a considerably larger sum of self-doubt. My parents had withdrawn all financial support, including medical insurance, when I refused to come home after college. I was now on my own; doubtful that I would even pass my first semester courses, hopeful merely that I would make it through an M.A. A year later, I was slightly less anxious, and engaged to a graduate student in history. He was smart, witty and, most important, emotionally stable: self-confident, from a well-knit and well-to-do family, he knew what he wanted to do – be a scholar and teach history. We set up house together without telling our parents, and planned to marry in June. It seemed that I had finally escaped my mother and survived the minefield of sex.

When I wrote home that I was going to be married, however, a firestorm erupted. With my mother leading the attack and my father in full complicity, what began as a wrangle over the proprieties of whose parents we would visit and how we would travel turned into a spying operation that revealed the "moral turpitude" of our shared household. My parents broke our secret in lengthy letters to my future in-laws that vilified me and threatened (implausibly, but disturbingly) to ruin my career and that of my fiancé. Mortified, terrified of what they might do next, and in order to stop them, we were married the day after Christmas by a slightly tipsy judge in the San Francisco City Hall. With a few friends we went to the movie "Tom Jones" and out to dinner; the next day we were back in the library.

It now seems to me that my parents went temporarily insane, in effect, when they realized that the *legitimate* sexuality of marriage would remove me from their control; prying into my illicit living arrangement was only a means of staving off the greater catastrophe of my departure into another family and a home of my own. In 1962 it didn't even occur to me that all this was happening because I was a daughter and not a son; because my sex and my sexuality, my parents were authorized to think, demanded constant surveillance. I was susceptible to that surveillance, and had even internalized it to a great degree; marriage was a guilt-ridden act for me, though it took years for that to reach the surface. I was susceptible because as a daughter I was subjected to and by the mothering relationship – in my case, an intensified and distorted one, but structurally typical in the terms established by Nancy Chodorow and others. According to Chodorow, women gain their first sense of femaleness through identification with their mothers rather than, as Freud has it, from turning toward their fathers and wanting babies from them as penis-substitutes. Mothers, in turn, tend to identify with their daughters as extensions of themselves, and to prolong a version of the mother–infant symbiosis into their daughters' adolescence (Chodorow: 1979). In my case, the blurring of ego boundaries between my mother and me in the culturally legitimated sphere of mothering meant that she could establish a symbiosis that crippled the identity it augmented. It meant that she had a lot of power over me.

*

I first came to Freud in my mid-thirties, through reading on my own and through psychotherapy, before the feminist revision of psychoanalysis that became the theoretical base of my work had begun. Though the Oedipus complex seems a reasonably accurate parable of how male gender identity develops in a phallocentric world, it cannot serve for women. But lodged in one of Freud's essays that feminists have rightly criticized, a shrewd insight caught my eye when I was beginning to suspect there was something wrong with my marriage. In "Femininity," asserting that a woman tends to choose her love objects "according to the paternal type," he notes that a certain residue of her earlier attachment to her mother may reassert itself, so that

> The woman's husband, who to begin with inherited from her father, becomes after a time her mother's heir as well. So it may easily happen that the second half of a woman's life may be filled by the struggle against her husband, just as the short first half was filled by her rebellion against her mother. When this reaction has been lived through, a second marriage may easily turn out very much more satisfying.
>
> (Freud 1933: 91)

Since I had never resolved my quarrel with my mother, never detached myself enough from her not to feel guilty about my own sexual maturation, my husband was bound to become "my mother's heir."

When I became pregnant, I knew I wanted a boy; only much later did I realize why – not to recuperate that symbiosis, not to inherit *that* power. At that time, I had nearly finished my Ph.D., I was planning to get a job, and relations with my mother had settled into an uneasy truce. When I took up a tenure-track position in 1971, I was the mother of a two-year-old son and had little idea of how to pursue an academic career: about all I knew was that I had to publish. Because an article that I had written, based on my thesis, was rejected by one journal, I assumed it was unpublishable, together with the thesis. Then some feminists in my department invited me to contribute an essay to their anthology, one of the very first to offer a feminist perspective on literature. To me as a novice Shakespeare scholar casting about for a topic, *The Taming of the Shrew* seemed a good place to look. I wrote the essay, and its publication gave me the confidence to keep on looking at Shakespeare from a feminist position. Those same colleagues, however, belonged to a consciousness-raising group that decided it couldn't admit me, or any other new members. A newcomer with a child and a more than full-time job, I was shut out from the personal connection to feminism that might have strengthened me and deepened my work. It was through publication and a scholarly network, then, that I formed that connection.

But you can't just publish, you have to teach as well, and when after a year at my first job I moved to Wesleyan, my teaching was a disaster. I was assigned the first half (Chaucer to Dryden) of the required majors' survey that I later learned had defeated the senior colleagues who taught it before me. I treated the under-graduates like graduate students, assuming they already understood concepts like period, convention, genre, lecturing them to death and allowing no time for discussion. They rebelled, and I landed in therapy. The issue, if years of dredging up what's been buried alive can be reduced to an issue, was talking – the Word, which as I had experienced it belonged not to the Father but the Mother. I couldn't help associating the authority of speech with my mother's non-stop volubility and insistence that her obsessions were received truth. Her conversation resembled her letters (just as wacky and bulky as ever, they still arrived several times a week, still critical of me and many others, but now focused on the problems of ageing). Once I timed her: how long could she talk to me while I remained silent? At the end of forty-five minutes I gave up, and said something. Mute during college (I spoke in class exactly three times), nearly so in graduate school, when forced to assume professorial authority, I had mimicked hers. The mimicry concealed a terror of what I would call the erotics of teaching: the flow of discussion in which students and teacher exchange the pleasures of discovering what they think, what can be thought. And that terror echoed a fear of sexual pleasure that also shadowed my marriage.

In those fifty-minute therapy sessions of halting, choked efforts to speak my feelings, I dealt not only with my classroom fears but with the articles I was trying to write on Shakespeare's early narrative poems, *Lucrece* and *Venus and Adonis*. In 1974, there was hardly any feminist literature on rape to help me explain why Lucrece, the rape victim, committed suicide because *she* felt "stained." It was through therapy and the psychoanalytic logic it taught me that I came to realize that Lucrece's desires weren't hers – they belonged to her husband; that her rhetoric of stain and guilt voiced not "her" subjective response, but the patriarchal ideology of female chastity. (Analogies to myself got clearer and clearer.) What-ever the errors of psychoanalysis as a phallocentric system of thought, it was the only system I could then find that offered a theory of gender; of how, as Gayle Rubin says, "the sexes are divided and deformed, or how bisexual androgynous infants are transformed into boys and girls ... a feminist theory manqué" (Rubin 1975: 184–5). In *Venus and Adonis*, an inward-turning youth winds up metamor-phosed into a flower and tucked into the bosom of a wordy, maternal goddess he died resisting. Reading it in psychoanalytic terms, tracing Adonis's fear of eros as a male fear of maternal engulfment, I read myself too. I over-rode the boundaries of gender ascription, appropriating the genius of two canonized males in order to understand my problems as a woman.

At the same time, the feminist movement and feminist theory supplied me with a critique of Freudian thought. I employed that critique not to interpret Shakespeare's women but, rather, to interpret his plays as representing dilemmas of masculine selfhood revealed in the design of the whole play. I saw the dilemmas as stemming from "the simple fact that most children, male or female, in Shakespeare's time, Freud's, or ours, are not only borne but raised by women." Setting aside the flattening of historical difference in that quotation from the book I published in 1981, I now hear an echo of Simone de Beauvoir's "One is not born, but made a woman." I focused not on the making of women but on the raising of men for two reasons, I think. First, it was too scary, too close to home, to write about women and their mothers – I had to displace my dilemma onto men. Second, given the kind of mother I had – oblivious to me as a person, engulfing, domineering – my dilemma was in fact closer to a man's than to a woman's. To found my gender identity on identification with my mother was to lose any identity of my own, in much the same way that, as Robert Stoller explains it, the boy's "still-to-be-created masculinity is endangered by the primary, profound, primeval oneness with mother" (Stoller: 1974, 358). What Stoller, in classic psychoanalytic fashion, regards as "primeval" I was able to see as patriarchal, the result of specific historical developments, because of Nancy Chodorow's *The Reproduction of Mothering* (1979) and Dorothy Dinnerstein's *The Mermaid and the Minotaur* (1977). Neither work takes an explicit or consistently historical perspective on mothering, but they both treat it as a social rather than natural arrangement, a division of labor within the family that might be different.

Over the decade between 1972 and 1982, I wrote the articles and the book – on masculine identity in Shakespeare – that gave me my own identity in far more than a professional way. I also helped start the Women's Studies Program at Wesleyan, and moved out of the male canon into courses on women fiction writers and feminist theory. During those busy, tense years of learning how to teach and how to mother my son, of getting tenure and getting divorced, work moved to the center of my life. It gave me not just financial security but also a sustaining community, of colleagues at Wesleyan University where I taught and all over America of feminist Shakespeare scholars. The career that had seemed almost out of reach to me as a timid, self-doubting graduate student became the warp and woof of my life. The ongoing synthesis I constructed from psychotherapy and feminism gave me a measure of rational control where before there had been only turmoil, anxiety, guilt. In the difficult years after divorce, that synthesis was the key to recasting my life.

But I cannot say that it enabled me to resolve my relationship with my mother. When, to my astonishment, my father divorced her (in the late sixties), she was forced to scrimp more than ever, and age began to diminish her formidable energy. I moved toward the role of caretaker and she became more dependent on me, but her phone calls and letters could none the less reduce me to tears. She still rode roughshod over anyone's feelings, and I was the most liable to be hurt because, notwithstanding the insight and strength therapy gave me, and my professional successes, I wanted her to recognize me. I wanted *her* gaze to confirm and validate my separateness from her, and that I could never get. When she suffered a heart attack, she was expected to recover, and I didn't fly to her side. Within a week, she died, and we never said goodbye.

In March 1983, nearly two years after my divorce and almost a year after my mother's death, I gave a paper titled "The Absent Mother in *King Lear*," at a conference in Hungary. The paper, later published, deals with a cluster of related ideas: hysteria as an expression of female subjectivity in patriarchal society, the mother's role in the formation of male as distinct from female identity, the play's imagery of children eating parents and parents eating children, and, most of all, "the absent mother" – Lear's repressed identification with the maternal and his "searing sense of loss at the deprivation of the mother's presence" (Kahn 1986). A rather perceptive colleague passed a note to me; it bore a little drawing of clouds dumping rain on a barren place below, a phrase from my paper like the one I've quoted, and a message to the effect that Lear's trauma bore some resemblance to my own recent losses. At that moment I began to realize that my book, which traces the problems of achieving male identity in a patriarchal world as a re-enactment of the first psychological separation from the mother, crucial in establishing the individual self, was about me as much as about Romeo or Macbeth. I suppose the book could be called "an adaptive response," a way of living with your hang-ups or even making them work for you.

In the decade since the book appeared, I have moved away from psychoanalytic methods, toward a more historically oriented criticism that is also shaped by Foucauld and Lacan. I continue, however, to work on constructions of male subjectivity in Shakespeare and, through them, to chart some of the ideological processes of the early modern period that gave gendered shape to what we call selves. In writing this essay, I have begun to realize that, whatever her nascent ambitions and desires may have been, like countless other women my mother had to pursue them within the dominant, masculinist ideology of the post-Victorian era and the genteel class that formed her. In raising me, she did what her education and experience had taught her to do as a mother. She transmitted a sense of the dangers to be faced by a woman making her own way in the world – but she did so through intimidation and surveillance. She thought she was preparing me to find a better place than she had found in the bourgeois family. I have probably given her less credit than she deserves for her departures from its norms and constraints.

The chapter on *Coriolanus* I recently wrote for a book on masculinity in the Roman works turns out – no surprise – to focus on his mother, Volumnia. My upcoming project is editing and writing an introduction for Thomas Middleton's *The Roaring Girl*, a seventeenth-century play about a woman who dresses like a man, never conceals her female identity, defends women against men, and refuses to do what all women are supposed to do: get married. The mother empowered through patriarchal ideology, the independent woman striving to get free of it: in my mind, these contrasting figures evoke my mother and myself, still ambiguously linked.

*

I wish to thank Avi Wortis, Emily Leider, Phyllis Mack, Gayle Greene, David Gullette and Margaret Gullette for their generous and perceptive readings of this essay.

REFERENCES

Chodorow, Nancy (1979) *The Reproduction of Mothering: Psychoanalysis and the Sociology of Gender*, Berkeley and Los Angeles: University of California Press.

Freud, Sigmund (1933) "Femininity," in Jean Strouse (ed.) *Women and Analysis: Dialogues on Psychoanalytic Views of Femininity*, 1974, New York: Grossman.

Kahn, Coppélia (1981) *Man's Estate: Masculine Identity in Shakespeare*, Berkeley and Los Angeles: University of California Press.

——(1986) "The Absent Mother in *King Lear*," in Margaret W. Ferguson, Maureen Quilligan, and Nancy J. Vickers (eds) *Rewriting the Renaissance: The Discourses of Sexual Difference in Early Modern Europe*, Chicago and London: University of Chicago Press.

Rubin, Gayle (1975) "The Traffic in Women: Notes on the 'Political Economy' of Sex," in Rayna R Reiter (ed.) *Toward An Anthropology of Women*, New York: Monthly Review Press.

Stoller, Robert J. (1974) "Facts and Fancies: An Examination of Freud's Concept of Bisexuality," in Jean Strouse (ed.) *Women and Analysis*, New York: Grossman.

Chapter 12

Getting gendered

Carolyn Porter

Among the many, by now clichéd, terms of opprobrium to emerge from feminism's career in academia is "male-identified," or "honorary male." There is a difference between these labels. The first tends to carry at least an implicit sense of sympathy, as if it specified a minor but lifelong disease over which its victim had only partial control – say, an allergy. The second, by contrast, evacuates sympathy altogether, dismissing its target as beyond all help; the "honorary male" has been so bountifully rewarded by a male-dominated academic culture that she is permanently fixed in false consciousness. But both charges are themselves charged with the guilt of the accuser, who knows that to some degree she shares the condition she names in her accusation. The feminists of my cohort and generation in the academy rarely use these terms about each other except in an ironic tone, one that deflects as it acknowledges self-recognition.

I'm reminded of the irony with which we on the left used to use "politically correct" among ourselves – not only to acknowledge our own failure to live up to our social and political ideals, but also to register our sense of that failure's inevitability, of the impossibility of being "p.c.," as we called it. Once an in-house joke we made with each other at our own expense, "p.c." has since become a right-wing slogan, its ironies reified for battle in the culture wars now attracting so much public attention; our joke has been turned into a joke on us. Already a cliché, "p.c." will soon become an anachronism – or so one hopes, at least. In so far as being "male-identified" is one way of being "not p.c.," it may already sound anachronistic. But in so far as it still registers our sense of failure and our fear of its inevitability, the term retains its salience among those members of the academic feminist community who are old enough to react with despondency to the announcement of the "post-feminist" era. If we have grown accustomed to acknowledging our male-identification, is it because we finally lacked the political courage and strategic intelligence to overcome the gender ideologies we discovered all around us? In the language of the sixties, did we simply "sell out," or as Marcuse warned, was the "system" endowed with an infinite cunning that rendered our every move always already a co-opted one? In the more current Foucaultian language, did the power of the gender system produce feminist resistance only in order to recontain it? Perhaps. Perhaps not. What is in any case clear is that we were deeply formed by the gender system we were trying to challenge and reform.

Certainly the more we struggled against the limits imposed on women by the gender system, the more clearly we saw that we were still well within it, and further, that it was within us. Having rejected feminine roles, we found we had been playing male ones. Rejecting these limited options, we set out to understand why and how our culture had set them up this way. We analyzed patriarchy, phallocentrism, misogyny we sought the causes of gender discrimination in history, the family, the economy, within and across cultures; we recuperated many women's voices, lives, stories. But we did so, still, within an academy that itself embodied and perpetuated the gender hierarchy we sought to undermine. Our work often effectively reinstated the very gender oppositions it had aimed to deconstruct. Our efforts to build Women's Studies led to the familiar impasses of marginalized irrelevance versus mainstreamed neutralization. Our attempts to alter pedagogical practice too readily imploded; as a friend of mine confessed, "after all these years of building a sense of my intellectual authority as a teacher, now I'm supposed to give it up in the name of feminist pedagogy?" Or, as another friend summed it all up, "First you slay the dragon, then you faint."

Such complaints point as directly as any I can recall to the dilemmas we faced as feminist academics. Having grown up in the 1950s and entered college in the 1960s, we had arrived in graduate school by virtue of our very resistance to getting gendered as female in the first place. In other words, our goal was precisely to become honorary males, although we had no means of understanding this at the time. It was not only difficult, but deeply confusing, to realize that the professional authority one had spent years fighting for was contaminated, suspect, wrong. Resisting the force of a gender system we had no means of understanding, we had become living examples of the contradictions it generated. And we still are. For whether we set about struggling to redistribute authority from the masculine to the feminine position and redeeming the category of "woman," or whether we tried to pry gender loose from its moorings, to transform it into a critical tool that would enable escape from the gender system altogether, we kept finding that the structure and force of gender always turned out to be deeper than we had expected. The more we learned about the gender system, the clearer it became that our lives – as scholars, teachers, administrators, mentors, "role models,"– were shaped by the contradictions it generated.

At least mine has been. But then I was a latecomer to feminist scholarship. I have no right to be using "we" here at all, in fact. All the work I've been referring to was done by women who made the move from being feminists to being feminist scholars at least a full decade before I did. But if my story has any interest or relevance for readers of this collection (and I am by no means sure it does or should), it is perhaps for this very reason – in taking so long to cross the line between a commitment to feminist politics and the intellectually rejuvenating discovery of feminist scholarship, I may fill out a small corner of the picture being composed by these essays.

As Ann Snitow has recently reminded us, feminism could liberate you in two, opposed ways. You could emerge from the revolution it effected in your perspective saying either "Thank God, I don't have to be a woman," or "Thank God, it's all right to be a woman." This polarization marks a well-known political division among feminists in this country, but it also, I believe, speaks to the contradictions within us, at least those of us who live multiply conflicted lives as feminists of a certain age in the academy. For I, at least, have often felt both of these opposed kinds of relief, and it may be of some use to the next generation of feminists to know what this meant.

CONFESSIONS OF A MALE-IDENTIFIER: HOW TO GET OFF TO A CONFUSING START

I never set out to be a literary critic. I arrived in graduate school in 1968 by a haphazard route. I hadn't even majored in English, for example, but in philosophy. Notable among the reasons for this choice was the fact that a degree in philosophy by definition foreclosed any chance of getting a teacher's certificate – a goal dear to the heart of my parents and easily the norm among my female friends. As I worked my way through Plato, Hume, Kant, I had little idea of where I was headed. No doubt this was part of the appeal of studying philosophy; working out the twists in a Socratic dialogue brought not only almost ecstatic pleasure in itself, but also welcome relief from having to think about the future. Whenever I was forced to think about it, I was clear about one thing – I didn't want to become a school-teacher, a prospect that felt like fate and so demanded resistance. My resistances to various imperatives have often taken perverse forms, but they never took a more ridiculous one than when, upon graduation, I married precipitously and joined the Peace Corps. Both projects swiftly proved failures. A specialization in medieval metaphysics had ill-prepared me for teaching elementary school in a West African village, population 500, never mind marriage to someone I barely knew. Once I had read the 300 or so books provided in our Peace Corps foot-locker, including every page of the Fanny Farmer Cook Book, I simply went mute. For two weeks, I was unable to speak at all. And so they shipped me home.

It now strikes me that if I ended up treating the Fanny Farmer Cook Book as a form of literature rather than as a practical guidebook, it was at least partly because its culinary focus on traditional American meals made it as esoteric with respect to Bumbuna, Sierra Leone, as Averroes had been with respect to the Texas in which I grew up. An apprentice housewife in a mud hut, a devotee of Wallace Stevens searching out ambiguities and tensions in recipes, I was unwittingly straddling contradictions of which I had remarkably little knowledge, and no understanding at all. Straddling contradictions was commonplace among Peace Corps volunteers in the sixties; I remember the one Black volunteer in our training group describing his dilemmas as an Afro-American being seen by Africans as white, as simply American. An inverted Oreo, he called it. As it turned out, he dealt with this particular version of what we had been taught to call culture shock with the same savvy, street-smart irony he had displayed during six weeks of training in Washington, DC, gently teaching all of us white, middle-class, liberal arts majors how to negotiate our way through ghetto territories every bit as alien to us as Africa would turn out to be to us all. He had long since passed Fitzgerald's test of a first-rate intelligence, although he would never have melodramatized it in such terms; he would have called it merely survival tactics. I, on the other hand, could have recited large chunks of Fitzgerald by heart at the time, but I didn't yet know I was living in contradiction.

Within a year of graduation, I found myself back in Texas, ending the marriage while teaching English in junior high school. Fate had descended; every hour from 8 a.m. to 3 p.m., forty students assembled in front of me, expecting to be taught something. I developed a low-level flu which lasted the semester. Even worse than my sense of incompetence was the mounting terror I felt at the prospect that this was to be my life – one stuck forever in the groove I had wanted so insistently to skip past and escape. Graduate school offered a second chance, and I seized upon it as if I'd been a prisoner offered a reprieve. But there was a parole period first: my parents agreed to pay my tuition for the first year if I would agree, while working toward a graduate degree in English, to take the Education courses necessary to acquire a teacher's certificate. I took the courses, but never completed the requirements; by the year's end I had a fellowship. I had escaped, and I never looked back.

To look back now is to recognize that, like my resistance to marriage for the next seven years, my resistance to the role of school-teacher had as much to do with gender as with a rebelliousness well-established in childhood. Marriage was easy to resist. For one thing, it was the sixties. Those few people one knew who were married were either visibly bewildered or increasingly alien – either they lived in communes raising children along experimental lines, or they had receded into the bizarre domain of garden apartments, land of handmade toaster-covers and tufted bedspreads. But it wasn't only the sixties that made marriage both unappealing and unnecessary. All men, or at least all of those I knew during the years I was in graduate school, expected women to compromise their careers in favor of their husband's. Having found both joy and an identity in the work I was doing in literary studies, I was not about to compromise. Which is no doubt one reason I was never to succeed as a wife; not until becoming a mother did I meet with a seduction forceful enough to compel compromises over work. As for school-teaching, the scene has changed so profoundly over the last twenty-five years that it may be worth trying to account for my desire in the early sixties to avoid it at all costs.

In my view, school-teaching, from grammar school through high school, is almost the only profession in our culture worthy of the term "noble." As I get older, I agree more and more with Henry Adams' statement that there are only two sacred duties – bringing new life into the world, and educating it once it is there. Nevertheless, obstetricians do not rank high in the medical world, and teachers do not get paid well, compared with other doctors, lawyers, bankers, or bureaucrats. But it was not such social and economic realities that had provoked my resistance. Rather, it was the gendered inflection through which these realities spoke that had direct and lasting impact.

Until I left high school, all my teachers – every single one – were women. With a few exceptions, these were extraordinarily bright, talented and accomplished people, people who took their jobs with a seriousness, and performed them with a dedication, that still astonishes me in view of how little they were paid and how little social recognition they received. They should have been my role models, as we were later taught to label such figures.

But the problem is, that's precisely what they were, or at least what they were to me by the time I left high school. For me, that is, the role of school-teacher was not only limited and limiting, it functioned *as* a limit in the social imaginary. It was not only that teaching was one of the few professions open to women, along with nursing and a few others. (I recall a very bright friend in high school who one day announced to me with a thrill that she had discovered something called a "paralegal" – a job she had decided to set her sights on. She was simply unable to imagine herself as a lawyer, and this despite – or perhaps because of – the fact that she was a star on the debate team, surrounded by young men already fantasizing their courtroom performances in three-piece suits.) More fundamentally, school-teachers occupied the site which marked a norm for respectable, middle-class women's professional aspirations; as such, it formed a boundary that one might cross, but cross at risk. There were functional reasons for this boundary; most obviously, one could be a schoolteacher before, after, or even during, marriage and motherhood. But by the time I reached college in 1963, such practical considerations had become encapsulated for me in the description of a teacher's certificate as an "insurance policy." If something went wrong in the pre-set agenda of my life as a woman – to marry and have children – school-teaching would provide something "to fall back upon."

My mother's career as a high school math teacher was regularly presented as evidence in support of this point. Financially speaking, the evidence was compelling. My mother's job had proven crucial over the years, since from the beginning of their life together, my father's health was seriously threatened by Crone's disease. Major surgery was virtually an annual event in my family, and the possibility of my father's death an always imminent prospect. (By the time he died at 79, my father had survived forty operations.) My mother's job was thus a form of life insurance – or *in*surance, as Texans pronounced it – as well as an indispensable source of income in a family headed by a man who had taken his first job as a laborer on an oil rig in West Texas.[1] When you add to this picture the financial exigencies of the Depression era during which my parents were starting out, it is little wonder that they kept insisting that I "get certified."

But in fact, my mother's teaching career represented much more than a second income or an insurance policy, as I knew but lacked the terms for understanding at the time. As a role model herself, my mother outstripped, and thereby undermined, the role of teacher she urged upon me. For my mother's is a success story

– a young woman from the provinces story – and as such, it pushed the limits of the gender code.

Graduating in 1929 from a small teachers' college in central Texas, my mother immediately began teaching in a junior high school on the outskirts of Houston – the biggest city in sight for her at the time. When she retired in 1973, she was the Assistant Superintendent of the Houston Independent School District. In between time, in the meantime, she made the most of her opportunities. Resisting my father's marriage proposals for seven years, she spent the summers getting her MA, travelling the country with friends, playing the piano professionally and basketball semi-professionally (as an All-American point guard on a full-court, mind you). Soon transferred to the best high school in town, she rapidly won recognition among students and faculty alike as its best math teacher, making a series of programs for the local educational channel. (These half-hour lessons in geometry and algebra were shown one day a week at 6.30 a.m., and my father insisted that my brother and I watch them. Too young at the time to know what she was talking about, I spent those early morning sessions getting a head start on developing "math anxiety," let alone sibling rivalry – my brother was already a designated "genius" in math.) Meanwhile, she raised two children while coping with my father's illness, not to mention his family. He was one of nine children, seven of them boys. Most of his brothers descended sooner or later on Houston to make their fortunes, a couple of them with the boundless energy and the moral perspective of adolescent criminals. In the mid-fifties, when she was promoted to her first administrative post, my mother had just completed the building of the house in which she still lives – one she single-handedly designed, contracted, and then supervised the construction of, day by day, one summer.

Among the many milestones in the years that followed, her promotion to the post of Director of Secondary Education stands out, for in this position she was the person to whom some thirty high school principals answered, and all of them were men. The fact that she had never served as a high school principal herself, had simply been catapulted past an entire section of the administrative ladder, only exacerbated the resentment she had to face from those men. The tale of how she not only faced, but effectively dissolved that resentment, is only one of many episodes in a story that could serve to demonstrate the salience to my mother's life of an oft-quoted feminist line: "Anything women do, they must do twice as well as men to be thought half as good. Luckily, this is not difficult."

I could go on, but you get the point: my mother's very success rendered problematic the role of school-teacher she urged upon me. To me, accepting that role meant giving up on the very promise it had held out for her – the promise of maximizing freedom, independence and the chances of accomplishment, despite the limits imposed by being born female. But then, finding another role was not easy. Beyond the boundary marked by school-teacher lay very little in the way of options. If marrying and joining the Peace Corps in one month had been a way of staying legitimate while keeping options open, or at least refusing to accept how limited they were, divorce and re-entry had returned me to square one, and the contradictions did not disappear, not even when I bracketed marriage, got my Ph.D. and a good job as well.

The spring when I was finishing my dissertation and preparing to move to Berkeley, I had two encounters in which gender told – if I'd only been able to understand its language fully and clearly. The first took place at a party at a professor's home, a large, drinking party of the kind once typical of faculty and graduate students, at least at Rice. A faculty member's wife, whom I had admired for years for her brash outspokenness, made a point of coming up to me late in the evening and announcing, "You know why you got that job, don't you? Because you're a woman." Infuriated and dumbfounded, I didn't think of a suitably cutting response until the next morning, when I decided that I should have replied, "Yes, and your husband got his job because he's a man." Not for several years did it sink in that such a response, though not inaccurate, would have entirely missed the point. For her part, whatever jobs I or her husband had gotten, the point was that *she* hadn't one of her own, that she had no position in the world other than faculty wife. For my part, the point was equally simple and straightforward – no matter how hard I had worked in graduate school, no matter how thoroughly I had mastered certain critical and professional skills, in short, no matter how willing and able I was to play Calamity Jane, demonstrating to myself if not to an all-male faculty, "Anything you can do, I can do better," I was still a woman. Even if I was not, like Calamity Jane, destined to turn pink in the arms of a Howard Keel, I was clearly not going to be allowed to shoot and ride with impunity. Not unless I grew a phallus to go with all my masculine ambitions and attitudes.

The second encounter took place at a family gathering later that spring, where I overheard my mother explaining to an aunt, "The difference between Don's dissertation and Carolyn's is that his is original and hers isn't." The way gender ideology was at work here cuts deeper than one might expect, and certainly beneath the obviously gendered register of Math versus English. My mother's own M.A. was in English. Nor was her B.A. in Math; she had majored in Spanish. The stellar career she had begun as a math teacher stemmed from the fact that math teachers were in short supply in 1929, and she had taken the necessary math courses in college to qualify for the few teaching jobs available. Gender ideology operated here, I came to see, not in terms of intellectual value, but of career prospects. For her, there was no intrinsic difference in value between Math and English as fields. If her son had a Ph.D. in Math, and her daughter one in English, she was certainly equally proud of both. And further, technically, the distinction was quite accurate, of course. She meant no harm in offering what she viewed as a neutral description of a difference in kind, not quality; she made the comment openly and within my hearing. Asked by an uneducated sister-in-law to explain what a dissertation was, exactly, and how one written in Math compared with one written in English, my mother was searching for some simple and yet not inaccurate terms to answer her. Dissertations of any description no doubt loomed up before this particular aunt much as Gothic architecture would have – as an admirable, but surely alien, and probably suspicious achievement.

In part, then, my mother's problem was how to express her pride across the class lines she had herself crossed, without sounding snobbish. For this task, she was fully equipped with all the necessary social and rhetorical skills, as she had demonstrated on countless occasions. If professionally, she knew how to still the resentments of the men she outranked, she was equally adept at forestalling any social resentments among the family's extensive rural branches.[2] But she was truly disturbed and apologetic when I cut into her conversation in fury at her invidious comparison. Neither of us at the time, I believe, could have found the terms to understand what had happened. But later, it became clear to me that the primacy of my brother's achievement, which I believed to be exposed so blatantly in her comparison, was a function not of favoritism, but of ideology.

For one thing, I think it highly likely that in labeling my brother's work original and mine secondary, my mother was unconsciously trying to protect her *image* of me, at least, from the threat posed to it by my professional choices. As if to say, "what she's doing is not serious, at least not serious enough to keep her from marrying and having children, from being happy." If she could not easily imagine a "happy" future for me as a professor, it was at least in part because the gender ideology she had herself stretched to its limits nevertheless provided no register for imagining that future, much less measuring its possible value. By the same token, what I imagined at that point to be my future was laughably off the mark. In her fears, she proved far more astute than I was to prove in my naïve faith.

But it is to this question of measure that the incident speaks most deeply, if indirectly. In her effort to simplify things for my aunt's benefit, my mother had tapped into, and made visible, a social imaginary where a man's professional achievements counted. There was a social measure by which these could be judged, but no such measure could be found for a woman's. So, in this case, the man's achievement had itself been turned into the measuring stick. Such a maneuver resonated powerfully, once I saw it at work, for what had my graduate career been but an exercise in learning how to use that same ruler? And what had feminism taught me but that in the process, I had come to be ruled by it?

GETTING SERIOUS

I have been suggesting that if I am a male-identified feminist, this contradiction may stem from the same roots in my childhood that made me fight against "getting gendered" in the first place. In this, my father's curiously anomalous faith in equal rights for women played as strong a part, no doubt, as my mother's remarkable example. Somehow, growing up in the arch-masculinist and deeply homophobic culture of West Texas, he had emerged with the fierce conviction that women had been the victims of discrimination . On the one hand, he would preach equal rights for women, and he practiced what he preached, too. Whether it was cooking or car-pooling, fixing broken lamps or broken spirits, he was there, at least so long as he wasn't sick. On the other hand, he held the full pack of cards when it came to playing out the codes of sexual difference, as a result of which he sent forth some remarkably contradictory signals. For example, he always wanted me to become a lawyer, but it was by no means a matter of career choices which led him to insist that I withdraw from ballet lessons at an early stage because he believed that toe-dancing would give me ugly calves. For Christmas, the year I turned twelve, he gave me a shotgun and a camera . (I never did learn to shoot the gun properly, but then neither did I ever learn to like being shot with a camera.)

There is, I believe, a decipherable cultural logic to my father's conflicting attitudes and beliefs about women, but tracing it would only take me deeper into his past and mine. All that is pertinent here is that he too contributed, powerfully if ironically, to my determined resistance to the disempowerments entailed in being "feminine." Feminism called such disempowerment into question, but it took me a long time, I now see, to overcome my fear that feminist scholars were disempowering themselves.

In the early to mid-seventies, as I began my teaching career at Berkeley, feminism for me was a political faith, not an academic field. Like many others of my class and generation, in what is by now a familiar story, I had come to be a feminist as a result of the civil rights and the anti-war movements of the 1960s. And, like others, I had been jolted into the realization that the "personal" was "political." But the lectures I began writing for courses in American literature registered little, if any, of this feminist perspective. These courses focused often on race, and addressed works by Richard Wright, Ralph Ellison and James Baldwin together with others by Herman Melville and William Faulkner. Aside from Gertrude Stein, Emily Dickinson, Edith Wharton, and eventually Kate Chopin, there were precious few women writers on my syllabuses. Meanwhile, the book I was struggling to write on four male authors was framed by Marxist theory and fueled by my desire to challenge the ahistorical bent of American literary criticism. Not the slightest echo of feminism could be heard in this book, finally published in 1981. Yet throughout the 1970s, I thought of myself as a feminist, and openly aligned myself with feminist causes. How could I have been so bifurcated?

One answer to this question is both simple and abject: I did not know how to teach the women writers who were being recovered by feminist scholars, so thoroughly embedded had my literary training been in the masculine tradition of American literature. When I began teaching Chopin, and later Cather and Jewett, I found it extremely difficult, for reasons that by now are all too obvious. Their work did not fit into the prevailing literary topoi of my field – indeed, that was a large part of its interest and challenge, but then, you could not, as we used to say simply add women and stir. New recipes had to be found, new questions had to be developed. Ultimately, of course, the entire concept of gender had to be addressed and rethought. By now, thanks to the stellar work done by countless feminist critics, theorists and literary historians, it has become much clearer what needs to be done if we are going to remap this field. At the time, however, I was too invested in the effort to secure a critical understanding of, not to mention some authority within, a field whose gender limits I could not see.

Once those limits began to come into view, furthermore, I resisted re-educating myself. Such resistance had many sources, but, looking back, it seems to me one of the most salient was the issue of being, and being taken as, "serious." As one of four women in a department of sixty-five or so faculty, I felt a virtual obligation to demonstrate that women should be taken seriously. But more pressing and immediate were the voices of my peers. Among the younger faculty I came to know in these years, the term "serious" had as much currency, and a good deal more weight, than "p.c." We judged each other's intellectual work, assessed each other's minds, in those days, according to standards in some ways far more demanding than those our senior colleagues would have used. The worst thing you could say about another scholar, in your field or anyone else's, was that he or she was "not serious," and that's how feminist scholars were usually seen.

It was primarily the work of feminist historians that opened my eyes at last to the fact that feminist scholarship *was* serious – dead serious. Not yet often *taken* seriously by those in positions to award the recognition of the academy's masculine authority, these women had none the less been doing serious work for years. Asked by the Provost to determine whether Women's Studies as a field offered evidence of what he liked to call "intellectual distinction," I found myself virtually buried by that evidence. In every field and discipline they had entered, feminist scholars were using the tools of logic and research in which they had been trained, to produce an astonishing bounty of new knowledge and understanding. The "intellectual distinction" of the best of this work was impossible to doubt, but further, the intellectual energy it displayed was impossible to measure. And once I began to work with feminist scholarship and not just alongside friends who were feminist scholars, I realized why they were so charged with energy. They had real questions, vast domains of uncharted territory to explore, and a genuine sense that knowledge might not be power, it might not change the world, but it certainly could change the view.

Working as an academic feminist, however, also reopened the old contradictions. You could do feminist research without becoming a "woman," that is seriously, in which case you were after all an "honorary male." Alternatively, you could try to redefine "woman" as someone capable of doing serious research, by doing it yourself and by demanding recognition for others who were doing it, but to succeed at this meant that you were, again, an honorary male. The only domain in which you could be a woman and a serious scholar at the same time was among other feminist scholars; here, at least and at last, you could be a woman with impunity. But this domain was limited and vulnerable. You could not work there all the time, and beyond this marginal enclave you got split in two. I vividly recall running into a feminist colleague of mine several years ago as she was returning to her office from a local bookstore, carrying a large stack of books under each arm. A specialist in modern poetry, she had just bought several books of recent feminist criticism in her field – these were under one arm – as well as the "regular stuff," as she put it – these were under the other arm. Never a complainer, she none the less on this occasion allowed herself the remark that feminist critics seemed to bear a double burden of keeping up as scholars, a burden of which her male colleagues were enviably ignorant.

By now, of course, such ignorance is far less legitimate in my field. Feminist critics and scholars have deeply affected the way in which literature is read and taught. Male scholars who, a decade ago, could at best be expected to be tolerant of feminists, could at best be counted upon to respect their work as separate but equal, can often now be counted on as co-workers in "gender studies." But with such progress, as every academic feminist knows, have come new splits and conflicts in the face of what Tania Modleski has recently called "feminism without women." Academic feminists are being reminded by their political activist friends these days, often in justifiably angry tones, that while we sit by exploring theories about "double lack" and "performing gender," women are increasingly at risk, politically, economically, physically. Whether it's a matter of backlash or backsliding, the advances made by the feminist movement with regard to women's rights, sex discrimination, abortion, sexual harassment, comparable worth, etc., are quite obviously under siege. Meanwhile, within Academe, feminist scholarship has established its legitimacy, at least in some disciplines, but at what price to its ethical and intellectual commitments to women? "Race, class and gender" has achieved the status of a cliché, at least in many fields within the Humanities, and affirmative action has worked at least effectively enough to raise an outcry on the political right. Meanwhile, feminists are as subject to academic class stratification as everyone else, but for those of us with the class privileges of tenure at research universities, the irony of "success" runs deep. For it is still the case, I believe, that the more seriously you are taken as a scholar and teacher, the less seriously it counts that you are a woman. One is, it seems, always getting gendered.

More personally, academic feminists of my cohort are not only split and conflicted, we are also very tired. A feminist friend and colleague of mine recently told me, in sympathetic response to my apology for failing to make a meeting of a committee she was chairing, "If it weren't for the fact that I'm team-teaching one of my courses, I wouldn't be making it this semester. But by working sixteen hours a day, I'm just keeping up." Another reported, just this week, that when she said to her husband for the third night in a row that she had to chair a meeting and wouldn't be home for dinner, he replied, "That's OK, I'm getting used to it." He may be, but she's not. Indeed, on the rare occasions when we have the chance to see each other outside committee rooms, the senior feminists I know relentlessly recite some version of the same question: I used to have a life. What happened to it?

A good deal of this overwork and fatigue is attributable to the budget crunch which has recently depleted the ranks of the faculty, but, needless to say, not the number of students we are supposed to teach, advise, mentor, and evaluate, and certainly not the number of committees that university administrators deem necessary for the whole operation to proceed along its magisterial course. There is, in other words, what labor unions used to call a speed-up in the academic workplace, and it affects everyone there. But what such pressures have called forth and made visible to my feminist colleagues is a set of strains which have been building for years. Many of us want desperately, now, after years of working to make a space in the university for feminist research and Women's Studies programs, to pursue our own long-delayed research projects, but we cannot refuse the insistent demand that comes from both within and without us, to devote our time and energy to defending that space. So we try to do both, and often we do neither very well. We are torn in fact in many directions: between the obligations we have assumed as senior faculty directing dissertations in our own fields, and our commitment to teaching undergraduate Women's Studies courses, between our accumulated responsibilities as mothers of small children, mentors of women students, members (still often token ones) of multiple committees, and the need to find time to read, write, think. We now have, many of us, a room of our own, but we have no time to spend there, and no energy left for productive work even if we could find the time. And we are the privileged ones; we know this all too well. Whatever stresses and strains we may complain of, they are as nothing compared to those faced by the many feminist scholars we know both close to home and across the land, teaching twice as many courses for half the pay, with no possibility of time off for research. Compared with them, we are taken very seriously indeed. They are taken as school-teachers.

Getting gendered is a "varying offensive," to return to a Fitzgerald phrase: you can't win for losing. Fighting against getting gendered female, I suppose I succeeded, but the gender hierarchy prevails, and I am on the wrong side still. This is not a complaint, but a confession. No sooner do I write that line than I recognize how it gives me away once again. After all, complaint is a female genre, isn't it?

NOTES

1 West Texas, where my father was born, is not merely Texas. It is, or at least it was, a distinct culture, another state entirely, of mind, body, spirit, flesh and dust.

2 This is not to imply that my mother lacked the capacity for tart responses, when appropriate. She was once informed by one of my father's more outspoken, ill-mannered and perennially unemployed brothers that he would never allow *his* wife to work. A wife, he opined, should stay at home and "sweep the floor." "That's fine," my mother replied, "as long as you provide her with a floor to sweep."

Chapter 13

Loss and recovery
Homes away from home[1]

Carol Thomas Neely

In my beginning is my end. . . .
Home is where one starts from. As we grow older
The world becomes stranger, the pattern more complicated
Of dead and living. . . .
In my end is my beginning.

T. S. Eliot, "East Coker", *Four Quartets*

I think how I just want to feel at home, where people know me; instead I remember, when I meet Mr. Boone, that home was a place of forced subservience, and I know that my wish is that of an adult wanting to stay a child: to be known by others, but to know nothing, to feel no responsibility.

Minnie Bruce Pratt, "Identity: Skin, Blood, Heart"

Reading has always been for me about the certainty of loss and the possibility of recovery. What is most crucially lost and recovered is, of course, love, and home is the central symbol of that painful loss and hoped-for recovery. It is this theme which I have repeatedly sought and found (and analyzed) in literature: in my avid readings of *The Bobbsey Twins* series when I was 5 and 6;[2] in a 1956 high school exam essay written on the Eliot quote above and drawing on the male modernists who were my first literary loves (Yeats, Eliot, Auden, Faulkner); in a senior honors thesis written at Smith College in 1961 on "Iris Murdoch's House: Art and Reality"; in a Yale University Ph.D. thesis finished in 1969 on *Shakespeare's Use of the Elements of Pastoral Romance*; and in my 1985 book, *Broken Nuptials in Shakespeare's Plays*, which evolved from earlier articles on *Othello* and *The Winter's Tale* and was completed as my marriage of nineteen years was coming apart.

When I read Kate Millet's *Sexual Politics* in 1970, I first understood sexual difference and gender as categories of analysis. I had my first lesson in the connections between the personal (love, family, "home"), the political (social and political structures and change), and the professional (literature, literary theory, teaching), connections which had remained unexamined or suppressed throughout my education. In the twenty-one years since then, largely through the developments in feminism and feminist theory, I have learned to attend to the assumptions, exclusions and inequalities which protected and circumscribed the literal and literary homes in which I sought recovery and reconciliation. In this essay I want to try (following the lead of Minnie Bruce Pratt) to look at the way in which my family, educational institutions, critical theories, and Shakespeare – a literary "home" at least since 1964 when I started working on my dissertation – have not only participated in the exclusions which protected me but also provided me with the resources to challenge them. Tracing this process may suggest some ways in which I can function as a professor of Women's Studies and Renaissance Studies in a multi-gendered, multi-cultural, multi-national environment more disparate and discordant than the one in which I grew up.

Yours in Struggle: Three Feminist Perspectives on Anti-Semitism and Racism includes essays by Elly Bulkin, an "Asjkenazi Jew," Minnie Bruce Pratt, a "white, Christian-raised Southerner," and Barbara Smith, an "Afro-American"; in the preface the three authors hope that their co-operation on the project will support feminist community organizing and coalition work (Bulkin 1988: 8). In her essay, Pratt locates herself at a number of precise geographical and historical co-ordinates by evoking journeys away from and (in memory) back to her childhood home in a small Southern town, and by depicting specific encounters during a walk out from and back to her present home near H street NE in a tense, racially mixed area of Washington DC:

> When I walk out in my neighborhood, each speaking-to another person has become fraught, for me, with the history of race and sex and class; as I walk I have a constant interior discussion with myself, questioning how I acknowledge the presence of another, what I know or don't know about them, and what it means how they acknowledge me. It is an exhausting process, this moving from the experience of the "unknowing majority" (as Maya Angelou called it) into consciousness. It would be a lie to say this process is comforting.... By the amount of effort it takes me to walk these few blocks,... I reckon the rigid boundaries set around my experience, how I have been "protected."
>
> (Bulkin 1988: 12, 13)

By examining the privileges based on exclusions which made home safe (these first eroded when Pratt came out as lesbian and had her children taken from her), and by learning about the parts of her childhood town formerly invisible, Pratt can exploit the resources home gave her to change herself and the world in which she grew up.

Martin and Mohanty argue that the notions of "identity" and "home" which Pratt evokes are concrete, changing and open to question. Therefore they are not blindly exclusive, restrictively personal or prematurely unified – hazards which attend both feminist identity politics and feminist autobiographical essays like this one. I use Pratt's scrupulous self-examination as a model to ask whether homes and traditions (family, education, literature) may be resources for growth as well as sites of exclusion. I want to explore how the ideals they represent might be expanded and toughened rather than simply abandoned.

My original influential homes were my Republican, upper-middle-class family (doting grandparents, lawyer father, housewife mother, and younger sister) and Germantown Friends School, the coeducational Quaker day school I attended in Philadelphia from kindergarten through high school (1944–57). Some tension existed between the two since my family was utterly conventional and, in the context of the political and social climate of the forties and fifties, GFS was radical in most respects. There, intellectual life was consistently connected with politics and with the possibility for social action. Suburbia, the man in the grey flannel suit, McCarthyism, foreign policy, the Cold War, and capitalism were vigorously criticized. I remember sending a tape to our companion school in France (in English of course) explaining and justifying the 1955 Supreme Court Desegregation decision; I also remember writing a history paper on why Third World countries needed revolutions like the anti-colonial American revolution. In two excellent English classes, literature was directly tied to personal values and political action; senior year we read Plato's "Apology," Thoreau's *Walden* and Shakespeare's *Hamlet*, and debated the necessity and difficulty of acting out of conscience in opposition to the beliefs of the majority, a central Quaker principle. I never felt excluded myself at home or at school; I identified as easily with Thoreau, Hamlet and male English teachers as with my adored grandmother, mother and sister.

But looking back now, I see blindnesses and exclusions within this politically aware school. Home – love, gender, sexuality and family – were excluded from the school's critique, and it was itself protected from the racial and political tensions analyzed there. The atmosphere at GFS was clearly more positive for girls than at most schools in the fifties. Female varsity athletes (like me) had more prestige than did cheerleaders; school offices were held jointly or successively by girls and boys; everyone went to college. Gender difference or discrimination, although clear in the structure of the school where the principal and most high school teachers were male and all the elementary teachers were female, was only once raised as an issue. When a small group, all women as it happened, read Woolf's *To the Lighthouse*, questions were raised about inequities in the Ramsays' relationship. I ignored these and idealized Mrs Ramsay and the unity and harmony she created with her *boeuf en daube* (prepared by the cook and served by the maid).

The starkest sign of gender inequality was that virtually all of my teachers – from kindergarten through graduate school – were married men or unmarried women; the latter were typed by students as "spinsters." The wedding to which my fourth-grade teacher invited the whole class is a vivid memory, perhaps because her mid-year marriage was a disruption of an otherwise absolutely gender-polarized system; it hinted that a woman *could* be a teacher and a wife, have a husband and a job, be Mr *and* Mrs Ramsay. My willed blindness to the bleak implications for my own future of the gender polarities around me grew, I think, out of the fruitful tension between home and school, between their opposite and equally appealing conceptions of fruitful productivity, one private, one public: one maternal, one artistic/activist. My positive identification with both spaces

perhaps accounts for my never remembering feeling compelled to choose between marriage and graduate school, career and motherhood, choices many
women of my generation felt forced into by prevailing social codes.[3]

Ethnic, racial and sexual differences were slightly more visible than those of
gender, but the school was more progressive about race in theory than in practice.
Although it celebrated its centenary in 1945, it did not desegregate until the late
forties and early fifties when a few isolated black students were admitted. We
learned about and countered racism working with residents to restore homes
during Quaker weekend workcamps in the Philadelphia slums or working on
Quaker community projects with Native Americans during summer workcamps
at Mesa Verde, but these were far from home. Although the school was in a racially
mixed neighborhood, there was no interaction of any kind with nearby public
schools, no scholarships or use of the facilities for area residents. (All this has
changed.) But in spite of such exclusiveness, my legacy from the school was the
acknowledgement of injustice and a commitment to social change.

Attending Smith, a women's college, thirty years after my mother,[4] ten years
after Betty Friedan, and five years after Gloria Steinem, widened the split between
my social and academic life (between private and public) and provided the
impetus for becoming a literary critic and a Shakespearean. The powerful formalist education I received at Smith and Yale laid the groundwork that determined
how I would read the plays, removing them from the oppositional political
context in which I had first encountered them and concealing the ways in which
reading did and did not serve personal needs. Even in high school, where what
we would now call the ideological work of literature was emphasized, I had always
been something of an instinctive New Critic. I never cared about authors' lives
or even their names (let alone their gender, race, or class or historical specificity).
I had always ignored boring historical background; at Smith I avoided professors
who took a historical or biographical approach (mostly older women, hired as
new Ph.D.s in the twenties and thirties in the so-called first wave of the contemporary feminist movement) and sought out those who favored eloquent New
Critical analysis of complicated poetic texts (mostly younger men, often recent
Yale Ph.Ds).

More important than any specific introduction to Shakespeare was my modernist and New Critical literary education. This theoretical approach assumed the
autonomy of the art work and celebrated art's unity, congruence and plenitude
and superiority to life;[5] art, it was asserted, was "all discrimination and selection"
while life was "all inclusion and confusion" (James 1934: 120); art was, in James
Joyce's formulation from *Ulysses*, "the postcreation" (1934: 385).[6] Most of the
papers I wrote throughout college and graduate school were on appearance and
reality, art and life, or language and truth. My honors thesis on Iris Murdoch (a
woman author I discovered for myself) was an Existentialism-driven close reading
of her first four novels; I took understanding art as a metaphor for loving and
analyzed house (home) as a metaphor for the self's satisfying relation to objective
reality.[7] Perhaps one reason for my fascination with the topic of appearance and

reality was that I always felt slightly fraudulent; my passion for literature and its corollary, my academic drivenness, seemed inauthentic. This feeling, shared to be sure by many adolescents, may have had to do with the particular unseemliness of such commitments for girls in the fifties – even in unusually supportive Quaker schools and women's colleges. This theme also allowed me to displace and reconcile my contradictory roles and commitments. By equating maternal procreation with artistic creation and covering over gender difference, I was able to keep the realms of the personal and professional separate and at the same time symbolically resolve stark oppositions between Molly Bloom and Stephen Dedalus, Mrs Ramsay and Lily Briscoe, Mrs Ramsay and Virginia Woolf.

My honors seminar on Shakespeare was with Charles Hill, a true gentlemen of letters then approaching retirement, an editor of our edition of the plays, and a wonderful teacher, scholar and friend. His class bridged the methodological divide between "New" and historical criticism. Without pushing a particular method, his meticulous opening remarks summed up the best in the standard approaches of the day (see note 8 for a sampling), and our close readings of the texts debated these interpretations. Several features of this course decisively shaped my future engagement with Shakespeare. A paper I wrote on "Appearance and Reality in *Hamlet*," traced, in exquisitely intricate detail, the ambiguities and paradoxes of "act" "seem" and "show" which made action with integrity difficult or impossible for Hamlet (and me). After finishing it, I came across Maynard Mack's essay, "The World of Hamlet,"[8] which took up, with far more brilliance and sophistication, the same Shakespearean lines, themes and topics. This powerfully exciting and depressing experience let me imagine that I could analyze Shakespeare and be a literary critic – and encouraged me to conflate the two activities. I also remember vividly reading *The Winter's Tale* straight through on a cold December night (while baby-sitting) and being astonished and exalted by Hermione's renewal (an advantage of skipping introductions I have long remembered). Driven by this exhilaration, I wrote a final paper on "Good and Evil in *Othello* and *The Winter's Tale*," showing how all the elements which drove toward loss and chaos in the tragedy – art, nature, love, friendship – generated reconciliation and renewal in the romance, symbolized by Hermione's gradual recovery of physical life. Finally, the seminar itself – held during evenings in the living room of an old New England frame house, comfortable with fireplace, book-lined walls, and offering tea and homemade cookies served by Mrs Hill at the break – provided me with a seductive ideal of the academic life, one whose class and gender subtext I would not notice or ponder until I had lived out my identifications with Mr and Mrs Hill.

At Yale, the gender subtext was starker, for there was only one woman (unmarried) in the English department, and she was one of only two women on the entire graduate faculty of the University. I ignored such demographics and felt fortunate to be studying with the New Critics I idolized: Cleanth Brooks on modern literature, Louis Martz on Renaissance poetry, W. K. Wimsatt on literary criticism, Maynard Mack on the eighteenth century. Since Mack did not teach the graduate Shakespeare course, I attended his spellbinding undergraduate lectures and bought the notes mimeographed by undergraduates (my mainstay later when I started teaching Shakespeare). I was not aware then of gender discrimination, and even with hindsight I find little to complain of in terms of individual treatment. Indeed it was generally acknowledged – by faculty and students – that in my "class," the women were better than the men.

But, late in my stay at Yale, three signs of systemic discrimination were registered – without surprise or objection. I was told by the Director of Graduate Studies that there was a quota on admitting women; they could not make up more than 50 per cent of any entering class. "Otherwise," he said, "we could fill up each class with first-rate women applicants." Second, a fellow student who was about to leave New Haven to follow her further-along husband to a job at a major State University asked her dissertation director what she would do for a job when she finished (nepotism laws being very much in force then). He assured her that she could get a job as a "crack secretary" in the Department – where the real power was! Third, when I announced that I was going to follow my future husband to the University of Illinois where he already had a job in another department, I was told by several of my professors, matter-of-factly, "The Illinois English Department doesn't hire women." Confirmation was swift. In 1965 (still an era of college teacher shortages), I applied to Illinois. My letter was never answered, and the English Department hired twelve entry-level assistant professors; all of them were male.

Yale never required nor did I wish specialization. Although I originally intended to write a dissertation on modern literature – perhaps on Murdoch – my excellent Renaissance courses, Yale's assumption that modern literature should be a hobby (a second field rather than a dissertation topic) and Mack's interest in directing, propelled me toward a dissertation on Renaissance tragedy and romance, on Sidney, Spenser and Shakespeare. Although my original interests were in the contrasting forms and themes of the Old and New *Arcadia*, Books I and VI of *The Faerie Queene*, and Shakespeare's tragedies and romances, this sweeping topic was eventually whittled down to a focus on *The Winter's Tale*. The dissertation took a long time to write; eventually it was completed on my older daughter's first birthday. Its optimistic conclusion was propelled by my favorite analogy, no longer merely academic – that between female reproductive fertility and male artistic fertility: "Shakespeare's art, like Perdita's, has coerced us into believing, for the moment, and against all reason, that shame, estrangement, loss, even death, can be overcome through desire and control and grace – that within the realm of art and nature, man can achieve integrity and integration, and time can be redeemed."

I wince now at this generic use of "man," and at the time when my dissertation was finally completed in 1969 my "home" only seemed to integrate work and life, time was in short supply, and the formal analysis I excelled at was no longer completely satisfying. I was married, teaching at the University of Illinois as an invisible faculty wife (and mother), was active in anti-Vietnam protests, and had begun teaching anti-war and Black Power poetry in my Introduction to Poetry course. But Vietnam protest, family life, and writing and teaching on Shakespeare remained compartmentalized. I had no framework to connect them until the following year when (on summer vacation) I read Millet's *Sexual Politics* and understood immediately how the personal was political, how my family life, job, writing and political activity demanded feminist analysis. I could face and respond to what Adrienne Rich calls "re-vision" only gradually; it took several years, two more children, the loss of my job, and the energy of repressed anger to enable me to apply systematically to Shakespeare what I was learning about patriarchy and women's oppression from reading Germaine Greer, Shulamith Firestone, Betty Friedan and Simone de Beauvoir. When the time came, I found myself well prepared to do so by the Quaker legacy of opposition to inequality, the resources of close reading honed at Smith and Yale, the rich responsiveness of Shakespeare's text, and years of meditation on love, authenticity and action.

My essay, "Women and Men in *Othello*: 'what should such a fool / Do with so good a woman,' " (written in 1973–4, a year marked also by the loss of my job and the birth of my third child) began to breach some of what Pratt calls "the rigid boundaries" which had encircled the plays for me: prescriptions about the autonomy of the art object, the focus on formal analysis, the erasure of gender conflict. In my dissertation, teaching, and my first published essay, I had translated gender and class into stylistic and symbolic categories and approached what I would learn to call Leontes' misogyny through careful analysis of his stylistic habit of translating particulars (Hermione) into abstractions (whore). Now I confronted such issues directly. The *Othello* essay, although written in complete isolation from the profession, turned out to be paradigmatic of seventies' American feminist literary criticism. I attacked critics and male characters (indiscriminately) for their sexism, and idealized the women characters. My polarized, densely argued analysis of (essentialized and universalized) "women" and "men" in the text, was influenced by feminist critiques of sexism and by psychoanalytic paradigms of men's divided attitudes toward women.[9] Identifying with Emilia's realism and courage, I ignored her complicity with Iago.

Writing this essay changed me and allowed me to initiate other changes. It is hard now to remember how frightening, exhilarating and, most of all, uncharted that writing was, although it is easy enough to see its blind spots. I did not deal with (or notice) Othello's race, (although the Leslie Fiedler essay that catalyzed my rage was called "The Moor in Shakespeare").[10] I did not think about Emilia's class, or about Iago's and Othello's homoerotic bond; to do so would have been to disrupt the neat division between good women and bad men I had so satisfyingly established. And I did not extend my critique to other plays, place it historically or implicate Shakespeare. Attacking *Othello* provided an enabling outlet for feminist anger without at first requiring me to confront directly men I knew or to challenge the familial, professional and critical practices which both protected and circumscribed me. Defending Desdemona's strength and integrity allowed me, indirectly, to defend my own without examining the privileges of race and class which we shared or acknowledging differences other than gender difference which were played out in the tragedy – the racial difference between Iago and Othello or the class differences between Desdemona, Emilia and Bianca. Writing the essay allowed me to identify with women through the women in the play while acting like a man – leaving home for the tiny library carrel where (in Adrienne Rich's exact formulation) I lived as "no one's mother" (Rich 1976: 30) and wrote an essay which would be published and would restart my stalled career. So although my overtly acknowledged identification was with Emilia, I wonder now if perhaps my covert and unacknowledged identification was with Iago – whose situation of being professionally passed over, emotions of concealed rage and strategy of indirect attack I (unknowingly) shared.

In an essay on *The Winter's Tale* (1978) which followed the *Othello* essay and in the book on *Broken Nuptials in Shakespeare's Plays* (1985) which grew out of them, Shakespeare was a resource which allowed me to examine the gender conflicts, inequities and anxieties (sexual, emotional, social) which attend courtship, marriage and motherhood, analyzing these through the many forms of broken nuptials represented in the plays. Influenced by a range of historians, critics and theorists while writing the book,[11] I came to see that to analyze the social relations of the sexes in the plays without simply circumscribing them within the confines of contemporary feminist analysis, I needed to understand better the place of women in early modern culture. In the book's introduction, written last and segregated from the discussions of the plays, I begin to interpret the historical context. Also, in a general discussion of the romances, I begin to problematize the endings by acknowledging the oppressive configurations which make their final reconciliations possible: the deaths of mothers – that is of women who, combining sexual power, reproductive power and maternal power, threaten the hierarchies of patriarchy; the idealization of female chastity; the losses of Mamillius, suspected bastard, and Antigonus, henpecked husband. But the need to finish a coherent book blocked out full exploration of the historical contexts or the limits of formalism.[12] I found for the book – again – a kind of happy ending, again through the conclusion of *The Winter's Tale*, in the moments of mutual acknowledgment which moved me at my first reading and still continue to move me. These are the gradual onstage stage restoration of Hermione's breath, "Skin, blood, and heart," (in Pratt's words), Leontes' acknowledged recovery of her warmth, "an art / lawful as eating" (5.3.110–11), and Hermione's reunion with her daughter Perdita: "I have preserved / Myself to see the issue" (127–8).

Seven years later, through reading feminist theory, teaching "Introduction to Women's Studies" and women writers, and hence listening to a range of voices utterly outside of the "Renaissance" as it comes down to us – African-Americans, Native Americans, lesbians, Third World women[13] – I have a more broadly contextualized sense of what is privileged (and what excluded) at the end of *The Winter's Tale*. There, male bonds and female friendships are decisively subordinated to the idealized contract of heterosexual marriage, an institution which, in the play, is dynastic, patriarchal, western – although it feels odd to characterize it

188 Carol Thomas Neely

in this way. What is restored and celebrated prefigures our current (limited and limiting) notions of what is allowed to count as "family": father, mother, daughter and, lacking the son, a son-in-law.

Other kinds of alliances and homes are represented as viable in the play's fourth and fifth acts: the unconventional families of the old shepherd, Perdita and clown; of Polixenes, Camillo and Florizel; of Leontes and Paulina; of Hermione and Paulina. These get swept away unacknowledged in the recovery of Hermione and the arranged marriage of Camillo and Paulina. Irregular triangles and asexual pairs are reconfigured as heterosexual married couples with Polixenes as the conventional odd man out of Shakespearean comedy and romance. This characteristic figure may serve to signify, in both comedy and tragedy, the imperfect symmetry and incomplete integration of the endings. In *The Winter's Tale*, although the shepherd and clown have been reborn as "gentlemen," and although Autolycus is granted a place with them, these lower-class characters are not present to mar the homogeneity of the royal family reunions. But to focus on what is excluded, subordinating what is attained, and denaturalizing the happy ending, makes me uncomfortable. This response may reflect my inability to face squarely the "forced subserviences" which define the homes I sometimes still long for. Or it may be because such suspicious readings seem to impose their own limits, to preclude or deny responsiveness to the pleasures of escape, identification and wish-fulfillment which the text can provide.

The conflicts this essay traces within the personal and professional realms – between the desire for a secure identity or "home" and the desire to dismantle that identity and repudiate the exclusions of that "home" – are played out in contemporary debates in feminist theory, in the academic profession and in popular culture. In current feminist theory, one important debate is usually articulated as that between essentialism and anti-essentialism; one of a number of attempts to mediate between the two sides is sometimes called strategic essentialism (Spivak 1988, 1990). In "A Gender Diary," Ann Snitow examines the debates between "maximizers" who want to emphasize gender differences and retain the category "woman" and "minimizers" who want to minimize gender difference and undo the category. In the terminology of its current manifestation, anti-essentialist postmodernism, by theorizing multiple selves, identifications, and instabilities in self, language and world, seeks to explode the rigid boundaries of traditional gender roles and of the potentially claustrophobic rooms an identity politics relies on for personal and political empowerment.[14] However, as Pratt, and, through her, Martin and Mohanty argue, unifying constructions of identity and community, variously derived, may be crucial to self-awareness, empowerment and social change. Hence some theorists while declaring their allegiance to postmodernism, acknowledge the power of categories such as women or gay on which social movements for liberation depend, and formulate flexible or provisional concepts of situated identities which connect theory and practice, acknowledge agency, and permit challenges to oppressive institutions and systems.[15]

Meanwhile, the gender, race, class and sexual identities theoretically called into question by postmodernists and social constructionists seem increasingly important and reified in professional and pedagogical practice. Calls for a more inclusive academy and curriculum and the pressure of ethnic group identifications have created widespread assumptions that scholars' identities should be congruent with the subjects they research and teach and the students they instruct.[16] Administrators and students agree on the value of, for example, African-American female professors researching and teaching black female writers which provide understanding and role models for black female (and male) students. Meanwhile Shakespeare, it is perhaps assumed, can be left to and for white males. Such ghettoization, while its creation of mini-canons has produced a more inclusive, intellectually richer and theoretically more rigorous academy, may create its own rigid boundaries. Such authorizing allegiances, narrowly construed, contradict postmodernism's claims about unstable, fissured identity, intertextuality and the possibility of multiple identification, with texts and varied strategies of appropriation. That Shakespeare is white, male, heterosexual, early modern, English, middle-of-the-road does not encompass him, exhaust the possible uses and meanings of his plays, or imply that those embodying none of the above can find nothing to identify with, be moved or enlarged by, in his plays. It seems foolish to assume that readers can only learn from or be empowered by writers and works which provide stabilizing reflections of themselves; sometimes one learns more by leaving home than by staying there.

Finally, as Susan Faludi meticulously details in *Backlash*, the US media in the 1980s and 1990s have inundated us with messages about women that are exactly those I grew up with: gender roles are or should be fixed and complementary, women belong in the confines of the private sphere, and career and family are incompatible for them (men, of course, are guaranteed both). The cultural onslaught the book documents reinscribes the myth of the mutual exclusiveness of childrearing and professional life, of "artistic" and maternal productivity – one which I usefully suppressed, which the women's movement convincingly denied, and which the growing number of "working" mothers belies. In doing so the backlash blames the imputed "success" of the women's rights movement for the frustrations that its dismantling causes women: "the rhetoric charges feminists with all the crimes it perpetrates" (Faludi: 1991: xxii).

These conflicts between essentialism/anti-essentialism and between fixed and multiple identities play themselves out for me now within my joint appointment in women's studies and English and on both sides of it. When I teach "Introduction to Women's Studies," I first teach the students that they are women and that they are oppressed, but powerful; once they understand that I turn around and try to teach them that there is no such thing as women, that "woman" is a malleable social construct and a dangerously divided political identity group. I focus on the differences of race, class and sexuality which divide women – and which can create deep divisions within the class. "Men," however, tend to become an overly unified category in women's studies classes. On the side I try to fit in doses of history and a crash course in close and resistant reading.

In teaching Shakespeare and Renaissance studies, I am interested in challenging traditional idealizations of Shakespeare and Spenser while (of course) insisting on their interest and value. I emphasize the presence of women writers, the status and roles of women in the period, and the importance of the controversy over them. Reversing the dynamics of women's studies courses, in disunifying Shakespeare and male authors, I reunify women. In teaching Shakespeare I continue to try to break down the rigid boundaries which restrict him (and me). A central strategy in research and teaching is to contextualize the plays in order to dislodge prefabricated assumptions and open them up for debate – just as did my high school Shakespeare experience. I have examined Shakespeare and the female characters in the plays in relation to the middle-class women he grew up surrounded by in Stratford – his mother, eight aunts, sisters, cousins, daughters (Neely 1989b). I have looked at the plays' participation in the construction of female sexuality (or rather, heterosexuality) in the early modern period (Neely 1989b). In my "Epilogue" to *Women's Revisions of Shakespeare* (Neely 1990), I explore how women writers have drawn on, appropriated and revised Shakespeare in accord with their own different cultural homes, in particular by their authorship of feminist romance. In teaching *Othello* now, I emphasize the issue of Othello's blackness and its erasure by critics like myself, providing historical context by talking about the arrival of blackamoors in England, and about racism in the Muslim slave trade[17] or looking at the interlocking representations of various Mediterranean "others" in *Othello*, *The Merchant of Venice*, Marlowe's *Jew of Malta* and Elizabeth Cary's *Tragedie of Mariam*: Jews, women, servants, Turks, slaves, "mongrell edomites," Arabs, Moors. In such research and teaching, the breadth of material which now needs coverage often crowds out readings, the extended, original close analyses of texts which must ground claims about literature and culture if they are to have weight and value.[18] Some days I get tired of self-reflection. Some days I am overwhelmed by the demands of two units, the burgeoning canons in Renaissance, women's studies, and theory, and the lack of hegemonizing structures to simplify my choices. Some days I long to feel "at home, where people know me," where I know them.

To acknowledge and challenge the exclusions on which home is based, to leave home, is to risk the loss of the self called up by Othello's "And when I love thee not, / Chaos is come again" (3.3.91–2) and to fear the separation from the community which Brabantio characterizes as monstrous in Desdemona: "and she, in spite of nature, / Of years, of country, of credit, everything / To fall in love with what she feared to look on!"(1.3.96–8). But it is also to "arrive where we started / And know the place for the first time" (Eliot 1952: 145). This new knowing, Minnie Bruce Pratt asserts, is a gain of changing and working for change:

> I am trying to learn how to live, to have the speaking-to extend beyond the moment's word, to act so as to change the unjust circumstances that keep us from being able to speak to each other; I'm trying to get a little closer to the

longed-for but unrealized world, where we each are able to live, but not by trying to make someone less than us, not by someone else's blood or pain.

(Bulkin, Pratt and Smith 1988: 13)

This "longed-for world" embodies reconciliations achieved through effort and loss, not entirely unlike those figured in Shakespearean romance where Leontes and Prospero live "by someone else's blood and pain," but Leontes must atone for his denial of Hermione and Prospero must discard power to achieve reconciliation and must confront (ambiguously) his relationship to the enslaved Caliban, his child, his servant, his subject, and his dark double: "This thing of darkness I acknowledge mine." Likewise, Hermione, in *The Winter's Tale* does not simply experience motherhood but must claim it by her potent withdrawal, her calculated reappearance, and her urgent reforging of connections with her daughter: she invokes the gods, questions Perdita, and asserts her own self-sustaining identity: "I have preserved myself to see the issue."

NOTES

1 My title alludes to that of Martin and Mohanty (1986), "Feminist Politics: What's Home Got to Do with it?" and both my concept of "home" and my use of Minnie Bruce Pratt's narrative are indebted to their influential piece. An earlier version of my essay was written for a seminar, "Gender and Cultural Difference" at the Sixth International Shakespeare Congress in Tokyo in August 1991. I am grateful to Madelon Sprengnether, who proposed and organized the session, for the opportunity to participate, to the other participants, and especially to Amanda Anderson and Gayle Greene for their crucial questions and suggestions. Reading successive drafts of Anderson's essay, "Crypto-normativism and Double Gestures: The Politics of Poststructuralism," has helped me to understand more clearly the theoretical implications of my narrative.

2 This Laura Lee Hope series was initiated in 1904, and by 1945 included forty-nine titles, for example, *The Bobbsey Twins at Home, The Bobbsey Twins at the Seashore, The Bobbsey Twins on a Houseboat*. The books depict 9-year-old Bert and Nan, who are tall, slender, and dark-haired; 5-year-old Flossie and Freddie, who are short, fat, and blond; Mr and Mrs Bobbsey (who, as parents and authority figures have no given names and no physical characteristics); Dinah, the big, fat, colored (*sic*) cook, who speaks in pronounced dialect; Snap, the (male) circus dog; and Snoop, the boring female cat. As even this brief account makes clear, the series' humor and adventures revolve entirely around stereotypes of gender, race, class, age and body type. The books often end with the restoration of families, especially the recovery of long-lost brothers and the reunions of lost boys with their parents.

3 Cf. Greene's essay in this volume; narratives in Friedan (1963); many essays in Ruddick and Daniels (1977), including those by Stimpson (pp.73–5) and Keller (p.89); and Snitow (1990). In effect, I kept putting off making a choice between career and motherhood (telling myself, "Next year I'll stop working and stay home with the kids") until it was irrelevant (my three children are now grown). I never remember feeling on one side or the other of the polarity between "maximizers" and "minimizers" (Stimpson 1980), between being glad to be a woman and glad not to be a woman, which Ann Snitow evokes so powerfully in "A Gender Diary" (1990).

4 Although my mother put in my application for Smith at birth, I resisted her pressure to attend and only made the decision to go (on what felt like my own initiative) one weekend

when she was out of town. I see this decision now as one stage in my complex identification with and disidentification from my mother. We both benefited, although in quite different ways, from the college, and it was a pleasure to join her there last June for our respective thirtieth and sixtieth reunions.

5 Especially influential directly and indirectly were Monroe Beardsley's *Aesthetics*, Cleanth Brooks' and Robert Penn Warren's *Understanding Poetry*, Elizabeth Drew's *Poetry*, and W. K. Wimsatt's *The Verbal Icon*.

6 My Jewish Smith roommate and I jokingly nicknamed each other Bloom and Dedalus, reflecting our passion for Joyce's *Ulysses* and our identifications with these characters; we loved Molly Bloom's soliloquy, especially when read by Siobhan McKenna (Caedmon), but our identifications with this minor character were perhaps too taken-for-granted to register.

7 The novels were *Under the Net* (1954), *Flight from the Enchanter* (1956), *The Sandcastle* (1957), *The Bell* (1958). The relation I explored, that between self and other, is now a matter for sophisticated conceptualization and debate – for example about "intersubjectivity." Cf. Anderson (1992); Benhabib (1986, 1987).

8 The Mack essay is reprinted in Dean (1961). This volume of reprinted essays serves as a perfect introduction to the Shakespeare criticism I grew up with; it includes essays by C. L. Barber, M. C. Bradbrook, E. K. Chambers, W. H. Clemen, Northrop Frye, Harley Granville-Barker, Alfred Harbage, G. Wilson Knight, Robert B. Heilman, Caroline Spurgeon, E. M. W. Tillyard, D. A. Traversi; only A. C. Bradley is missing.

9 My developing feminist critique was supported subsequently by the work of friends and colleagues engaged in similar projects, among them C. L. Barber, Peter Erickson, Charles Frey, Gayle Greene, Coppélia Kahn, Marianne Novy, Phyllis Rackin, Madelon (Gohlke) Sprengnether, Carolyn Swift (Lenz), Richard P. Wheeler.

10 Loomba rightly calls me on this exclusion (1989: 41,60) and on my failure to notice the racism of Fiedler's discussion as well as its sexism. Cf. Fiedler (1972: 139–96).

11 Cohen (1987: 23–5) usefully characterizes my book. Some of the many Renaissance critics I learned from then (and since) are Catherine Belsey, Jonathan Dollimore, Margaret Ferguson, Steven Greenblatt, Jean Howard, Joan Kelly, Louis Montrose, Steven Mullaney, Marilyn Williamson.

12 It is an academic myth that the purpose of research and publishing is to enable (force) scholars to grow or "keep up." It may be that working on long-term book projects is in fact likely to retard or halt intellectual growth because of the deep necessity to protect the coherence of the project by not challenging its assumptions, thus jeopardizing its completion. Our self-validating "book" may too often be a home that protects us rather than a journey that shakes us up.

13 Especially influential have been the essays in Moraga and Anzaldúa (1981), Bulkin, Pratt and Smith (1988), and Anzaldúa (1990b).

14 Cf, also many feminists who call for coalitions across the lines of identity politics, for example, Reagon (1983), Anzaldúa (1990a) and Lorde (1990).

15 For some useful and varied examples see Alcoff (1988), Anderson (1992), de Lauretis (1990), Martin (1988), Sedgewick (1990), Smith (1988), Snitow (1990).

16 See self-mapping of multiple identities in Sedgewick (1990: 63) and Anzaldúa (1990a: 380).

17 Useful resources include Loomba (1989), Lewis (1990), Bartels (1990) and Barthelemy (1987).

18 Cf. Berger (1988: 459). Harry Berger's discussion of his "reeducation" (454), explored in his "Afterword" to *Revisionary Play*, a collection of essays written in the sixties and the eighties, intersects with mine in informative ways. I too have tried to "de-aestheticize New Critical practice" (453), and could describe myself as a "reconstructed old New Critic" (460). His summary of the postulates of New Criticism and their fate in

contemporary discourse is especially useful (460–1, summarizing Berger 1986) as is his analysis of the ways in which the theoretical developments of this period "facilitate the breaching of those boundaries that New Criticism drew around interpretation and its 'object' to distinguish the specifically literary or aesthetic transaction from others" (454).

REFERENCES

Alcoff, Linda (1988) "Cultural Feminism Versus Post-Structuralism: The Identity Crisis in Feminist Theory," *Signs* 13 (3): 405–36.

Anderson, Amanda (1992) "Cryptonormativism and Double Gestures: The Politics of Poststructuralism," *Cultural Critique* 21 (spring), 63–95.

Anzaldúa, Gloria (1990a) "La conciencia de la mestiza: Towards a new consciousness," in Anzaldúa (1990b).

——(ed.) (1990b) *Making Face; Making Soul: Creative and Critical Perspectives by Women of Color*, San Francisco: Aunt Lute Press.

Bartels, Emily C. (1990) "Making More of the Moor: Aaron, Othello, and Renaissance Refashionings of Race," *Shakespeare Quarterly* 41:433–54.

Barthelemy, Anthony (1987) *Black Face Maligned Race: The Representation of Blacks in English Drama from Shakespeare to Southerne*, Baton Rouge and London: Louisiana State University Press.

Beardsley, Monroe (1958) *Aesthetics: Problems in the Philosophy of Criticism*, New York: Harcourt, Brace.

Benhabib, Seyla (1986) *Critique, Norm and Utopia: A Study of the Foundations of Critical Theory*, New York; Columbia University Press.

——(1987) "The Generalized and the Concrete Other: The Kohlberg-Gilligan Controversy and Feminist Theory," in Seyla Benhabib and Drucilla Cornell (eds) *Feminism as Critique: On the Politics of Gender*, Minneapolis: University of Minnesota Press.

Berger, Harry (1986) "Reconstructing the Old New Criticism," *Journal of Comparative Literature and Aesthetics* 9:1–14.

——(1988) "Afterword." *Revisionary Play: Studies in the Spenserian Dynamics*, Berkeley: University of California Press: 453–73.

Brooks, Cleanth and Robert Penn Warren (1960) *Understanding Poetry*, 3rd edn, New York: Holt, Rinehart, Winston.

Bulkin, Ellie, Minnie Bruce Pratt and Barbara Smith (1988) *Yours in Struggle: Three Feminist Perspectives on Anti-Semitism and Racism*, Ithaca, NY: Firebrand Books.

Cohen, Walter (1987) "Political Criticism of Shakespeare," in Jean Howard and Marion O'Connor (eds) *Shakespeare Reproduced: The Text in History and Ideology*, New York and London: Methuen, 18–46.

de Lauretis, Teresa (1990) "Upping the Anti [*sic*] in Feminist Theory," in Hirsch and Keller (eds) (1990).

Dean, Leonard (ed) (1961) *Shakespeare: Modern Essays in Criticism*, New York: Oxford University Press.

Drew, Elizabeth (1959) *Poetry: A Modern Guide to its Understanding and Enjoyment*, New York: Dell.

Eliot, T. S. (1952) *The Complete Poems and Plays: 1909–1950*, New York: Harcourt Brace.

Faludi, Susan (1991) *Backlash: The Undeclared War Against American Women*, New York: Crown.

Fiedler, Leslie A. (1972) *The Stranger in Shakespeare*, New York: Stein and Day.

Friedan, Betty (1963) *The Feminine Mystique*, New York: Dell.

Hirsch, Marianne and Evelyn Fox Keller (eds) (1990) *Conflicts in Feminism*, New York and London: Routledge.

James, Henry (1934) *The Art of the Novel*, reprinted 1984, Boston: Northeastern.

Joyce, James (1934) *Ulysses*, New York: Modern Library.

Keller, Evelyn Fox (1977) "The Anomaly of a Woman in Physics," in Ruddick and Daniels (eds) (1977), 77–91.

Lewis, Bernard (1990) *Race and Slavery in the Middle East: An Historical Enquiry*, Oxford: Oxford University Press.

Loomba, Ania (1989) *Gender, Race, Renaissance Drama*, Manchester and New York: Manchester University Press.

Lorde, Audre (1990) "I am Your Sister: Black Women Organizing Across Sexualities," in Anzaldúa (1990b), 321–5.

Martin, Biddy (1988) "Lesbian Identity and Autobiographical Difference(s)," in Bella Brodski and Celeste Schenck (eds) *Life/Lines: Theorizing Women's Autobiography*, Ithaca: Cornell University Press, 77–103.

Martin, Biddy and Chandra Talpade Mohanty (1986) "Feminist Politics: What's Home Got to Do with it?" in Teresa de Lauretis (ed.) *Feminist Studies/Critical Studies*, Bloomington: Indiana University Press, 191–212.

Millet, Kate (1970) *Sexual Politics*, Garden City: Doubleday.

Moraga, Cherríe, and Gloria Anzaldúa (eds) (1981) *This Bridge Called my Back: Writings by Radical Women of Color*, Massachusetts: Persephone Press.

Neely, Carol Thomas (1977) "Women and Men in *Othello*: 'what should such a fool / Do with so good a woman,'" *Shakespeare Studies* 10: 133–58.

——(1978) "Women and Issue in *The Winter's Tale*," *Philological Quarterly* 57: 181–94.

——(1985) *Broken Nuptials in Shakespeare's Plays*, New Haven: Yale University Press.

——(1989a) "Constructing Female Sexuality in the Renaissance: Stratford, London, Windsor, Vienna," in Richard Feldstein and Judith Roof (eds) *Feminism and Psychoanalysis*, Ithaca: Cornell University Press, 209–29.

——(1989b) "Shakespeare's Women: Historical Facts and Dramatic Representations" in Norman Holland, Sidney Homan, and Bernard J. Paris (eds) *Shakespeare's Personality*, Berkeley: University of California Press, 116–34.

——(1990) "Epilogue: Remembering Shakespeare: Revising Ourselves," in Marianne Novy (ed.) *Women's Revisions of Shakespeare*, Urbana: University of Illinois Press, 242–52.

Pratt, Minnie Bruce (1988) "Identity: Skin, Blood, Heart," in Bulkin, Pratt and Smith (1988), 11–63.

Reagon, Bernice Johnson (1983) "Coalition Politics: Turning the Century," in Barbara Smith (ed.) *Home Girls: A Black Feminist Anthology*, New York: Kitchen Table Press, 356–8.

Rich, Adrienne (1976) *Of Woman Born: Motherhood as Experience and Institution*, New York: W. W. Norton.

Ruddick, Sara and Pamela Daniels (eds) (1977) *Working it Out: 23 Women Writers, Artists, Scientists, and Scholars Talk about their Lives and Work*, New York: Pantheon.

Sedgewick, Eve Kosofsky (1990) "Introduction: Axiomatic," *Epistomology of the Closet*, Berkeley: University of California Press, 1–63.

Smith, Paul (1988) *Discerning the Subject*, Minneapolis: University of Minnesota Press.

Snitow, Ann (1990) "A Gender Diary," in Hirsch and Keller (eds) (1990), 9–43.

Spivak, Gayatri Chakravorty (1990) "Strategy, Identity, Writing," Interview (1986) in Sarah Harasym (ed.) *The Post-Colonial Critic: Interviews, Strategies, Dialogues*, New York and London: Routledge, 35–49.

——(1988) "Subaltern Studies: Deconstructing Historiography," in *In Other Worlds: Essays in Cultural Politics*, New York: Routledge, 197–221.

Stimpson, Catherine R. (1980) "The New Scholarship About Women: The State of the Art," *Annals of Scholarship* 1 (2): 2–14.

——(1977) "On Work," in Ruddick and Daniels (eds) (1977) 72–6.

Wimsatt, W. K. (1954) *The Verbal Icon*, Lexington, Ky: University of Kentucky Press.

Chapter 14

Being the subject and the object
Reading African-American women's novels

Barbara Christian

If memory serves me right, the first novel by an African-American woman I'd even held in my hand came from a second-hand bookstore in Harlem. It was 1967. I was a graduate student at Columbia, and an English instructor in the SEEK program at CCNY, a program designed to uplift apparently uneducable black and Puerto Rican youth by giving them the skills to enter city colleges. In ways I'd not consciously calculated, I was pursuing two different tracks of training. At Columbia, I was working on a paper on Wallace Stevens, a concession to me from my professors who, mostly, were immersed in British literature and who barely touched on American contemporary writers, the writers in whom I was most interested. At SEEK, I was fast discovering African-American writing (in response to which my students suddenly exhibited the writing capacity they were not supposed to have) and was planning classes on *Invisible Man*. Using African-American literature in the classroom sent me on regular treks to black bookstores where I could sometimes find out-of-print books, the category it seemed to which most African-American books then belonged.

So it was, that I saw the image of a brown girl on the cover of a cheap Avon paperback and noticed its title, *Brown Girl, Brownstones*. I'd been in this country, and had studied literature long enough to know that brown girls did not usually appear on book covers nor did they figure prominently in novels. My curiosity aroused, precisely because I was a brown girl, I bought the book for fifty cents, and put it away until at some future date, after I'd completed the Stevens paper, I could read it.

The world I entered into in Paule Marshall's brownstones was unlike any other I'd encountered in books, not even that of James Baldwin or Richard Wright, LeRoi Jones or Ishmael Reed. Perhaps because I am a Caribbean woman living in the United States, *Brown Girl, Brownstones* resonated for me on many levels, some of which I cannot yet articulate. Reading this novel was, for me, an intensely personal and emotional experience. It was not that I'd grown up in Brooklyn, as Selina had, for I'd spent my childhood in the Caribbean. Nor that my mother and father resembled Silla and Deighton – quite to the contrary. Yet I recognized, *knew* Marshall's characters – the Boyces, the Chancellors, Suggie, Clive; I spoke their language with its *Wunna's* and *beautiful-ugly's*. I'd experienced their cultural context without being able to really articulate it, for it was the world view in which

I was raised. I'd tasted every day the gritty dilemmas with which they were contending – without having named them. Marshall's first novel insinuated itself into my emotional psyche and compelled me, in spite of myself, to remember the rich, sometimes frustrating complexity of my own people, a complexity many of us wanted to ignore, forget about in the black revolutionary fervor of 1967.

In particular, Silla's woman-voice constantly interrupted my mind-voice. Her anguish-rage warned me of trials I might have to face. Like a lioness she stalked the corridors of my imagination even as she challenged the ideal of black womanhood enunciated by ideologues of the sixties. Her fate called on me to act, lest my life resemble hers. Her wonderful and terrible deeds mocked the simplicity of many of the views I held.

For at that time, many young black women like myself thought ourselves free enough to be all we could be, at least in the Struggle – only to find that we were enclosed, even in our own communities, in cages of misrepresentations as to who a black woman should be. As many of us were beginning to value, to celebrate the black culture our mothers had been instrumental in creating and passing on, we found ourselves entangled in contradictions about black motherhood, and silenced by versions of history in which we were said to have undermined our own.

Supposedly we'd been domineering matriarchs, powerful furies who'd brought the race down and who needed to come down off our high horses so that our men could ascend to the throne – in much the same way that the ancient mother goddesses of pre-history had had to be tamed by the enlightened male gods who vanquished them. How else were black people to survive in the male-centered world of America? As Selina tossed one of her silver bracelets, the symbol of her West Indian heritage, on to the American landscape, I fondled the bracelets I still wore and wondered what my fate would be.

Whether or not we young black women ascribed to the ideals of womanhood in this society, we could not achieve them and survive, given the racism we daily encountered. In fact, rather than being powerful matriarchs, we made "our mouths a gun" precisely because we were the least of the powerless, caught up as we were by the demands of survival for our families, demands which were sometimes in conflict with our own desires and personalities. We were often blamed for the sacrifice of self even as we were called upon to make the sacrifice. No wonder, like Silla and her women friends, we'd traditionally sought the company and solace of each other, for which we were again criticized in this western society focused on the male/female couple.

Marshall did not resolve our dilemmas. What she did was to name them, embody their complexity in the language, the gestures of her characters, in their relationships with one another. By carefully sculpting her characters' forms within the space in which they actually moved, she illuminated the intricacy of the reality behind their apparently simple appearances. Why, for example, did so many of the black men I knew appear to be hedonistic, irresponsible ne'er-do-wells? Marshall's deft analyses of Deighton and Clive's characters exposed the rage, the aura of deep-felt impotence behind their pose. Why did so many black women appear to be hard, scheming, embittered bitches? Marshall's tender but precise probing of Silla and her women friends revealed the vulnerability of their existence, the woman-impotence and rage with which they contended. What could brown girls like Selina, like myself *become*, given the society's view of who we were? Could we disentangle ourselves from the intersections of oppressions we moved in, or were we doomed to relive the life of Silla?

For me, *Brown Girl, Brownstones* was not just a text, it was an accurate and dynamic embodiment both of the possibilities and improbabilities of my own life. In it I as subject encountered myself as object. In illuminating so clearly, so lovingly, the mesh of my own context, Marshall provided me with a guide, a way to contemplate my own situation and gave me back the memory, the embodied history of women like myself who had preceded me. *Brown Girl, Brownstones* was not a book I read in order to write about, or to answer smart questions about. It was crucial to a deeper understanding of my own life.

When I met Paule Marshall a year after I'd read her novel, I was not surprised to hear her say that she'd written *Brown Girl, Brownstones*, not so much with publication in mind as to unravel her own knots. Years later when I read an interview with Toni Morrison, in which she said that she wrote what she did because *she* needed to read it, I recalled Marshall's comment about her reason for writing *Brown Girl, Brownstones* and my response to it. If there is any one reason why I write literary criticism (and there are times when I wonder why I do), it is because of the need I feel in African-American women writers to craft experience informed not only by their intelligence but also by *their* imagination and *my* need to respond to that crafting. African-American women interpret, create their own experience even as that experience might have been critically affected by forces outside them.

For although the *idea* that there is a shared experience between African-American women's history and the reality of African-American women's lives is now being challenged, *my* experience is that we have known both a collective life as well as individual variations that are ours and ours alone. That both these ideas are true does not mean that either is not true.

While some may say that the reason I responded to *Brown Girl, Brownstones* as I did was due to the West Indian origin I share with Paule Marshall, I did not have that same kind of connection with the characters of *The Bluest Eye*, the first novel by an African-American woman, about which I wrote. I'd never been to Lorain, Ohio, nor had I migrated from the Southern United States to the Midwest. As with *Brown Girl, Brownstones*, however, reading Morrison's first novel was for me intense, emotional. That was due, of course, to Morrison's remarkable language, which sounded so much like black music, and to the themes she chose to craft.

If there is any experience black women in this hemisphere have in common it is the way our physical appearance, our bodies, have been held against us – how the norms of beauty as self-worth for a woman have systematically been denied us. When Pecola sees the disgust in the eyes of the Polish storekeeper when he tries not to look at her dark face, her kinky hair, her Negroid features, I know what she is feeling. That look is a look that was burnt into my psyche from my youth and embellished even by my own community's comments about "good" and "bad" hair. As late as the 1980s the usually astute Stevie Wonder could use as one of his lyrics in a popular song: "She's dark *but* she's pretty." Every black girl in this hemisphere *knows* the feeling of schism from watching the fly-a-way hair and true blue-eyed imitation blonde TV icons of beauty. And despite the "black is beautiful" slogans of the late sixties, one can open up any popular black magazine today and *see* the unbelievable ways in which black women are still drastically altering their physical selves.

What Morrison dramatized so beautifully in *The Bluest Eye* was the relationship between the value of woman's physical self and philosophical concepts about the society's definition of the good and the beautiful. How societies are fixated on *The Body* rather than valuing the fact that there are many bodies. How we create hierarchies of worth based on *The Body* as a manifestation of class, wealth, virtue, goodness. And because black women's bodies have been the object of systematic abuse for all of this century's history, it stands to reason that our bodies would be placed lowest in the hierarchy. Although Pecola is a tragic victim, Morrison achieves a triumph in giving her, who has never had a voice, a story in her own right, in situating her who has been the margin of the margin, at the center of a narrative. In doing that, Morrison challenged the concept of physical beauty as monolithic, and as an ideal, not only as it relates to brown girls but to all women, to her fair-skinned Maureen Peal, and to societal icons of beauty such as the Shirley Temple girl doll of her novel.

In one of her talks, Morrison said that she created Pecola because she'd known Pecolas – the ones with no voice whose stories are not acknowledged, and that she'd written *The Bluest Eye* partly because she did not recognize the black people in much of the literature of the 1960s. For many of us at that time wished to forget about the Pecolas – those who had not survived the madness of this society – and preferred to focus on the Afro-coiffed beauties of the time.

Interestingly, *The Bluest Eye* was published at the end of that decade, in 1970, a date it shares with another pivotal African-American women's novel for me – *The Third Life of Grange Copeland*. Alice Walker's first novel shares with *The Bluest Eye* a focus on types of black people hardly mentioned in the literature of the decade that preceded it. In dramatizing the life of a family of black sharecroppers that moves in time from the 1910s to the 1950s, Walker reminded us that all blacks did not live in the Northern urban ghettoes. For her rural blacks, the "violent" revolutionary rhetoric of the period had little meaning. Yet violence was very much a part of her characters' lives – not only the institutionalized violence of racism and segregation that contained them, but violence within their own families.

In the sixties of my youth, the black family was one of the most idealized icons of the movement – from the Muslim messages to the cultural nationalist images of the neo-African family. Yet I wondered, as Walker did, "why people in [black] families are often cruel to each another and how much of that cruelty was caused by outside forces such as various social injustices, segregation, unemployment, etc." That question was not an abstract one for me. I'd lived in Harlem where one could nightly hear and sometimes witness the rage and violence that black men and women, often in families, turned on each other. And as any West Indian can tell you, the Saturday night yard fights of husbands and wives were common occurrences of communal life. I did not want to remember the *internal* violence we inflicted on one another for it led so easily to racist stereotypes about the innate violence of black people. Yet in trying to forget it, not speaking about it, I ignored the destruction of so many people, particularly of women I knew.

What I responded to most personally in *The Third Life of Grange Copeland* were the many black women who were destroyed within their own families, Mem and Margaret Copeland, Josie – and how that destruction went against the monumental image of the strong black woman who could bear anything, would bear anything, an image so often invoked by black society. Because I am a black woman, that quality of indomitable strength had often been attributed to me, more accurately laid on me sometimes as an excuse as to why I should put up with, endure that which no one should have to endure. Why could we not be like other human beings who could only bear but so much? Why were we not valued? Walker's graphic portrayal of Mem Copeland reminded me that we did not always endure – that many of us were destroyed within and by our own families.

For it seemed to me in 1970 that Walker was directly asking us, black women of my generation, whether women were valued in the idealized black family that political ideologues promoted, where the black man was head of the house, the black woman, the black madonna, clearly an imitation of the Western Christian family. I knew that American society promoted power and money as the measuring sticks of manhood, attributes to which few black men had access. And that, like Grange Copeland, in believing in this conception of manhood, many black men too felt powerless and vented their frustrations on us, the only ones over whom they felt they could exert some power. In not understanding this situation, in acquiescing to that control, black women participated in the destruction of themselves and their families. I did not acknowledge what I knew was happening all around me until I read Walker's spare incisive analysis of Grange Copeland's first two lives. Walker's novel was a novel, to use one of her own titles, "for everyday use."

Walker's novel reminded me how important family history was – not the abstract history of text books, but the remembering those who came before us, the means they used to hold on to their humanity, and the ways in which they failed. Even as many of us in the sixties invoked images of a romantic Africa that never existed, we tended to forget those who'd recently preceded us, the sharecropping grandmother, the uncle in the sugarcane plantations, the generations who'd preceded us in this new place of pain and had something to tell us that we needed to know. Grange's conversations with her granddaughter Ruth about their family history, the land they cultivated, the dances they danced, were conversations *with me* as well, about the recent past and the wisdom embodied in it.

Like Marshall and Morrison, Walker both criticized and celebrated those who came before them, before me, and in languages that my ancestors, I myself, had helped to create, languages that were ours and affected me not only in intellectual terms but in that deep part of myself – in feeling ways. Their voice, their many voices sounded so authentically like mine, like ours, like the calypso, like jazz, like country blues, and their different uses of tone, pitch, timbre emanated from a deep part of themselves as women. They dared to remember the recent past, and show how it continued to affect the present, the history we are now making, not only through intellectual concepts but through those shared sounds, gestures, nuances, that cannot be completely dissected. Like Claudia and Frieda as they listened to the grown-up women in *The Bluest Eye*, we not only hear the words but sense the "truth in timbre."

How does one respond to a language that is tonality, dance, to these voices without mutilating them and turning them into logical progressions, mere intellectual concepts? How does one shimmy back to forms that soar beyond philosophical discourse or jargon? How does one respond to the nuance, windings, shifts, the turning of the music that is this literature? That is the goal I am still seeking.

Chapter 15

Generational differences
Reliving mother–daughter conflicts

Madelon Sprengnether

> I am talking here about a kind of strength which can only be one woman's gift
> to another, the bloodstream of our inheritance. Until a strong line of love,
> confirmation, and example stretches from mother to daughter, from woman
> to woman across the generations, women will still be wandering in the wilder-
> ness.
>
> Adrienne Rich, *Of Woman Born*

Adrienne Rich has a wonderful phrase to describe the failed nurturance of women
under patriarchy: she says we are "wildly unmothered" (1986: 225). This is very
much how I once felt, not only in my own family, but also in the larger institutional
family of academia. It was feminism, I was initially convinced, that would save
me from this dual dilemma. Filled with seventies' idealism, I believed that we
feminists in academia would repair our mutual orphanhood through sisterly
understanding and co-operation. I thought that we really could transform the
academy if only we put our minds to it: from a place of patriarchal rivalry to one
modeled on an ethic of empathy and care.[1] In time, we would be the "good
enough" mothers to our successors which we had so craved in our own child-
hoods and careers.[2] Needless to say, this goal has proved elusive, if not downright
foolish in its failure to acknowledge the very real differences (of class, race, sexual
preference) that distinguish and often divide us.

One difference that is not much discussed, however, is precisely that of age,
how it is that older and younger feminists relate to each other across generations,
a process which can evoke troubled memories of mother–daughter conflict.[3] I
want to describe some of the more obstructive aspects of this process as I have
observed it in myself and in my relations with younger colleagues, in the hope of
promoting a more positive and useful dynamic. In order to do this, I will need to
interweave information regarding my own experience of being a daughter and a
mother both in and outside of the academy.

Although I became a mother (in the middle of my first year teaching) when I
was 27, I had difficulty seeing myself as one and for many years believed that I
was a failure. This had to do with my assumption (based on my reading, my social
environment, and my early childhood experience of a traditional family) that only

a full-time mother could do the job right.[4] It also had to do with the disappointments of my growing up and my subsequent inability to internalize a positive
maternal image. For, while I had felt loved and cared for by both parents as a
young girl, the sudden death of my father when I was nine dramatically altered
the nature of our family life. My mother, who was emotionally traumatized by the
loss of my father, was almost equally distraught at the prospect of taking his place
as breadwinner. This double burden made her seem remote, anxious, depressed,
to the point that I sometimes felt I had lost, not one parent, but two. Bravely, she
managed to keep us together as a family and to earn a living, but not without a
cost. While materially we did well, even prospering over time, I perceived her as
distracted, distant. As a consequence, I felt my mother missing from the most
intimate aspects of my growing up. Later, when I tried to summon an idea of what
mothering should be, I had only scraps of memories to draw on in combination
with feelings of absence or sadness. Mostly I thought about mistakes I wanted to
avoid, when I wasn't feeling simply frightened or inadequate.

For all of these reasons it was easier for me to think of myself as a daughter
than as a mother. Institutionally, of course, this was encouraged. As a graduate
student in the late sixties, I felt this in both enjoyable and disturbing ways. All I
had to do as a daughter was please my academic fathers, a duty which I found
easy enough to perform. If anything, I basked in the atmosphere of paternal
approbation which I had so lacked because of my own father's untimely death.
Only gradually did I become aware of signs of disapproval, all focused on the
issue of my intended marriage to a fellow graduate student. "But you have such
promise," I was told by one advisor, "you don't want to ruin your career." "Think
of what your life will be like," said another, in the middle of a discussion of my
fiancé's problematic draft status. "You wouldn't want to be a camp follower."
Getting married, I slowly began to realize, was somehow destroying my credibility
as an ace student.

No doubt my professors thought their advice was simply realistic. Married
women, after all, were supposed to follow their husbands, produce children, and
immerse themselves in domestic routine, none of which was conducive to writing
scintillating articles, much less great books. But I have come to suspect another
motive as well. By stepping out of the daughter role, I was violating an implicit
pact. In order to continue to receive paternal approval I was expected to remain
an *ingenue*, a case of arrested development. I was confirmed in this impression
when, many years later, I acquired access to my confidential personnel file (a result
of the passage of the Minnesota Data Practices Act) and had an opportunity to
read my graduate school recommendations. While generally pleased at their terms
of praise, I was somewhat rattled by the overall impression they conveyed. I appeared smart and promising enough but also rather characterless, like a trembling
and starry-eyed Miranda, in need of mature guidance. Choosing finally to ignore
my marriage, my professors had reconstituted me (discursively at least) as perpetual daughter.

There is yet another way in which I came to understand my institutional identity as daughter. I left graduate school believing that my professors had done their job and I was now on my own. The concept of mentoring was not only something I had never heard of, but was wholly oblivious to in my environment. It took me years to realize that what I had to learn, laboriously, through trial and error, was simply the patrimony of many of my male colleagues. Magically, they seemed to know things I did not: how to write grant applications, where to send articles for publication, how to read papers at scholarly conferences. What I stumbled into once again was the position of daughter, this time as anomalous outsider. While permitted to grace the graduate classroom, I was never really expected to succeed and hence received no practical instruction about the workings of the profession. By the time I understood that my ignorance of these things was not a sign of inherent unfitness, I no longer needed the Oedipal circuit from which I had been so neatly excluded.

Luckily, I found other women. When I arrived at the University of Minnesota in 1971, after a brief stint at a small liberal arts college where I was the only woman in my department (and one of a mere handful on campus), I discovered the pleasure of women colleagues.[5] Though studiously ignored by the senior men in my field (three full professors complexly bonded through shared history and ideology), I was openly and warmly received by the two women who had preceded me at the assistant and associate ranks. Together, we created our own small society, sharing information, not only about departmental politics and the mechanics of the profession, but also about our most intimate hopes and dreams. From the heart of this alliance, we drew strength on many levels. All three of us assisted in the creation of the Women's Studies Program, and later in the establishment of our own departmental subfield, Feminist Studies in Literature, which in turn formed a nucleus of the editorial collective for *Hurricane Alice: A Feminist Quarterly*. Both of my colleagues have chaired the Women's Studies Program, and one currently directs the Center for Advanced Feminist Studies, on whose board of graduate examining faculty all of us have served. Two of us have been active on the editorial board of *Signs* since it has moved to Minnesota, and one has recently been appointed to co-direct a university-wide program on "Excellence and Diversity in Teaching." I do not believe that we could have achieved these things without the basis we created for each other of mutual and sustained trust.[6]

Adapting Adrienne Rich's phrase, I would say that my women colleagues and I were "wildly unmentored." Abandoned by our institutional fathers, we had even less chance of finding an institutional mother, at a time when the rare woman full professor did not "identify" with other women. While the prevailing model for peer professional relationships might have suggested competition over co-operation, we actively chose differently. The two of us who were untenured, for instance – who might have seen each other as rivals for a single coveted position – decided to assist each other's progress instead. Later, the strength of this bond helped us to collaborate successfully on a book project. I mention these examples as a contrast to what one of my male peers, who had just advanced to tenure, once advised me. "As I see it," he said, "it's like we're all in this big swimming pool with a shark and the question is who can swim the fastest."[7]

I do not mean to imply that my women colleagues and I never experienced tension or conflict, but rather that when faced with these disagreeable emotions, we have made efforts to confront them, assuming that we can work our way through to a better understanding. Throughout, I believe that we have each held a deep conviction: that the continuity of our friendship matters more than any specific instance of disappointment or irritation. So far, this implicit faith has been rewarded. Our relationship has survived twenty years of growth and change, generously accommodating our differences of sexuality, regionality and class background, while teaching us over time how to continue negotiating these differences so as to integrate them more fully into our knowledge of one another.[8]

Given our closeness in age, my women colleagues have seemed more like sisters to me than mothers or daughters, though there are no doubt occasions when any one of us might offer the kind of support one could think of as maternal, coming, that is from someone older and wiser than a peer. For the most part, however, we tend to complement each other in our individual temperaments, talents and moments of energy or fatigue. When one of us is down, at least one other will be in a better frame of mind and able to help. If two of us pair off for a while, or seem to become temporarily more intimate, it is never for long or to the exclusion of the third. The flexibility and resilience of our friendship depends on the flow of energy among all three of us, and I am convinced that we know this as deeply as we know anything.

Given our history of successful alliance, we looked forward to the arrival of younger women colleagues, not only in our own department, but also across the university. While many of these relationships have developed smoothly and proved rewarding over time, others have run into some surprising snags. Thinking about the latter has persuaded me that some of the more intractable problems I have encountered are rooted in a mother–daughter dynamic so insistent, yet obscured, as to defy all but the most thoughtful and committed efforts to address.

While gradually gaining confidence in my capacity to mother my own daughter (more a matter of ethics, I think, than biology), I still did not see myself as a "mother" at work, where I was more likely to be reminded, on any given day, of my filial status in the department. Wishing, moreover, to subvert where possible the hierarchical structures that kept me knowing my place, I first tried to approach younger women as sisters, or peers. I imagined them as eager to receive the information that I and my friends had so laboriously gleaned. Unlike my senior male colleagues, I would not choose to hoard what I knew but generously to put it into circulation. What I failed to take into account, however, was not only the difference in age between me and my younger colleagues, but also the difference of rank. As first an associate, then a full professor, I had a say in their future employment, and while I might pooh-pooh this distinction, it was none the less real and something of an impediment. My desire for open and full communication, I came to see, was unrealistic. As someone with the power to vote on tenure,

I was not immediately perceived as an ally, not automatically trusted. Given that my critical temperament had been formed in a different era, moreover, I was looked on by some as behind the times. I wasn't necessarily considered an authority for today's feminists.

As unpleasant as these realizations were, the one I have found most painful derives from what I will call "academic matrophobia," borrowing Adrienne Rich's word to describe not the fear of mothers *per se* but the fear of becoming *like* one's mother (1976: 235). Looking literally less like a *soror* than a *mater* to some of my young colleagues, I believe that I evoked, at times, their unexamined, yet deeply felt, attitudes toward their own mothers.[9] While I can only guess at the individual histories that may have informed these responses, I can describe some of their effects.

What I often felt was that junior women saw projected on to me an image of the mothers who had disappointed them: through their failure to confront or to wield authority, through their repression of their daughters' spirit and energy, or through their inability to grow old in challenging and dynamic ways. Viewed through any one of these lenses, I could seem powerless in the university hierarchy and hence pitiable, overly controlling and hence to be resisted, or stultified in my opinions and hence irrelevant. Doubtless I have been all of these things on occasion, yet the wall of suspicion or indifference I sometimes encountered felt both inappropriate and excessive.

If I had thought of myself as a mother at all in relation to my younger colleagues it was in an idealized way – as someone who wanted her surrogate daughters not only to succeed, but also to have an easier time of it. In exchange (although I did not fully articulate this to myself at the time), I wanted some kind of recognition or gratitude. What I felt instead was that I had been cast in roles I had neither created nor desired yet was somehow destined to play. No matter who I tried to be, I kept turning into someone's "bad" or disparaged mother.

Despite my best efforts at learning how to mother, my own daughter had a stormy adolescence. She was often sullen or angry, threatening behavior she knew I disapproved of or openly defying me. It seemed at times that she was determined to reject everything I represented or had to offer. Occasionally, I felt something like this (in much milder terms, of course) from younger women colleagues. It was as though I simply didn't count. My pain at feeling ignored by my daughter was echoed in this way, albeit in a lesser mode. Gradually, I learned to understand better my own participation in this cycle (on both personal and academic levels) and hence to begin to alter it.

My loneliness as a child, due in part to the loss of my father, in part to my mother's distraction, left me with a legacy of need. As a result, I was more than usually sensitive to signs of indifference or rejection. When my daughter, exercising her adolescent desire for independence, began to turn away from me, I felt panicked, afraid that I had lost her love for good. Only gradually did I recognize that our struggles were not entirely wasteful. Paradoxically, by quarrelling we actually learned to communicate better, although this required that I accept her feelings as she expressed them and begin in a deep way to give her my attention.

Slowly, I realized that I could tell her what I thought, but I couldn't any more tell her what to do. When I reached this understanding, not only did I stop resisting what my daughter said to me, but I also began to talk more honestly about myself, how I came to the opinions I held, or simply how I felt. Through this kind of conversation – what I think of now as listening and letting be – my daughter and I have come to a more open and trusting place. Once I began to relax, moreover, what I could see was that my daughter, even as a teenager, had good judgment. Today, as a young woman of 22, she is not only more thoughtful than I was at her age, but also more poised, outgoing and generous.

There are some obvious parallels between my relations with my daughter and with my younger women colleagues. In both instances, my anxieties about being liked, accepted or needed (loved in the case of my daughter) interfered with the process of knowing another person. Yet it has taken me longer to understand this in my academic than my personal life, perhaps because of the greater immediacy and urgency of the latter. As a result, I have only recently begun to incorporate the lessons I learned as a mother into my professional life.

Getting to know someone takes time as well as insight, neither of which can be rushed. Slowing down, stepping back, restraining my impulse to offer gratuitous advice, have all helped me to feel more at ease with myself (less like someone's projection or parody) and to develop more dignified and comfortable relations with younger women colleagues. At the same time, I am aware that any developing relationship involves two partners, requiring a willingness, or openness to possibility on both sides. While I feel this with some younger women, with others I do not. Instead of finding fault with myself for this lack, I now see it as largely out of my control, due to factors that may be hidden, which may or may not have anything to do with me.[10]

Yet I feel some concern for our collective future. Whether or not older and younger feminists are friends matters less than that we be able to work together toward some agreed-upon aims. For this, we need to foster an atmosphere of mutual respect. Not only do we need to try to see each other as clearly as we can apart from our personal histories of mother–daughter relations, but we also need to acknowledge that some degree of cross-generational alliance is necessary for the continuing existence of our multiple feminisms. One painful contra-indication I see for this possibility is the phenomenon of what I will call "careerist feminism," the version of academic feminism that focuses on individual achievement as its primary goal, disavowing the very value of collectivity in its definition of feminism.

Believing in the relative stability of academic feminism, some younger women, I think, are overly confident about its future and hence somewhat passive about sustaining the bonds among women that made it happen in the first place. In this sense, they not only benefit from the struggles of us older feminists, who created the fields and markets that allow their work to flourish, but they also underestimate the levels of resistance that remain and are actually on the rise.[11] Neglecting the work of collaboration and mutual assistance in favor of the heady rewards of individual fame is a short-term strategy of little long-term benefit. Yet today it is quite possible to make a tidy career in academic feminism without the labor of getting to know other women. If this is the career model that prevails, I do not see that we are much better off than we were when I started out. Increasingly, however, I find women graduate students pointing to just such a career pattern as the one they hold in awe, the one they seek to emulate. This feels to me like coming full circle – a reversion to the model of competitive individualism that seventies feminism (however limited in other ways) sought to transform. It was never our goal to challenge the patriarchal fathers, simply to take their place.

Yet I do not wish to romanticize the past, any more than I wish to sentimentalize the mother–daughter relationship. On the contrary, I believe that to the extent that we idealize this bond we will be prevented from recognizing its capacity to trip us up. At the same time, I think that it is possible to incorporate an *ethics* of relationship, based on what we know about mother–daughter interaction, into the academy in order to offset the effects of unexamined projection. Now that institutional mothers actually exist, it would be a shame to blow this opportunity. As feminists, we owe it to each other not simply to relive our scripts of mother– daughter conflict, but to change them.

NOTES

1 Whereas in the seventies I would have stressed the "empathy and care" aspect of this statement, I would now place the emphasis on "ethic." I take this to be Sara Ruddick's point in *Maternal Thinking* (1990), although people who have not read her carefully may think she idealizes women's innate capacities for nurturance.

2 The phrase "good enough mother" comes from D. W. Winnicott's attempt to define an ordinary mother's ability to care adequately for her child. In the context of object relations theory generally, however, it tends to refer to a fantasy ideal of a mother's near-total absorption in nurturing her infant. I confess to a certain fascination with this fantasy ideal in the heady days of early seventies feminism, when I had less understanding both of my own limitations (for which I castigated myself) and those of mothers generally. While I continue to believe that children need sustained and loving care, I no longer think that mothers can or should be responsible for everything. Somewhere along the line, I realized that the way I lived my life was also providing an example for my daughter. As Adrienne Rich puts it, "the quality of the mother's life – however embattled and unprotected – is her primary bequest to her daughter, because a woman who can believe in herself, who is a fighter, and who continues to struggle to create livable space around her, is demonstrating to her daughter that these possibilities exist" (1986:247).

3 Evelyn Fox Keller and Helene Moglen address this issue, among others, in their insightful essay "Competition: A Problem for Academic Women." They observe that the frequency with which the mother–daughter analogy is invoked "attests to the extent to which our relations with older women who are not in fact our mothers, and with younger women who are not in fact our daughters, remain haunted by the residue of unresolved conflicts from another domain" (1987:26). They also point out that the idealism of the seventies was based, at least in part, on academic women's shared sense of marginalization. Now that some of us have achieved some of the traditional rewards of academic success, our relations with each other have become more openly competitive and conflictual. I agree with the authors' recommendation that we strive to understand our difficulties with one another instead of denying that they exist. Erika Duncan, in "Mothers and Daughters" (1987), writes compellingly about the taboo subjects of

hatred, envy and competition between actual mothers and daughters. I am moved by the honesty and the generosity of both of these essays.

4 My daughter was born in 1969, in the middle of the upheaval of the Viet Nam war, but well before the development of an academic women's movement. Needless to say, the concepts of maternity leave and day care were as yet unimagined. If anything, my social environment was even more conservative than the norm for the country at large. There were no other regular women faculty at the small liberal arts college where I taught who were also mothers of young children. I was such an anomaly that the chair of my department even suggested that I might want to "retire" after giving birth – this after less than one year teaching.

5 I believe there were only two tenured women on the faculty when I was teaching at this college. Fired with enthusiasm after reading Kate Millett's *Sexual Politics*, I tried to enlist one of them in my efforts to raise campus consciousness about faculty women. While admitting that her own experience had been grim, she told me that she wanted to put the past behind her rather than re-experience the pain of that time; hence she could not help me.

6 My colleagues are Toni A. H. McNaron and Shirley Nelson Garner. This is only a partial list of their (and our) accomplishments.

7 This man had just been elected Director of Graduate Studies. He went on to chair the department for six years.

8 While we are all three white and currently members of the academic middle class, our other differences are not negligible, nor are they easily summed up by category.

9 I was first alerted to this possibility by a young woman from another department, who was brave enough to tell me her own story of mother–daughter conflict and how it had affected the way that she viewed older women academics. Her confidence in me allowed me to think more clearly about my own history and its problematic inscription in my relations with younger women colleagues.

10 The process I am describing requires some degree of self-reflectiveness on both sides, in addition to a willingness to entertain the possibility at least of unconscious motivation. Some people, in my experience, are either oblivious to their own thought processes and behavior, or they are too absorbed in other pursuits to bother. Where there is conflict in relations with such people, it may not be possible to accomplish much in the way of mutual understanding.

11 Younger women, for instance, mindful of feminist job descriptions, curriculum changes, and publication outlets, may not be aware of the "glass ceiling" which some of us older feminists are encountering as we rise to the rank of full professor. None of us should be complacent, moreover, about the program of the National Association of Scholars, which targets academic feminism in its anti "political correctness" campaign. For evidence of reversionary tendencies in society at large see Susan Faludi's *Backlash*.

REFERENCES

Duncan, Erika (1987) "Mothers and Daughters," in Valerie Miner and Helen E. Longino (eds) *Competition: A Feminist Taboo?*, New York: Feminist Press, 131–40.

Faludi, Susan (1991) *Backlash: The Undeclared War Against American Women*, New York: Crown.

Keller, Evelyn Fox, and Helene Moglen (1987) "Competition: A Problem for Academic Women," in Valerie Miner and Helen E. Longino (eds) *Competition: A Feminist Taboo?*, New York: Feminist Press, 21–37.

Rich, Adrienne (1976) *Of Woman Born: Motherhood as Experience and Institution*, New York: W.W. Norton.

Ruddick, Sara (1990) *Maternal Thinking*, New York: Ballantine.

Winnicott, D. W. (1971) *Playing and Reality*, New York: Basic.

Part IV

Connections and contradictions

Part three

Connections and contractions

Chapter 16

Stormy weather
A memoir of the second wave

Leslie W. Rabine

Among the thought-provoking questions sent to contributors to this volume, one struck me in particular: "A major strength of feminist scholarship is the vital connection between lived experience and theory. How would you describe the connection between your work and your life?" The question struck me because my work and life have been so haunted by the multiple disconnections between and within theory and experience: in my life as an academic, versus my research as a critic, versus my experience in academic feminism, versus my experience in community feminist and peace groups.

These disconnections, untraceable to any simple cause, are overdetermined and become so acute for the very reason that feminism is not just a set of ideas, but permeates every area of our lives. They are, moreover, symptoms of contradictions inherent in contemporary feminism, not incidental to it, but shaping it and pushing it beyond itself. Since these contradictions grow out of the historical conditions in which second-wave feminism emerged in the late sixties and early seventies, it does seem that a critical examination of our experiences then can increase our understanding of them. But having made this assertion, I have to ask: To what extent are my own conditions general, and to what extent personal to my own case? The impossibility of answering this question is what makes it so difficult to write this essay, which revolves around my first attempt to work as a feminist critic in 1971–3, when these contradictions joined to shape my relation to feminist criticism.

At that time, I was finishing my graduate studies at Stanford while the Viet Nam war and social movements at home were reaching a crisis point. At Stanford, civil disobedience against war-related recruiting and military research had become weekly occurrences. My husband's professor, a tenured member of the English Department, and a charismatic leader of the campus movement, was being fired in a precedent-setting disciplinary proceeding, and my husband, who had abandoned graduate studies, was working full-time on his defense. Many people we knew were being arrested in early morning raids on their homes by the FBI, and others were being threatened with arrest if they did not testify before grand juries. At our own home, the phone rang constantly with pleas for support in organizing demonstrations, writing articles, setting up legal defense, or going to witness these early morning raids. All this demanded a level of energy and commitment to which I felt completely inadequate. I was not much more sanguine about the dissertation I was trying to write at the same time on women writers of mid-nineteenth-century France.

These two realms of my life not only clashed with each other, but also made my feminism enter into contradiction with itself. With respect to the Marxist revolutionary movement, feminist theory offered a weapon against the leaders' aggressive pressure to conform to an excessively macho ideal of politics, and my feminist research offered a haven and respite. Each day, I would escape from the storm raging around me to my office, where I would close the door as if I were closing a security blanket around me, and turn to my beloved feminists of the 1830s, who had gone through all this before me. But as I would start to write, my attempts to articulate a feminist analysis of their texts became the source of my sense of inadequacy. Thus feminism, experienced as a guilty pleasure in the context of the Marxist movement, was experienced as anxiety in my academic life.

Although feminism goes with me everywhere, it takes conflicting forms in different contexts. And in one way or another, my research has always investigated this issue, asking why feminism should be so divided within itself, why a feminist should be so divided within herself. Ironically, this essay itself epitomizes the contradiction in that after having repeatedly treated this issue indirectly through a critique of linear narrative as repressive of feminine subjectivity, I now find myself treating the issue directly through just such a narrative.

That narrative begins in the mid-sixties, when, like many in my generation, I welcomed these conflicts, if only as a necessary by-product of the chance to participate in extraordinary historical processes. They at least represented a relief from the stultifying vacuum we lived in during the 1950s. As an undergraduate at Cornell, I edged toward the civil rights and anti-war movements, attending the early protest marches and teach-ins. But the idea of a *movement*, of people joined together, collectively and deliberately to bring about social change, was at that time completely unknown to me.

During this time at Cornell, feminism seems to have been unthought and unthinkable. There were, to be sure, protests against the strict dress codes and curfews for women, which disappeared sometime between my freshman and senior years. But one of my sorority sisters became the object of horrified gossip when she had an abortion. The mystery of why she had to work at two jobs to pay off enormous debts was solved when the house mother found her unconscious, hemorrhaging in a pool of blood. The cause of her near-death was laid solely to her personal responsibility and never connected to a wider pattern of oppression. When I first heard the expression "women's liberation" a couple of years later, I felt uncomfortable, not knowing whether to giggle or get angry. I thought the speaker was belittling women's rights by a sarcastic and hyperbolic play of words on "national liberation" and "black liberation."

At Stanford in 1970, my old friend Merle from high school and Cornell (and my future husband), a leader in the campus student movement, suggested that I go to the new women's liberation meetings. "Why don't you go?" he would say. "You really ought to go." (He has urged me into most of the dubious decisions of my life, including the decision to write this essay.) But at first I resisted. I thought about Vietnamese peasants fleeing from their invaded ancestral villages, about Black ghettos I had seen in Cleveland, Virginia and Oakland, and compared them to my own material comfort.

I also measured the distance between my present life as a graduate student and my adolescence in 1950s suburbia. My exhilarating advance toward relative freedom seemed to have taken me so far, that my limited imagination could not envision a greater liberation. Was I not doing what I wanted, far more than I had dreamed myself capable of, and the very possibility of which I had not known existed in high school? What else was there? I was far from seeing the power of phallocentrism underlying war and imperialism, not to mention the very movements supposedly intended to fight against them. I was also far from understanding how racism depends on sexism for its deep unconscious penetration, although I had seen countless examples of this interdependence during my year spent teaching at Hampton Institute, a Black college in Hampton, Virginia, the year before I went to Stanford.

The job at Hampton, something I drifted into not out of a dedication to civil rights, but in order to fill the void of my indecision about graduate school, coincided with that historical turning-point year of 1967–8. While I may have been only dimly aware of the tiny new women's liberation movement that was being born in the US that year, I did confront a rush of new questions and discoveries without which I would not have been led to graduate studies or to feminism. Hampton was a college of African-American students run by members of the white elite. It was intended to offer the students a certain minimal level of education that would encourage them to imitate white culture, but not too perfectly, and permit them a certain place in white society, but not one inch beyond. Captive to the myth that Blacks are immoral, campus life was blanketed under that the same pall of authoritarian moralism and hypocrisy described by Ralph Ellison in *Invisible Man*. The conditions of squalor in the dorms and dining halls were appalling.

But in spite of the censorship that hung over the college, the older faculty and administrators could not keep out the tidal wave of Black liberation movements. During that year, Black leaders were moving beyond civil rights to broader, deeper, more radical theories of Black Power. When an orator such as Stokely Carmichael or H. Rap Brown came to campus, the whole student body would turn out to hear him. I had seen only the demonizing treatment of these men in the white mass media, and went expecting to hear some slogans and nothing more. I was all the more impressed by their brilliant analyses of American culture and politics, analyses to which our future feminist theories would owe so much.

The notion that apolitical women can become radicalized through feminism has become such an accepted principle that we tend to forget its converse: that second-wave feminism, like its nineteenth-century predecessor, grew out of radicalism, and, specifically in North America, out of Black radicalism. Stokeley and H. Rap Brown gave the students tools for analysis; they explained that Black oppression and racism were fundamental to the US capitalist economy and the white American sense of self. They exposed the inextricable connections between Black oppression in the US and the invasion of Southeast Asia. Going beyond the ideology of civil rights, they convinced the students to reject being measured according to white standards of value as universal and superior, to stop looking to whites for approval, and to develop instead a Black culture.

These ideas were all new to me, and very exciting, but each time I attended one of these speeches, I would also feel a prick of unease as I awaited the inevitable moment when the speaker would bring up the question of women – Black women and white women. At this point it became clear that the speaker considered himself to be addressing an audience of men. He would talk first, intensely, and at length about the danger that sexual relations with white women represented for the development of a strong Black manhood. As the only young, single white woman in the crowd, I would sit very still, trying not to breathe, and hoping no one would notice me. Then the speaker would talk more briefly, less vividly, and with a great deal less interest about the need to relate better to Black women, who were, as Muhammad Ali kept repeating in one speech replete with extended metaphors about planting seeds and plowing, "our field."

This problem has since been treated from a feminist perspective by African-American women, who analyzed the hardships placed upon Black women by the Black man/white woman pattern, and the destructive stereotype of strong Black women as unfeminine in a culture that idealized femininity as white and frail. The spokesmen of Black Power, however, were preoccupied with the development of Black manhood as centerpiece of a revolutionary culture. Stokeley's famous quip that "the only position for women in SNCC is prone," was not just an isolated comment but the expression of a theory that excludes women as subjects of history. Those speeches, then, offered the first of many experiences with one of the major contradictions inherent in feminism. Feminist theory draws upon other theories (Black nationalism, Marxism, psychoanalysis, deconstruction, etc.) that are in some sense inimical to feminism.

The word "inimical" hardly expresses the level of anti-feminism in the anti-war movement during that year of 1967. I was told that at the march on the Pentagon in the fall of 1967, a woman had stood up in front of the microphone to give the first public talk about women's liberation, and some male anti-war protesters in the crowd had yelled, "Take her off the stage and fuck her!" I was at the march but was too overwhelmed by the enormous crowd on this my first trip to Washington to see or hear anything. I was also preoccupied with other matters, that while only indirectly related to the dramatic events engaging sisters I did not yet know, were leading me in their direction.

Having driven a group of students to Washington, I was responsible for them as the unwilling representative of Hampton's heavy-handed *in loco parentis*. We parked at Howard University and boarded the bus for the Pentagon. On the way, we ran across the radical Black march that had separated itself off from the white demonstration. The students could not contain their excitement. "Oh, please, please can we join that march?" they begged me, and, when I said OK, they immediately jumped off the bus at the next traffic light. I had sinned enough against Hampton's codes of respectability – by living alone as a single woman in the Black section of this segregated Southern town, by wearing mini-skirts "to lure the students," as rumor had it, "into radical activity" – and so I spent most of the demonstration worrying about what would happen to me if anything happened to them.

The year at Hampton was the beginning of my education in the political logic of power relations, and I had a lot to learn. At 23, I was the same age as many of my students, but far less worldly-wise. My age, my ethnic background, my inexperience and naïveté combined to make me completely superfluous to the education of my students. They needed young Black instructors like the two energetic, smart women with whom I shared my office.

Strangely enough, my very superfluity turned out to be one of the things that made this the happiest year I had ever spent. As a complete outsider to both the Black and white communities, I lived for one year the feminine dream, often expressed in women's literature as a kind of corollary to having a room of one's own, of living outside of culture. Freed of pressures to conform to social codes that had always left me feeling both inept and suffocated, freed of expectations weighing upon me, I began to feel I might be capable of getting a Ph.D. In any event, contract renewal time came, and all of my friends, the talented, dedicated young instructors who were dramatically upgrading the poor quality of educational at Hampton, received termination letters. Probably because the administration feared my Cornell connection, I received no termination letter, but also no contract. In any event, I could not justify my happy but useless presence at Hampton, and so the fall of 1968 found me a graduate student at Stanford.

What was now being called the "Movement" was exploding in too many directions to keep track of, and I, as usual, hovered at the fringes. But in the spring of 1970, I finally joined a women's consciousness-raising group, through which I could overcome my reticence and take a more active role in organizing. Paradoxically, however, the association with a group of women that allowed me to participate more deeply in the Movement also led me into the conflict between feminism and this male-led anti-imperialist movement. I could not understand supporting struggles against one type of oppression without also supporting struggles against the other, but the war between the two movements was heating up.

This was mainly because of the ambivalence of Movement men towards women's liberation. While they had to acknowledge its legitimacy on an abstract level, they could not admit that it had anything to do with their own male chauvinism, or with what we would now call their own status as subjects. They arrogated to themselves the prerogative of defining women's liberation as a set of reduced, distant, objectified, externalized issues which had nothing to do with them personally. It was forbidden to discuss male chauvinism in any way that might unveil the men's use of left politics to secure an illusory masculinity, expressed through their infatuation with guns in the name of armed struggle, their ostentatious mimicry of Black and Cuban revolutionary leaders, their obsession with sexual conquest of Movement women, and their refusal to take responsibility for domestic work.

In their denied anxiety to exorcise women's liberation, Movement men abandoned the dialectical method, even while assuming superior authority over its use, and took refuge in the analytical logic of static, closed categories and hierarchies of oppression, whereby some groups could be quantitatively measured as "more" oppressed than others. To all our arguments, they endlessly intoned the same triple litany, delivered with great authority: "Women's oppression is a secondary contradiction; it's a bourgeois question; and Third World women are more oppressed than white women, proletarian women more oppressed than bourgeois women." As if fighting against one's own oppression did not leave room for fighting against others, or as if they were not all interdependent.

The Movement men at Stanford thus retained leadership, adopting a posture of lofty disinterest from which to criticize our concerns as selfish. They took the role of noble spokesmen for more oppressed – and more distant – victims. The Marxist Movement produced its own sanitized ideal of women's liberation for our emulation. Appearing on posters and buttons, it was the image of a Third World woman nursing a baby while carrying a rifle on her back. She could be Vietnamese, African, or Latin American, but she was anonymous, schematic and silent. A liberated woman was one who proved herself as tough as a man while accepting all the traditional burdens of womanhood. Her image affirmed phallocentric values while making no demands on men to change themselves.

Anyone who attempted to criticize patterns of sexual oppression within the Movement would immediately be accused of the worst heresy, that of claiming that "men were the enemy," when everyone knew that women's oppression came from "the system," as if men were completely outside of "the system." As in other times and places, these men used a rhetoric of objectivity as a kind of armored vehicle for projecting masculine subjectivity. It seemed to me in the early seventies that the hypocritical deployment of this weapon was driving radical feminists into separatism. Caught as ever in contradiction, I sympathized and identified with them even as I moved closer to joining a Marxist organization. But I could not follow radical feminism into the theory that all women were sisters in oppression.

The few women of color whom I knew personally or whose political essays I had read were very critical of radical feminism for ignoring their needs and perspective. The first feminist book I read, *Sisterhood is Powerful*, in 1970, contained an essay, "Double Jeopardy: To Be Black and Female," by Frances Beale, that expressed this perspective, and was to be the first of many. I wanted to support the struggles of Third World women, and it seemed to me that my only chance for doing so was through the Maoist organization that was leading the Movement at Stanford. It had some Chicano collectives in working-class communities near Stanford, and its chair was a Chicana. Yet Marge Piercy's essay in *Sisterhood is Powerful*, a searing exposé called "The Grand Coolie Damn," which showed how mixed Movement organizations reproduced in exaggerated form the sexual oppression in capitalist society, struck me as absolutely accurate, if not understated, in every detail.

To compound my conflict, the new radical feminist theory, in spite of its tendency to universalize a white perspective, was soaring with an intellectual boldness absent from Marxist feminism. Freed from the desire for male approval, the radical feminists I read with amazement in *Sisterhood is Powerful* and *Notes from the Second Year: Women's Liberation*, also published in 1970, stripped away the naturalizing veil of daily life to reveal the heretofore invisible political power system permeating it. Pallid indeed by comparison with this dazzling transformation of our world-vision seemed the decorous efforts of Marxist feminists to legitimize women's liberation through plodding debates on such subjects as whether or not housework produced surplus value.

By the spring of 1971, most of the women in my first consciousness-raising group had discovered their lesbianism and were leaving Stanford for San Francisco, where they could commit themselves more deeply to radical feminist separatism, at the same time that I was preparing to get married and join the Maoist organization. I envied the wholehearted enthusiasm they gave to their political commitment and which I found dismayingly absent in my own. And although throughout my brief and stormy membership in the Maoist organization, I harbored a secret enthusiasm for this heresy banned beyond the pale, I could not join it for reasons at once personal, political and theoretical.

Personal reasons included my lifelong attachment to my future husband, who had been my most dependable friend through my difficult adolescent years, and whom I could not imagine leaving even for a woman, as well as my incurable romanticism, which I was vainly trying to exorcise through my dissertation on women of the Romantic movement. Political reasons contained their own conflict: on the one hand my revolutionary desire to involve myself more in anti-war and anti-racist struggles, and on the other my bourgeois desire to get a Ph.D. and become a literary critic. The theoretical reason was my attachment to Marxist theory, which had been as thrilling a discovery a couple of years before as radical feminism was now, and without which the radical feminist analysis could not have been thought.

I kept hoping that Marxist feminism could take similar advantage of the possibilities in dialectical materialism to go beyond a static, fragmented, empiricist view of gender relations, but I think it was prevented from doing so by the heavy-handed censorship in New Left organizations. They banned any formulation that went beyond talking of women's "special" oppressions or their "special" needs" within national or class struggle, thus safely reducing sexual politics to detachable units that could be added on to a central (men's) struggle without fundamentally changing it. Since then, I have not been able to hear the word "special" without mentally cringing. It served to provide an alibi for not thinking about the interconnections between various kinds of oppression, through the comfortable ruse of hierarchizing them as compartmentalized unities, lest one's own subjectivity, thought processes, and desires be implicated as socially constructed means of oppression themselves.

In secret, intense discussion with one or two other women in the Maoist organization, we arrived at the conclusion that this treatment was not dialectical materialism. For us, dialectics made interconnections come before unities and change before stasis. We saw as the fundamental principle of Marxism (a Marxism that has unfortunately never been put into practice) not the notion of class struggle or national liberation, but the notion of history as a process of multiple contradiction, especially as Mao Tse Tung's essays "On Contradiction," and "On Questions of Philosophy," reinterpreted it outside of a Hegelian tripartite enclosure. If the New Left had used the Maoist theory of primary and secondary contradiction to serve its own metaphysics of statically hierarchic oppressions, to us it made dialectics more complex. Rather than a single process of contradiction, history could be seen as struggle over different relations of domination, all dialectically related to each other, so that primary and secondary, or framing and subordinate, were always changing into each other.

Needless to say, we never persuaded our male comrades to take this interpretation seriously. And so we remained in conflict – with ourselves and with the disconnected realms of our world. "You're selling out," my radical lesbian friends would tease me with an affectionate smile. "It's a secondary contradiction, a bourgeois issue," my male comrades would lecture us in ponderous tones. But I was unable to analyze this particular conflict in terms of contradiction. In spite of my enthusiasm for the notion of a dialectic with no third term, and thus no unifying synthesis, I kept hoping for a synthesis between radical and Marxist feminism which, according to the very theory that I used to link them, was impossible.

If Marxist and radical feminism are no longer in contradiction, it is not because they have synthesized, but only because they have been taken beyond themselves to new theories, in a larger context provided by the rise of Third World feminisms, both heterosexual and lesbian. Since the sixties, feminists of color have been developing a new transformation of our entire world vision, while the white, male left has steadily declined in its pretense to provide an all-inclusive umbrella for oppressed groups. The western, masculine assumption of universalism, even in the left, made all other oppressions seem particular, and led us to compartmentalize Third World women or lesbians of color into "triple" or "quadruple" oppression. In their own writings, however, the struggles of women of color appear as a complex context within which our partial forms of oppression can be thought.

Since the sixties, moreover, the influence of poststructuralism, while creating a new contradiction with feminism, has shown me the futility of my old wish for a synthesis between Marxist and radical feminism to form a perfect whole. All theories, even those that one is most passionately committed to, would be inadequate, harbor an explanatory lack, since none could provide a totally accurate representation of social processes from a universal point of view. Moreover, any critical theory must be formulated against another theory, and thus would need a supplement.

By the spring of 1971, I was also trying to come to terms with the problem of my dissertation. The original topic, a formalist analysis of Stendhal, had been retreating beyond a misty distance as the feminist and anti-war movements enveloped us with greater intensity. As a literature student, I had been so exclusively trained in textual formalism that I did not even know it was a methodology among others, but I had discovered by my senior year at Cornell that I could get the highest marks simply by locating the place within the text where it reflected back on its own formal processes. By the time I started studying at Stanford, I was weary of its mechanical predictability, and looking for something else. Although the new texts by Barthes and Derrida were being introduced into some courses, they were assimilated to North American formalism, divorced from any social or historical dimension, and so did not seem so different from the method I had been taught. It would only be through Marxist theory that I would find entry into the exciting newness of poststructuralism.

I had begun reading Marx's political texts on my own around 1968. During my time at Cornell, texts by Marx and the major Marxists seem to have been banished from the curriculum. Even a course called "Marxist and Structuralist Sociology" assigned only texts by Talcott Parsons and anti-Marxist sociologists. Marx's texts brought me a heretofore unexpected way of thinking the world, and Marxist analyses of the Viet Nam catastrophe seemed infinitely more intelligent than the liberal explanation of a "tragic error," a blunder by naïve but well-meaning policy-makers.

But my studies in Marxist politics seemed unconnected to my literary problem of how to go beyond the New Critical formalism that had become intellectually meaningless, and conceive a political approach that went deeper than thematics while treating literature as text rather than social document. This problem began to resolve itself at the very moment that my dissertation seemed to fade the furthest away. In the spring of 1970, the US invasion of Cambodia brought about a national student strike. Instead of going to classes, students would be attending teach-ins. One afternoon, I was walking across campus with Merle, who was describing to me how, in an effort to change education and make it more relevant to the world around them, students and faculty were planning to present every possible subject from a radical perspective. He and some other graduate students in English were going to present a teach-in on Marxism and literature. "You mean," I said, trying to keep the astonishment out of my voice, "there's a Marxist literary criticism?"

The leading Marxist critics of that time, Georg Lukács and Lucien Goldmann, have since been thoroughly criticized for a multitude of metaphysical sins. Yet Lukács' *Studies in European Realism* and Goldmann's *The Hidden God* and *Towards a*

Sociology of the Novel provided the promise that one could not only read literature in relation to history, but that one could read textual *form* in relation to invisible historic processes and structures. What seems obvious now was a revelation in face of the tyrannic hold of New Criticism.

Yet by the beginning of 1971, my dissertation was still not being written. Preoccupied with the newness of feminist consciousness, I could not focus on Stendhal, in spite of Simone de Beauvoir's praise of his feminism. I had heard that some women somewhere were teaching something called women's studies, giving courses on women authors rather than the "great classics" (I was unaware of such a thing as a socially constructed literary canon). Tempted to change my dissertation topic, I unfortunately knew of no other woman author in my period than George Sand, and her cult of the unique superior woman, always seen through the eyes of men, repelled me. Somehow, I would have to find other women writers.

But I would also have to get permission to change topics from my very traditional advisor, to whom, I feared, my request would sound frivolous indeed. After walking around his office building several times, I finally summoned the courage to confront him. "It would be all right with me," he told me gravely, "but do any such writers exist?" By going through some obscure literary histories, I found mention of the names Hortense Allart, Daniel Stern and Flora Tristan, but their books were almost impossible to find. Researching the historical background for a textual study of these authors, I also came across a group of fascinating French proletarian women, socialist feminists and sexual radicals, who had published a journal in Paris, from 1832 to 1834, and then again during the Revolution of 1848.

In Paris I finally immersed myself in the writings of these women at the Bibliothèque nationale and at a tiny, hidden, feminist library, named after the French suffragist Marguerite Durand. During long, still afternoons, in this old room, usually peopled only by me and a lone elderly librarian, I read with a sense of uncanny recognition the women's literary and political texts of the 1830s. And I repeatedly came up against the same question: they had experienced what we were experiencing, reacted as we were reacting, and had formulated thorough and brilliant critiques of male supremacy in all of its manifestations. Then they had been repressed into an almost total oblivion. The nineteenth-century cartoons that ridiculed them were more famous than they. Would we share their fate?

My dissertation director approved my proposal to write on the novels and memoirs of Sand, Allart, Stern and Tristan, but balked at the inclusion of the proletarian feminists, who, he said, were not real authors writing real literature, nor, as proletarians, relevant to my analysis of the texts of bourgeois and aristocratic women. The women who interested me the most had to be squeezed into a few furtive paragraphs of my dissertation.

And writing my dissertation itself had to be squeezed into the furtive hours that I could steal from my work in the women's and anti-war movements. The Maoist organization expected its members to be at the forefront of what had become an all-consuming campus movement. It is difficult to transmit the atmosphere of immersion in ongoing history in which the choice to participate in such an organization could flow logically from one's situation, for even though this atmosphere engrossed the campuses only a generation ago, it seems less another time than another temporal dimension. At a time when everyone felt the summons to leave life-as-usual for a larger involvement, and the future was a question mark, this organization represented commitment and exercised real leadership. Its members were respected and followed even while they were criticized for their elitism, their ultra leftism, their closed, secretive membership policies, and their heavy-handed, self-righteous vanguardism.

The good and bad reasons for which I joined – the need to test myself? the fear of missing some essential core of my generation's historical experience? peer pressure? – are too numerous and too mixed to discuss here. The contradictions it threw me into are also too numerous to discuss fully, but as they established a pattern for me as a feminist critic ever since, I will briefly mention some of them. A few of the other women in the organization also experienced a conflict between their desire to be feminists and the pressures to reject this "petty bourgeois" consciousness. We had heard that socialist feminists in Chicago and Boston had formed women's unions and, in an attempt to resolve our contradiction that only deepened it, decided to form one at Stanford.

While we saw the women's union as a chance to gain some autonomy and breathing space from the Maoist organization, so that with other women we could search for a feminist alternative to male chauvinist socialism, the men in the organization had a completely different idea of what we were supposed to be doing. They made it clear that our purpose was to bring the other women to the "correct" line as quickly as possible. We were constantly interrogated to make sure we were "raising" them to a more lofty political consciousness. By contrast, one of the white male students in the organization belonged to a Black and Chicano motorcycle club called the Soul Brothers. When I finally met the Chicano auto mechanic who had founded both the Soul Brothers and the Chicano wing of the Maoist organization, he was astonished that I thought any kind of progressive politics whatever went on in the Soul Brothers. Yet, needless to say, the male student had an aura of heroism around him and was left in complete freedom from interrogation. After about a year and a half, I left the organization in a storm of protest.

But in the meantime, my membership forced me to confront the issues of militancy and violence, which left me with questions still unresolved. On the one hand, second-wave feminism has tended to assume that a feminist politics would be pacifist. And indeed, from a feminist point of view, war is an outmoded and thoroughly horrifying contest over who has the biggest phallus. Yet my experiences with civil disobedience both at Stanford and later have led me to the conclusion that for white, middle-class people, it is tinged with hypocrisy. My two arrests have only served to confront me with my privileged status. We are free to commit civil disobedience in support of Third World people who do not have the pacifist option. Where we are arrested by jovial police relieved to be dealing with us rather than dangerous criminals, people in Third World countries would face a very different fate. When I was finally suspended from Stanford in 1972–3 for civil disobedience, I suffered no ill effects. When I had to look for jobs that year, everyone at Stanford covered for me, including my professors and even the director of the placement service in whose office we had staged weekly sit-ins to protest war-related recruitment. By contrast, a Singaporese student who was suspended with me lost his student visa and had to go back home. He was last heard of being tortured in a Singapore jail. This is not to say that my suspension did not affect my future course as a feminist critic. It did, but in ways that I will talk about later.

On the other hand, I could never overcome my ambivalence toward the skirmishes with tactical squads. While I hated these excursions, one part of me believed in taking the greater risk involved and in using this tactic to raise discussions about violence. This invariably happened when the very people who vehemently condemned breaking windows as "violence" reacted with compla-cency to dropping uncounted tons of napalm, guava bombs, pineapple bombs, fragmentation bombs, and defoliants on Asian peasants and their land. But another part of me watched with horror the fine line between militancy as an austere tactic and militancy as an ecstatic ritual of male bonding for the pure pleasure of the chase; and my lack of physical courage made me unable to trust my perception as to when this line was crossed.

Many people must have felt as I did, because the Women's Union decided to form a women-only "affinity group" (a group which acted as a closely knit unit at demonstrations), where women could feel comfortable, find support and protection, and try to articulate a feminist practice and theory of militancy. The affinity group, called Rosa, grew and grew, finally even rallying around its red silk standard many men in quest of a haven from phallic frenzy, and became by far the largest affinity group in the Movement.

Our prominence in the anti-war movement, however, plunged the Women's Union into controversy with a formidable opponent. The Women's Union had entered into an uncomfortable alliance with the Stanford YWCA Board, which counted among its members several wives of major industrialists in the Bay Area military-industrial complex. The YWCA had luxurious facilities but a woefully lagging membership, and the Women's Union had ambitions to establish a women's center. We increased the YWCA's membership tenfold and brought them gobs of money in dues, but when the United States escalated its bombing of North Viet Nam, and students went on strike all over the country, many board members objected strenuously to the women's center's decision to double as a strike center. In the ensuing negotiations, they told us they objected only because the anti-war movement was "violent." We raised the issue of their husbands' violence. We also lost the women's center. The experience left us with profound doubts about the universal sisterhood of women at the present juncture.

Similar doubts were raised around the same time by another experience, which in a deeper way brought my feminism into conflict with itself. The Women's Union decided to teach some women's studies courses, but because we were students, we had to find faculty members to act as titular officers of instruction. To our dismay, all the women faculty members, both senior and junior, whom we approached, with the single exception of one junior professor, refused, and we had to turn to male professors to sign for these women's studies courses. Perhaps the women did not want to appear to be associated with a subject that was generally scoffed at and, worse still, associated with radical and Marxist feminism.

In the past twenty years, the complex process of establishing women's studies has simultaneously made it respectable and gained inclusion for Marxist and radical feminism, developing them into other theories beyond their early opposition. Indeed, among the contradictions inherent in academic feminism today, that between desires for institutional respectability and desires for theoretical radicalism is one of the most difficult to probe into, and one which I will discuss briefly in the conclusion. But at Stanford in 1972, that contradiction had not even emerged. The professional women's movement, to the extent that it existed there at all, foreclosed any theoretical reflection that connected the issue of individual advancement to the larger questions that were then being raised, and specifically the questions about Stanford's involvement in the war. As a result, it reduced women's liberation to even more narrowly defined and hermetically sealed issues than the Marxist organizations. Strange as it may seem, discussion and argument about these connections were more censored in the professional women's movement than in the New Left, where we were at least supposed to "struggle" over them.

I, too, was at that time unable to make the connections I have since learned to understand. Although I greatly desired a university post, I could not connect anything as exalted in my mind as women's liberation with personal advancement in a career. I connected the anxiety surrounding my work less to insecurity about a "career" than to inadequacy in face of an ideal of literary knowledge and critical insight. I had been inspired with this ideal since my first French literature classes at Cornell, when it had seemed that my professors held the key to what I then called the mysteries of life. A job where one was paid to delve into these mysteries seemed the happiest of privileges. Amazingly, I, or at least that part of me not consumed with anxiety about the institutional pressures that ensnare us, still believe this.

This internal division, one that I earlier traced back to my first experience of feminist theory as both exhilaration and anxiety, has never gone away. It has merely become more multi-faceted as the position of my generation of feminists in the university has changed. It inheres in a unique quality of feminist criticism as a profession. Our job allows us on the one hand to make a living pursuing the utopian vision I had as a student, and on the other hand requires us to practice an institutional politics of competition for prestige, and to instrumentalize human relations with each other in violation of those ideals. The utopian vision includes a searing critique; it implies taking risks and avoiding the illusion of security, while the institutional practice advises playing it safe, and avoiding critiques that might offend those in power. What makes us unique is that women in other professions – business, law or medicine, or even biological and physical science within the university – do not have to theorize, as a daily condition of performing the tasks of their profession, the reasons they should not belong to it.

We find ourselves in a split between theory and practice more often than not, and this can create a profound ambivalence toward identifying with our profession. Feminism requires disrespect and irreverence toward phallocentric institutions. Behaving as a professor requires scholarly decorum. But how much, I must often ask myself, does this sense of a web of contradictions come from the particular circumstances that took me through the hiring process while under suspension, and how much can I generalize it? I have talked to scores of women who believe that a "fraud complex" is generally shared among feminist academics, but in my case the fraud complex was literalized, since I was not, literally speaking, a student at Stanford when I interviewed for jobs.

Like the other feminist academics of my generation, I can hardly count myself a young rebel, but must see myself as a senior faculty member (at my admittedly young campus), with the necessity to reflect upon the privilege and the responsibility to other women that this entails. Yet the sense of not quite succeeding in carrying off a precarious masquerade has never left me. Perhaps this is because whatever seemingly impossible dreams have succeeded, the overriding dreams of second-wave feminism remain an endangered utopia. On the one hand, I became a feminist critic, and wrote as many pages as I desired about the proletarian feminists of the 1830s. But like so many other women professors, I have to work very hard to fight off despair in face of the ominous imbalance between our tiny but hard-won gains and the forces amassing to take them away. Thus our present situation continues to engender contradictions. But these await future accounts, if we are fortunate enough to be around to write them, in the story of the split (or should I say fractured?) personality of feminism.

REFERENCES

Although footnotes do not seem appropriate for an essay of this kind, readers might be interested in seeing the list of texts mentioned in it and/or consulted in its writing:

Cade, Toni (ed.) (1970) *The Black Woman: An Anthology*, New York: Signet.
Carson, Clayborne (1981) *In Struggle: SNCC and the Black Awakening of the 1960s*, Cambridge: Harvard University Press.
Ellison, Ralph (1952) *Invisible Man*, New York: Random House.
Evans, Sara (1980) *Personal Politics: The Roots of Women's Liberation in the Civil Rights Movement and the New Left*, New York: Vintage.
Goldmann, Lucien (1975) *Towards a Sociology of the Novel*, trans. Alan Sheridan, London: Tavistock.
——(1977) *The Hidden God: A Study of Tragic Vision in the Pensées of Pascal and the Tragedies of Racine*, London: Routledge & Kegan Paul.

Lukács, Georg (1964) *Studies in European Realism*, New York: Grosset & Dunlap.
Mao Tse Tung (1967) "On Contradiction," *Selected Works*, I, Peking: Foreign Language Press, 311–47.
——(1974) "Talk on Questions of Philosophy," in Stuart Schram (ed.) *Mao Tse-Tung Unrehearsed: Talks and Letters: 1956-71*, Harmondsworth: Penguin, 131–47.
Morgan, Robin (ed.) (1970) *Sisterhood is Powerful*, New York: Vintage.
Notes from the Second Year: Women's Liberation: Major Writings of the Radical Feminists (1970) New York: Radical Feminism.
Piercy, Marge (1979) *Vida*, New York: Fawcett Crest.
Sale, Kirkpatrick (1974) *SDS*, New York: Vintage.
Viorst, Milton (1974) *Fire in the Streets: America in the 1960s*, New York: Simon & Schuster.

Chapter 17

On having a personal voice

Elizabeth Ermarth

For Carol Pierce and Elizabeth Gay

One of my oldest commitments is a belief in the broad political importance of those issues that, since the Enlightenment, we have called "literary" or "aesthetic." From many sources and from my earliest years I have had a sense of the material intensity of intellect and language, and an awareness of the constructed nature of personhood. Increasingly I have learned to see the close affinities between my interest in language and art on the one hand and my interest in feminism on the other. I began working on literature because I loved my language – the positively kinetic plenitude of Elizabethan English, and the linear extensions of it in modern, especially nineteenth-century narrative – and because I sensed the challenge of achieving in language the multivocality, the power to surpass narrow explanations that I loved in painting and music. I began working in the women's movement for similar reasons, though the similarity did not strike me at the time. I sensed that my potential life surpassed the narrowed one I was increasingly being offered by college placement officers and by professors who descried women, to the extent they did so at all, dimly as if at the bottom of a well.

But my feminism has not been merely a natural outgrowth of other interests, nor primarily a theoretical issue, abstracted from particular experience and its pressures. In the late 1960s and early 1970s I connected with the women's movement by contributing to it (one doesn't exactly "join" such a movement as if it were a club). I was drawn to it by two very different kinds of experience, each in its own way necessary: on the one hand, my frustrating experiences as a graduate student in the patriarchal establishment; on the other hand, and in quite a different, more lasting and creative way, my experience of support from women's networks.

First, the opposition. In 1965 and mid-way through my doctoral work, I voluntarily transferred (I look back on this incredulously) from Berkeley to the University of Chicago as a result of my marriage to someone who was keen to study there. I was 24 and had a lot to learn about the politics of academic sexism, beginning with the fact that this particular move is a classic one for a woman.

When I arrived at the Chicago English Department the fairly small graduate faculty was composed entirely of men, most of whom accepted as gospel an Aristotelian variant of New Criticism and appeared numb or even hostile to other theoretical influence. While I found New Criticism to be a useful training tool I thought it had serious problems of justification, to say the least, as a methodology for anyone interested in history or practice. But I was not particularly vocal or organized about this dissatisfaction, just looking for more comprehensive alternatives, and I was even adept enough at the in-house method to win, one year, the department's annual prize for original criticism. When I discovered in phenomenology and phenomenological criticism (Merleau-Ponty, Gaston Bachelard, Georges Poulet and Hillis Miller) a new method of writing about nineteenth-century literature that seemed to me interesting and fruitful, I employed it in my dissertation. Though this dissertation was greeted by the professoriate, to the extent that it was noticed at all, as "too much under the influence of Hillis Miller," subsequent graduate students (I was told several years later) appreciated it as proof that there was an alternative to the local method.

While I was writing this dissertation in 1968 and 1969 I was also making a life-threatening commute during rush hour, twice a day, three days a week, from the south side of Chicago along Lake Shore Drive to Northwestern in order to teach my first classes. As a pre-doctoral instructor I taught nine courses a year to Freshmen (there was an occasional upper-level variant for good behavior) and graded 1,080 freshman compositions. I had plenty to do and I liked doing it; I was full of confidence and I trusted my own strengths.

No one in the department at Chicago (I can hardly call it "my") department ever said to me a single word about getting a tenure-track job, especially the all-important first job, or ever helped me to get one, although graduate students after my time told me that subsequently the department has been quite happy to hold me up as an example of the employability of Chicago graduates in tight job markets. Apart from one very general informational meeting for all graduate students, the sole communication I ever received from my department concerning jobs – a misaddressed invitation to a pre-convention meeting for the department's job candidates one year in the late sixties – reached me several weeks too late. My advisor's contribution was the advice to be as good as possible so "they" can't touch you, advice that has a certain Boethian value but is scarcely what a job-candidate needs most. The one member of the department who was in my field of narrative theory (he was in administration at the time and unavailable as a dissertation advisor) and who, as a member of my orals committee, was supposed to read my thesis, did not do so, although he did apologize and he reportedly thought the oral "delightful." As he hadn't read my work before my oral, I asked him to read it afterward and to mail me his comments; more than a year later the dissertation appeared one day in my mailbox in a brown wrapper; no comments were enclosed.

When I began looking for a tenure-track job in 1969–70 the job market was just beginning to get pinched. My application letters produced sixteen requests for a dossier so, in order to establish one, I dutifully asked my two dissertation advisors (both men, there being no women) to write letters for me. My first reader, a shy senior professor, I knew a little and respected as a teacher; I knew my second reader, an untenured newcomer, scarcely at all. My dossier went round to more than a dozen departments and produced only a few requests for interviews. Given my experience with the so-called "profession" up to that time, and given the general paucity of interviews among my peers that year, this result did not seem odd to me. It was not until two years later that someone on an interviewing committee told me I had a negative letter in my file. Sure enough, my second reader had responded to my request for a recommendation with a three-liner calculated to turn off any first-rate possibilities. Thanks to the Buckley Amendment, I was able to read the letter myself and to have it removed from my file. Too late, alas, for the important first job. It was little consolation to me that the twerp was fired soon after and went on to his permanent professional mausoleum in a small English department elsewhere. He had managed to damage many of my initial job prospects.

What is most important, however, is the fact that he did not act alone. He took his cues from a department, and from a collegial atmosphere in which such condescension to women was and, for all I know, still is accepted practice. In short, he had the support and encouragement of a large departmental and institutional apparatus of unacknowledged sexism.[1]

Why, you might ask, didn't I go flaming into the department chairman and demand my rights? Good question, and the answer says a lot about the so-called profession, women's place in it, and the value of networks for professional women. In 1970 I knew no one who could help me to verify that my experience was a common one for women, not exceptional or unique to me. In addition, I did have a life with the usual amount of energy-absorbing demands: a teaching job, poverty, solitude, unworkable first marriage. I contributed to this general misconnection a certain naïveté, perhaps even a wilful naïveté. I went into the profession because I was interested in books and in art and in people and in theoretical problems and I expected accomplishment to carry me.

Full of confidence and notwithstanding my experience at Chicago which I carelessly concluded was anomalous, I rejected an interesting job prospect in California and went off jobless with my husband to Dartmouth College on the strength of verbal assurances to me and a lucrative job offer to him. Confidence of a certain kind is careless of details, and I chose to believe the prophecy that a job for me would materialize in the English Department there the following year. What did I expect? This is the question raised by Jill Conway in her autobiography. Did I expect "that I could, by some special merit [or extra effort], leap over the barriers society placed in the way of serious professional work for women" (Conway 1989: 194)?[2] The answer is, "yes, I did." Why? Because otherwise I would have to reconceive my belief that effort and achievement are worth the sacrifices they entail.

Naturally, when I arrived in New England I was a bird in the hand and, as every academic search committee knows, that is worth much less than two in a bush. Instead of a job, there was a lot of humiliating dithering during two separate job searches about whether to hire me or not. In the end, the male chauvinist section

of the all-tenured voting committee, especially under pressure from the knowledge that the entire junior faculty supported me (no junior faculty could vote on
hiring), refused even to *read* my dossier (on one occasion the chairman, who
apparently had never even looked at the dossier, called a well-known personage
who happened to be one of my referees asking her to suggest candidates for their
position; he was stunned to silence at hearing her say, "What about Betsy
Ermarth?"). I had discovered the local axiom: that there was no possibility of
regular tenure-track employment for a "faculty spouse" – a sort of third sex
which includes mainly but not exclusively women and which generally appears in
those academic environments where misogyny seeps from unsavory private
situations into the professional one. I am happy to record here that among those
in that department who supported me, the one person with the most to lose by
it, an untenured woman in a field near mine, took a significant and sustained risk
with her own future by joining the effort to hire me; she told me later that she
decided she had to live with herself.

A little counsel from my graduate department might have been timely, but I
sought none and none was offered. I was by that time busy with other things:
things separate from but hardly irrelevant to my professional history as a woman,
and things worth mentioning because any "history" that selects one or two tracks
from the lived, material rhythms of a life is in danger of rationalizing the very
existential tensions that specially define it. For instance, nothing is said here about
the medical misogyny thanks to which I was the unknowing recipient in 1973 of
a Dalkon Shield and the prolonged miseries it entailed: a "detail" that expanded
to put pressure on every other aspect of my life, including the professional.

A certain amount of adjunct teaching and one divorce later I published my
first articles on George Eliot in 1974 and 1975. A leading scholar in the field, a
man whom I had never met and who turned out to have been a reader for one of
the articles, wrote to me a letter I still treasure, saying "You have published one
of the best articles on George Eliot that has ever been written." (Thank you,
Gordon Haight, wherever you are.) Such relatively disinterested feedback and
encouragement is rare in American academic life, and that rarity is one of
academia's greatest weaknesses because it disadvantages anyone who depends for
recognition primarily on their actual work.

There is much, much more of this kind of history to retell, but its gist remains
the same. I pretty much figured it out by myself, and the kind of treatment I
received from "the profession" shook even my self-confidence. Women reading
this can match me, I know, story for story.

Left to myself and my individual resources – and like how many other women
and with what effects on the profession? – I certainly had received the signal:
"Give Up"; or, more precisely, "Give Up, Sweetheart." But in the late 1960s
something else was gearing up that taught me the most valuable lesson of my
professional life: that what was happening to me didn't have much to do with me
as an individual; nor was it a just or even adequate measure of my professional
achievement or promise. That something else was the women's movement.

While I was doing adjunct teaching at Dartmouth and writing articles, I also got involved with women's groups: first, as the founding chairperson in my state for the National Women's Political Caucus; then in women's consciousness-raising groups, especially groups run by leaders from the national training center in Washington; and finally as a member of the Faculty Women's Caucus where I helped to write Dartmouth College's first Affirmative Action document. This was an experience with many facets, one of the more salutary of which was the illuminating period of weeks I spent in the library collecting the data from publications by the Bureau of Labor Statistics on the Ph.D.s granted to women across academic fields during the twentieth century, data that formed the statistical basis of that affirmative action document. (The major degree-granting institutions, the very ones who claimed most often that there were no women Ph.D.s and that they therefore couldn't find good women to hire, had themselves been conferring degrees on women at a substantial and regular rate since the early 1900s, and doing so, I suspect, in much the same spirit that Chicago conferred its degree on me.) Not all these experiences with women were free of exclusionary tactics and hierarchical competition, but those that were gave me an opportunity to share my experience with other women in a most productive and life-affirming way, and that experience had and continues to have a powerful effect on my intellectual life. The experience of support from other women raised my consciousness in a new and far more powerful way than opposition had.

Consciousness-raising, as an historical term, applies to a particular phase of the women's movement in the US. But it is much more than that. It is a continuing process, a quotidian effort, renewable each day, and requiring considerable if not constant vigilance. Initially women's consciousness-raising groups were formed, like other such groups, because they provided critical support in the difficult effort to change destructive habits. I was fortunate to encounter strong, creative groups with the kind of direction that made it possible for participants to change habits rather than merely to reinscribe them. The best of these experiences took me outside academia where I met women from a wide spectrum of social, economic and professional circumstances. Our ostensible differences paled considerably as we began to tell each other our histories. We would probably have disagreed about presidential candidates and the rest of those "issues" that belong to the prefabricated world of borrowed opinion, but together, word to word, face to face, we could agree about our experiences as women because, as we discovered with some wonder, we had lived very similar lives. We had infinite variations to tell but it was always the same story. What a relief, what a mutually enabling moment it was – and still is – to have discovered that this is so.

This experience of mutually supporting action among women produced not only documents and ostensible "action," but a far more profound result: the construction of a truly *feminist* experience. There is so little agreement about the term "feminist" at this time that it needs some specific comment and definition. I am a feminist, and to me the term "feminist" means one thing only: a woman who likes and trusts other women.

That only sounds simple.

For women who have been trained since birth to compete with each other for male attention as the primary means to achieving social and discursive status, actually to like and trust other women requires major ontological readjustments, not merely a correction of opinions or views. Feminist talk is cheap; feminist behavior is something else again. It is so difficult because we have learned from our cradles to *internalize* this mistrust of women and have fatally learned to mistrust ourselves. We have not learned to collaborate as equals, we have learned to compete for favor at each other's expense. To like and trust other women means investing in true networks, with their resistless equalities, and avoiding the whole gambit of hierarchical exclusion that makes differences into grounds for envy and resentment.

All this is a matter of cultural construction, and not something individuals can either make or break alone. Internal versions of that old, old competition between women are the chief instruments of patriarchal maintenance; by these divisions women support patriarchal suppressions and by them they learn to mistrust their own powers. (They learn this with a lot of help. Freud's theories, for example, show the extent to which competition among women is a *sine qua non* of patriarchal society.) To overcome the division in whatever way, however briefly, is to glimpse a world of power and opportunity that never again can be eclipsed. "Chloe liked Olivia," said Virginia Woolf, going as usual straight to the feminist point and to the radical, world-changing fulcrum (Woolf 1929: 86ff.). This "liking" is solidarity; it is political, which is to say "personal" in the special sense I will define here.

Learning to like and trust other women meant learning to like and trust myself; for me this meant learning first of all how little, *really,* I knew how to do that, all my self-confidence and strengths notwithstanding. "Have you ever been in a consciousness-raising group?" a woman asked me at the beginning of this period. "No," said I, privately thinking that consciousness-raising was not for me. "It shows," said she. I was dumbstruck. *What* "shows"? I concluded that if a lack of consciousness-raising showed, maybe I should explore the matter: especially since, at that time, I was the state chairperson of the National Women's Political Caucus. I soon learned, once I overcame my initial resistance, that this form of self-discovery through sharing my history in a particular way was liberating in unforeseeable ways. This kind of careful, mutually supportive effort made it possible to learn new forms of expression, new forms of restraint; it was possible to move beyond the dualistic negations of oppositional politics and beyond the constraints of victim behavior to entirely different kinds of social experience with other women.

An example of the difference such groups make has to do with the problem of power. To have the power to direct my life, I must be free of unspoken prohibitions and prejudice, not only in the conduct of other people but also in my *own* actual, material practice. I must begin by affirming, not what I wish I *might* do, but what it is I actually *do.* Support, including self-support, begins there. For me this has meant accepting responsibility for my discursive function as a woman, a wife, a sister; it has meant knowing that, as we used to say in the sixties, if I'm not part of the solution, I'm part of the problem. If I do not collaborate in my own suppression, I cannot really be suppressed; but I cannot stop collaborating and assume a constructive role until I acknowledge my actual constructions, look at them, and see whether they are any good. To take that latter, critical step, I need other women because only they share my problem, my discursive identity, my particular woman's "I."

The experience with new power relationships that I had in such groups has been valuable in many contexts, especially in my teaching. As an academic facing daily the temptation to speak from a podium, if not a pulpit, my experiences in women's groups continue to remind me of the importance of speaking not just to an audience but to a group of speakers: that is, of recognizing the dynamic function of language that makes even silent auditors into participants. For many teaching situations the Big Bow-Wow style of lecturing is simply dysfunctional because it is careless of a simple fact about learning, that one learns best by doing. This is probably common sense to all good teachers, who know that a student who can talk as well as listen learns more than one who simply sits passively taking notes – but patriarchal models do not necessarily foster common sense. Students who have been raised entirely on the filling-station model of education expect, even prefer, the no-obligation, no-engagement lecture that prevents anything from happening. The discussion that creates obligation and engagement, however, does throw one on the mercy of fate to a certain degree; there is always the unexpected drift, the surprising question. As a woman facing the continuous deflections of patriarchal culture, one learns how to improvise; as a feminist, one learns how to trust that ability, how to use that gift.

It's an important political step, to acknowledge our place in discourse, and to acknowledge that we have *not* been absent during the 2,000 years of patriarchal metaphysics, *not* merely helpless and suppressed but, for many reasons and in many ways, collaborators. Liking, trusting, working with other women, blows up the law that says women can be conquered, as they always have been, by division. To take responsibility for my participation means that perhaps for the first time I can make a real difference: that I can avoid the trap of merely reproducing, only with female personnel, the same, same old stories of power.

This difficult step is impossible without networks. One cannot do it alone. A soloist feminist is a contradiction in terms, although this contradiction is one fostered eagerly enough by the patriarchal establishment within the university and outside it. Among the many familiar gambits of patriarchy for preserving its hierarchical exclusions, one of the most seductive, apparently, is the patriarchal compliment: "You're different," which translates, "You're like us, not like them." A feminist – that is, a woman who likes other women with all that entails politically – is not comfortable with this praise in any explicit or implicit version. She is uncomfortable being "the woman" in the senior ranks, on the job list, the panel, the committee. A feminist is never a soloist who acquiesces in, accepts, even delights in the implicit message, "you're different" and makes for herself a separate peace. To accept the patriarchal compliment, "you're different," is to accept a posture of competition with other women of the kind that perennially has undermined women's solidarity. It always has worked, and it still seems to work, like a charm.

To my perception the development most damaging to the expanding influence of the women's movement for all women has been various forms of permanent separatism. Temporary separatism – quite a different thing – gives women space and time to recognize the very issues and agendas that I have mentioned, especially the feminist agenda of learning to like and trust other women.[3] By temporary separatism I mean women joining with other women for specific work, from consciousness-raising to electing women: something not unlike Lyotard's temporary contracts without absolute status. I would argue that such temporary separatism is the only way to overcome the divisions that have kept women economically and politically powerless. But unlike temporary separatism, which has the effect of supporting and strengthening women, permanent separatism has the very different effect of reinscribing patriarchal structures with female personnel.

Permanent separatism occurs when one group of women, sometimes quite a small one, define themselves by excluding other women and in much the same way that men have always done. This effect of permanent separatism is produced whenever a group totalizes a limited issue. For example, there are issue separatists – those who make an exclusive agenda of an issue such as abortion, or the right to vote, or lesbian rights, or "my career," or some other achievable result detachable from any broader social problematic. The problem with this tactic is obvious: once the goal is achieved the effort is over and no broadly based constituency has been built.

This is where networks come in. Networks are headless and footless sources of support and influence, sources of information and suggestion. They are never closed systems of exclusion like the familiar power hierarchies. Always, and above all, networks are available to anyone who needs them. Networks are not producers of capital, yours or mine; their product is their process, and when you need the product, you show up for it, and you provide the same support for other women, all other women. It's that simple and that complex for women who have never had any relation to another woman except a competitive one.

And this Chloe liking Olivia, incidentally, has nothing to do with sexual preference; a lesbian is not automatically a feminist, nor is a feminist automatically a lesbian. A feminist is a woman who can resist the many temptations to fall into competition with other women for favored slave status: it does not really matter whether a woman is old, married, single, lesbian, young, professional, mother, democrat or church-goer; what matters from the point of view of changing oppressive discursive constructs is whether or not she likes and trusts other women, and consequently herself, and whether she treats other women – all other women – with respect. Internecine squabbling among women over various forms of separatism – whose practices or life choices are most feminist, or most woman-like, or most ideologically pure – is a stupidity that women in the US have not learned to avoid, and such squabbling only serves the hierarchical structures that keep women barefoot and pregnant, culturally speaking.

By liberating women from destructive internecine competition feminism has given women a new *kind* of resource: a medium in which to lose the killing solitude that patriarchal practices have imposed on us. By establishing networks independent of conventional social structures, women have empowered themselves to bypass the narrow arena assigned to them in patriarchal discourse and, consequently, are having profound effects on that discourse as well as on the terms of their own social construction. Where women maintain really vital networks they not only construct new kinds of personhood for themselves, they also create a new kind of cohesion in a culture plagued by increasingly simple-minded and destructive oppositions between (so-called) "individual" and "social" life.

For me it was an empowering moment and a great relief to give up enervating competition with other women: and competition for what, I began to ask myself, for a chance to strike a patriarchal attitude? We are constructs, but also constructors of the problem, and consequently agents and producers of change. Feminist activity, whether its context is domestic, or political, or academic, seems to work best when the historical moment of consciousness-raising is succeeded by some form of sustained collective effort of a personal kind. Never the one without the other. Awakening to oppression is a necessary beginning, but only the beginning; any change in consciousness, especially one that has lasting social consequences, does not take place once, or in solitude, or merely in opposition, and such change is not an individual affair.

These definitions raise certain problems when I come to the phrase "feminist scholarship." If a feminist is a woman who likes other women, it follows that feminism is a negotiation between women, among women. A man, for example, cannot be a feminist, however supportive he may be of a woman's personal and professional development, for the simple reason that no man is culturally constructed as a woman and thus no man is qualified to engage in this particular dynamic between women.[4] This point may be worth making in an academic context where some men, having seen the power of feminism, are here and there hopping on the bandwagon as if a couple of articles with woman-friendly topics could make them feminists.

So if feminism is essentially a private matter between women (albeit one with massive cultural implications), then what exactly is a "feminist scholar"? Is she a feminist who is also a scholar? Is she a scholar who writes mainly about women (in which case, why may the scholar *not* be a "he" as well as a "she"?) Can a woman hold a position in the academic hierarchy and still be a feminist? Can a feminist scholar work on issues that affect women – for example, issues such as the construction of historical consciousness – and yet not focus directly on women writers or do what has become defined academically as "women's"? This latter question has special importance to me because, although I often have written and spoken on conspicuously feminist subjects (women and representation, the solitude of women, women's time, feminist theory as a practice, George Eliot, feminist theory and postmodernism, etc.), I have also written a book on the construction of historical consciousness as a discursive practice from Alberti to Henry James: an argument with vast anthropological importance for women, and for the culture that excludes many of their values and much of their experience, but an argument that has implications for more than women and one that does not fit conventional definitions of feminist scholarship.

Here is where the various forms of academic separatism – the kinds associated with the "women only" program – show their conservative side. While separatism is essential for women's consciousness-raising, it does not necessarily follow that it is essential for women's studies nor does it follow that women's studies necessarily involve consciousness-raising of the kind I have described, even though they often do introduce individuals to women's issues. Treatment of the women's movement and women's issues as "subject matter" tends to leave aside and untouched issues of personal and institutional practice, reinforcing the very disciplinary and discursive exclusions which the "women's" program supposedly investigates.

Women's studies has always had a problematic relation to university structures, and the situation remains problematic for women contemplating an academic career: if you do "women's studies" chiefly as subject matter, you can find your field quite circumscribed and methodologically conventional; if you attempt theoretical or methodological revision you may go unrecognized by patriarchs of both sexes who will not be able to recognize you as a "women's studies" woman. Even if you attempt and manage both, you may find yourself quite isolated as "the woman" or "the feminist" in a conventional academic department that finds one woman (or even, gasp, two) quite enough, thank you. Such problems are grounded in the discourse of a culture and are not solved by individuals.

I am, then, a feminist *and* a scholar: a feminist as a woman among women, and a scholar who, given that knowledge and commitment, works in whatever ways my particular leading takes me. I teach in women's studies programs, I have done the work that was required to get such programs institutionalized, and I have done other institutional work concerning the reformation of sexist practices like establishing affirmative action and sexual harassment policies. But these feminist and scholarly activities do not take place in a vacuum; they take place in a world where women's issues are among the most pressing, but not the only pressing issues. I do think that many so-called "national" and "international" issues, certainly issues of economic and social dysfunction in the US, *are* in effect women's issues, but they don't "belong" only to women. As a feminist I am interested not so much in sticking to "women's" issues as I am interested in exploring the bearing of certain social and theoretical issues on women, issues such as the construction of historical consciousness, the primitive condition of childcare in the US, and even the connection between those two issues. When such things as these are considered in broadly social terms, that is, in terms that include those who have been ignored and repressed, one sees in new ways the urgent need for discursive reconstruction for the sake of general renewal in a culture much in need of it.

I said above that the feminist difference is not fundamentally an individual affair. Behind that generalization lies a theoretical insight that I would like to spell out in concluding this autobiographical reflection because it focuses the problems that my experience has presented to me and that I have raised here both as personal and as larger theoretical problems.

Feminism really works only through networks. But there are networks and networks. As my experience repeatedly has taught me, a really healthy network, the kind with vitality enough to provide broadly accessible support to women, differs completely from the so-called network of influence that is really a disguised hierarchical power structure of an all-too familiar kind and one that depends for its existence on systematic exclusions. A true network is headless and footless; it is a material system of linkages that operates without reliance on subordination, which is to say without hierarchy. A living network is infinitely democratic, and always local. Anyone who wants to join such a network can do so; no one is excluded. The point of such a network is literally occasional; it provides the occasions where individual women exercise the mutual support that empowers them in their practical lives whatever their occupations or opinions may be. A living network such as this differs fundamentally from those ossified networks of influence that we all know so well and that define themselves by exclusion (dualism, hierarchy, World Historical Greatness) and various forms of rarefaction (they are always Elsewhere, always Other and somehow never local or locatable) that effectively block that general circulation of nourishment which, in the end, keeps the entire system alive in the first place. For example, and not to put too fine a point on it, the patronage system in US universities, a function that keeps alive a very old hierarchy, is one form of such blockage, although women in general seem to have resisted succumbing to it and in many cases maintain a healthy hostility to it. Finally, a true network makes room for laughter: another fundamental distinction between it and the sobersides converse or elliptical aggressiveness characteristic of provincial celebrities.

It is important to be able to distinguish a living network from a dead one because a living network has for women one crucial, indispensable benefit: it supports what I would call the personal voice, one that differs from both the individual voice and the public or professional voice. There is a crucial difference between the person, which exists socially and discursively or not at all, and the so-called "individual", a being which seems to me more a somatic than a social designation and which, as a social designation, has operated as a phantom ruse of certain totalizing mechanisms. For example, one of the many interesting differences between "personal" and "individual" is the question of taste. An "individual" conceived as something unique (for example, a body, with its fingerprint) cannot precisely have "taste" because taste is a matter of shared value, which is to say a matter of aesthetic judgment. The public or professional voice also expresses shared value, of course, but in gross ways and without the particular distinction conferred by this or that voice. By supporting this personal voice a living network thus supports the nexus between individual and collective life with effects that may be profound, especially where there is so deep a separation between individual and public consciousness as we find in the United States today. This kind of personhood does not receive much press in the US, where we seem to prefer a simple dualistic distinction between a grossly conceived collective totality (the people, the country, Republicans, women, etc.) and the so-called "individual" conceived primarily in terms of deviation from that totalized and featureless norm.

A living network, then, encourages the power to say "I" in a particular way, one that allows latitude for individual expression and, at the same time, posits that expression in collective terms. A network acknowledges by its very nature that to say "I" – I think, I know, I believe – is to say something profoundly social, as distinct from merely "individual." The power of this "I" is collective; it is not merely the individual identity, "miserable treasure,"[5] so broadly valorized by empiricist culture over nearly five centuries: it is not unique, not individual. This power to say "I" is in other words not a soloist's achievement but, instead, a power conferred by a constituency. As such, this "I" and its expressions are fundamentally inaccessible to what I would call "logocheck": the rationalist instrument of enforcement.

There are many different kinds of networks in the US that in various, always specific and temporary ways, support this power to speak a collective "I" by dropping the usual identifying terms like last name, profession, address, date of birth, race, national origin. Perhaps we are a culture particularly suited to this kind of constituency; perhaps in the absence of other cultural depths it is one of our special privileges. In any case, such networks, and their particular affirmation of personhood, tend to work in ways not easily assimilable to the simple and increasingly uncreative opposition between individual and social that is popular in our public rhetoric: a schematism that frames culture not by other versions of culture but by "nature," and that consequently tends to obscure the constructed basis of social distinctions. The personal voice is not definable as one, essential thing; it is more like a power to vary between what is uniquely individual and what is general and public; it is a power crucial to sociality, and a power that must be learned.[6]

The women's movement is testimony to the creative power of ideas to make incarnate what was not there before. In my experience as a woman working with women, that creative power cuts across customary definitions, including the peculiar boundary between academic and public life that exists in the United States. In women's networks I joined an effort to construct a social syntax that would exercise a new sense of personhood, one repressed by the prevailing structures in which I found myself. This sharing and building of networks is slow, unglamorous and satisfying work. It is an effort for the long term and, as such, it is vulnerable locally to the quick rip-off; it requires generosity and courage. But such work is hardly selfless because, *un*like the disguised hierarchy, a living network conserves energy. The more energy that goes into it, the more energy it generates, so that the generous effort defeats pinched competitiveness, if not by direct combat then by altering the atmosphere in which competition is conceived.

NOTES

Thanks to Jo Ann Argersinger and to Thomas Vargish for their helpful comments on this essay.

1 He was not even the first, and certainly not the most intelligent among my oppositional acquaintances during my student years. While I was in college at a small, pious, prestigious private institution in the midwest, an English professor who was himself something of an outsider and not at all the greasy careerist, responded to a paper I wrote on Dickens – one, it turned out, that was publishable – by asking me whether the paper was my work. I was so shocked and baffled by the question I didn't even feel stricken, until later. I had no experience that would help me to feel how thoroughly this response was *his* problem, not mine; few of my peers among women students spoke of professional ambitions, and none of us in the late 1950s yet knew anything about the feminine mystique or any related issues that would make mutual awareness as women a potential protection against this kind of patriarchal *Anschluss*.

2 Conway continues,

> How could I have studied the newspapers every day where jobs were advertised in segregated lists, or listened to people's disparaging remarks about women doctors or their jokes about bluestockings, and not realized they were about me? I used to dismiss Dr. Johnson's often quoted remark about a woman talking in public being like a performing animal as a sign of the benighted attitudes of the eighteenth century, but they were around me every day in my fellow students' comments about the tiny number of women faculty.

3 Luce Irigaray has argued a similar point in her recommendation that women go on strike "long enough" to learn how to "escape their proletarization on the trade market," but not with the goal of permanent separatism or exclusion from men which is really only a repetition in "reverse of the existing order"(Irigaray 1981: 106).

4 It remains an interesting question why men who tried consciousness-raising in the seventies found it essentially impossible to maintain networks for discussing the manifest problems of being a culturally constructed "man."

5 Julia Kristeva uses this phrase from Claude Lévi-Strauss (Kristeva 1980: 127). The translated phrase, "personal identity, miserable treasure," uses "personal" in a different sense than the one I'm developing here.

6 Certain theoretical issues attach to the construction of this personal voice that are worth mentioning here. This construction takes place in tension with the "individual" and "human" definitions that we have codified for at least five centuries. This "common" or "human" denominator has become increasingly confused with more limited and patriarchal norms as empiricism has increasingly valorized physical and material difference and, most importantly, as empiricism has universalized its particular conceptions of space and time. I have made these arguments elsewhere (Ermarth 1983, Ermarth 1992); I mention them here to reaffirm that the issues of women's private lives have social and cultural importance that is immediate and extensive. What is important here is the compound identity of the personal voice. It remains inseparable from what Nabokov in *Ada* calls the "unique poetry of an individual life" and yet remains acutely aware of its own dependency on collective achievements; it remains materially specific but at the same time inextricably defined in terms of a collective medium.

REFERENCES

Conway, Jill Ker (1989) *The Road From Coorain: Recollections of a Harsh and Beautiful Journey Into Adulthood*, New York: Alfred A. Knopf.

Ermarth, Elizabeth Deeds (1983) *Realism and Consensus in the English Novel*, Princeton: Princeton University Press.

——(1992) *Sequel to History: Postmodernism and the Crisis of Representational Time*, Princeton: Princeton University Press.

Irigaray, Luce (1981) "This Sex Which is Not One," trans. Claudia Reeder, in Elaine Marks and Isabelle Courtivron (eds) *New French Feminisms: An Anthology*, New York: Schocken Books.

Kristeva, Julia (1980) "From One Identity to An Other," in her *Desire in Language: A Semiotic Approach to Literature and Art*, ed. Leon S. Roudiez; trans. Thomas Gora, Alice Jardine and Leon S. Roudiez, New York: Columbia University Press.

Woolf, Virginia (1929) *A Room of One's Own*, New York: Harcourt, Brace, & World.

Chapter 18

Asians in Anglo-American feminism
Reciprocity and resistance

Shirley Geok-lin Lim

This essay I write as an "Asian" woman owes its presence to an invitation from Anglo-American feminists. The agency which permits my presence in this text has an authority that legitimizes me and that my presence in turn validates. Its authority presides because certain epistemic bodies have privileged it to *speak for* women. So I have permission to speak, but permission to speak as and for a minority; not as an *individual* which is an ideologically majority construct in the United States, but as a *re-presentation* of a minoritism of specified color and race.[1] One can read this already given inequality between Asian women and Anglo-American feminists as that of the moon to the sun, a smaller, unfueled planet illuminated by the atomic radiance of a self-propulsive star. Or perhaps as that of an even smaller orbiting fragment, illuminated by the pale glow of the moon, a light borrowed of a light borrowed of a patriarchal sun.

For an Asian like me, the personal and social significance of "owing," social indebtedness, the unequal relation of being a taker with the implied promise of making a return, is very strong. The bonds of reciprocity are an idealized social construct in both Confucianist and traditional Malay societies. The Filipinos call the construct *utang na loob*, a functional relation in a feudal and patronage-based society whereby the patron, the landlord, the rich man, the mistress, assists the serf, the tenant farmer, the poor woman. In return, the taker is obligated to return that "social capital" in any number of ways: giving his labor when needed, offering a share of his crops and his livestock, showing due respect and proper distance at all times.[2] Reciprocity as a pre-capitalist function that is as materialist and economically penetrative as colonially introduced capitalism is not simply good or bad; it is a way of constructing social relations when capital is not available to many of the constituents in that society.

As a child growing up in the British colony of the Federated States of Malaya, I was constantly reminded of how much gratitude I owed to all kinds of people. To my father for keeping us children with him when our mother abandoned us. To my stepmother who cooked and cleaned for us. To the nuns of the Convent of the Holy Infant Jesus who taught us the Catechism and how to pass exams. To my many aunts and uncles who gave us an occasional dollar or meal. To the British administrators who gave us the railroad, the macadam roads, piped water, electricity, law and order and civilization.

I was always aware of how much I "owed" family, adults and white people, in that order of importance. And I was expected to moderate my behavior in accordance with these debts. Not merely in saying "thank you" often and sincerely, or holding my posture in a deferential manner, but in what I said, judged, evaluated and believed. If I were properly grateful, I would not say what I thought, that so and so was a foolish and selfish person. In fact, I would not think negatively – for example, that the British were a racist lot who believed themselves superior to others. Nor would I question the unequal relation of creditor and debtor – does a charitable meal offered to a hungry child make the giver a morally superior being or the child wolfing down the meal a morally inferior creature?

Now that I'm an adult, a mother and an "Asian American", I am still confused by this miasma, this entangled, entangling net of bonds of gratitude that arises almost involuntarily when white feminists recognize me. Mentoring, that positive spin given to a corrupting old-boys' network, is inevitably, for me, shaded in with the ideal of *utang na loob*.

In order to write an essay on feminism, a term made popular and authoritative by Anglo-American women, I have first to understand wherein and why my relationship to feminism is tangled with those early cultural ideals of gratitude and obligation, and how those ideals, embedded in a Confucianist/Malayan/ Catholic background, a colonized/British imperialist mentality, and an Asian patriarchal society, still command the relations between western feminists and, in my case, an Asian woman.

Filial duty. Gratitude. *Utang na loob*. Obligation. Indebtedness. These terms are not synonymous although they circle around a common set of paradigms: the child to the parent, the wife to the husband, the peasant to the landowner, the colonized non-citizen to the colonizing administrator, the debtor to the capitalist. These paradigms are predicated on unequal relations, between one who is lesser with one who is greater. The child is dependent on the parent's wisdom, the wife on her husband's protection, the serf on the landlord's plenty, the colonized subject on the administrator's rule, the debtor on the capitalist's loan.

What is missing from the paradigm of reciprocity ironically embedded in unequal relations is the notion of injustice. The analogous relations are constructed around apparently "natural" phenomena, specifically that of dependent child and protective parent. The "naturalization" of these social and political structures, their ideological propagation, serves to mask their economic purposes. With social reciprocity, dependants do not perceive their powerlessness as caused by the others' agency. The peasant does not understand the landlord's exploitation of his labor; the colonized subject the colonizer's abuse of his land and people to enrich the "mother country"; the wife the husband's possession of her body and services. Instead, dependants perceive chiefly their weakness and the others' power to assist them; and align themselves with the stronger as the means to empowerment. In systems of social reciprocity, oppression is seldom an overt and single act of domination; rather it is comprised of systematic, multiple, repeated, pervasive acts of injustice in which the complicity of the oppressed, their silence, passivity and – yes – co-operation, support and contribute to the power of the oppressor. The "natural" gratitude owed by child to parent becomes enlarged, reified, and ideologized as those Confucianist social hierarchies of family position and state power, just as the British colonialists exploited the Christian ideal of gratitude owed to a good Samaritan to explain the loyalty subjugated natives owed them for their civil government.

At a political and social level, I was raised a colonized child, abandoned by my mother and left to my father's heavy-handed care. According to family legend, my father, who kept all the children with him after our mother ran away, favored me, the only daughter, above his five sons. But he did not hesitate to take a rattan cane to me when, as they said it then, he "lost his temper." Corporal punishment in the 1950s and early 1960s was perhaps more prevalent than in these enlightened times. But to a child of 8 or 10 or even 15, slaps, blows, and caning on the arms and legs that raise bloody welts can never be rationalized. My first experience of patriarchy, in its most immediate domestic manifestation, made me sharply ambivalent about any future relations with men. I learned that love and brutality existed simultaneously in the "protection" that men offered; but I also learned that there was nothing outside of this social structure to which a weak child could appeal. My mother having blithely abandoned us for the bright lights and freedom of a big city, I also learned that my father's protection, his attachment to the patriarchal family, was absolutely necessary for my simple existence.

What I understood, even as a child, was that my father's brutality should have been mediated for me by a mother's presence. Even where constraints make it difficult for women to act against men's power, there are strategies available to lessen that abuse of power. These strategies have usually developed over centuries of social formation.[3] My mother, however, like Ibsen's Nora, chose to live for herself. Displacing the Chinese tradition of the good woman as the dutiful mother, she grasped the prickly principle of duty to self.

At the age of 8, I had not read Ibsen. The central experiences of my childhood shaped me to understand not one set of injustices – that of a patriarchal world where men have power to do good and evil to women – but another set seldom discussed by feminists: that of a women-for-women world where women, deciding on their duties to their children, also have power to do good and evil. My early lesson, learned as it were at my absent mother's knee, is that feminism, like patriarchy, is open to critique.

Feminism, as defined in the United States, as ideology, movement and personal practice, is predicated on the belief that women suffer injustices simply by the fact of their gender. Feminists concur in an activist vision of correcting these injustices wherever they occur: in the home or workplace, in bed or out on the streets. The social and political agenda has assumed, perhaps inevitably, a universalist program, that feminism speaks for all women and works for the good of all women.[4]

Women of color increasingly have queried this assumption.[5] Hooks criticizes contemporary United States feminism, initiated by Friedan's *The Feminine Mystique*, as dealing with "the plight of a select group of college-educated, middle and upper class, married white women" and ignoring "the existence of all non-white women and poor white women" (1984: 1–2). To hooks, "White women who dominate feminist discourse, who for the most part make and articulate feminist theory, have little or no understanding of white supremacy as a racial politic, of the psychological impact of class, of their political status within a racist, sexist, capitalist state" (ibid.: 4). An instance of US feminism failing black women is its intensification of male sexism.[6] Black women do not join the feminist movement, hooks says, not because they cannot face the reality of sexist oppression, but because "they do not see in feminist theory and practice ... potential solutions" (ibid.: 75).

For hooks, as well as for the Anglo-American feminists who are the objects of her critique, a key concept for feminist struggle resides in the term, "deprived."[7] "Deprived," with the prefix "de-" functioning as a signifier, connotes an act of theft, oppression, upon a set of rights. It suggests not merely a negative state but also a causal agent behind that condition. When you are "deprived," the assumption is that you have had certain items that rightfully belong to you taken away from you by someone or some force. A deprived child in contemporary America is one who should rightfully have more – care, food, shelter, education. Someone or some force has robbed the child of her rights, and, if we are so minded, we can act in concert to return these rights to the child.

It is easy for many women in the US, politicized by anti-colonial, anti-establishment movements, to recognize the Confucianist, feudal, patriarchal paradigms as misleading, distorted, incorrect and incomplete. In place of the benevolent protection that these false consciousnesses of reciprocity had asserted in an earlier colonialist era, Anglo-American feminists posit instead a malevolent inequality of power constructed on economic, military and political oppression. In place of social reciprocity or bondage, they insist on democracy, individual freedom, and equal rights for women.

The first set of paradigms was pervasive when I was a child. The British colonial system, particularly as conveyed to me through the teaching of missionary women from Ireland, constructed an ideology that in its paternalism supported and replicated the patriarchal, sexist, feudal and capitalist aspects of pre-Independence Malayan society. In contrast to colonialist propaganda, Aimé Césaire's unrelenting critique of colonialism provides no space for compromise: "Between colonizer and colonized there is room only for forced labor, intimidation, pressure, taxation, theft, rape, compulsory crops, contempt, mistrust, arrogance, self-complacency, swinishness, brainless elites, degraded masses" (1972: 21).[8] To Césaire, colonized societies are "drained of their essence, cultures trampled underfoot, institutions undermined, lands confiscated, religions smashed, magnificent artistic creations destroyed, extraordinary possibilities wiped out" (ibid.). All this was true of colonized Malaysia, despite the construction of macadam roads, railways, hospitals and schools. The British-style institutions that replaced native customs quickened the pace of alienation, which was made irreversible for populations that lost their original languages and became largely monolingual English-speaking. The alienated elite were assimilated into western culture and were chiefly disaffiliated from any sense of Asian solidarity. The poets quoted T. S. Eliot's *Waste Land* and wrote from a colorless, that is, western imagination (ibid.: 75). I was vaguely aware of this alienation and the need to return to Asian sources of culture before I left Malaysia, immediately after the riots of 13 May 1969, when hundreds of Malaysian Chinese were killed by Malays who resented the Chinese push for electoral representation. My analysis of my homeland's political future then was that of inevitable race-based state power empowering the majority Malay and the increasing economic and social marginalization and dislocation of the minority Chinese. It was clear to me in 1969 that there was no place in Malaysia for a Chinese Malaysian woman who was temperamentally suited only to a democratic polity. In Boston of the early 1970s, completing my doctorate at Brandeis University, in place of my youthful aspirations for full Malaysian cultural participation I decided instead on a future as an alien exile in American society.

In my life, therefore, it was not feminism that radicalized me. Instead, it was experiences within Confucianism, colonialism, feudalism, patriarchy and neo-colonialism that led me to feminism. In the United States in the 1990s, the second paradigm that I had been "civilized" in, the paradigm of unequal power, with one pole of the race, class and gender category oppressed by the other dominant pole, has become *au courant*. The shift from the first to the second paradigm is usually what is meant by the term "radicalized." When one becomes radicalized, the first naturalized ideological universe tilts, as it were, left. Usually, the radicalized person comes to view the conserving powers of capitalism, imperialism and patriarchy as an undifferentiated epistemic oppression of dispossessed groups.

But as an already multiply colonized subject, I do not see these oppressions as coming from a hegemonic center. Instead, I see a colonial subject as the cultural site for the contradictions inherent in the intersections of multiple conserving circles of authority. These authoritarian domains overlap each other but not sufficiently so as to preserve the illusion of totalization. Ironically, therefore, I experienced those liberatory movements precisely *where* Confucianism, Catholicism, feudalism and colonialism intersected.

To give an example. An internally consistent system such as Catholicism possesses oppressive weight for the individual enmeshed in its social networks. But its consistency becomes a point of departure or becomes itself a disruptive force when it intersects and destabilizes another ideological system, such as Confucianism. Within the stable relations constituted by Confucianism, the female is always subordinate to the male, the younger to the older, the outsider to the insider family member. In the social hierarchy constructed in a Confucianist family, all members of the family know where they stand in relation to everyone else, in an order of social importance that is reiterated in naming (Eldest Brother, Second Uncle, Third Sister, for example) and replicated in official and institutional constructions outside the family. To a young female in this family, the dogmatic constructions of Catholicism can very well take on the lineations of a liberationist theology. The ideals of an order made in Heaven, rather than embedded in familial hierarchies, of loving your neighbor as yourself (and as your parents and siblings!), are frankly subversive, almost anarchic in their effects on retrograde Chinese chauvinists.

That was how I read the role models of those tight-faced, hooded virginal nuns in the Convent of the Holy Infant Jesus. At the age of 7 or 8, I saw them as dangerous women, living outside the protection of the Confucianist family, Asians and whites together, thriving in open defiance of what centuries of Chinese civilization have shaped as natural for humans. They lived without men, outside of marriage, without children of their own, doing the kind of work that men do. They were women who were like men. That I was given to their care every day from 7.30 a.m. to 2 p.m., that Chinese parents were deferential to them, were intimidated and made smaller by their presence: these facts did not pass by me unremarked. In Catholicism as lived by these nuns I saw a larger power than Confucianism, and so very early, even before my mother's flight, the Confucianist construct of the good wife and mother lost any significant hold on my imagination.

However, the ideal of the ascetic single lives of cloistered women, women who had unerringly destroyed the possibility of Confucianist upbringing for those good little girls entrusted to them by foolish parents, never exerted its ideological power over me. Instead, what fueled my imagination were the multiple lapidary colors of cross-cultural worlds created by a history of colonialism. The Federation of Malaya, a minor protrusion off the southeast corner of the Asian landmass, was all of the world I knew. Malacca, the town in which I spent the first nineteen years of my life, like a frog in a well who measures the night sky and stars from the roundness and depth of her well, was a microcosm of cultures. Beginning as a Malay fishing village, it attracted Portuguese, Spanish, Dutch and English colonizers, drew Arab, Indian and Chinese traders, and was visited by Irish and French missionaries. Australian tourists drank beer in its few bars, American soldiers on R&R drove politely through the narrow streets.

Growing up, I knew a town of small untidy houses and large families, and shops in which cloths, foodstuffs, cosmetics, hair ornaments and other gimcracks were displayed in single rows or heaps. I knew nothing of boredom. The scale of experience in Malacca for a child was near perfect. The few cars sped at twenty to thirty miles per hour on the open roads outside town. In the town itself, crowded with cyclists, trishaws and occasional bullock-drawn carts, the cars moved at ten to fifteen miles per hour. Walking in the short winding lanes, you could see the faces and postures of passengers as the cars passed slowly beside you. It was a town that a child could map on her imagination, could hold in the palm of her mind. Here one's family knew a banker, a rubber estate owner, a Malay government official, a schoolteacher, a trishaw man, a noodle peddler, a temple trance devotee, a gangster, a madman, a doctor, a gambler, several unfaithful husbands, a hen-pecked man, people much richer than oneself, indigents to be pitied, snobbish Eurasians who thought too highly of themselves, alcoholic Ceylonese, chauvinist Chinese who talked of returning to China: an entire society englobed in one's immediate experience. There was more of color, activity, and bustle in the little town, more that could be grasped by a child sent spinning among its circles of gossips, its sphericities of class and race, than could be contained within the walls of the convent. And it is that contingent aspect of colonialism, its anarchic, entrepreneurial free-for-all of cultures encountering, breaking down, breaking through to others, that re-positioned Catholicism and its universalist apparently gender-free spirituality, so appealing against a Confucianist patriarchal kinship system, as small, provincial, and unattractive to a 13-year-old.

The irony of my present feminist state is that it owes as much to Confucianist patriarchy (a father determined to keep his family together), Roman Catholicism (nuns who offered another model of woman as unmarried and professional), and colonialism (a political system that produced a commingling of radically different races and cultures) as it does to Anglo-American feminist theory. However, it is not these systems but their intersections that offered me points of escape. Situated as I was in Confucianist, Malay feudal, Roman Catholic, British colonial cross-ways, I was exposed not to systematic political oppression but to continual upheavals. As Fanon points out in his phenomenological critique of colonialism, "There is a zone of nonbeing, an extraordinarily sterile and arid region, an utterly naked declivity where an authentic upheaval can be born" (1967: 10).

My cultural world was not monological but multilogical. Given the multiplicity of cultures, the extraordinary subjective feature remained that none of them offered the girl-child a stable, established, supporting society. Each system, oppressive alone, became interrogative and subversive in the matrix of multi-culturalism. Their values and beliefs did not co-exist in parallel structures but reacted on each other, calling in to question their differences. None was domi-nant, there was no mainstream, each system was marginal to the other. As subject, agent and object, I resisted the identity given to me by each of them. I remained between and outside the statements of these systems: non-male, non-Malay, non-Catholic, non-British-colonial. Involuntarily, I moved from my Chinese extended family where uncles, aunts, cousins, and even strangers were endowed with familial and honorific status – third paternal uncle, first maternal aunt, eldest brother – to a missionary school where a Mother Superior ruled over Irish sisters – Sister Finigan, Sister Patrick, Sister Alexis. From the South Seas community known as Nanyang Chinese and the Irish Convent (locally known as the French Convent), I moved on to a high school whose Principal was a Sandhurst Military Academy Englishman. Colonel Wade presided over prefects in the imago of characters from *Tom Brown's Schooldays*, characters already phantasmically related to Roman senators traced through a classical Latin imaginary. Trained intellectu-ally on the British model of parliamentary debate, we moved suddenly to the phenomenon of *Merdeka* (Independence) with a Malay Royal Prince, Tengku Abdul Rahman, as the first Prime Minister and nine Malay Sultanates all standing in line every five years to rule as feudal kings over our now Malaysian nation.

Significantly, I experienced none of these systems as closed. They were present as contradictions opening multiple counter-possibilities, offering questions rather than answers, divergences rather than oppressions, ferments rather than ideologies. Cultures (not Culture), differences (not Centrism), form the base of inquiry for me. Before coming to the US, before coming to feminism, I understood pluralism as the ground of experience. Thus, although the ethos of American democracy is relatively recent to me, a by-product of an interracial, international marriage and of immigration, and although feminism in its western form is even newer, a still evolving force that has reached me via academia, the media, and theory, they bear the traces of something familiar and ancient, the lineations of civilizations rising from the crossroads where natives and travellers are indistinguishable, trading, babbling in a multitude of languages, and engaging in activities both seductively mysterious and dangerously alien to each other.

The attack on patriarchy as an entrenched political system preserving the privileges of one gender on the back of another is for me also an anti-colonialist position. Men have colonized women, exploiting their labor for their own purposes, creating a society of unequals, and reifying these injustices through a series of legislative acts. Women, passive, long-suffering, complicit, have been colonized subjects for centuries. The critique of patriarchy not merely parallels but reinforces and broadens the critique of colonialism, moving it from a historical specific moment to a profoundly ahistorical theoretical acknowledgement of the relations of power and powerlessness. Having had my being always already on the margins of circles of power, I recognized this construction of (male, colonialist) power over (female, colonized) subject as authenticated in and authenticating my life. Theory and experience match in this moment of feminist consciousness.

But what keeps me going as a feminist in the United States is the promise of community that Anglo-American feminists hold out to women of color like myself. Unlike Malacca of my childhood, the United States is a continually hegemonizing society. By that I mean that political, institutional and social forces are continually contesting for a foreground, and that American culture generally is defined as and defines itself as a conflict of centrisms. Not to name oneself as centric is already to accept marginalization. And the material, professional, and social rewards and privileges accrue generally to centric positions. Even young children in the United States are trained in observations of centric positioning, especially as manifested in material behavior. Possessing specific brand-name items, sharing in specific activities and behavior, can create a sense of being in the mainstream. But other determinable aspects also dictate the individual's position in American society, among them race, color, national origin, class, gender and language-possession. As if to counter the pluralistic immigrant influx, American society has constituted hegemonic cultural processes, through education, employment, the media, the military, governmental and social agencies, so that millions of Americans while they recognize their marginality are continually pressed to give it up to assimilate into a cultural center that is Standard-American-English-speaking, European-civilization-based, and middle-class in consumption and aspiration. American feminism appears to offer a counter-community. Commanded by its rhetoric of the privileging of difference, it promises a community that paradoxically is constructed not on commonality but on difference.[8]

Already a feminist in my post-colonial progressive marginalizations, two significant events mark my entry into an overt commitment. The first was my coming to motherhood at 35; the second my summer at Barnard working with the prominent feminist scholar of French Literature, Nancy Miller. No feminist, I believe, can understand woman's special position of social enslavement/social empowerment without understanding the psycho-social dynamics of maternality. The maternal role entails the kind of physical labor, daily drudgery and social bondage that equalizes most women with the working poor and, in a different era, with slaves. But it also enables an ideal of noble sacrifice, a social bonding that functions as referent for human behavior, that has almost universally made a mystique of motherhood. Becoming a mother late in life, and determined to maintain my professional position, I soon discovered the needs for woman-bonding, for woman-centered community, that an academic career can ignore. Mothers who can baby-sit, mothers who share information on child-care, mothers who understand the stresses, guilts and joys of raising children – I hungered for these contacts as much as I had hungered for books in my impoverished childhood.

This need for woman-centered community took a theoretical shape in 1987 when Nancy Miller gathered twelve women in Barnard to discuss feminist issues in literary criticism.[9] Among the twelve were three women of color; and it was the white women whose community dominated. Perhaps the most meagre place to look for community is among competitive and research-oriented academic women; but Miller offered an intensely brilliant summer when the decade-old conversations among feminists were replayed for us. If a colonized, Confucianist, feudal apprenticeship prepared me for the zone of upheaval, difference and question, Miller's readings provided me with the language that shaded me as a feminist ideologue.

But it is this very shading, this feminist vocabulary, that I now interrogate, for I see in my relation to Anglo-American feminism the same troubling imbalance of power that characterized my earlier experiences. Fanon, from his own situated colonized experience, noted that

> Every colonized people – in other words, every people in whose soul an inferiority complex has been created by the death and burial of its local cultural originality – finds itself face to face with the language of the civilizing nation; that is, with the culture of the mother country. The colonized is elevated above his jungle status in proportion to his adoption of the mother country's cultural standards. He becomes whiter as he renounces his blackness, his jungle. In the French colonial army, and particularly in the Senegalese regiments, the black officers serve first of all as interpreters. They are used to convey the master's orders to their fellows, and they too enjoy a certain position of honor.
>
> (1967: 19)

I hold similar ironic observations of myself. Adopting the rhetoric of feminism that allows me to be heard by white feminists, I am also at the same time elevating the culture of that "mother country." Speaking of Asian experience to white feminists or of feminist agendas to Asian Americans, I am also serving as mediator and interpreter, conveying the "mother-culture's" position to my fellow Asians. In that mother-culture of feminism, have I not buried my own original "jungle status," that local piecemeal of plural civilizations manifested in the South Seas Chinese–Malay–British cultures-in-process and in-contact?

Feminism that predicates its viability on a recognition of gender difference has yet to make space for the plural cultural utterances of gender differences. Feminism as ideology leaves no space for gaps of being in which psycho-social upheavals can occur. It has yet to listen to the voices of colonized women from deep within their oppressions, to recognize the divergent race, national, class, religious and linguistic selves among women. Too often, as hooks argues, in its Anglo-American form it serves careerist, middle-class white women and, as complicit servitors, those women of color admitted into this professional feminism.

Yet, in its liberatory mission, US feminism has served me well. In the ideal of sisterhood, it has given me a sense, an affect, of community larger than nation, race, religion or class. In the "conversations" of women from Nancy Miller to bell hooks and Catherine Stimpson, it has provided me with the analytical tools that permit me finally to segue through the intersecting systems of twentieth-century oppression that have directly borne upon me (Stimpson 1988). More importantly, it has made a space for women of color like myself to be heard. As in this essay. How easy then to be grateful to one's sisters, to commit oneself to the community of women.

None the less, the Asian woman who comes to feminism via Anglo-American theory would do well to resist the Asian cultural pressures of reciprocity and the historical colonial construction of inferiority that paradoxically support each other in her induction into the ideology. The relation between Asian woman and Anglo-American feminist theory must be continually interrogative and provisional as long as it remains a relation of unbalanced power, with Anglo-Americans formulating the theory and Asians consuming it. Fanon argued that colorless literature produced by black people was a manifestation of their colonized imaginations; similarly, we should read "colorless" feminism, feminist theory that ignores the place of cultural and racial difference in women, as an expression of Anglo-American-centric colonialist theory. A feminist canon of foremothers that centralizes Anglo-American writers such as Gertrude Stein and Virginia Woolf and constructs a theory out of their privileged white upper-middle-class oriented lives and works can only speak marginally to my concerns. When such a theory is presented as essentially speaking for women, I perceive the same kinds of imperializing patterns that characterize white male culture.

It is especially distressing to observe how white feminists, arguing the model of sisterhood and shared narratives of oppression and victimization, have moved into postcolonialist discourses. My distress does not arise from perceptions of appropriation but of misappropriation. If white feminists were open to instruction about women of color, about women as diverse and different, their speaking for these differences would be welcomed. Instead, some white feminists, claiming to speak for postcolonial women, offer a discourse that takes only more white and privileged women – Olive Schreiner, Jean Rhys, Isak Dinesen and Nadine Gordimer – as women's voices from the Third World. The Eurocentric view prevails over and above the feminist critique. In light of such narrow, intolerant, culture-bound canons, it behooves the Asian feminist to read US feminism as yet another manifestation of Anglo-American imperialism. Until white feminists become embarrassed at the gaps in their critiques of society, and until feminism becomes a cluster of culture-specific practices, I will have to remain uneasily a resisting sister.

NOTES

1 I discuss the unease of speaking as representative of a color and gender in my lecture, "The Ambivalent American: Asian American Literature on the Cusp" delivered at Brown University, 1988; in *Reading the Literatures of Asian America*, ed. Shirley Geok-lin Lim and Amy Ling (Philadelphia: Temple University Press, 1992) p.1:

> I was conscious that the invitation to speak was addressed not just to me, as an individual but also to the group which I represent. I am a representative, I suppose, by fact of my origin and appearance, my yellow-brown skin and black hair, my birth in an Asian country … . It is difficult to be a representative. One must always be more than one is, and in like manner one is always less than one is.

Gayatri Spivak addresses it also in "Questions of Multi-culturalism," an interview with Sneja Gunew, in *The Post-colonial Critic*: "When *they* want to hear an Indian speaking as an Indian, a Third World woman speaking as a Third World woman, they cover over the fact of the ignorance that they are allowed to possess, into a kind of homogenization" (1990: 60).

2 See Fred Eggan (1971: 10):

> In one form or another reciprocity is basic to all social life everywhere … . The most important feature of this reciprocity system in the Philippines is that much of life goes on among relatives, and others, too, on a basis of just give and take, of agreements and compensations for agreements. If one goes beyond this and *voluntarily* performs a service or helps someone out of a difficulty, then he puts the individual he helps under a special obligation. It is an obligation which cannot be repaid in money, but which has to be repaid in services and should be repaid upon request.

3 Margery Wolf discussed women's strategies for influence and survival in traditionally structured peasant families in *Women in Chinese Society*. As Kay Ann Johnson (1983: 20) points out, "in fairly regularized ways the influence of women often went beyond their legitimate limits in informal and sometimes surreptitious ways."

4 See the kind of universalism appealed to in the introduction to *New French Feminisms*: "Feminism owes its existence to the universality of misogyny, gynophobia, androcentrism, and heterosexism. Feminism exists because women are, and have been, everywhere oppressed at every level of exchange from the simplest social intercourse to the most elaborate discourse" (Marks and de Courtivron 1981: 4).

5 For example, see critiques of white feminist theory in Mitsuye Yamada (1981: 71-5) and

Trinh T. Minh-ha (1989). Yamada asks uneasily for support from white feminists:

> this path (feminism) is fraught with problems which we are unable to solve among us ... . in order to do so, we need the help and cooperation of white feminist leaders, the women who coordinate programs, direct women's buildings, and edit women's publications throughout the country.
>
> (1981: 71)

Trinh addresses ironically the restricted role of difference that a Third World woman must play to her sponsors:

> Eager not to disappoint, I try my best to offer my benefactors and benefactresses what they most anxiously yearn for: the possibility of a difference, yet a difference or an otherness that will not go so far as to question the foundation of their beings and makings.
>
> (1989: 88)

6 See bell hooks (1984). Hooks points out that

> the poor or working class man who has been socialized via sexist ideology to believe that there are privileges and powers he should possess solely because he is male often finds that few if any of these benefits are automatically bestowed him in life
>
> (1984: 73)

The reluctance of black women "to publicly discuss sexist oppression" (74), she explains, comes from a fear that "it could simply lead to greater victimization" (76).

7 For example, hooks uses the concept of comparative deprivation to criticize the white feminists' privileging of work as liberatory, because it ignores the exploitative and dehumanizing aspects of many jobs held by people of color. Many Anglo-American feminists interpret work narrowly as professional careers, leading to an influx of bourgeois women into the marketplace. The success of these professional women has taken attention away from the fact that many more women, especially women of color, are still exploited and devalued in low-paying service jobs (1984: 95–105).

8 Feminist scholars, in attempting to rearticulate woman against traditional and patriarchal norms, privilege complexity, conflict and difference. See, for example, Gayle Greene and Coppélia Kahn, "Feminist Scholarship and the Social Construction of Woman" for a cogent review of feminist revisions in anthropology, history and literature that insist on "restor(ing) conflict, ambiguity and tragedy to the centre of historical process" (Fox-Genovese 1982: 28, cited in Greene and Kahn 1985: 21).

9 Nancy Miller's most recent book, one that she was completing during that summer, *Subject to Change: Reading Feminist Writing* (1988), demonstrates her witty feminist re-reading of "the text's heroine" and the refusal of the patriarchal plot in women's writing.

REFERENCES

Césaire, Aimé (1972) *Discourse on Colonialism*, trans. Joan Pinkham, New York: Monthly Review Press.

Eggan, Fred (1971) "Philippine Social Structure," in George M. Guthrie (ed.) *Six Perspectives on the Philippines*, Manila: Book Mark.

Fanon, Frantz (1967) *Black Skin White Masks*, trans. Charles Lam Markmann, New York: Grove Press.

Fox-Genovese, Elizabeth (1982) "Placing Women's History in History," *New Left Review* (May–June), 5–29.

Greene, Gayle and Coppélia Kahn (1985) "Feminist Scholarship and the social construction of woman," in *Making a Difference: Feminist Literary Criticism*, London: Methuen, 1–36.

hooks, bell (1984) *Feminist Theory: From Margin to Center*. Boston: South End Press.

Johnson, Kay Ann (1983) *Women, The Family and Peasant Revolution in China*, Chicago: University of Chicago Press.

Lim, Shirley Geok-lin (1992) "The Ambivalent American: Asian American Literature on the Cusp," in Shirley Geok-lin Lim and Amy Ling (eds) *Reading the Literatures of Asian America*, Philadelphia: Temple University Press.

Marks, Elaine and Isabelle de Courtivron (eds) (1981) *New French Feminisms*, New York: Schocken Books.

Memmi, Albert (1968) *Dominated Man: Notes Towards a Portrait*, New York: Orion Press.

Miller, Nancy K. (1988) *Subject to Change: Reading Feminist Writing*, New York: Columbia University Press.

Minh-ha, Trinh T. (1989) *Woman, Native, Other: Writing Postcoloniality and Woman*, Bloomington: Indiana University Press.

Spivak, Gayatri Chakravorty (1990) *The Post-colonial Critic: Interviews, Strategies, Dialogues*, ed. Sarah Harasym, New York: Routledge.

Stimpson, Catherine (1988) *Where the Meanings Are*, New York: Methuen.

Wolf, Margery and Roxanne Witke (eds) (1975) *Women in Chinese Society*, Stanford: Stanford University Press.

Yamada, Mitsuye (1981) "Asian Pacific American Women and Feminism," in Cherríe Moraga and Gloria Anzaldúa (eds) *This Bridge Called My Back* New York: Kitchen Table Press, 71–5.

Chapter 19

Growing up theoretical
Across the divide

Jerry Aline Flieger

Our generation of feminists has come of age – here we are in middle age, looking back, and forward, from the middle ground that society has taught us to dread and which we are trying to reassess. We are not only between generations, but between decades, approaching a divide between centuries and millennia, which makes us feel both hopeful and anxious. Now that we are the older generation of feminists, what do we say to our younger sisters?

It is easy to feel discouraged, faced with a women's movement in disarray, with official governmental hostility towards affirmative action, with no constitutional guarantee of equal rights, with old territory (reproductive choice) to defend yet again, with the hard discovery that it is perhaps after all not possible to "have it all" – family and career and social activism – without shortchanging something. Indeed with all the recent talk about postfeminism, it is easy to feel that we may be living in an age where our values are considered anachronistic. Most discouraging of all is the realization that, twenty years after "women's lib" became a household term, we feminists are perhaps more divided than ever – by issues of race and sexuality, by questions of strategy, by theoretical issues around difference and equality, by disagreements concerning the efficacy of theory to help us get where we're going. For there is no going back; the question is how to go forward.

As the editors of this volume suggest, some retrospective soul-searching may be in order, so that we may carry the lessons of "before" feminism – before the sweeping changes of the 1970s – into the "after," our collective and personal future. As mid-life feminist activists and intellectuals, we are perhaps in the best position to negotiate the divide between before and after, in order to heal some of the differences that separate us, or at least to get a certain perspective on them, from atop the wall. This is, after all, an age where walls, however firmly entrenched they may have been, are coming down.

To this end, Gayle and Coppélia have asked us to reflect on how we have come to be feminist critics, to do a brief personal intellectual history. For me, and for many of us I suspect, that history in retrospect seems to line up along a series of divides (middle age is merely the latest one). I want to focus on one of the most important of these divisions, which is increasingly evident in feminist academic circles: the divide between feminist theory and practice, or at least between proponents of theory and proponents of practice.[1] In the pages of our journals and at our conferences, "theoretical" feminists continue to be accused of aping male discourse, of adopting androcentric and ethnocentric intellectual habits, of paying insufficient attention to hard economic and social issues.[2] For those of us who do theoretical work, then, a question has persisted throughout our encounter with feminism: how to integrate our activism with our intellectual activity, which might seem elitist or out of touch.

This theory–practice split, in my experience at least, reflects a continental divide, first on this side of the Atlantic, between the coasts in the States – when I was a graduate student at Berkeley, theory was imported by teachers from the Ivy East – and second between continents. For the young faculty who brought continental theory to Berkeley in the seventies had in turn studied with the poststructuralist gurus from France, during the period when Derrida was frequently giving seminars at Yale. And this transatlantic divide parallels another division, which sometimes seems like a rift, between Anglo-American feminism and continental feminism. The tension between two veins of feminism – issue-oriented (American) activism versus highly theoretical (French) writing – persists to this day, and has even grown to a debate over whether French theory has usurped the term itself.[3] But this tension between French and American "theorists" and "activists" has been an issue for at least a decade, since it served as the focus for the classic 1981 issue of *Yale French Studies* where Gayatri Spivak, Alice Jardine, Naomi Schor, Shoshana Felman and other feminist theorists first addressed the question of the gap between the cerebral nature of French feminist theory and the practical, hands-on activism needed to effect changes in women's lives.[4]

In addition to these three divides of the last three decades – between East and West Coasts in the States, between European and American theory, between French and Anglo-American feminism – there is yet another continental divide that is pertinent to the debate around the efficacy of theory for feminists. It is the breach between the Third World and everyone else, and the related separation of the concerns of minority women from the concerns of middle-class white feminism. We are reminded by our sisters of color that theoretical speculation is a luxury which may be enjoyed only when basic needs of survival have been met. I am thinking of Barbara Christian's and bell hooks' recent criticisms of deconstructive feminist theory as being out of touch with the experience of racial and ethnic minorities; or Alice Walker's insistence that "womanism" is more meaningful to black women than feminism. Nor is the racial divide the only one that continues to face feminists today: differences over sexuality (lesbian versus heterosexual) are also reflected in theoretical splits between radical and liberal feminism.

I wonder if feminist theorizing, rather than continuing to divide us, may in fact help us to bridge some of these gaps, tying our past experience with our hopes for the future. First, then, in the spirit of this volume, I will do a little reflecting about the way my own life has been affected by the before and after of feminism

– as well as by exposure to French theory – and then I want to ask how theory might help us confront some of the divides that are facing us today.

BEFORE AND AFTER

The most decisive divide in my own life came in 1969 or 1970 – again between decades – when a rock came sailing through my classroom window at Berkeley. I was a new teaching assistant, conducting a class in beginning French, mildly interested by the uprising on the Berkeley campus about ROTC recruiting on campus – interested, sympathetic, but as yet uninvolved. And then, the rock was pitched through my window, my classroom was invaded by three young men who announced that the university was on strike, and who demanded that we dismiss class and join them. We did – out of solidarity? or embarrassment? – but this incident in any case was a dividing line in my life, marking my first real involvement in anti-war protest, or in protest of any kind. I had a fiancé in Viet Nam, and was biding my time at Berkeley, getting a Master's Degree in French with the intention of becoming a high school teacher, so that I could have a career I could always "go back to" after having a family (I have yet to have that family). In other words, I was waiting for a man to come home and shape my life. So to enter into anti-military protest with a loved one "over there" was a real watershed decision for me, entailing a break with my past and my projected future. My own prehistory, then, my "before," was before Kent State, before Cambodia, before Watergate. And it was just before the great swell of the seventies women's movement, which helped me make the decision to end my relationship, to go on with my own education, and to become politically active.

There was another aspect to this "before" and "after" divide in my experience: 1970 was just before the arrival of "French theory" at Berkeley – poststructuralism came to Berkeley in the early seventies with our new chair (Leo Bersani), who was also instrumental in hiring several brilliant young women who became role models for many of us (Ann Smock, Phyllis Zuckerman, Marie-Hélène Huet). It was these East Coast (or in Marie-Hélène's case, French) intellectuals who introduced my generation of graduate students to theory, in their seminars and reading groups. During the early seventies, a period that Geoffrey Hartman has called "the invasion of the mind-snatchers from the Continent," we were bombarded by waves of exciting new ideas, imported from the East Coast and beyond: French Freud, structuralism, poststructuralism, French feminism. Thus my personal "before and after" is intertwined with three encounters: my first exposure to French theory, my first involvement with politics, and my first experiences with feminism. It is impossible for me to disengage these various events: they all happened at Berkeley, and had something to do with the way the outside world came sailing through the window and crashed into my classroom.

In the following years I would attend protests, support strikes, participate in founding a faculty–student women's group in our department at Berkeley; and I would study theory, which has shaped my career. In the early seventies we converts to French theory – a friendly faculty spouse called us "the Young Hegelians" – held earnest discussions, reading *The Phenomenology of Mind* and trying to figure out just what Lacan's Mirror Stage was and what Kristeva and Bataille meant by absolute negativity. At just about the same time, several women in the department, faculty members and students, started a departmental women's caucus, which was a kind of intellectual consciousness-raising group, where we somewhat timidly shared our experiences as female academics, and where we read some essays and novels together – Simone de Beauvoir, Adrienne Rich, Monique Wittig, Freud's *Case of Dora*, Julia Kristeva's *Des Chinoises* and *La Poésie et la négativité*. (In fact, during a lecture-visit to Berkeley, Kristeva herself descended from the stratosphere of theory to come and talk to our group. We were dazzled by her intellect, her radical chic, and yes, her glamor.)

Our group also started the first women's studies course in the department, which I got to teach, and which was my first literature course as well. And we put out a feminist newsletter (*La Chimère*), in which we militated for the hiring of more women in the department. So I can think of my life with a before and after, but I cannot discern a division between the personal, political and intellectual aspects of my own "consciousness-raising." Perhaps that is why I have such a soft spot for theory to this day. My first meaningful political contact with other women was around academic and intellectual issues (What does Kristeva mean by polyphonic writing? What should be the topic of our new women's course? Should we give grades? What kind of format should the women's caucus meetings take? Should we even call it a caucus – with the oppositional connotations of the word – or something else?). However academic these questions might have been, they certainly felt like real-life issues to us, important and passionately engaging.

RAZING WALLS, RAISING CONSCIOUSNESS

What, then, did we perceive as the relation between practice and theory during those formative years as feminist academics? First of all, we set about the task of bringing down some of the walls – cultural and intellectual – that had hemmed us in, and of which we were just becoming aware. At a time when deconstruction was problematizing walls, binary oppositions, neat either/or categories and positivist reason, we were discovering that we were living the consequences of such divisions, as we set about trying to undo some of the restrictions of a sexist society. We had come of age in an era where the economic wall between men and women was reflected in pronounced social differences (it felt very liberating, for instance, to have women professors for the first time); furthermore, as children of the Cold War, we had grown up in an era of divisions, in the shadow of the Berlin Wall, in the certainty that "they" (the communists) were evil; and of course our personal lives had always been separate from our politics, even in the peace movement. Suddenly, some of these walls were being challenged or scaled; women were breaking into all-male enclaves; the New Left was embracing Hanoi; political issues (such as abortion, such as sex discrimination) were intensely personal (burn the bra!). In the spirit of these times, many of our first political exercises were attempts to bring down walls or to negotiate across them, or even to fence-sit (could you be a feminist and get married too? Do your own thing ...).

For instance, even while not wanting to offend the largely sympathetic male power structure in the department, or to exclude our male graduate student friends from our intellectual discussions, we none the less voted to exclude men from the women's caucus meetings: after passionate debates about whether male graduate students could come to our reading discussions, it was decided that they could not, "oppressed" though they were. For their sex put them on the other side of the wall, and bringing them over seemed to be an encroachment on our own intellectual space. This division between men and women, perhaps necessary in our first tentative efforts at female solidarity, was a new one for me, and was reinforced by some of the French theory I was reading at the time. I was particularly impressed by Simone de Beauvoir's concept of woman as existential "Other," as well as by the ideas of younger French feminists such as Annie Leclerc, with her passionate claim to a specific "women's speech," and Luce Irigaray, with her lyric and deeply partisan perspective on the biological divide, the essential difference between masculinist modes of reasoning – visual, discrete, monolithic – and feminist modes – tactile, fluid, plural. Reading Irigaray and Kristeva, as well as Freud, caused me to get interested in Lacan, where I found yet another formulation of an unbridgeable gender divide, this time cast in linguistic terms. I was fascinated and troubled by Lacan's characterization of the phallus as the Signifier of Signifiers, as well as by his infamous statements "There is no sexual relation," and "Woman does not exist." Thus I was relieved and grateful when feminists such as Jacqueline Rose and Jane Gallop, in the late seventies and early eighties, performed ingenious and persuasive readings of Lacan as critic of phallocracy, rather than advocate.

Through the work of many of these theorists, I was for the first time exposed to the wall of difference separating "us" from "them," even when "they" were sympathetic, progressive males, my friends. (Monique Wittig, who also spoke to our women's group, even asserted that heterosexual sex was equivalent to rape.) Of course, some feminist theory of this era did "deconstruct" essentialist notions of immutable differences between male and female – including the writing of Derrida, who professed writing as a process of "invagination," and Cixous, who was calling for a bisexual expression, as well as Kristeva, who voiced doubts about a too-negative, too-oppositional feminism, the mirror image of the order it was opposing. But other theoretical readings seemed to reinforce the notion of essential difference, and especially sexual difference (Irigaray, Bataille, some essays by Kristeva). As Lacan put it, human beings were born to take sides, to line up along the line of gender, as suggested by his famous illustration of the two familiar doors, one with the sign "men" and one with the sign "ladies," which separate the boys from the girls.

All of which led to some confusion: our feminist readings were positing a separate "women's speech" (Leclerc), a distinct "women's time" (Kristeva), even a women's space (Irigaray), while the fledgling women's center at Berkeley provided an actual physical space of refuge for women only. But at the same time, our encounter with theory warned us against too-simple, clear-cut distinctions, based on binary oppositions such as male/female, inside/outside, us/them.

Still all of the theorists we were reading at the time, whatever their position on sexual difference, were mounting critiques of reason, of positivism, and of certainty, and were celebrating the creative possibilities of equivocal thought and expression, of undecidability. This theory contained a new message about difference, a reassessment of old demarcations, exposing the traditional divisions as effects of binary logic often equated with masculine ideology, eroding the phallocentric absolutism of "either/or" logic (which Blanchot has called "the reign of light"). From Barthes, Derrida, Kristeva, Sollers, we learned to be wary of the wiles of the dialectic and of idealist philosophy, where one could be co-opted or synthesized or assimilated, even while staging the most vociferous opposition. These were theoretical discoveries – that rational Cartesian logic harbored a subversive genius, the unconscious; that origins are anything but original and that "last words" cannot have the final say; that what we want is implicated in a web of intersubjective contexts ("our desire is the desire of the Other"); that our clearest assertions are shadowed and undermined by our own unconscious, the *non-dit*. But we also made discoveries about "undecidability" directly and daily, sometimes painfully, through the contradictions in our lives, through the prevalence of "either/or" logic in feminism. (Either you take your husband's name or you forge a new one. Either you wear make-up, a sign of sexual servility, or you don't – well maybe just a little lip gloss.... . And what about the men in our lives; how did they fit into this feminist business?) Even as we brought down old walls and explored new territory, we discovered that the middle ground is shaky, that there is a price to pay in *not* being able to line up with an unequivocal position.

So even if our first theoretical efforts were about bringing down walls, erasing divisions, deconstructing certainties, living in the grey area of undecidability – and even if these efforts were compatible with our feminist efforts to deconstruct the assumptions of the past and to show that seemingly immutable ideological walls could be challenged or scaled – at the same time, our ventures in French theory and in our women's group caused us to uncover new divisions, perhaps insurmountable. (When it came to decisions about who could attend the reading group, for instance, you were, after all, male or female, in spite of all our discussions about the desirability of flexible gender roles.)

Sometimes our allegiances were in conflict, as we tried to line up on more than one side of more than one divide. How could we reconcile our push to be a big-time theory department – emphasizing individual credentials, publications, big names – with an egalitarian collectivist feminist impulse? Who would choose the person to teach the feminist course – the women's caucus, including graduate students, or the department chair and executive committee, who were interested in the "quality" and "rigor" of the course, including its theoretical content? We theoretical types, who were reading Bataille and Derrida and Barthes and Lacan as well as the French feminists, were sometimes viewed suspiciously as the lackeys of male ideology. On the other hand, those women who refused to participate in the theoretical conversion to poststructuralism, and who were doing dissertations, say, on the images of women in the canon, were considered by us "theorists" as copping out in some way, shying away from the difficult and intellectually demanding, and refusing to participate in the remaking of the department in a theoretical mould. So there was tension, in the women's caucus and in other areas of departmental life, between the theory converts, regarded by the more radical feminist scholars as intellectual groupies of sorts, and the "non-theoretical" students who were daring to use unfashionable modes of analysis (like character motivation or biographical criticism) in their dissertations, before feminist scholarship had gained acceptance in academe. Personally, I felt a great deal of admiration for those doing feminist work, but I none the less wrote a dissertation where not one woman was mentioned, because I felt that Bataille and Derrida were more "interesting" (a code word for intellectually rigorous).

In addition to dealing with internal differences in our department's women's group, those of us who were "French feminists" had to defend our readings of the likes of Kristeva and Cixous to members of the wider academic community, American feminists who felt suspicious of the squeamishness of Kristeva and company about the very word "feminist."

During the seventies, like many of my contemporaries, I struggled to stake out my own position – engaging in a kind of shuttle diplomacy between continental theory and American practice – as I became increasingly involved with theory on the intellectual level, even while I was devoting more and more time in my personal life to activism around women's issues. Then as now, the potentially liberating aspects of French theory had to be weighed against the charge of elitism, or even sexism, of that theory, perhaps especially as concerns French psychoanalytic theory. I have had to come to terms with the implications of French theory, and especially "French Freud," for feminism: although I feel that Lacanian theory may be read from a feminist perspective, which casts gender as a social position or linguistic construct, I have certainly had some explaining to do to my non-psychoanalytic feminist friends, about how "the phallus is what no one has," etc. (And certainly Lacan's choice of the Phallus as "Signifier of Signifiers," as well as such statements as "Woman does not exist," have not made the task an easy one.) More than once I have felt like an imposter unmasked, when political friends have discovered with consternation that I'm one of those "theoretical types."

And as any transatlantic feminist knows (I borrow the term from Alice Jardine, whose work has often dealt with the issue), the suspicion and ill-will dividing Yankee brass-tacks feminism and French theoretical feminism has come from both sides. In the late seventies, at a luncheon at Barnard, I remember hearing Hélène Cixous, decked out in the latest fashion, spike heels and pearls, disdainfully remark that "American feminists always look like they're ready to climb a tree." Although theoretical pioneers such as the contributors to the aforementioned *Yale French Studies* issue (*French Texts/American Contexts*) were confronting these divides, these differences, as did the Barnard seminar on "The Future of Difference" some years later, it became increasingly clear that American and continental feminism had some serious disparities, not the least of which concerned the ideological appropriateness of high-sounding theory in a movement that sought to be a mass movement and to make real changes in real lives. Could American pragmatist–activist "tree-climbers" ever see eye to eye with French radical chic?

In our first encounters with international feminism, we seventies feminists discovered that not all divides could be erased by good will. In addition to the theory–practice, American–French divide, there were other walls that proved equally resistant to "deconstruction" of any sort. How could one be both married and not? What names did one use? (Monique Wittig for instance was calling herself Theo at the time, a name of her own invention and choosing, to get out of the patriarchal chain.) If we married, did we hyphenate our patronym with that of our husband, separating our name from his with a symbolic wall of sorts? How could one compromise about the name of a child?[5]

Our experience with French psychoanalytic theory allowed us to confront some of these issues (like the Name of the Father, the Paternal Metaphor, the phallocentrism of Lacan) on an intellectual level, at the same time that we were trying to work them out on a practical, visceral level in our own lives. For instance, the "French Freud" of the Lacanian school, like the other theory we were reading at the time, was exciting and even personally liberating, with its emphasis on a divided, decentered Subject "on trial" (Kristeva's term), a Subject whose free-floating desire seemed to elude restrictions, appropriation by norms, the limits of a monolithic identity or a "monological" mode of expression devoted to the illusion of coherence, unity, and control. In other words, while as feminists we were trying to forge an "identity" and "get our lives together," much French theory was exposing the illusory nature of that "identity" and insisting that the dispersive force of desire was somehow more "desirable" and at least more poetic than the ideal of coherence. At the very least, French theory seemed to suggest the creative possibilities of contradiction, while the notion of "undecidability" permitted us to enjoy (intellectually at least) the complications of various positions, even while tensions and contradictions in our own lives remained.

What I personally found most interesting in all of French theory was Lacan's "return to Freud," which centered on yet another divide, another bar, the bar between consciousness and the unconscious (which Lacan made an analogue for the linguistic bar between signifer and signified, in his ingenious treatment of metaphor as repression). We learned from French psychoanalysis that the unconscious could not be cleared up or wished away, that the bar between conscious and unconscious could not be abolished, but that it could be crossed, on poetic visits from the other side, in a kind of creative cross-pollination. (As Lacan suggests, this crossing of the bar is not unlike the workings of metaphor itself, the finding of similarity in difference.) Indeed, the conscious/unconscious interaction as staged by Lacan and others still seems to be an illuminating paradigm for the maintenance of creative difference, enabling an exchange across divides.

French theory introduced us to other intriguing and useful models of difference – there was Kristeva, for instance, who not only talked of the interpenetration of the thetic and the semiotic, in a poetic dance of meaning, but who applied this kind of interchange as a principle in her own life, writing a lyric tribute to the work of her mate Sollers, insisting that heterosexual love was not a violation but a source of interchange. Reading this kind of work, with its emphasis on splitting, pluralism, diversity – as well as Foucault's writings on the complicity of marginality with system – helped us to think about the complications of the era, to grapple with the contradictions in our own lives, and even to be able to take uncomfortable, even illogical, positions ("Here we draw the line.... You cannot attend our seminar – it's for women only. And if that's reverse sexism, so be it – logic is not the final criterion here").

In other words, while our experience with both feminism and with poststructuralist theory sometimes seemed to be about undoing or deconstructing divides, it was also, paradoxically, about creating new divides, both theoretically and in real life. Indeed, every act of solidarity among women seemed built on new schisms – between the female "us" and the male "them," a schism reinforced by theories of a specific feminine expression, grounded in the body (*l'écriture féminine*). My Black friends were living similar problems with their own struggle for intellectual identity within the university. They did not want the help of white friends, however sympathetic. And for the most part, alas, our French feminist group remained white, except for one or two visits from the only black female graduate student in our department at the time. She must have felt very uncomfortable, since she did not return. Here, we certainly did not do enough to cross the divide, making the easy assumption that gender was enough of a bond to overcome the divide of race.

One wall was however successfully deconstructed by our women's group: the divide between students and faculty. Our meetings were well attended by both groups, with little sign of academic hierarchy in our decisions and discussions. Nearly twenty years later, that wall has reappeared in my life, a generational divide between me and my students. (When did I stop being Jerry to them? At first it was as startling to be called Professor Flieger as it was to be called Madame for the first time in France, alerting me that I had crossed some ineffable boundary.) I look back now to those days as a student at Berkeley and try to remember how our shared experiences as women academics were able to provide a common ground between faculty and students. For the task now is to pass our experience on, to cross this generational wall from the other side, from the side of accomplishment and authority, and to decide where we go from here.

In my own life, as the seventies ended, I crossed another continental divide, turning down a job in California for one in the East: like a reverse pioneer, I packed up my VW bug, with cat and plants, and headed across the Rockies, bound for the mecca of theory, the Eastern deconstructive-psychoanalytic enclave. I am still living the ramifications of those early choices: now I am tenured (after a battle) at an Eastern university, married for only three years, trying to make the difficult choice about children before it is too late, as all my contemporaries seem to rush to the maternity wards. Above all, I am keenly aware that my position as a female teacher in mid-life entails a constant contact with the next generation, and I am mindful of my position as role model for my students, as my women professors were for me. Sitting on the wall between decades and between generations, between career and family choices, I am looking for a way to connect my past with my students' future.

FENCE POSTS (FRENCH "POSTS"?): MAKING LINKS

Today we are faced with new dilemmas, intellectual, political, professional, not the least of which are the divides that continue in the feminist movement in our day: radical/essentialist versus liberal/cultural feminism; the oppositional mentality of what Betty Friedan calls "first stage" feminism versus a more accommodating "second stage" attitude of co-operation with the opponent. There are also the divides within the feminist intellectual community about how theoretical feminist discourse should be, which are in turn reflected in the divide between women's studies and the rest of the university, which demands theory and research credentials as proof of "seriousness." On the theoretical level, we are faced with a proliferation of "posts": post-feminism, post-structuralism, postmodernism – and at least one "new" ("new historicism," delineating itself from the old). All these hyphens and qualifiers, all these rather uncomfortable posts in the wall of our middle age, suggest that we are once again witnessing a significant divide in intellectual history.

Theory, I suggest, may provide a kind of connection between past and present, or offer some possibilities of crossing some of the divisions that splinter our experience; and I think we feminists would do well not to reject it as elitist or androcentric. The feminist project is inherently revisionist, sifting through layers of inherited culture, reclaiming, reshaping, changing the perspective and the emphasis. Does a theorist like Derrida do otherwise? Deconstruction really *re*constructs the past, the heritage, gives it new possibilities, freeing us from rigid categories and simple causality, even opening up a role for chance. (As Derrida suggests in the essay "Mes Chances," history is always at least in part a game of chance, a roll of the dice.)

Still, two decades of feminist practice have taught us that theory alone will not suffice to bring about change: if economic and social rights have been won, it is because of hard political work. Yet surely theory is not inimical to action and to ethics, but can help provide a base for choices we make. One example: Derrida's now infamous statement, "there is nothing outside the text," which has too often been read as an invitation to intellectual solipsism, may also be read as a statement of implication , with "text" understood as a social fabric, and *écriture* understood as a metaphor for human interaction. And if, as de Man suggests, "every reading is a misreading," this does not mean that we cannot take a position, but rather that we must be willing to recognize that every perspective has a blind spot and every position a consequence (as his own history demonstrates).

Since we are speaking from and of our own experience, let me close by making a personal link between theory and practice, testifying to what "French theory," feminist and otherwise, has brought to my own practice as a feminist academic. From the likes of Derrida and Foucault I have learned the value of a radical skepticism *vis-à-vis* "power," consistent with the political climate in which I came of age (Michael Sprinker, Michael Ryan, Gayatri Spivak and others have made intriguing connections between the "question authority" political climate of the New Left and the "deconstructive" intellectual climate of the sixties and seventies.) More importantly, reading these thinkers teaches us that the powers that be are agents of power-systems with which we often collaborate, even when we think we are in opposition.

Second, from French theory, I have acquired a critical attitude toward the companion notions of "canon" and "coverage" – the idea that an education means covering a certain ground and claiming it as our own – and that this territory must be the consecrated ground determined by generations of professors and academic tradition. French theory's emphasis on marginal or experimental texts suggests that there are criteria more compelling than that of "greatness" which determine whether a work is read.

Third, from all of this theory I have learned that it is all right not to know everything, not to aspire to a seamless view of the universe (a view which Irigaray has exposed as profoundly masculinist). One of the most important lessons of French psychoanalysis in particular is that the "subject [who is] supposed to know" (Lacan's term for the analyst, who is supposed to have all the answers) is always a mirage, a projection of our expectations. Perhaps I would have learned this simply from interacting with students, without having read Lacan's *Ecrits* or Foucault's *Archeology of Knowledge* or Derrida's *Writing and Difference*, all of which see "writing" (or human thought) as a contextual play, where no one gets the last word. But my exposure to theory has helped the process along, inviting me to practice what I teach, and to be wary of the temptation to take myself for the authority, simply because I have been formally vested with the right to do so. This is a useful lesson, now that we seventies feminists are part of the establishment.

Fourth, my encounter with theory has caused me to ponder the difference between cultural and essentialist feminism, and to line up pretty much with the first camp. "A woman is not born, she is made," that capital insight of de Beauvoir, is a gift of French theory, even if it is in direct opposition to the stance of other French feminist writers (like Irigaray or Chantal Chawaf) who seem to argue not only for an essential biological difference between the sexes, but for a whole biologically determined mode of cognition and expression. In contrast to these biocentric views, Simone de Beauvoir's formulation of gender as social acquisition is, I think, similar to what Lacan argues later (albeit in a hypertheoretical way): gender is a construct, linguistic and social, an effect of our relation with the other gender as Other. This is how I read Lacan's concept of locus – the "feminine" position, socially and linguistically – the position of object, is one which we all occupy, alternately and successively. Theorists as different as de Beauvoir, Irigaray, and Lacan all argue that there will always be a difference between the genders, but cultural perspectives insist that the nature of that difference will change, and that what matters in this view is the conclusions we draw from that difference, the use we make of the space between "us" and "them".

What I draw from French feminist theory, be it "cultural" or "essentialist," is the valorization of difference – *vive la différence!* – and the emphasis on sexuality *as* difference. Much of French theory insists that difference opens the very possibility of communication, the space in which words may be exchanged and just perhaps understood: the abolition of difference in one seamless Truth is not only impossible (an "Imaginary" construct, in Lacan's terms), but undesirable. We feminists have come to the same conclusion by a different route: after the euphoric mirage of sisterhood as sameness and unity, we have learned that deep differences among women can make solidarity complicated or difficult. But from a theorist such as Kristeva, who valorizes "negativity" as a creative resource, we may learn to cherish difference as a source of enrichment, rather than as a barrier. Not that the appreciation of diversity can wish away real conflicts. But it can at least suggest ways of arguing that negotiate the "either/or" impasse, by not insisting on simply winning out over the opposite point of view.

In other words, poststructuralist thinking – and all good theory for that matter – is metaphoric thinking, which crosses the bar, the divide, between two apparently unlike terms, making a connection that manages to include them both, even while gaining in force from a maintained tension between the terms. We might say that this poetic model "deconstructs" the divisive use of the word "and" (them and us; then and now), reconstructing it as a space of contact. This transforms restrictive "either/or" logocentric thinking to creative "both/and" logic, the profoundly poetic language of the unconscious, as revealed by French Freudians like Lacan and Lyotard. This mode – a perspective consistent with the feminist valorization of "choice" – provides an alternative to the agonistic model of interaction, where the goal is victory over the opponent or assimilation of the Other.

French theory proposes other enabling spaces, other divides that provide a playing field: in psychoanalysis, the divide in the ego (*Spaltung*) – and Lacan's related notion of the self as divided or multiple – has caused us to rethink the demands of "identity" and "ego" (in view of Lacan's notion of a unified identity as an Imaginary construct, necessary for mental health, but illusory). Which means we feminists can search for an "identity," as long as we remain aware of the impossibility of private ownership ("Our Bodies, Ourselves") of that identity; it is always "overdetermined" and plural, implicating the Other. The divide (bar) between consciousness and the unconscious, between self and other, is what makes us profoundly human; it is the condition of our ability to repress, rework, recall, *between* two spaces (conscious and unconscious) that may never be fully transparent or assimilated one to the other.

I see this as a comic or poetic use of difference – indeed, for French theory, this freeplay between spaces is what defines art and literature. Maintained difference may deploy the possibilities of a life which has many facets, but which does not pretend to "have it all" in the manner of dress-for-success corporate feminism, avid for every possession and every experience. Instead of trying to live my mother's life, as well as that of the feminist generation, I have come to understand that my choices may divide me from the life of my parents. But that doesn't mean we can't visit across the divide.

A final insight from French theory continues to shape my current work. French theory has provided creative paradigms for crossing over genre lines, cross-pollinating autobiography, fiction and theory, and challenging traditional dividing lines between subject and object, self and other.[6] In so doing, this theory has made us better readers, more attentive to the implications of our own investment in the reading process.[7] Along the way, French theory has shown us the importance of a sense of humor, in its proclivity for pun and its decidedly slippery, playful, ironic tone – the distance it takes from itself and its own project, enjoining us to humility and playfulness, not defeatism. (This theoretical valorization of playfulness provides an alibi for one of my own contradictions: the divide between the intellectual at my word processor, and the low-brow who slips away to watch soap operas between writing sessions.) Lacan's work, and Derrida's, demonstrate that divides are a source of play – the playground of the *Fort*! and the *Da*! – engendering meaning in the space between the correct use of a word and its punning deformation.

Where, then, do these theoretical insights intersect with feminism? Feminism, as much or more than any other social movement, has had to grapple with the question of difference, especially sexual difference. Feminism wants at once to deny difference (I'm just like you) and to proclaim it (but women are different from men) – an insoluble dilemma. But if feminism has given us choices that are painful, opening up more room for difference, it has also given us more ways to connect. French theory too has given us ways of celebrating difference, of resisting appropriation, even while it cautions us to modesty about our gains. It paradoxically deconstructs divides and shows that they may never be bridged: the diacritical gap between words is what makes meaning possible, just as sexual difference engenders sexuality, and the divide between human beings engenders social interaction.

In this spirit, I find that the pedagogical use of certain provocative theoretical texts actually provides a way to open a dialogue with my students, to get a rise out of them, to bridge the gap between us, to sound a political chord without preaching. I find, in this post-feminist age, that the easiest way to connect with students is still through theoretical discussions on sexual politics, using theory as a vehicle to cross the generational divide.

The best in feminism, like the best in "French theory," teaches us to live with difference in tension, to be shuttle diplomats, to proliferate choices, rather than closing them off. It does not mean one answer is as good as another, nor does it give us license not to take a stand. But it does help us perhaps to distinguish between positive enriching differences, which invite interplay, and insurmountable battle lines (the Reagan–Bush Supreme Court versus women and minorities) and make judgments accordingly. However "undecidable" truth may be in the abstract, feminism has taught us that we must be able to say, "I believe that is the wrong position – because of the effects it has on people." We can't permit our interest in theory to allow us to shy away from ethics as too "positivist."

For if the political is personal, the theoretical is too, since it is an interpretative handle on what we call real life. Surely there is a way to use the lessons of theory without jargon and elitism – and here again teaching has taught me. If I can't explain "French theory" to my students, then I ought to discard it. But as long as it gives me more angles from which to teach and read, I'll continue to shuttle between theory and practice, across the divide.

NOTES

1 Several recent collections have addressed the political ramifications of feminist theory. See, for instance *The New Feminist Criticism*, ed. Elaine Showalter (New York: Pantheon, 1985); *Sexual/Textual Politics: Feminist Literary Theory*, ed. Toril Moi (London and New York: Methuen, 1985); *Making a Difference: Feminist Literary Criticism*, ed. Gayle Greene and Coppélia Kahn (London and New York: Methuen, 1985); and *Feminist Criticism and Social Change: Sex, Class, and Race in Literature and Culture*. eds. Judith Newton and Deborah Rosenfelt (New York and London: Methuen, 1985). For a review dealing with all of these works, see June Howard, "Feminist Differings: Recent Surveys of Feminist Literary Theory and Criticism," *Feminist Studies* 14.1 (spring 1988), 167–89.

2 For a fascinating series of articles on the theory debate, and particularly on the ramifications of deconstruction for feminism, see *Feminist Studies* 14.1 (spring 1988).

3 See for instance the exchange between Joan Wallach Scott and Linda Gordon, in *Signs* 15.4 (summer 1990), around the importance of French poststructuralism for feminism, and the question of whether more explicitly political or sociological approaches may be considered equally "theoretrical."

4 Collette Gaudin, M. J. Green, L. Higgins, M. Hirsch, V. Kogan, C. Reeder, N. Vickers, (eds) *Feminist Readings: French Texts/American Contexts*, special issue of *Yale French Studies* 62 (1981).

5 Many of these divides are symbolized in what Lacan calls the Name of the Father, our patriarchal label, and are central issues for French psychoanalysis.

6 I am thinking of such essays as Roland Barthes' *Le plaisir du texte* (Paris: Seuil, 1974); Kristeva's interactive writing on the work of her mate Sollers (*Polylogue*, Paris: Seuil, 1977); Derrida's essay on Freud ("Coming into One's Own," in *Psychoanalysis and the Question of the Text*, ed. Geoffrey Hartman, Baltimore: Johns Hopkins University Press, 1978).

7 One of the best feminist essays in this vein comes from Madelon Sprengnether ("Ghost Writing: A Meditation on Literary Criticism as Narrative," in *The Psychoanalytic Study of Literature*. ed. Joseph Reppen and Maurice Charney, Hillsdale, New Jersey: Analytic Press, 1985, 37–49). In this piece, Sprengnether comments on the autobiographical element of Derrida's essay on Freud, arguing that all writing is, in a sense, autobiographical ghost writing, where we mourn our absent others, and speak for them.

Afterword

Carolyn Heilbrun

In telling the stories of their lives writers create a form for the actuality: sometimes they recreate the reality itself. This is not to say that they make it up, as did a delightful character in a novel by Majorie Allingham:

> When Mr. William Faraday sat down to write his memoirs after fifty-eight years of blameless inactivity, he found the work of inscribing the history of his life almost as tedious as living it had been, and so ... he began to prevaricate a little upon the second page, working up to downright lying on the sixth and subsequent folios.

The women whose histories make up this book had just the opposite problem – too much rather than too little to write about, and none of it blameless inactivity. Their lives were remarkably untedious, and they have had to find a way to endow them, or a piece of them, with form. Doing so, they have discovered the trajectory of their stories, the spirit of their narratives.

The importance of these essays arises precisely from such an endeavor: to discover how being academic women, and feminists, has shaped the careers, the lives, and the loves and friendships, sometimes indistinguishable, of women whose generation saw the flowering of academic feminism. To me, roughly a decade and a half older than these women, the stories are both strange and achingly familiar. Strange because by the 1950s when, as the introduction says, "most of us came of age," I was already married, having children (three, as it turned out, since the last two were twins) and organizing my life around them (no double parenting in those days, even from fathers who might have been willing: a woman hardly dared threaten that delicate, vital masculinity). There was the guilt of working, the rushing back and forth, the home-bound evenings (how could one be gone part of the day and the evening too?) By the time the sixties came, indeed, the autumn before they came, I was working full-time as an instructor (a position since largely abolished), and while I clearly understood *The Feminine Mystique*, I was no longer in it. Indeed, in miraculously avoiding the suburbs, I passed from its major dangers. (Why do I say miraculously? Because the refusal to move out of the city was maintained with a resistance utterly inexplicable to my family or my husband's; I quite simply knew it would be the death of me. If a miracle can be defined as the individual strength to resist an overwhelming, universal convention, it was a miracle.) The fifties were fearsome for me: Ann Snitow has evoked them well:

> [Today] ... forces are at work, half the time threatening us with loneliness, half the time promising us rich emotional lives if we will but stay home – a double punch combination designed to make the 1950s look, by contrast, safe. The 1950s were not safe, not for me, anyway, and they don't become so with hindsight.

In 1957, I published "The Character of Hamlet's Mother" in the *Shakespeare Quarterly*. It was my first publication and I mention it here because many of the contributors to this collection chose Shakespeare and his time as their first area of concentration. They did so for reasons that I think Gayle Greene, in her essay, incisively sets forth. She also says that she didn't begin looking at the women in Shakespeare for quite a while; that I was looking at them in the 1950s suggests to me that I somehow understood the "safety" of women in the fifties to be more or less equivalent to their "safety" in Shakespeare's tragedies. Maybe one needed to be simultaneously an academic and in the throes of "a woman's traditional life" not to suppress the problems women faced in academia: except in childhood, some experiences are too palpable for suppression.

At any rate, I was in the 1950s fully of age, and found the women in my "social life," – there were, to all intents and purposes, none in academia – not only universally boring, but also unwilling to admit that there were any serious pressures in their lives. One of my most brilliant college friends said to me: you complain too much; you should be grateful for your three beautiful children. She eventually had three beautiful children, told me she couldn't bear talking to me any more, and a few years later, committed suicide; a terrible loss, but there were to be others, equally as frightful. That was the fifties and early sixties for my cohort. Those years are largely a blur, but I remember when I was teaching full-time at Brooklyn College, a man asked me what I did with my children while teaching: I told him I locked them in a closet. Or perhaps I only *wanted* to tell him that. Anger seethed, and went on seething until the seventies and early eighties.

*

In the sixties, much remained unchanged. Gayle Greene reports her experience at Columbia's graduate school, identical to mine a decade earlier. Her dissertation, she says, was a project that

> turned out to be self-directed. (No one wanted to touch it ... though [my sponsor] eventually did read and rubber-stamp it and set up a defense committee and smuggled me out the back door.) It now strikes me as stubborn and perverse to have persisted in doing Shakespeare with everyone advising against it. Perhaps it had to do with Steven Marcus scaring me off George Eliot by naming every German philosopher she'd ever read and assuring me that I'd have to master all of them to write on her.

That was the story of my dissertation too. I wrote on the Garnett family; no one cared, no one directed it, except that Jerome H. Buckley, before moving to Harvard, performed for me what Greene's advisor did for her: I was smuggled out the back door with a Ph.D. Two years later, when I was already teaching at Columbia, my dissertation was published. I didn't mention it to anyone at the university: there was no one who would have been remotely interested.

The seventies and early eighties are the times during which, the introduction tells us, "feminist lit crit rose and burgeoned." These were the years when my life and the lives of the women writing in this collection coincided. Older than they, I was, I suspect, happier, if only by contrast. Suddenly the world, and above all the place of women in that world, righted itself and began to sing. When I published *Toward a Recognition of Androgyny* in 1973, it was greeted by men as though I had been advocating S&M. But that was the year of Roe v. Wade, and Billy Jean King beating Bobby Riggs: anything seemed possible. *MS Magazine* published a book on the seventies called *The Decade of Women*; it seems to me now that, if in the fifties I worried and seethed, in the seventies I rejoiced. But something else was happening around me, something the essays in this volume make clear, and I was unaware of it until I read them.

The astonishing fact revealed by this collection is that a great number of the women who would become the leading feminists of their generation passed through Columbia in either the English or French departments, and *Columbia kept not a single one of them*. They all, like Gayle Greene, expended "enormous energies trying to get the attention of people who turn out not to have been looking, over what turns out not to have been the point," in an environment "unbelievably hostile to what we do." I list their names here (and I may have missed some) with a grim, perhaps morbid sense of the idiocy of it all: Nina Auerbach, Carolyn Burke, Barbara Christian, Rachel Blau DuPlessis (who provided most of this list in a note to her essay), Kate Ellis, Judith Kegan Gardiner, Sandra Gilbert, Gayle Greene, Alice Jardine, Myra Jehlen, Constance Jordan, Alice Kaplan, Nancy Milford, Nancy Miller, Kate Millett, Lillian Robinson, Naomi Schor, Catherine Stimpson, Susan Suleiman, Louise Yelin. I was the only declared feminist who stayed, although I wasn't a declared feminist when I got tenure in 1966. It was reported to me, however, that Lionel Trilling had his suspicions, and the only reason I made it was because in the sixties everyone made it who hadn't done something foolish, like publishing detective novels under one's own name or annoying the males in Columbia College. (I didn't annoy them because they hadn't really heard of me; women didn't teach in Columbia College, as Rachel DuPlessis tells us, until the year I got tenure. I've made up for it by annoying them unceasingly ever since.)

The price of being older than those who have written these essays was loneliness: the lack of female friendships. My friends from graduate school were men, and it is, I think, simultaneously a tribute to them and to me that of the four close friends from those years, three have become active feminists and have encouraged their formerly housebound wives to develop a career. The fourth, I regret to say, is in favor of star wars and other enlightened endeavors, but even he keeps in touch. The seventies and eighties brought me women friends, all younger (the few academic women feminists my age are not in New York, and not, alas, often met up with.) Their friendship has sustained me through bad and good times. The first half of the eighties seemed like good times, by which I mean that the forces on *our* side still seemed to be making some progress; if we worried about "political correctness," it was within the feminist community that we worried, not in fighting off the radical right. I don't know what the nineties will ultimately be seen to have brought us, but at their beginning I can say only that they don't look promising.

Columbia, which seems to run like a thread through an account of the growth and decline of academic feminism, is back in the hands of the men whose primary loyalty is to Columbia College and each other. Even the new male professors brought in – and there have been, since the early eighties, more than twice as many men as women hired – seem to climb up into the tree house and help the guys to tack on the sign: "no girls allowed." This year the department threatens to turn down for tenure a brilliant feminist woman in a field where we are short of staff, in favor of a white male member of the tree-house gang in a field where we already have *five* tenured professors. When, not long ago, I tried to persuade the department to hire one of the absolutely top feminists in the country (who would have been willing to come to Columbia, as many are not), I was voted down: she was too threatening as, I suppose, am I. Margaret Mead is supposed to have said: "I have been honored everywhere but at Columbia." I would frame that and put it in the women's room, if we had a women's room in Philosophy Hall big enough to hold it.

As I write this I am, appropriately (it is such a relief occasionally to be appropriate) at a different place from those who have written herein. Columbia has stopped hurting me, but like someone who has escaped a battering marriage – and the analogy is, in many ways, not a far-fetched one for feminist women faculty – I cannot wipe out the terrible years. I cannot change the isolation of all my time at Columbia. But the friendships I have found among women, and what is referred to still as my private life, have made that isolation, if not welcome then benign, as a tumor is benign: it's not cancerous, but it doesn't do anyone any good.

What has done good, to me, to feminist literary criticism, and to feminism generally, has been the expansiveness that has come into the materials I teach. These days all feminist courses, and certainly Americanist courses, include great writers who are neither white nor upper class. In teaching both the novel and women's autobiography, I use the pivotal texts of writers who are women of color. The names – Toni Morrison, Alice Walker, Maya Angelou, Harriet Jacobs, Maxine Hong Kingston, to list only the most obvious – have offered the prime texts in both genres. My courses now include these novels and autobiographies not only because of their excellence and my wish to expand the canon, but chiefly because these texts serve to illuminate the area where feminism most readily takes hold: at the intersection between gender and other marginalities.

Feminism's wonderful capacity for change and for expansion and inclusion made this diversity possible. If this capacity was not evident as early as it should have been, at least in recent years, more slowly in personnel than in course content, but inevitably, it has manifested itself. Even in studying the major British novels of the eighteenth to twentieth centuries, canonical, white, upper-class though they be – new interpretations of imperialism and racism have come to the fore. Although diversity has taken too long to become visible, feminism's capacity for it has been there from the beginning, and is now one of its major strengths, to which essays in this volume bear witness.

Just as the texts in my classes have expanded from the white, western, male canon, so in recent years has my effort to reach out from my isolation at the University to an audience in the world of intelligent women and men, either non-academic or in other academic disciplines than mine. I have particularly enjoyed meeting women (like those in this book) who are just now entering upon the second half of their lives. Because that time of life for women has come to interest me so profoundly, I have found the study of women's biographies and autobiographies compelling, and have been able to lead seminars in these genres at Columbia and elsewhere.

At the same time, I am trying to write the biography of a woman, Gloria Steinem, of the same generation as the contributors to this book, whose life must be the text because she offers no extensive texts for analysis. Her life has been with feminism, and in writing it I hope to understand more about those born in the fourth and fifth decades of this century, who saw feminism flourish and then fragment, and who are, as I am, not without hope, but aware that they live in what my friend Nancy Miller calls, simply, a bad moment.

Index